RISK-TAKING BEHAVIOR

Wiley Series
Human Performance and Cognition

Acquisition and Performance of Cognitive Skills
Edited by Ann M. Colley and John R. Beech

Stress and Performance in Sport
Edited by J. Graham Jones and Lew Hardy

Training for Performance: Principles of Applied Human Learning
Edited by John E. Morrison

Sleep, Sleepiness and Performance
Edited by Timothy H. Monk

Risk-taking Behavior
Edited by J. Frank Yates

Further titles in preparation

RISK-TAKING BEHAVIOR

Edited by
J. Frank Yates
The University of Michigan,
Ann Arbor, Michigan, USA

JOHN WILEY & SONS
Chichester · New York · Brisbane · Toronto · Singapore

Other Wiley Editorial Offices

John Wiley & Sons, Inc., 605 Third Avenue.
New York, NY 10158-0012, USA

Jacaranda Wiley Ltd, G.P.O. Box 859, Brisbane,
Queensland 4001, Australia

John Wiley & Sons (Canada) Ltd, 22 Worcester Road,
Rexdale, Ontario M9W 1L1, Canada

John Wiley & Sons (SEA) Pte Ltd, 37 Jalan Pemimpin #05-04,
Block B, Union Industrial Building, Singapore 2057

Library of Congress Cataloging-in-Publication Data:

Risk-taking behavior / edited by J. Frank Yates.
     p. cm. — (Wiley series, human performance and cognition)
   Includes bibliographical references and indexes.
   ISBN 0-471-92250-1
   1. Risk-taking (Psychology) I. Yates, J. Frank (Jacques Frank),
1945- . II. Series: Wiley series in human performance and
cognition.
BF637.R57R57 1992
155.9—dc20   91-21229
                                      CIP

British Library Cataloguing in Publication Data:

A catalogue record for this book
is available from the British Library

ISBN   0-471-92250-1

Typeset in 10/12 Times by APS, Salisbury, Wiltshire
Printed and bound in Great Britain by Biddles Ltd, Guildford, Surrey

For our families

Contents

List of contributors

Nancy Adler

Professor of Medical Psychology and Director of the Health Psychology Program, University of California at San Francisco, USA. Professor Adler received her PhD in social psychology from Harvard University, and currently conducts research on the uses and limitations of "rational" models of behavior for understanding health-related behaviors. Address: Center for Social and Behavioral Sciences, University of California at San Francisco, 1350 7th Avenue, San Francisco, CA 94143, USA.

Philip Bromiley

Associate Professor of Strategic Management and Organization, University of Minnesota, USA. Professor Bromiley received his PhD from Carnegie Mellon University. His research interests have included the influence of organizational decision processes on strategic choices, the determinants of corporate risk taking, and the influence of risk taking on performance. Address: Curtis L. Carlson School of Management, University of Minnesota, 271 19th Avenue South, Minneapolis, MN 55455, USA.

Shawn P. Curley

Assistant Professor of Information and Decision Sciences, University of Minnesota, USA. Professor Curley received his PhD in psychology at the University of Michigan. His professional interests relate to decision and judgment processes under uncertainty, belief processing, forecasting under uncertainty, and medical decision making. Address: Curtis L. Carlson School of Management, University of Minnesota, 271 19th Avenue South, Minneapolis, MN 55455, USA.

James H. Davis

Professor of Psychology, University of Illinois, USA. Professor Davis received his bachelor's degree from the University of Illinois and his MA and PhD degrees from Michigan State University. He has held previous appointments at Miami University and Yale University. His long-term research focus has been on small, task-oriented groups, especially the consensus process achieved by members holding initially disparate response preferences. Address: Department of Psychology, University of Illinois, 603 East Daniel Street, Champaign, IL 61820, USA.

Baruch Fischhoff   Professor of Decision Sciences, Carnegie Mellon University, USA. Professor Fischhoff received his PhD from the Hebrew University. His current interests span several areas of judgment and decision behavior, including adolescent decision making, risk perception, and the teaching of decision making skills. Address: Department of Social and Decision Sciences, Carnegie Mellon University, Pittsburgh, PA 15213, USA.

Janice L. Genevro   Doctoral Candidate in Health Psychology, University of California at San Francisco. Ms Genevro has worked in the fields of child development and maternal and child health since the completion of her undergraduate degree. A special focus of that work has been the behavioral and psychosocial risk associated with poor perinatal outcome. Her additional research interests include personality development and occupational stress in health care providers. Address: Center for Social and Behavioral Sciences, University of California at San Francisco, 1350 7th Avenue, San Francisco, CA 94143, USA.

Tatsuya Kameda   Instructor of Social Psychology, University of Tokyo, Japan. Dr Kameda received his BA and MA degrees from the University of Tokyo and his PhD from the University of Illinois at Urbana-Champaign. His research focus has been on collective judgment and decision making, social influence processes in small groups, and Bayesian approaches to individual inference. Address: Department of Social Psychology, Faculty of Letters, University of Tokyo, 7-3-1 Hongo, Bunkyo-ku, Tokyo 113, Japan.

Susan M. Kegeles   Research Psychologist, University of California at San Francisco. Dr Kegeles received her PhD in social and health psychology from the University of California, Berkeley. Her current research focuses on AIDS prevention behavior and reproductive behavior. Address: Center for AIDS Prevention Studies, Box 0886, 74 New Montgomery, #600, University of California at San Francisco, San Francisco, CA 94143-0886, USA.

Leon Mann   Professor of Organizational Behaviour and Decision Making, University of Melbourne, Australia. Professor Mann holds an MA in social psychology from the University of Melbourne and a PhD in psychology from Yale University. He has held previous appointments at Harvard University, the University of Sydney, and Flinders University of South Australia. His interests have included choice and conflict and also methods of teaching decision skills to high school students. Address: Graduate School of Managament, University of Melbourne, Carlton, Victoria 3053, Australia.

Peter J. Neumann   Special Assistant to the Administrator, US Health Care Financing Administration, and Doctoral Student in health economics and health decision sciences at the Harvard University School of Public Health. Mr Neumann earned a master's degree in economics from the University of Pennsylvania. He has worked previously as a health policy analyst at the Project HOPE Center for Health Affairs. Addresses: Health Care Financing Administration, 200 Independence Avenue, S. W., Washington, DC 20201; Department of Health Policy and Management, Harvard School of Public Health, 677 Huntington Avenue, Boston, MA 02115, USA.

Peter E. Politser   Visiting Scientist, Operations Research Center, Massachusetts Institute of Technology, USA. Dr Politser received his MD at Northwestern University and his PhD in mathematical psychology at the University of Michigan. He has held faculty appointments at the University of Michigan, Case Western Reserve University, and the Harvard School of Public Health. His interests include various topics in decision analysis and behavioral decision making in medicine, management, and policy. Address: Operations Research

Center, Massachusetts Institute of Technology, Cambridge, MA 02139, USA.

Gordon F. Pitz   Professor of Psychology, Southern Illinois University, Carbondale, USA. Professor Pitz received his PhD from Carnegie Mellon University. His research has been concerned with the processing of probabilistic information and descriptive models of decision making. Most recently he has studied the effectiveness of decision aiding systems, especially those based on multiattribute utility theory. Address: Department of Psychology, Southern Illinois University at Carbondale, Carbondale, IL 62901-6502, USA.

Mark F. Stasson   Assistant Professor of Psychology, Virginia Commonwealth University. Professor Stasson received his bachelor's degree from the University of Wisconsin and his master's and doctoral degrees from the University of Illinois. His primary research interests are centered around individual and group judgment and decision making, and the effects of collective decision making experience on group members' subsequent decision making strategies. Address: Department of Psychology, Virginia Commonwealth University, Box 2018, Richmond, VA 23284-2018, USA.

Eric R. Stone   PhD Student in Psychology, University of Michigan, USA. Mr Stone received his bachelor's degree in mathematical sciences and psychology from the University of Delaware. A member of Michigan's Judgment and Decision Laboratory, his interests include risk perception, individual and group judgment processes, and statistics. Address: Department of Psychology, University of Michigan, 330 Packard Road, Ann Arbor, MI 48104-2994, USA.

Willem A. Wagenaar   Professor of Experimental Psychology, Leiden University, The Netherlands, Professor Wagenaar received his PhD at Leiden University. Before returning to Leiden, he held appointments at the University of Utrecht and the Institute for Perception TNO. Among his research interests are decision making, human factors, and memory, including applications to gambling, accident prevention, and psychology and the law. Address: Department of Psychology,

Leiden University, PO Box 9555, 2300 RB Leiden, The Netherlands.

J. Frank Yates Professor of Psychology, University of Michigan, USA. Professor Yates received his PhD from the University of Michigan. He has held visiting appointments at Rice University and Peking University. As a member of Michigan's Judgment and Decision Laboratory, his current research emphasizes risk and probability judgment, including cross-national differences, judgment and decision making under stress, and techniques for improving decision quality. Address: Department of Psychology, University of Michigan, 330 Packard Road, Ann Arbor, MI 48104-2994, USA.

Series preface

The earlier Series on Human Performance was designed to provide clear explanations of issues affecting human performance. The volumes dealt with topics such as the analysis of human skills, the effects of sleep and biological rhythms, sustaining attention during vigilance performance, the effects of noise on human efficiency, the changes resulting from aging, and the consequences of sex differences in human performance. In each case, however, it became evident that it was necessary to take account of the cognitive processes that underlie the overt expression of human performance variables.

The new Series in Human Performance and Cognition was therefore designed to devote more attention to cognitive processes, and to the relevant research findings. The extended Series now has a broader scope, which gives explicit recognition to what was hitherto implicit. The change provides an opportunity to offer books dealing with a much wider range of topics, potentially ranging from cognitive science to cognitive ergonomics. Thus far, new volumes have been devoted to the acquisition of cognitive skills, to the effects of stress and arousal in sport, to cognitive approaches to learning and training, and to the problems of sleep and sleepiness. The new series attempts to preserve those distinguishing features, such as clarity of exposition, that accounted for the success of its predecessor.

Many of the books in this series take the form of edited volumes. However, the end products of the editing process are not haphazard collections of papers, but systematically organized texts that utilize the advantages of multiple authorship. Although writing a monograph is often regarded as the more difficult assignment, producing an edited volume presents a considerable challenge. On one hand, it provides an opportunity to bring to bear on the subject matter a concentration of expertise that would otherwise be unavailable; on the other hand, the need for a multiplicity of contributors carries with it the risk that the overall result might lack coherence. In the present series, every effort has been made to counter the potential disadvantages of the edited format while preserving the positive advantages that stem from the opportunity to draw on specialized knowledge. The individual chapters have been commissioned in accordance with an integrated plan for each volume, information about chapter content has been circulated among the contributors to ensure cohesiveness, and editorial control has been extended to the level of difficulty as well as to the format of each text. These books have thus been designed to combine readability with high standards of scholarship.

In accordance with these principles, the present volume on risk-taking is both readable and scholarly. It outlines the concept of risk, stressing the possibility of loss as central to many of the overlapping definitions. It deals with techniques for optimizing risk, showing how utility theory can be adapted to provide precise predictions of choice behavior, but also shows how people arrive at subjective assessments of risk in sometimes ill-defined situations. Of course there are individual differences in risk-taking, although these are not easy to pin down, while the differences between older and younger risk-takers do not necessarily follow one's preconceptions. It also seems that the risks one will accept depend partly on group pressures, although the research story contains several twists and turns. Risk is interlinked with stress and mood changes, and its acceptance is a prominent issue in health contexts, where large samples of behavior have been studied. When dealing with accident causation, the book raises the question whether people really take risks at all, or whether they simply fail to perceive the dangers. Finally, the book draws attention to the responsibilities of designers and managers, who are often better placed to evaluate risks than the eventual sufferers.

It can be seen that *Risk-Taking Behavior*, like many of the other volumes, successfully combines both theoretical and practical objectives. Thus, the book clearly explains the use of abstract models for well-defined situations, but also explores risky behavior in the real world. Readers will find that this volume is informative, sympathetic, comprehensive, and useful. Its broad perspective results from careful editing of the combined expertise of a representative group of risk researchers from various backgrounds, demonstrating the potential strength of the edited format. The skillful blend of information and explanation exhibited in this volume ensures that it will fully contribute to the aims of the Series in Human Performance and Cognition.

Dennis H. Holding
University of Louisville

Preface

The following are comments and questions that might be overheard in various situations:

- "I'm a doctor myself; I've *seen* what can happen. That's why I'm scared to death about trying to have my first baby now, when I'm forty years old."
- "After careful consideration, we concluded that the potential benefits of putting the new plant in this country far outweighed the risks."
- "If we parole Decker, how do we know he won't go out and rape some other woman—or even kill her?"
- "How in the world did we get into this incredible S&L mess? How could any rational banker *possibly* make the kinds of loans those folks made and expect to get their money back?"
- "I see in the paper here that they're still planning to put that new chemical waste dump in our township. We could become another Love Canal! I think somebody ought to start a petition drive against this thing, don't you?"
- "Given the hazards involved, it was obviously reckless for Carol to have tried that stunt. So why did she do it?"
- "We're furious with McNeilab for sending free samples of Tylenol Gelcaps in the mail. Didn't they realize that at least *some* kids would get ahold of that medicine before their parents did?"
- "Barnes is the kind of guy who hates taking chances. For that reason alone, I seriously doubt that he's right for this job."

Risk, the possibility of loss, is the common denominator of all the situations implied in the previous remarks. *Risk-Taking Behavior* is about how people act in such situations. The diversity of the illustrative scenarios underscores the fact that risk permeates our everyday private and public affairs. This pervasiveness, in and of itself, is sufficient justification for making risk taking an essential object of study by behavioral scientists, one of the book's prime audiences. The examples also highlight the seriousness risk can assume. In fact, people's risk-taking behavior in situations like those above is so critical that it is a central concern in a host of fields. Among them are product design, personnel management, insurance, health care, and hazard control, to name but a few.

Practitioners in these areas thus constitute another natural audience for the text; for these individuals, a good understanding of how people deal with risk can spell the difference between the success and failure of their enterprises.

Why a book on risk taking at this time? In view of the commonness and significance of risk, as noted above, one would expect the literature on risk-taking behavior to be vast, and thus a book like this one would seem redundant. Considerable scholarly and practical attention in fact has been devoted to risk. However, in many instances, such as in finance and insurance, the focus has been on normative rules that should guide institutional decisions under well-circumscribed conditions. Markedly less emphasis has been placed on the actions of real people when they are confronted with risk. To be sure, actual risk-taking behavior indeed has been studied systematically and from several perspectives. For instance, risky choice has a secure position in work on behavioral decision making; almost every decision text devotes one or more chapters to the topic (e.g. Bazerman, 1990; Dawes, 1988; Hogarth, 1987; Yates, 1990). And there have been several excellent monographs describing research on special risk problems (e.g. MacCrimmon & Wehrung, 1986; Viscusi & Magat, 1987). However, there is no single source that critically reviews and synthesizes scholarship on risk-taking behavior that cuts across multiple contexts and points of view. One consequence is that an individual seeking a comprehensive understanding of the subject must track down and struggle through widely scattered and often difficult original materials. Another perhaps more serious consequence is that risk researchers within any particular paradigm are unable to exploit the insights of investigators who have examined risk taking from other vantages. As contributors, we hope that *Risk-Taking Behavior* will help fill the void.

Following is an overview of what our book contains:

Chapter 1, by J. Frank Yates and Eric R. Stone, is called "The Risk Construct." The objective of this chapter is to elaborate the concept of risk and how it has been understood in the diverse arenas where risk taking has been studied. It thus sets the stage for the remainder of the text.

"Risk and Optimality," Chapter 2, is by Peter J. Neumann and Peter E. Politser. In many areas of human endeavor, most notably in finance and commerce, risk has been a major practical concern for centuries. Thus, disciplines like economics and statistics have developed carefully reasoned conceptions of optimality that serve as guides for sensible behavior in risky situations. Chapter 2 summarizes and critically evaluates dominant notions of optimality and how those principles are continuing to evolve.

As is emphasized in Chapters 1 and 2, in many—if not most—situations, we are hard-pressed to identify anything like "objective" risk. Instead, risk is often characterized subjectively. Chapter 3, "Risk Appraisal," by J. Frank Yates and Eric R. Stone, reviews research about how people arrive at their assessments of the risk that is present in given situations.

Philip Bromiley and Shawn P. Curley wrote Chapter 4, "Individual Differences in Risk Taking." Many of us have the impression that some individuals are reliably less prone to taking risks than are others. Similarly, we often hold beliefs that some groups of people are generally more or less inclined toward risky actions than those in other groups, for instance, men vs women. How valid are these impressions? And, to the extent that various risk-taking propensities do exist, how can they be explained? These are the kinds of questions pursued in Chapter 4.

Parallel to our intuitions about other group differences, most of us believe that risk taking tends to differ in character for people of different ages. For instance, the stereotype is that the young are reckless and the old timid. But what really *are* the changes in risk taking over the life cycle and what lies underneath these changes? Baruch Fischhoff examines approaches to these issues in Chapter 5, "Risk Taking: A Developmental Perspective."

James H. Davis, Tatsuya Kameda, and Mark F. Stasson are the authors of Chapter 6, entitled "Group Risk Taking: Selected Topics." Beginning around 1960, social psychologists directed considerable attention to the possiblity that individuals' risk-taking behavior differs qualitatively depending on their social contexts. At first, research indicated that interaction with others encouraged risk proneness. Subsequent studies recorded instances of the opposite effect. Chapter 6 traces the history of this line of work, as well as research on the more general issue of risk taking in group settings.

Chapter 7 is called "Stress, Affect, and Risk Taking," and was written by Leon Mann. There is a constellation of affective constructs that includes stress, emotion, and mood. Is it possible that these constructs influence the nature of risk-taking behavior? Is it also possible that there are effects in the opposite direction, too, for instance, that risk taking reliably alters people's stress experiences? Chapter 7 tells what the literature has to say about such questions.

Nancy E. Adler, Susan M. Kegeles, and Janice L. Genevro wrote Chapter 8, "Risk Taking and Health." There is little that we can do to protect ourselves as individuals from some health hazards, for example, environmental pollution or some diseases such as pneumonia. However, other threats to our physical well-being in fact are influenceable by our personal actions, for instance, infectious diseases passed through the exchange of body fluids or diseases resulting from smoking tobacco. Chapter 8 discusses models and evidence concerning how people actually do behave in ways that affect their susceptibility to health threats.

Chapter 9, "Risk Taking and Accident Causation," was written by Willem A. Wagenaar. When accidents occur, we often assume that the culprit is faulty risk taking. Special theories of risk-taking behavior have been developed for the kinds of situations in which accidents often happen. Chapter 9 reviews such theories. It also critically evaluates the evidence that these theories, as well as more general notions of risk taking, indeed can adequately account for why accidents take place.

Chapter 10, called "Risk Taking, Design, and Training," is by Gordon F. Pitz. The activities of certain individuals have special risk significance. That is because these persons' actions affect the risk exposure of large numbers of people, not just themselves. Among these risk-critical individuals are designers of consumer products, equipment, and buildings, as well as managers of nearly every kind. Building on and going beyond the existing literature, including the preceding chapters, Chapter 10 develops concrete recommendations for how design considerations and personnel training can encourage more appropriate risk-taking behavior.

The "Epilogue" to the book highlights some of the more important themes that recur throughout the book. It also brings attention to especially significant gaps in our knowledge that should be the targets of future research on risk-taking behavior.

REFERENCES

Bazerman, M. H. (1990). *Judgment in managerial decision making* (2nd ed.). New York: Wiley.

Dawes, R. M. (1988). *Rational choice in an uncertain world.* San Diego: Harcourt, Brace, Jovanovich.

Hogarth, R. M. (1987). *Judgement and choice* (2nd ed.). Chichester, England: Wiley.

MacCrimmon, K. R., & Wehrung, D. A. (1986). *Taking risks: The management of uncertainty.* New York: Free Press.

Viscusi, W. K., & Magat, W. A. (Eds.). (1987). *Learning about risk.* Cambridge: Harvard University Press.

Yates, J. F. (1990). *Judgment and decision making.* Englewood Cliffs, NJ: Prentice Hall.

Acknowledgments

Special thanks are due to several individuals, without whose assistance the production of this book would have been far more difficult than it was. First, of course, are the contributors. The intellectual exchanges among the authors have been exciting and have led to insights that none of us could have achieved had they not taken place. Numerous readers provided invaluable criticisms and suggestions for individual chapters of the text, and are acknowledged in those chapters. In addition, however, several other friends were kind enough to offer similar commentary on other parts of the manuscript, including Nancy Adler, Kevin Biolsi, Nancy Johnson, Ju-Whei Lee, Paul Price, Steven Salterio, Karen Siegel-Jacobs, Eric Stone, and Carolynn Young. Mention must also be made of the bibliographic and production assistance of Kristin Blackburn, Andrew Parker, Nicole Willeumier, and John Gingrich. Finally, the list would be incomplete without recognizing the useful topical and organizational suggestions of the series editor, Dennis Holding, and of Michael Coombs of John Wiley and Sons, Ltd.

Partial financial support for production of the book was provided by the Arthur F. Thurnau Endowment at the University of Michigan.

J. Frank Yates

Chapter 1

The risk construct

J. Frank Yates and Eric R. Stone
The University of Michigan

CONTENTS

Fischhoff (1985, p. 89) observes that "People disagree more about what risk is than about how large it is." Such statements are common among risk experts. If we were to read 10 different articles or books about risk, we should not be surprised to see risk described in 10 different ways. How, then, can we achieve an understanding of risk-taking behavior when risk, the focal construct, appears to

Risk-taking Behavior. Edited by J. F. Yates
© 1992 John Wiley & Sons Ltd

be so slippery? Despite ambiguity about what risk is, research on risk taking has been demonstrably productive. Nevertheless, as numerous risk scholars have maintained (e.g. Weber, 1988), it seems that even more progress would occur if there were greater understanding and consensus about the risk construct itself.

It is conceivable that individuals who use the word risk in different ways are referring to entities that have no connection with each other. Consider, say, a trustee who reports that she takes "risk" into account when building clients' stock portfolios and a safety researcher who claims that "risk seeking" explains the behavior of the teenage drivers he studies. Although they are using the same expression, the trustee and the researcher *could* have completely unrelated concepts in mind. We doubt that such is often the case, however. Our thesis is that, instead, disagreements about the risk construct typically are more apparent than real. That is, we submit that a single construct underlies most risk discussions.

If the proposed thesis is correct, why does it *appear* that there is so little consensus about what constitutes risk? There seem to be three explanations. First, as we will argue, although there is indeed a widely accepted implicit risk construct, that construct has several distinct elements. Unfortunately, in practice people often refer to individual risk elements as the entire risk construct, as simply "risk." Second, risk manifests itself in different ways in different situations. The superficial differences in those situations make it hard to recognize that they have an important common denominator—risk. Finally, the illusion of disagreement arises from the fact that, as we will demonstrate, the risk in a given situation is inherently subjective, varying from one individual to the next.

Our aim has been to identify the basic risk concept through an analysis of how the risk expression is used across a variety of circumstances. The presumption is that commonalities and contrasts in such usage should reveal what is essential to the idea of risk. There have been numerous other analyses of the risk concept, each of which offers valuable insights, for instance, those by Fischhoff, Watson, and Hope (1984), Hansson (1989), Hertz and Thomas (1983, Chapter 1), MacCrimmon and Wehrung (1986, Chapter 1), Mehr (1977), and Vlek and Stallen (1980). Our analysis differs from the previous ones in several respects. The major difference, however, is that we have tried to take a broader perspective. Each of the prior analyses emphasized risk in a particular context, for example, public hazards or insurance. We have sought what is common *across* contexts. In this endeavor we are indebted to the earlier analyses, as they have helped illuminate what appears to be universal about risk.

We have found substantial consistency in diverse treatments of risk, and argue that this consistency rests on what can be legitimately called the risk construct. However, like others, we have also observed considerable variety in how risk is characterized. These variations highlight distinctions that, although they do not challenge the risk construct itself, are nevertheless significant in their own right. Each of these distinctions is acknowledged in some areas of risk scholarship though they apparently go unrecognized in others. Thus, the present analysis should be useful to risk specialists not only because it clarifies the focal construct, but also because it brings attention to aspects of risk those specialists might otherwise neglect.

The plan of the chapter is as follows. The first section addresses the role of risk in human activities: What *kind* of thing is risk? Why is it important? We will propose that the risk construct entails three critical elements: loss, the significance of loss, and the uncertainty associated with loss. Thus, the three succeeding sections respectively explore these elements in depth. The last major section of the chapter examines the notion of overall risk.

THE ROLE OF THE RISK CONSTRUCT

The topic of risk often arises, implicitly or explicitly, in the form of a question: "How much risk is acceptable?" For instance, when deliberating pollution control measures, we might ask: "Can we tolerate that much sulphur in our air?" Or when considering our personal finances, we might worry: "Is it really wise for us to reject this bid on our house, hoping that something better will come along?" Several authors have noted that, in isolation, there is no such thing as acceptable risk; because of its very nature, risk should always be rejected (e.g. Kaplan & Garrick, 1981; Slovic, 1987). This observation highlights two related facts. First, risk-taking problems are actually special kinds of decision problems. Second, these dilemmas are "problems" mainly because the relevant options entail other, complicating considerations besides risk.

In a decision problem a person selects an action with the intention of producing outcomes at least as satisfactory as those that would result from any other available option (cf. Yates, 1990, Chapter 1). When this goal is actually achieved, we say that the decision succeeds; otherwise, it fails. Thus, a "decision problem" is the challenge of making a successful decision. In risk-taking situations, risk is one—but only one—significant aspect of the available options. Accordingly, from the decision maker's perspective, the worth of such an alternative can be characterized as

$$\text{Worth} = f(\text{Risk, Other considerations}),$$

where the chance of an option being selected increases with its "worth." If risk is intrinsically repugnant, then the reason an alternative that contains risk is not rejected out of hand is that "Other considerations" must include attractive benefits, as well as perhaps additional negative features. For instance, a pollution control proposal that tolerates high sulphur emissions (significant disease risks) is taken seriously mainly because it also has advantages like low fuel costs and high employment rates for coal miners. So, in summary, the role of risk is that of one kind of negative feature that might characterize a decision alternative. Some might question the critical assumption that risk is indeed negative, something to be avoided. We will address this issue at the very end of our discussion of overall risk. We now examine what appear to be the essential elements of the risk construct.

THE ELEMENTS OF RISK

Dictionary definitions describe the meanings of words that are accepted by general consensus, or at least consensus among the language experts charged with establishing standard usage. Thus, such a definition seems a reasonable place to begin our analysis of the risk construct. A common dictionary definition of risk is "the possibility of loss."

Risk as loss possibility qualifies for the role prescribed in the previous section; the possibility of loss should certainly make a prospective action less appealing. Moreover, few of us would say that this definition conflicts with or is unrelated to what we mean when we use the word "risk." Indeed, a close examination of the many superficially different risk definitions and measures that appear throughout the literature leads to a similar conclusion. For instance, in their monograph on technological hazards, Fischhoff *et al.* (1981, p. 2) define risk as the "existence of threats" to life or health. In medicine and epidemiology, risk is the chance of some adverse outcome, such as death or the contraction of a particular disease (e.g. Kleinbaum, Kupper, & Morgenstern, 1982). And in the economic and business literature, opportunities whose returns are not guaranteed are commonly described as "risks" (e.g. Camerer & Kunreuther, 1989).

Unfortunately, risk as the possibility of loss falls short on essential detail. This definition does not elaborate what is meant by the components of the risk construct, that is, possibility and loss. And, although "the possibility *of* loss" is suggestive on the point, the definition is imprecise about how possibility and loss combine with each other to determine risk. A consistent but more refined characterization of risk seems to be required. We propose the following refinement: The critical elements of the risk construct are (a) potential losses, (b) the significance of those losses, and (c) the uncertainty of those losses. Further, these elements degrade an alternative's worth interactively (see Crouch & Wilson, 1982, Chapter 2). Thus, the effect of increasing the chance of a possible financial disaster on the riskiness—and hence unattractiveness—of a business venture depends on the size of the disaster. For instance, the risk implications of increasing the chance of a liability from 1 % to 5 % would be much greater if the potential liability were $2 000 000 rather than $2000.

In the succeeding sections, we explore the above risk elements and how they jointly determine overall risk. However, two important observations arise immediately from the present conception of risk. The first is that many measures and operational definitions of risk focus on only one of the risk elements. Such is the case, for example, when epidemiologists say that the risk of cancer in some population is 15 in 100 000, an indication of the uncertainty associated with a particular loss. This does not necessarily conflict with measures that focus on other risk constituents, say, an insurer's indication that providing coverage on a $250 000 house is riskier than providing coverage on one that costs only $100 000. These alternative measures are simply indicators of distinct parts of the same entity.

Our second observation is that, strictly speaking, risk is not an objective feature of a decision alternative itself. Instead, it represents an interaction between the alternative and the risk taker. In other words, risk is an inherently subjective construct. This is because, as we shall see, what is considered a loss is peculiar to the person concerned, and so is the significance of that loss and its chance of occurring. For instance, although being admitted to University X would be an honor for one student, having no recourse but to attend the same school would be a disappointment for another student.

LOSSES

A perspective

Most risk-taking situations involve alternatives that, if selected, would eventually produce not just one outcome that matters to the decision maker, but a host of them. It is useful to keep this fact in mind as we further review the risk concept. As an example, imagine an individual who is trying to choose among several job offers. For concreteness, we will call her "Jane Smith." Each of her potential jobs could be described with an "outcome matrix" like the one for Job A displayed in Figure 1.1. There we see that there are numerous categories of outcomes that are pertinent to Jane Smith's satisfaction and which might be realized at a given point during her tenure on Job A, such as her salary, her assigned location, and so on. We also see that various specific outcomes might really occur within those categories, for instance, $45 000, $50 000, ..., for salary, and Chicago, Detroit, ..., for location. The particular matrix that is shown applies to the circumstances five years into the future. Since our job seeker is actually concerned about an entire career, we recognize that the present characterization is a gross simplification. As implied by the outlines of additional outcome matrices shown in Figure 1.1, for every other time period there is another collection of outcomes that are significant to the person involved. Despite its impoverishment, the current view does serve our purposes.

Jane Smith's eventual satisfaction with Job A would depend on which outcomes in the various categories are actually realized, an "eventual reality." Such an eventual reality can be seen as a collection or vector of outcomes (cf.

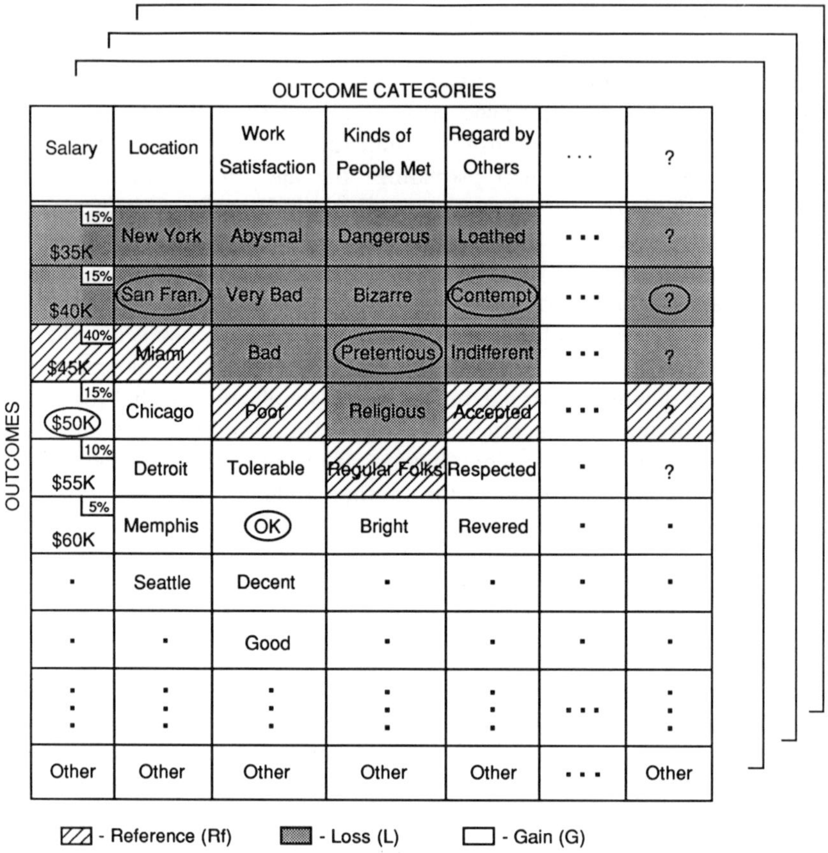

Salary	Location	Work Satisfaction	Kinds of People Met	Regard by Others	. . .	?
15% $35K	New York	Abysmal	Dangerous	Loathed	▪ ▪ ▪	?
15% $40K	San Fran.	Very Bad	Bizarre	Contempt	▪ ▪ ▪	?
40% $45K	Miami	Bad	Pretentious	Indifferent	▪ ▪ ▪	?
15% $50K	Chicago	Poor	Religious	Accepted	▪ ▪ ▪	?
10% $55K	Detroit	Tolerable	Regular Folks	Respected	▪	?
5% $60K	Memphis	OK	Bright	Revered	▪	▪
▪	Seattle	Decent	▪	▪	▪	▪
▪	▪	Good	▪	▪	▪	▪
⋮	⋮	⋮	⋮	⋮	▪ ▪ ▪	⋮
Other	Other	Other	Other	Other	▪ ▪ ▪	Other

▨ - Reference (Rf)   ▪ - Loss (L)   ☐ - Gain (G)

Figure 1.1. An illustrative outcome matrix: Job A for Jane Smith, five years hence. Outcomes that actually would be experienced are circled.

Kaplan & Garrick, 1981). For the sake of argument, imagine that the outcomes that are circled in Figure 1.1 are those that actually happen. Then the eventual reality would be

($50 000 salary (G), San Francisco location (L), OK work satisfaction (G), largely pretentious acquaintances (L), held in contempt (L),...)

where the Gs and Ls denote gains and losses, respectively, as defined below. As we shall see, outcome matrices facilitate the discussion of losses as well as other risk issues.

References

When we experience a loss, we are deprived of an outcome we already possessed or might have acquired; further, we are left with an outcome that is less appealing than the one that was taken away or precluded. Thus, implicit in the loss concept is the notion of a *reference outcome*, or simply a *reference* (cf. Kahneman & Tversky, 1979). This is the focal outcome that is taken away or denied. Any outcome that is preferred to the reference is a gain; one that is less preferred is a loss. As suggested in Figure 1.1, Jane Smith's salary reference (Rf) is $45 000. Any salary lower than $45 000 is a loss (L), and any higher salary, such as the $50 000 she actually earns, is a gain (G). In terms of location, we see that the reference outcome is Miami, Jane Smith's present location, and that her actual location in Job A, San Francisco, is a loss.

Our example implicates two classes of reference outcomes, *status quo references* and *non-status quo references*. A status quo reference is whatever a person presently has, for instance, Jane Smith's current residence in Miami. Being a student, Jane Smith earns nothing. This implies that her $45 000 salary reference is clearly a non-status quo reference. The example also brings attention to the inherent subjectivity of reference outcomes and hence losses. Given her $45 000 reference, Jane Smith's actual salary of $50 000 is a gain. But if that reference had been $55 000, her real earnings would be regarded as a loss.

How is it determined what is a reference outcome and, by implication, what is considered a loss? In various practical situations, practitioners simply declare reference outcomes by fiat, so they can get on with their work. For instance, in finance, the implicit reference is sometimes the investor's current wealth. On other occasions, it is the amount of money the investor might have earned in the most conservative investments, such as bank deposits. We often see "objective" risk measures being constructed from these standard reference outcomes. Such objectively defined references, losses, and risk measures have been retained over the years because the analyses that rely on them have been considered beneficial. For example, financial analyses that use the kinds of objective risk measures described later in the chapter are thought to have facilitated the assembling of more profitable investment portfolios. Most frequently, however, it seems that references are adopted by individuals for various psychological reasons. Hence, most of them form the foundations of subjective rather than objective risk. Examples include the following:

Personal average references: These are outcomes representative of those an individual has experienced most often in the past and therefore reasonably might expect in the future. They are sometimes known as *adaptation level references*. Notice in Figure 1.1 that "Poor" is the work satisfaction reference for Jane Smith. This might be a personal average reference, because "Poor" is, sadly, the level of work satisfaction Jane Smith usually experienced in her previous jobs.

Situational average references: These references are similar to personal average references. The difference is that the average applies to the situation rather than the given individual. For instance, since Jane Smith has never held Job A, she has no basis for establishing a personal average for the kinds of people encountered on that job. However, friends who have occupied the position might tell her that the typical person encountered is "a regular guy," hence her reference of "regular folks." Situational average references are commonly employed in the risk measures used in finance (e.g. expected returns on investment).

Social expectation references: These are outcomes that people who are important to an individual indicate they expect that person to achieve. Perhaps Jane Smith's salary reference of $45 000 is such a social expectation reference, induced by her parents' ideals.

Target references: A target or *aspiration level* (Lopes, 1987) is an outcome a person actively works to attain, say, holding the number of defective parts produced by a manufacturing process to no more than 0.5 %. Some targets are established solely by individuals for themselves. In other situations, targets are set by other people. For instance, it is not unusual for corporate managers to impose profitability targets on the division heads who answer to them (cf. Payne, Laughhunn, & Crum, 1980).

Best-possible references: This kind of reference is the most attractive outcome that is possible in the given situation. An example would be a grade of "A-" in a certain course, established as a reference because the professor says he cannot imagine any student deserving anything better than that.

Regret references: A regret reference is the outcome an individual would have attained—or at least the outcome the person *thinks* he or she would have attained—had a competing alternative been selected. For instance, suppose Jane Smith thinks that, had she chosen Job B instead of Job A, other people would regard her with acceptance. This might account for why "Accepted" is Ms Smith's reference for the outcome category of "Regard by Others" in Figure 1.1. A loss implied by a comparison against competing options is sometimes said to induce *regret* (cf. Bell, 1982; Loomes & Sugden, 1982), hence the present terminology. (Also see Dowling, 1986, on the related concept of "choice risk.")

Loss multiplicity

The multiplicity of potential outcome categories—and thus classes of losses—that are possible in risk-taking situations is recognized in several areas of risk research. Consumer behavior is an example where the idea has special prominence. Bauer (1960) was among the first to suggest that risk is a major determinant of whether a consumer buys or rejects a given product; the greater the perceived risk, the less likely the purchase. Many of us experience apprehension—sometimes bordering on terror—when we contemplate large purchases like cars, especially used cars. Bauer attributes these feelings to the risk inherent to those transactions. Research subsequent to Bauer's paper has shown that the risk that affects consumer purchasing comes in several varieties, which correspond to various distinct kinds of losses a person might suffer as a result of buying a given product. The risk taxonomy developed by Jacoby and Kaplan (1972; Kaplan, Szybillo, & Jacoby, 1974) is the one that is mentioned most often in research on consumer choice. According to that system, the losses a prospective purchase might produce fall into the following categories:

Financial loss	The consumer loses money, either because the product will not work at all (and presumably must be replaced), because it costs a lot to keep it in good condition, or because an equivalent or better product is available at less cost.
Performance loss	There is something wrong with the product or it does not work properly.
Physical loss	The product is unsafe, that is, harmful to one's health.
Psychological loss	The product disagrees with the buyer's self-image or self-concept, the way the buyer thinks about himself or herself.
Social loss	The product adversely affects the way others think about the buyer.
Time loss	The product wastes the buyer's time and causes inconvenience because it must be adjusted, repaired, or replaced (from Roselius, 1971).

Bearden and Mason's (1978) study of consumers' inclinations to buy or reject generic prescription drugs is a concrete illustration of how this conception of distinct loss categories has been used. These investigators found that concerns about performance, financial savings, and safety were among those that determined individuals' drug preferences. Carroll, Siridhara, and Fincham (1986) performed a similar analysis, but from the perspective of pharmacists who might recommend either generic or brand-name medicines. They discovered that concerns about the risks of generics—specifically, how well those drugs might perform—had significant effects on pharmacists' willingness to substitute generic for brand-name products. Such findings are valuable because they allow us to focus attention on those aspects of a risky situation that have major effects on people's behavior and not waste time on those that do not.

Two important ideas are implicit in the recognition of loss multiplicity. The first is that, all other things being equivalent, the greater the number of distinct losses that are incurred, the worse off is the risk taker. For instance, referring back to Figure 1.1, we see that Jane Smith suffered losses in three of the five outcome categories that were explicitly acknowledged—Location, Kinds of People Met, and Regard by Others. Things clearly would have been worse had, say, work satisfaction been a loss, too. The second idea is related but distinct. Alternatives differ in the numbers of significant outcome categories they entail, for instance, carpets, which are simple, versus computing systems, which are much more complicated. Again, all else being the same, we might expect that the potential for consequential losses—and hence risk—increases as the number of significant categories increases, for example, greater risk for computing systems than for carpets.

SIGNIFICANCE

Risk researchers and laypersons assume that, the more significant the potential losses in a situation, the greater the implied risk. Subjectivity affects this role of loss significance in two ways. We have already seen that reference outcomes can easily differ from one person to the next. Thus, an outcome that is a loss for one individual might well be a gain for another. But even if two individuals both consider the same outcomes to be losses, there is still room for differences in the significance of those outcomes, differences that have bearing on risk. Consider the Location category in Figure 1.1. Imagine a second job seeker besides Jane Smith, "Mary Jones." Like Ms Smith, Mary Jones also feels that locations in San Francisco and New York are losses. But, whereas Jane Smith regards New York as worse than San Francisco, Mary Jones feels the opposite. This could affect the riskiness of accepting Job A. For example, suppose that an assignment to San Francisco is more probable than one to New York. Then, by some conceptions of risk (see the section below on overall risk), accepting Job A would be riskier for Mary Jones than for Jane Smith.

Often potential outcomes are quantified, say, salaries or concentrations of pollutants. Typically, greater magnitudes are preferred to lesser ones or vice versa. For instance, we all prefer making more money to less, but we desire the smallest possible concentrations of pollutants in the air. On the other hand, there also exist quantified outcomes for which some intermediate amount is most preferred, amounts of fluoride in drinking water being an example. For any given quantified outcome, although loss significance is greatest for either maximum, minimum, or intermediate amounts, there can still exist important distinctions in loss significance from person to person.

As an illustration, consider Figure 1.2, which shows value functions for monetary losses for three different individuals, all of whom, of course, prefer having more money to less. Person A's linear value function says that the rate of change in the significance of losing money is constant. For instance, as depicted, losing an additional $10 always reduces Person A's satisfaction by the same amount, denoted D. In contrast, Person B's convex value function indicates diminishing marginal significance as loss magnitude increases. This implies, as suggested in the figure, that losing an additional $10 matters less to Person B

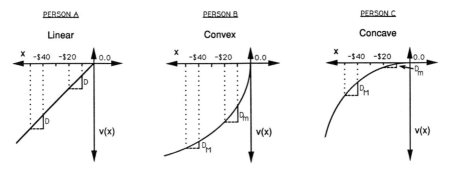

Figure 1.2.   Alternative value functions for losses.

when he has already lost a lot rather than a little, D_M vs D_m. Person C's concave value function describes the opposite pattern of loss responses. These different value functions for losses imply corresponding differences in how Persons A, B, and C would appraise the riskiness of alternatives that might result in financial losses. There are also theories of risk taking, such as expected utility theory (see Chapter 2, by Neumann & Politser) and prospect theory (Kahneman & Tversky, 1979), for which these distinctions imply either risk-seeking, risk-aversive, or risk-neutral behavior, in senses that will be defined below.

UNCERTAINTY

Every conception of risk requires that there must be uncertainty about the outcomes of prospective actions; if the outcomes are guaranteed, there is no risk. However, various risk conceptions differ in precisely *how* uncertainty affects risk. At least four roles for uncertainty are commonly discussed, as described presently.

Risk *as* uncertainty

Sometimes risk is said to exist whenever the outcomes of an action are not assured. That is, risk effectively *is* uncertainty. This is implied, for instance, when economists refer to any prospect with unguaranteed returns as a "risk" (e.g. Camerer & Kunreuther, 1989). Note that, in order for this viewpoint to be consistent with the notion of risk as the possibility of loss, the worst potential outcome must be less attractive than the reference. For example, imagine a business deal in which the best that could happen is that one earns $5000 and the worst is a return of $1000. To legitimately say that this deal is risky must mean that the reference is more than $1000.

Risk as uncertainty is the risk conception implicit in many discussions of risk-taking behavior within decision analysis (cf. Keeney & Raiffa, 1976; Winkler, 1972). Consider Gamble G, which captures the essential features of how alternatives are characterized in decision analysis. Gamble G promises a prize of $10 if a coin toss results in a head, and nothing otherwise. The expected value of a gamble is simply the sum of all the potential payoffs, each multiplied by its probability. It can be shown that the expected value is the mean payoff a gamble would yield over the long run. So, assuming a balanced coin, the expected value of Gamble G is

$$EV(G) = (1/2)(\$10) + (1/2)(\$0) = \$5.$$

If Gamble G were played hundreds of times, the average outcome of these plays would be very close to $5. Suppose an individual is given a choice between a gift of Gamble G and a gift of a $5 bill. The following terminological conventions are typically applied: (a) a preference for Gamble G is described as "risk seeking"; (b) indifference between Gamble G and the $5 bill is called "risk neutrality"; and (c) a preference for the $5 bill is termed "risk aversion."

More generally, risk seeking is evidenced by a preference for an uncertain prospect over a sure thing equivalent to the expected value of that prospect; indifference between those alternatives implies risk neutrality; and preference for the sure thing indicates risk aversion. As far as long-run considerations are concerned, the alternatives in such comparisons are indistinguishable. The above conventions imply that one interpretation of the "risk" that might be avoided or sought in situations like that described is simply the uncertainty about the payoff from any single implementation of the decision maker's choice.

Uncertainty about loss categories

Figure 1.1 suggests that there exist other categories besides those explicitly listed but which nevertheless are capable of affecting Jane Smith's satisfaction with Job A. The blank spaces and question marks highlight an important reality. Decision makers typically are unable to anticipate every significant outcome category. For instance, it might well turn out that, if Jane Smith took Job A, the quality of clerical support would be a major source of comfort or grief, although it never crosses her mind when she is trying to decide whether to accept the position. Generalizing, situations differ in the extent to which potential outcome categories—and therefore possible losses—are apparent. The riskiness of those situations increases with the uncertainty about what the categories of losses might be.

Sometimes the locus of uncertainty about loss categories resides in the alternatives themselves. Take the case of public hazards. Laypersons, at least, consider the newness of a technology (e.g. genetic engineering vs coal mining) to be a significant contributor to its riskiness (Slovic, Fischhoff, & Lichtenstein,

1985). In effect, a new technology is risky partly because no one knows what kinds of losses it might produce.

In other circumstances, the uncertainty about loss categories is a reflection of the risk taker's naïveté. Consider the activities of professional risk analysts in business and hazard management (cf. Hertz & Thomas, 1983). A major task of such analysts is unveiling the myriad ways a proposed business venture or public project conceivably could turn out badly. The intent of these exercises is to prevent clients from being "blindsided," that is, experiencing losses whose possibility never even occurred to them. The very surprisingness of these losses makes them all the more devastating. Blindsiding is not confined to business and public affairs; examples from personal situations abound. Take the case of AIDS (Acquired Immune Deficiency Syndrome). Not in their wildest dreams did it cross the minds of AIDS victims in the early 1980s that an incurable, fatal disease was among the hazards of their sexual or drug-taking activities or their receiving blood transfusions in the hospital.

Uncertainty about which losses will occur

Even if it is recognized that losses in a given category *can* occur, there is still uncertainty about *whether* those losses will occur. We assume that, short of loss being guaranteed, the greater the chance of a loss happening, the greater the risk. For instance, suppose that in Job A the chance of Jane Smith being assigned to one of her "loss" cities, San Francisco or New York, is 15%. If the corresponding chance for Job B is only 10%, then Job B is less risky, in that respect, at least.

As noted earlier, loss chances are the standard way of characterizing risk in medicine and epidemiology, for example, with disease mortality rates. Accounting is another arena in which risk is routinely described as loss chances. The end result of an audit performed on a firm's financial statements is a written opinion about whether those statements fairly present what they purport to present, for instance, that stated account balances and inventories do not differ significantly or "materially" from what is claimed. Such opinions are essential for the interests of several parties, including a firm's potential investors. Auditors recognize that their opinions can be erroneous. That is, the auditor might attest that a firm's statements are fair reports when they actually are not, or vice versa. The chance of either error occurring is called *overall audit risk*. Reporting an inappropriate opinion is disastrous for an auditor's reputation, resulting in the loss of future business. More immediately, inappropriate opinions expose the auditor to damaging lawsuits. Accordingly, auditors seek to limit overall audit risk to no more than 5% (Sullivan et al., 1985).

There is an additional important form of uncertainty associated with loss chances. In Figure 1.1, observe that no specific cities are listed underneath Seattle in the Location category. Instead, other potential locations are subsumed under the heading "Other." Some probability might be assigned to the

Other grouping. However, that assignment would not capture the uncertainty embodied in the fact that the constituents in the Other group are not identified explicitly. For instance, suppose that the other possible assignment locations are actually St. Louis, New Orleans, and Salt Lake City. Most of us would say that leaving these cities obscured within an "Other" category constitutes a variety of uncertainty in and of itself. That uncertainty, which contributes to riskiness, is analogous to, but different from, that associated with unspecified loss categories.

Levels of uncertainty

Imagine Surgical Procedure A, which has failed in 200 out of 1000 previous attempts, and Surgical Procedure B, which has failed in one of its total of 5 trials. These procedures are being contemplated for patient "Ronald Davis." Most people would say that the chance of failure for Mr Davis is the same for both procedures: 20%. At the same time, however, they would say that Procedure B is riskier. This example implicates the importance of levels of uncertainty in risk characterizations.

In the present context, the expression "levels of uncertainty" pertains to the firmness of the basis on which loss chances are designated. In the case of Procedure A, the basis is secure, but it is considerably less so for Procedure B. Decision researchers acknowledge a continuum of uncertainty levels, as noted in Figure 1.3. At one extreme, termed "ignorance" by Luce and Raiffa (1957), there is no basis whatsoever for assigning loss chances. At the other extreme of the solid portion of the continuum, the chances of those outcomes are well established by informed consensus. These chances are sometimes described as *canonical* or *objective probabilities*, and in some circumstances are also known as *actuarial* or *aleatory probabilities*. A good example is provided by American legal trials. Thirteen jurors might hear all the evidence in a case. However, only twelve of those individuals actually participate in the jury deliberations and make a decision; one of the original thirteen jurors is randomly selected by lot to be excused. All of us would agree that the chance of any one of the jurors being dismissed is 1/13. Interestingly, Luce and Raiffa referred to the level of uncertainty entailed in this example as merely "risk." To avoid confusion, we will call it "objectivity." Between ignorance and objectivity are various states of what Ellsberg (1961) has described as *ambiguity*.

Uncertainty levels clearly affect people's behavior (e.g. Becker & Brownson,

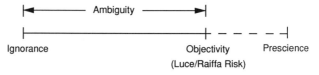

Figure 1.3.   Levels of uncertainty.

1964; Yates & Zukowski, 1976). In an illustrative study, Curley, Eraker, and Yates (1984) asked medical patients and hospital visitors about a treatment for stiffness and pain. They found that large numbers of the respondents who would accept the treatment when its chances of success were described as "5 in 10" rejected it when those chances were characterized as "somewhere between 3 in 10 and 7 in 10" (pp. 505–506). Although ambiguity is generally avoided, it is sometimes sought, for instance, when the odds of realizing a gain are remote (Curley & Yates, 1985).

Regardless of what people actually do, there is not general agreement among risk specialists about what role, if any, levels of uncertainty should have in a proper characterization of risk, or even in decision making. Some (e.g. Raiffa, 1961) maintain that ambiguity avoidance or ambiguity seeking should be prohibited because such behavior violates expected utility theory, which is often taken as a norm of rationality. However, Hazen (1990) has shown that ambiguity preferences can be reconciled with utility theory for decisions that will be implemented repeatedly.

Relatedly, surveys indicate that business executives make a sharp distinction between "risk taking" and "gambling" (March & Shapira, 1987). These executives contend that, although risk taking is an essential part of their responsibilities, gambling is something they avoid. The executives' conceptions of gambling situations appear to involve at least two things. First, in gambles the probabilities of losses are unacceptably high and the chances of gains are too slight. Second, and more importantly from our perspective, beyond a certain point it is impossible to learn anything to reduce the uncertainty in a gamble.

As an example, consider the card game of blackjack. In principle (though no casino would allow this), a player could use a computer to follow the course of play and calculate the actuarial probabilities of particular cards appearing on every drawing, say, determining that $P(8$ or better$) = 43\%$ for a given situation. This would almost certainly improve the player's winnings, because the player's unaided judgments are virtually guaranteed to differ from the actuarial probabilities. And it can be shown that these unaided judgments should lead to choices that, in the long run, produce worse payoffs. However, by the very nature of random drawings, our computer-assisted player cannot approximate the foresight of a clairvoyant, who would *know* what card would appear on every selection from the deck. Such constraints on knowability are intolerable to executives. Thus, a large part of executive risk handling involves discovering more about what would happen if a given action were taken, for instance, by acquiring intelligence about competitors' abilities to respond to one's initiatives, thereby lessening the risk. If a situation does not permit this kind of discovery, executives avoid that situation if they can. (See also Wehrung *et al.*, 1989.)

Executives' remarks about the reducibility of uncertainty suggest that levels of uncertainty beyond objectivity should be acknowledged. As implied by the dotted line extension to the continuum in Figure 1.3, in some cases it is indeed possible to do better than merely reaching objectivity. Or perhaps it is more appropriate to say that we can sometimes achieve versions of objectivity that more closely approach "prescience," wherein one literally knows whether a loss is going to occur.

To continue the previous blackjack example, imagine that the situation that resulted in the computed probability $P(8$ or better$) = 43\%$ were repeated 1000 times. We should expect a card with value 8 or better to be drawn on approximately 430 of those occasions. Unfortunately, our blackjack player cannot anticipate *which* of the 1000 occasions would be the ones with the high-value cards. Now, if a clairvoyant were to report probability judgments for each of the 1000 card drawings, the clairvoyant would indicate $P'(8$ or better$) = 100\%$ on precisely those 430 occasions when a card of 8 points or better is drawn and $P'(8$ or better$) = 0\%$ in the remaining 570 instances. Thus, for both the mortal blackjack player and the clairvoyant, the probability assignments are "objective" in that their average values match the actual relative frequency of the focal event. However, the clairvoyant's assignments are clearly superior. Executives cannot hope to always attain the prescience of a clairvoyant, but they see it as eminently reasonable to strive for such perfection.

OVERALL RISK

As noted previously, in various practical and research situations, risk specialists often index risk according to only one of the elements distinguished above, for example, loss probabilities. This does not mean that these individuals believe that such measures fully capture the risk construct. It is just that, for the limited purposes at hand, those measures are sufficient. For instance, mortality rates are adequate risk measures in many public health discussions because it is taken for granted that deaths from the pertinent diseases represent significant losses to society. Moreover, death from one cause is considered the same as death from any other. In our terminology, since there is no variability in the significance of the relevant losses, significance can be ignored and the focus can be placed on uncertainty. (But suppose a disease affects mainly one segment of the population, such as children or drug addicts. This could well change how the situation is regarded.) So, beyond the demands of particular situations, how should various risk elements combine with one another to determine overall risk? Here we describe the major positions that have been taken on the issue, first presenting the underlying concepts and then how they have been expressed in the literature. (Also see Libby & Fishburn, 1977; and Yates, 1990, Chapter 11.)

The core ideas: interaction and independence

At the heart of the combination principles we will consider are two basic ideas. The first applies to how the significance and uncertainty associated with a given loss jointly affect overall risk. Suppose we let the uncertainty associated with specific $Loss_i$ be represented by its probability, $P(Loss_i)$. And let us characterize the significance of that loss by the importance index $I(Loss_i)$. The first risk combination notion is then captured by the following conceptual equation (cf. Crouch & Wilson, 1982, Chapter 2):

$$Risk_i = P(Loss_i) \otimes I(Loss_i) \tag{1.1}$$

We see here that the loss likelihood and loss significance constructs are combined by an operator $\otimes$ that behaves essentially, though not completely, like multiplication.

As indicated earlier in the chapter, the prevailing view is that uncertainty and significance should combine interactively. Thus, constant differences in significance should have little influence on overall risk if the chances of the pertinent losses are small, but should matter a great deal if those chances are substantial. This notion is well captured by a multiplication-like operator. Risk specialists sometimes hedge on fully accepting multiplication operators because there are instances where such operators contradict intuitions about how risk should behave. For instance, Kaplan and Garrick (1981) contend that it is difficult to equate (as implied by Equation 1.1) the riskiness of a low probability-high damage scenario (e.g. breaking a leg) and a high probability-low damage scenario (e.g. getting a cold). In fact, there is some evidence that multiplication operators do not faithfully represent conceptions of how loss chances and significance combine, among laypersons, at least (e.g. Bettman, 1975).

The second idea that recurs in risk combination principles applies to situations in which more than one loss might occur. It says that the effects of those losses are independently cumulative. That is, in contrast to the interactive combination of significance and uncertainty, the contribution to overall risk made by one potential loss is always the same, regardless of the other potential losses that might accompany it. Suppose, as suggested above, that the risk involving potential $Loss_1$ is denoted by $Risk(Loss_1)$, that with potential $Loss_2$ by $Risk(Loss_2)$, and so on. Then the second risk combination concept is embodied in this conceptual equation:

$$\text{Overall Risk} = Risk(Loss_1) \oplus Risk(Loss_2) \oplus \cdots \tag{1.2}$$

In this equation, the operator $\oplus$ is equivalent to addition. Thus, the overall risk implied by a collection of potential losses is an accumulation of the contributions made by each of them.

Note that the above cumulation principle precludes context effects. That is, the risk contribution of any given potential loss is always the same, no matter what other losses might be combined with it. For instance, the effect of financial risk on the overall riskiness of a prospective action is the same, whether the other potential losses entail physical injury or social embarrassment. Curiously, there seems to have been no controversy over the legitimacy of this notion.

Exactly how the ideas of interaction and independence have been operation-alized in risk research and risk management is illustrated in the overall risk representations described below (see also Yates, 1990, Chapter 11, for further discussion, including numerical examples).

Expected loss

Expected loss is the overall risk characterization that captures the previous principles most directly. The expected loss concept is most easily described as it applies to quantified outcomes. Let us denote by L the loss implied by a given outcome X and reference Rf. More explicitly.

$$L = Rf - X, \qquad (1.3)$$

Further, let $P(L)$ describe the probability of that loss. Then the expected loss (EL) is simply the sum of all potential losses, each weighted by its probability:

$$EL = \sum P(L)L, \qquad (1.4)$$

where the summation is taken over all outcomes considered worse than the reference. As a specific example, consider Jane Smith's six potential salaries in Job A, as described in Figure 1.1. The percentages associated with the respective salaries are their probabilities. It is easy to show that, given Jane Smith's reference salary of $45 000, the expected loss is $2250.

A variant of expected loss applies to nonquantified outcomes. It takes the following form:

$$EL = \sum P(L)IR(L), \qquad (1.5)$$

where $IR(L)$ is an importance rating assigned to the loss L represented by outcome X, and the summation is taken over all the outcomes considered worse than the reference. Imagine that location is Jane Smith's sole consideration in choosing jobs. Suppose that in Figure 1.1 there are probabilities 0.10 and 0.05 that Ms Smith would be assigned to San Francisco and New York, respectively, her only "loss" locations. Further, suppose that Ms Smith considers it worse to be sent to New York, with loss importance ratings of 6 and 8 attached to San Francisco and New York correspondingly. Then the expected loss would be 1.0 rating points (since $0.10 \times 6 + 0.05 \times 8 = 1.0$). If a similar calculation indicated that the expected loss for another position, Job B, is 1.6 points, then we would say that Job B is the riskier prospect.

Semivariance

One could argue that the risk associated with quantified losses should not increase directly with the magnitude of a loss, but instead should grow more dramatically. The *below-reference semivariance* (*Semvar*) is a risk measure that captures this requirement:

$$\text{Semvar} = \sum P(L)L^2, \tag{1.6}$$

where the notation is the same as before. In the case of Jane Smith's salary on Job A, the semivariance would be Semvar $= 18.75 \times 10^6$, in squared dollar units.

Is it reasonable to think that for most people loss significance grows with the square of the loss? Some theories of decision behavior (e.g. Kahneman & Tversky's, 1979, prospect theory) suggest not, that in fact losses generally exhibit diminishing marginal significance. The semivariance can be generalized to allow for this possibility by replacing L^2 in Equation 1.6 by L^a, where a is a constant less than 1.0 (Fishburn, 1977).

Variance

As suggested in our previous discussion of gambles, the expected value (*EV*), or mean, of any distribution is the sum of all the possible values of the pertinent quantity, each weighted by its probability. Thus, the expected salary for Job A in Figure 1.1 is $45 250. The expected value is the reference that is used in the most common overall risk measure in finance (Elton & Gruber, 1987), the *variance* (Var):

$$\text{Var} = \sum P(X)(X - EV)^2, \tag{1.7}$$

where the summation is taken over all outcomes X, not just the ones that are losses. Literally, the variance is a measure of how much the outcomes vary or differ from one another. It is straightforward to show that, for Job A salaries, Var $= 43.69 \times 10^6$, in squared dollars.

The variance is sometimes regarded as a flawed risk measure because it is affected not only by losses, that is, outcomes below the reference, but by gains, too. Thus, two alternatives whose outcome distributions are identical with respect to losses could nevertheless be considered to entail different amounts of risk. So what is the attraction of the variance? Mainly computational convenience and the fact that financial analyses relying on it have proved useful (cf. Levy & Sarnat, 1990, Chapter 9).

Overall risk when there are multiple outcome categories

Implicit in the overall risk characterizations described above is the assumption that there is a single outcome category, for instance, either salary or location. Suppose, as is typically the case, there are several categories. What then? Curiously, the issue is seldom explicitly discussed. But one domain where the question *has* been addressed is consumer behavior. There the suggested approach is a direct extension of the independent cumulation principle (e.g. Bearden & Mason, 1978). Thus, the generalization of expected loss as in Equation 1.5 would be

$$EL = \sum \sum P(L)IR(L),   (1.8)$$

where the second summation extends over all the pertinent outcome categories. For instance, in the case of Jane Smith's Job A, the expression for expected loss would look something like the following

$EL = (0.15)IR(\$50\,000 - \$35\,000) + (0.15)IR(\$50\,000 - \$35\,000)$

$\quad + P(\text{San Francisco})IR(\text{San Francisco}) + P(\text{New York})IR(\text{New York})$

$\quad + P(\text{Abysmal})IR(\text{Abysmal}) + P(\text{Very Bad})IR(\text{Very Bad}) + P(\text{Bad})IR(\text{Bad})$

$\quad + \cdots$

An assessment

How well do the present overall risk characterizations capture the essence of what people mean by risk? First of all, the various measures such as expected loss and variance do not necessarily even rank order different situations the same way as to their putative riskiness. That is, although according to expected loss, Alternatives A, B, and C might be ranked $A > B > C$ in riskiness, the ranking might be something like $B > C > A$ according to the variance. Thus, not every one of the overall risk descriptions can be a *perfect* risk representation. Beyond this observation, however, two complaints can be voiced about the very approach embodied in these accounts.

The first complaint lies in the reliance on probabilities for specific outcomes as a representation of uncertainty. The most obvious reason this is problematic is that it neglects other aspects of uncertainty, such as that which arises from not knowing which loss categories are possible in a given situation. It also ignores issues associated with levels of uncertainty and uncertainty reducibility.

The second objection rests on the observation that risk is multidimensional, that it entails numerous distinct elements. Some observers claim that the very idea of overall risk as a quantity is unreasonable. As Kaplan and Garrick (1981) put it: "a single number is not a big enough concept to communicate risk" (p. 25). Such a statement could mean several things. But one of those potential meanings is that overall risk cannot be "measured" in the sense that it might be impossible to consistently map risk appraisals from multiple dimensions onto a single continuum (cf. Roberts, 1979). Whether this is in fact the case is an important issue for future risk scholarship.

Aside from the question of whether risk appraisals *can* be reduced to a single overall risk indicator consistently, why would one want to do so? Has that aspiration been misguided, as might be inferred from Kaplan and Garrick's (1981) remarks? Probably not. One approach that is sometimes taken in making risky decisions is to trade off risk against benefits (cf. Crouch & Wilson, 1982). This strategy has several appealing features. However, it can be implemented only when risk is characterized by a single index (see also Fischhoff, Watson, & Hope, 1984).

Risk repugnance

We noted at the outset that most treatments of risk assume that risk is inherently repugnant. This assumption is not universal, however. Some analyses seem to allow for indifference or even attraction to risk. Others assert that individuals might have intermediate "target" levels of risk that they find most appealing. Thus, our review of the risk construct would be incomplete without addressing the risk repugnance issue.

Are there circumstances in which the consensus conception of risk does not require that risk be shunned? We propose that the answer to this question is "No." We submit that claims to the contrary only *seem* to be such. Consider arbitrary risky Alternatives A and B, with A riskier than B. In the scheme introduced previously, these options could be represented as

$$A = \text{(High risk, Other considerations)}$$

$$B = \text{(Low risk, Other considerations)}$$

To justify the claim that risk is not repugnant, in choosing between some such A and B, a risk taker must choose Alternative A, with the assumption that "*Other considerations*" *are equivalent in both options.* Our thesis is that most—if not all—analyses of risk-taking behavior that appear to reject risk repugnance describe situations where the alternatives in fact differ with respect to "Other considerations." More specifically, there is a confound, whereby the greater risk in high-risk options is offset by positive features missing from their competitors. These analyses also sometimes use special definitions of risk that disagree with the consensus notion of risk.

There is too little space available to present detailed arguments for our thesis for all the apparent risk repugnance counterclaims that appear in the literature. However, a few remarks about some of those proposals indicate the nature of the arguments.

Expected utility theory and decision analysis: As noted previously, expected utility theory, which is operationalized in decision analysis (see Chapter 2, by Neumann & Politser, and Chapter 10, by Pitz), allows for risk indifference and risk seeking. But also recall that the latter terms are defined in a restrictive manner in that context. Thus, to reprise our earlier example, an individual is said to be risk seeking if she rejects a $5 bill in favor of Gamble G, which promises $10 if a balanced coin toss yields heads and nothing otherwise. Notice that the risk characterization implicit in this example demands the kind of confound described above. When the decision maker selects the gamble, implying the possibility of "losing" money relative to the potential gain of $5, she simultaneously acquires the possibility of gaining $10, an outcome that is precluded by accepting the $5 bill.

Thrill seeking: As described by Bromiley and Curley in Chapter 4, and consistent with common experience, there are lots of instances where people seek out and relish high-risk games. The most obvious examples are sports like racing and mountain climbing, in which life itself is imperiled, as well as casino gambling, where financial ruin is not uncommon. Actually, risk seems endemic to almost all games, especially competitive ones. People say the games would be "boring" without the risk of losing. We note that, in all these cases, there is again a confound between the riskiness and benefits of the activities. Individuals are plausibly not attracted by the risk of those activities, in the sense of their loss potential, but instead by the prospect of the exhilaration which accompanies *escaping* from the potential loss. Moreover, such escapes typically are accompanied by significant auxiliary rewards, for example, prestige.

Target risk levels: Wilde's (1982) risk homeostasis theory seems to imply that people do not seek to minimize risk in activities like driving. Instead, the theory appears to say that we seek intermediate target risk levels. However, as argued by Wagenaar in Chapter 9, a more careful analysis of models such as risk homeostasis theory paints a different picture. The risk taker is actually portrayed as trading off risk against benefits (even if only implicitly), where the benefits of alternative actions increase with their riskiness. For instance, along with the greater risk implied by driving fast is the advantage of arriving earlier at one's destination. The results of these subjective risk-benefit analyses only appear to indicate intermediate risk targeting if one ignores the benefits.

Coombs's (1975) portfolio theory explicitly posits intermediate risk targets for monetary gambles, conditional upon constant expected values. Once again, varying risk while holding expected value constant requires the kind of confound between increased risk and potential gains that casts doubt on the legitimacy of the special meaning of "risk seeking" as the term is used in decision analysis. Moreover (see, for example, Lehner, 1980), portfolio theory provides a good description of the risk-taking behavior of very few individuals.

SUMMARY

At first glance, it appears that there is substantial disagreement among risk researchers and others about what should be understood as risk. This disagreement suggests that there might not be a core conception of risk that drives most research that purportedly examines risk-taking behavior. However, a careful analysis of how risk has been discussed and studied implies that there is indeed implicit general agreement about a fundamental conception of risk.

In this consensus view, risk is one among several considerations that can affect the subjective worth of the decision alternatives that people face. At its core, risk is the possibility of loss. There are three essential risk elements: (a) losses, (b) the significance of those losses, and (c) uncertainty associated with those losses. These elements are inherently imprecise and subjective. For instance, losses are defined relative to reference outcomes, which vary according to principles that are not only poorly understood but virtually unstudied. And loss uncertainty can reside not only in the chances of particular losses happening, but also in the very *kinds* of losses that are capable of occurring. The prevailing assumption is that the significance and uncertainty of losses contribute to overall riskiness in an interactive manner, while the risk contributions of several potential losses are implicitly assumed to be independent of one another. However, it is not entirely clear that the various acknowledged elements of risk can be consistently aggregated to form overall risk.

ACKNOWLEDGMENTS

It is our great pleasure to acknowledge the excellent criticisms and suggestions offered by the following friends on previous versions of this chapter: Kevin Biolsi, Baruch Fischhoff, Nancy Johnson, Ju-Whei Lee, Gordon Pitz, Karen Siegel-Jacobs, and Carolynn Young. Preparation of this chapter was supported in part by the Arthur F. Thurnau Endowment at the University of Michigan.

REFERENCES

Bauer, R. A. (1960). Consumer behavior as risk taking. In R. S. Hancock (Ed.), *Dynamic marketing for a changing world* (pp. 389–398). Chicago: American Marketing Association.

Bearden, W. O., & Mason, J. B. (1978). Consumer-perceived risk and attitudes toward generically prescribed drugs. *Journal of Applied Psychology*, 63, 741–746.

Becker, S. W., & Brownson, F. O. (1964). What price ambiguity? Or the role of ambiguity in decision-making. *Journal of Political Economy*, 72, 62–73.

Bell, D. E. (1982). Regret in decision making under uncertainty. *Operations Research*, 30, 961–981.

Bettman, J. R. (1975). Information integration in consumer risk perception: A comparison of two models of component conceptualization. *Journal of Applied Psychology*, 60, 381–385.

Camerer, C. F., & Kunreuther, H. (1989). Decision processes for low probability events: Policy implications. *Journal of Policy Analysis and Management*, 8, 565–592.

Carroll, N. V., Siridhara, C., & Fincham, J. E. (1986). Perceived risks and pharmacists' generic substitution behavior. *Journal of Consumer Affairs*, 20, 36–47.

Coombs, C. H. (1975). Portfolio theory and the measurement of risk. In M. F. Kaplan & S. Schwartz (Eds.), *Human judgment and decision processes* (pp. 63–85). New York: Academic Press.

Crouch, E. A. C., & Wilson, R. (1982). *Risk/benefit analysis*. Cambridge, MA: Ballinger.

Curley, S. P., Eraker, S. A., & Yates, J. F. (1984). An investigation of patient's reactions to therapeutic uncertainty. *Medical Decision Making*, **4**, 501–511.

Curley, S. P., & Yates, J. F. (1985). The center and range of the probability interval as factors affecting ambiguity preferences. *Organizational Behavior and Human Decision Processes*, **36**, 273–287.

Dowling, G. R. (1986). Perceived risk: The concept and its measurement. *Psychology & Marketing*, **3**, 193–210.

Ellsberg, D. (1961). Risk, ambiguity, and the Savage axioms. *Quarterly Journal of Economics*, **75**, 643–669.

Elton, E. J., & Gruber, M. J. (1987). *Modern portfolio theory and investment analysis* (3rd ed.). New York: Wiley.

Fischhoff, B. (1985). Managing risk perceptions. *Issues in Science and Technology*, **2**(1), 83–96.

Fischhoff, B., Lichtenstein, S., Slovic, P., Derby, S. L., & Keeney, R. L. (1981). *Acceptable risk*. New York: Cambridge University Press.

Fischhoff, B., Watson, S. R., & Hope, C. (1984). Defining risk. *Policy Sciences*, **17**, 123–139.

Fishburn, P. C. (1977). Mean-risk analysis with risk associated with below-target returns. *American Economic Review*, **67**, 116–126.

Hansson, S. O. (1989). Dimensions of risk. *Risk Analysis*, **9**, 107–112.

Hazen, G. B. (1990, June). *Decision versus policy: An expected utility resolution of the Ellsberg Paradox*. Paper presented at the Fifth International Conference on the Foundations and Applications of Utility, Risk, and Decision Theories, Duke University, Durham, NC.

Hertz, D. B., & Thomas, H. (1983). *Risk analysis and its applications*. New York: Wiley.

Jacoby, J., & Kaplan, L. B. (1972). The components of perceived risk. In M. Ventakesan (Ed.), *Proceedings of the Third Annual Conference of the Association for Consumer Research* (pp. 382–393). Chicago: Association for Consumer Research.

Kahneman, D., & Tversky, A. (1979). Prospect theory: An analysis of decision under risk. *Econometrica*, **47**, 263–291.

Kaplan, L. B., Szybillo, G. J., & Jacoby, J. (1974). Components of perceived risk in product purchase: A cross-validation. *Journal of Applied Psychology*, **59**, 287–291.

Kaplan, S., & Garrick, B. J. (1981). On the quantitative definition of risk. *Risk Analysis*, **1**, 11–27.

Keeney, R. L., & Raiffa, H. (1976). *Decisions with multiple objectives: Preferences and value tradeoffs*. New York; Wiley.

Kleinbaum, D. G., Kupper, L. L., & Morgenstern, H. (1982). *Epidemiologic research: Principles and quantitative methods*. Belmont, CA: Lifetime Learning Publications.

Lehner, P. E. (1980). A comparison of portfolio theory and weighted utility models of risky decision making. *Organizational Behavior and Human Performance*, **26**, 238–249.

Levy, H., & Sarnat, M. (1990). *Capital investment and financial decisions* (4th ed.). New York: Prentice Hall.

Libby, R., & Fishburn, P. C. (1977). Behavioral models of risk taking in business decisions: A survey and evaluation. *Journal of Accounting Research*, **15**, 272–292.

Loomes, G., & Sugden, R. (1982). Regret theory: An alternative theory of rational choice under uncertainty. *Economic Journal*, **92**, 805–824.

Lopes, L. L. (1987). Between hope and fear: The psychology of risk. In L. Berkowitz

(Ed.), *Advances in experimental social psychology, Vol. 20* (pp. 255-295). New York: Academic Press.

Luce, R. D., & Raiffa, H. (1957). *Games and decisions.* New York: Wiley.

MacCrimmon, K. R., & Wehrung, D. A. (1986). *Taking risks: The management of uncertainty.* New York: Free Press.

March, J. G., & Shapira, Z. (1987). Managerial perspectives on risk and risk taking. *Management Science, 33,* 1404-1418.

Mehr, R. I. (1977). *Life insurance: Theory and practice.* Dallas: Business Publications.

Payne, J. W., Laughhunn, D. J., & Crum, R. (1980). Translation of gambles and aspiration levels in risky choice behavior. *Management Science, 26,* 1039-1060.

Raiffa, H. (1961). Risk, ambiguity, and the Savage axioms: Comment. *Quarterly Journal of Economics, 75,* 690-694.

Roberts, F. S. (1979). *Measurement theory.* Reading, MA: Addison-Wesley.

Roselius, T. (1971). Consumer rankings of risk reduction methods. *Journal of Marketing, 35,* 56-61.

Slovic, P. (1987). Perception of risk. *Science, 236,* 280-285.

Slovic, P., Fischhoff, B., & Lichtenstein, S. (1985). Characterizing perceived risk. In R. Kates, C. Hohenemser, & J. Kasperson (Eds.), *Perilous progress: Managing the hazards of technology* (pp. 91-125). Boulder, CO: Westview Press.

Sullivan, J. D., Gnospelius, R. A., DeFliese, P. L., & Jaenicke, H. R. (1985). *Montgomery's accounting* (10th ed.). New York: Wiley.

Vlek, C., & Stallen, P. J. (1980). Rational and personal aspects of risk. *Acta Psychologica, 45,* 273-300.

Weber, E. (1988). A descriptive measure of risk. *Acta Psychologica, 69,* 185-203.

Wehrung, D. A., Lee, K., Tse, D. K., & Vernitsky, I. B. (1989). Adjusting risky situations: A theoretical framework and empirical test. *Journal of Risk and Uncertainty, 2,* 189-212.

Wilde, G. J. S. (1982). The theory of risk homeostasis: Implications for safety and health. *Risk Analysis, 2,* 209-225.

Winkler, R. L. (1972). *Introduction to Bayesian inference and decision.* New York: Rinehart, and Winston.

Yates, J. F. (1990). *Judgment and decision making.* Englewood Cliffs, NJ: Prentice Hall. Hall.

Yates, J. F., & Zukowski, L. G. (1976). Characterization of ambiguity in decision making. *Behavioral Science, 21,* 19-25.

Chapter 2

Risk and optimality

Peter J. Neumann and Peter E. Politser
Harvard University

CONTENTS

INTRODUCTION

Risky decisions have long interested researchers, many of whom have suspected that people often make choices "suboptimally." This skepticism has motivated many studies to help people improve their decisions. Such research has obvious appeal. All of us, from money managers deciding how to invest a portfolio to physicians deciding on a proper diagnosis and treatment, would like to make the "right" decision, or at least to correctly interpret the probabilities and risks involved. Recently, the US Congress has even begun discussing a broad research program to evaluate medical interventions that would include quantitative analytic techniques (Gradison & Stark, 1989). But after decades of research, as we later discuss, the use of decision analytic methods remains controversial.

Risk-taking Behavior. Edited by J. F. Yates
© 1992 John Wiley & Sons Ltd

This chapter describes "optimal" decision models and the current debate over their application. The first section clarifies why we need better decision making. The second reviews expected utility theory as a theoretical foundation for "rational" decision making and decision analytic tools. The third section discusses criticisms and limitations of the expected utility model. The fourth describes alternative techniques. The final section discusses the current state of the debate and the need for further research.

LIMITATIONS OF HUMAN DECISION MAKING

All of us confront an uncertain environment with many risky choices (i.e. those with uncertain outcomes but perhaps with known probability distributions). But we have limited abilities to process information. The following sections illustrate a few of the many ways that humans inadequately estimate probabilities and make risky decisions. Although their examples derive largely from physicians' medical decisions, most conclusions apply equally in other contexts.

Judgment

Experiments show that people may incorrectly use information or not use all the relevant information. When confronted with diagnostic tasks—like guessing why a car will not start—even experts typically generate a small fraction of the potentially relevant hypotheses (Fischhoff, Slovic, & Lichtenstein, 1978).

Similar judgment errors may impair physicians' treatment choices. Doctors typically face risks in making diagnoses, performing surgical procedures, and prescribing drugs. To improve their decisions, traditional educators taught physicians to pursue an "exhaustive" diagnostic strategy, i.e. to obtain as much information and consider as many diagnoses as possible (Politser, 1981). Evidence indicates, however, that physicians typically keep only a few diagnostic hypotheses in mind at any one time and, as a result, may retain incorrect hypotheses or ignore evidence that points to correct ones. Elstein, Shulman, and Sprafka (1978) have shown that physicians typically form tentative diagnoses from a small amount of data and sometimes ignore new information that contradicts the initial diagnosis. In other cases, physicians may remember only a diagnosis that is currently being entertained, thus overweighting recently acquired information (Wortman, 1972). Human frailties such as limited memory and inattention may cause other errors. Studies have shown, for example, that physicians preoccupied with a more acute condition have overlooked abnormalities like unexplained anemia (Cole, Balmer, & Wilson, 1974; Craven, Wenzel, & Atuk, 1975) or adverse drug effects (Shapiro, Slone, Lewis et al., 1971).

People also have limited abilities to estimate probabilities, and such limitations can lead to inappropriate decisions. For example, physicians' subjective probability judgments for diagnoses are often miscalibrated and do not match actual disease frequencies. Doctors also may equate the conditional probability of a test result given a patient's illness with the probability of an illness given a test result (Casscells, Schoenberger, & Graboys, 1978). In addition, people often ignore the effect of the sample size in a problem. For example, consider which outcome is more likely between Hospitals A and B in the table below. Assume that the probability of a surgical death is equally likely ($p = 0.5$) in each but that we find the following rates for two hospitals, a small one and a large one:

	% Male deaths	% Female deaths	Total no. of hospital deaths
Hospital A	60	40	100
Hospital B	60	40	1000

A statistical model predicts that the likelihood of such deviations from the expected 50% mortality rate is lower in the larger hospital because of its greater sample size. Thus, the rate observed in the large hospital is less likely due to chance and more likely due to poor quality of care, if the severity of cases in the two hospitals is comparable. However, in similar problems, many people intuitively believe that the outcomes are equally likely (Detmer, Fryback, & Gassner, 1978).

For several years now, research has been refining our understanding of these biases, asking how they depend on the context, and whether they are important in real-life decisions. However, many researchers believe judgment errors do exist and argue for prescriptive decision-making aids like Bayes's Theorem or regression analysis. In well-defined clinical problems, many studies already indicate that these aids improve predictions (Politser, 1981).

Choice

Studies also reveal that people often make poor choices in risky situations. Suppose, for example, a person must decide between two policies that insure against the risk of incurring a large expense resulting from a major illness or accident.

	Deductible	Monthly premium
Policy A	$400	$40
Policy B	$0	$80

Faced with these choices, many people express a preference for Policy B over Policy A because B has no deductible; therefore, it appears to guarantee the certainty of no expenses in the event of an illness. However, Policy A is a better choice because it is less expensive, regardless of whether an individual remains healthy or becomes ill. If he stays healthy during the year, Policy A costs $480 ($40 × 12 months) while Policy B costs $960 ($80 × 12). If he becomes ill and incurs a medical expense which exceeds the deductible, Policy A costs $880 ($400 + $480); Policy B costs $960. Thus, Policy A dominates Policy B—i.e. no matter what happens, it is better. This would appear to hold even if pessimistic assumptions were made about the timing of payments and adjustments for inflation.

Just as for judgment problems, researchers continue to debate whether and to what extent people make poor choices in real world problems. Some argue that gambles in experiments may inadequately represent such problems. Some economists have argued that "irrational" behavior may occur in insignificant problems but that, when faced with important decisions, people will act rationally.

Other investigators worry more about irrational choices. For example, people do not simply consider the marginal costs and benefits of their decisions, as economic theory predicts, but also consider what they have already spent—"sunk" costs (Thaler, 1980). Kunreuther, Ginsberg, Miller, et al. (1978) have pointed out that individuals often act irrationally when the probabilities of particular outcomes are very low. They found that home owners in flood plains failed to buy flood insurance at heavily subsidized rates even though they were informed about the availability of insurance.

Thaler (1980) has noted differences in the way people react to identical prices depending on whether they are labeled surcharges or discounts. Consumers are more willing to accept a price if it includes a discount rather than a surcharge because they value discounts as gains and surcharges as losses and because they attach different values to monetarily equal gains or losses. Some economists have argued that workers suffer from a money illusion—that in times of high inflation, people are willing to accept increases in nominal wages that do not protect their real wages but that they would vigorously resist equivalent wage cuts if there were no inflation.

THE EXPECTED UTILITY THEORY AND RATIONAL DECISION MAKING

Evidence that people often make poor choices in risky situations implies the potential to make better decisions. But how do we know if a decision is "optimal" or "rational?"

Investigators have asked how to make better decisions for at least three centuries, long before experimental evidence suggested that people often make poor choices under risk. Early studies of probability and decision making under risk originally sought to help gamblers improve their chances of winning (see, e.g. Machina, 1987). Seventeenth-century mathematicians assumed that gambles were evaluated on the basis of their expected values, reasoning that this approach followed from the law of large numbers (i.e. that in repeatedly played gambles, the long run average payoff converges to the expected value).

In the eighteenth century the Russian mathematician Nicholas Bernoulli observed that people do not merely evaluate gambles by their expected values. He illustrated this point with the now famous "St. Petersburg Paradox." Suppose we flip a fair coin until a head appears and the individual playing this game receives a value of $\$2^n$, where n is the number of flips of the coin necessary to produce a head. What would you pay to play this gamble? Bernoulli noted that most people would pay very little to play such a gamble, much less than its expected value. What is this value? To compute it, note that the expected value of the first flip is $\$1$ ($\frac{1}{2} \times \$2 = \$1$, where $\frac{1}{2}$ is the probability of producing a head and $\$2$ is the value the player receives if a head appears). If we get to it, which occurs with probability $\frac{1}{2} \times \frac{1}{2} = (\frac{1}{2})^2$, the second flip has an expected value of $\$1$ ($\frac{1}{2^2} \times \$2^2$), and so for the third ($\frac{1}{2^3} \times \$2^3 = \$1$) and others such that the expected value of the game is $\$1 + \$1 + \$1 + \cdots = $ infinity! Daniel Bernoulli (Nicholas's cousin) and others later explained the paradox of people's willingness to pay only small amounts for this gamble by hypothesizing that people possess a utility function for wealth and that they value gambles based on the expected *utility* associated with the outcomes, not the expected value (Bernoulli, 1738). For example, if the utility of money is a logarithmic function, the expected utility of the game can become a very small amount, more nearly consistent with people's willingness to pay.

In repeatedly played gambles, the gamble having the greatest expected utility will in the long run give us the highest utility. However, in real life, many gambles are not played repeatedly. Thus, we require another justification for the expected utility principle.

Von Neumann and Morgenstern justified expected utility for choosing non-repeated gambles in their classic work, *Theory of Games and Economic Behavior*, in 1947. They showed how the expected utility maximization principle derives from several underlying axioms. Decision analysts interpret these as principles for "rational" choice prescribing how people ideally should formulate preferences among gambles. We call these axioms completeness, transitivity, independence, continuity, and reducibility, and define them as follows (Coombs, Dawes, & Tversky, 1970, pp. 122–126):

1. Completeness. In evaluating two alternatives, x and y, an individual should prefer x to y, or y to x, or be indifferent between the two. Formally,

$$x \gtrsim_p y, \text{ or } y \gtrsim_p x, \text{ or both, i.e. } x \sim_p y, \text{ for all } x, y,$$

where $\underset{p}{>}$ indicates strict preference, $\underset{p}{\sim}$ denotes indifference, and $\underset{p}{\gtrsim}$ implies preference or indifference.

2. Transitivity. If alternative x is preferred to y, and y to z, then x should be preferred to z,

   i.e. for $x \underset{p}{\gtrsim} y$, and $y \underset{p}{\gtrsim} z$, then $x \underset{p}{\gtrsim} z$, for all x, y, z.

3. Independence. Outcomes that are not related to an individual's decision, such as some common potential outcome z combined with original options x and y, should not influence that decision. That is,

   if $x \underset{p}{\gtrsim} y$, then $(x, p, z) \underset{p}{\gtrsim} (y, p, z)$,

   where (x, p, z) denotes a gamble in which outcome x occurs with probability p and outcome z with probability $1 - p$.

4. Reducibility. Preferences depend only on final outcomes and probabilities, not the process involved in obtaining them (e.g. whether they are obtained in a one-stage or two-stage gamble):

   $$[(x, p, y), q, y] \underset{p}{\sim} (x, pq, y)$$

   In other words, obtaining gamble (x, p, y), with probability q, or y with probability $1 - q$, is equivalent to the gamble (x, pq, y), where x has probability pq and y probability $1 - pq$.

5. Continuity. If $x \underset{p}{\gtrsim} y \underset{p}{\gtrsim} z$, then there exists a probability p such that an individual is indifferent between the gamble (x, p, z) and outcome y.

These axioms, plus some other "technical" ones (Coombs, Dawes, & Tversky, 1970), imply the existence of a utility function, consistent with people's expressed preferences. That is, for an individual choosing "rationally" (i.e. according to the axioms), one alternative is preferred to another if and only if its expected utility is higher. Specifically, $x \underset{p}{\gtrsim} y$ if and only if $U(x) \geq U(y)$, and $U(x, p, y) = pU(x) + (1 - p)U(y)$, the expectation of the gamble. Decision theorists often claim that an "optimal" decision is one which *maximizes* this expected utility because only this principle can conform with people's preferences and with the axioms.

In the 1950s, Savage showed that the theory can be generalized to include *subjective* measures of probability (Savage, 1954). These measures have their own axiomatic foundations not unlike those of expected utility theory, though we will not discuss them here. The generalized model is called the subjective expected utility (SEU) model, since both probabilities and utilities are defined subjectively.

But what does it mean to say that a decision that conforms with the axioms is "rational" or "optimal?" It does *not* mean that different people faced with the same risks will or should make the same decision. As discussed by Bromiley and Curley in Chapter 4, people differ widely in their attitudes toward risk. Moreover, an optimal decision under risk may change with the circumstances even if probabilities remain the same. For example, as Dawes has pointed out, most of us believe it would be foolish to accept an even wager that a roll of a pair of unloaded dice will produce "snake eyes." Yet, if the person were in danger of physical harm or death at the hands of a loan shark and if the wager were the only way to raise money to avoid that harm, then the person might not be so foolish to accept the bet (Dawes, 1988, p. 7).

The expected utility concept of rationality asserts that people should make decisions by evaluating uncertainties without violating probability theory's rules, but also by considering the choices' possible consequences and one's preferences for them, according to the expected utility rule (which ensures that people obey the theory's axioms).

Consider a simple example. Imagine a student who is deciding whether to drive or to walk to class. Let us assume that there are two important uncertainties involved in the decision: whether it will rain or be sunny and whether there will be traffic. The studient faces a decision: should she walk or drive? Assume that she would prefer to walk if it is sunny because she enjoys the exercise. In addition, she dislikes driving when there is traffic. However, she does not want to walk in the rain. Assume that she cannot determine beforehand if it will rain or whether there will be traffic. What should she do in this "risky" situation? SEU theory says that the student's optimal choice is the one which maximizes her subjective expected utility.

Assume that we ask the student how much satisfaction she will receive from driving and walking in the event of the four possible scenarios presented in Figure 2.1. We can do so because von Neumann and Morgenstern's theory allows an arbitrary assignment of numbers (e.g. 10 and 100) to two of the outcomes, with any other outcomes' utilities measured in relation to these. Note that the utilities she attaches to the various scenarios depend on her attitudes and will differ for other individuals. Also realize that considering only these outcomes may oversimplify the real problem, but for pedagogical reasons let us proceed with this simple model. In addition, assume that the student has the subjective probabilities presented in the figure. These derive from her belief that there is a 50 % chance of rain and a 75 % chance that there will be traffic and that these events are independent.

Now we have the information needed to determine which option will maximize her subjective expected utility. If she drives, her expected utility is:

$$(100)(0.125) + (30)(0.375) + (50)(0.125) + (10)(0.375) = 33.75$$

If she walks, her expected utility is:

$$(20)(0.125) + (20)(0.375) + (60)(0.125) + (60)(0.375) = 40.00$$

Utilities:

	No Traffic/ Rain	Traffic/ Rain	No Traffic/ Sunny	Traffic/ Sunny
Drive	100	30	50	10
Walk	20	20	60	60

Subjective Probabilities:

P(No Traffic) = 0.25
P(Traffic) = 0.75
P(Rain) = 0.50
P(Sunny) = 0.50

P(No Traffic, Rain) = (0.25)(0.5) = 0.125
P(Traffic, Rain) = (0.75)(0.5) = 0.375
P(No Traffic, Sunny) = (0.25)(0.5) = 0.125
P(Traffic, Sunny) = (0.75)(0.5) = 0.375

Subjective Expected Utilities:

Driving: (100)(0.125) + (30)(0.375) + (50)(0.125) + (10)(0.375) = 33.75
Walking: (20)(0.125) + (20)(0.375) + (60)(0.125) + (60)(0.375) = 40.00

Figure 2.1.   Summary of the driving vs walking decision problem example. Subjective expected utility theory says that the optimal choice is the one that maximizes the decision maker's expected utility. The theory holds that the student should walk to school since this option yields the higher expected utility. Based on an illustration by Wright (1984).

   SEU theory says that she should walk to school since this option yields the greater expected utility. And even for more complex situations, if we can estimate all the student's utilities and subjective probabilities, expected utility theory should give us the optimal solution. Without such a solution, and faced with the need to consider many complexities, she might not otherwise make the best decision.

   Researchers have applied expected utility theory to more important and complex real world choices. For example, the theory has been used to help investors choose among assets with different rates of return, often called portfolio selection. The theory says that investors should choose among riskless assets with low expected rates of return and riskier assets with higher rates of return much as the student in the scenario above decided whether to walk or drive to work. Investors should evaluate the tradeoffs of risk against the expected return based on their expectations and their attitudes about risk.

McNeil, Weichselbaum, and Pauker (1978), have applied the theory to a lung cancer patient's decision regarding whether to undergo surgery or radiation therapy. At the time of the study, surgery offered a better chance of five-year survival and a prolonged life-expectancy compared with radiation, but also subjected patients to a small risk of immediate death. McNeil *et al.* elicited patients' risk preferences and discovered that most patients were "risk averse" throughout the entire period of survival studied (see Figure 2.2). That is, they preferred an assured survival time (say, 10 years) over a gamble with an equivalent life expectancy (say a 50:50 gamble between living 0 or 20 years).

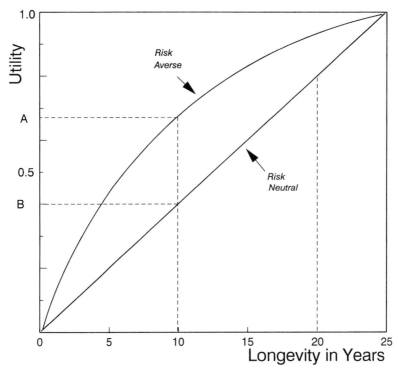

Figure 2.2. Utility on a longevity scale for risk-averse and risk-neutral individuals. (Adapted from Figure 7-16, Weinstein & Fineberg, 1980, with permission.) An individual is risk averse if his or her certainty equivalent for a gamble is less than the gamble's expected value. A gamble's certainty equivalent is the outcome along the scale such that the decision maker is indifferent between (a) that outcome being received for sure and (b) the gamble. Within the framework of expected utility theory, the risk-averse individual assigns utilities according to the concave utility function shown in the figure. In the example, the individual prefers the certainty of 10 years of life (point A) over the 50:50 gamble offering either 0 or 20 years (point B). A risk-neutral individual, whose utility function is linear, as shown in the figure, would be indifferent between the certainty equivalent and the expected value of a gamble.

According to expected utility theory and despite widespread use of surgery, many patients "should" have chosen radiation therapy, even though radiation has a lower five-year survival rate. The risk of immediate death from surgery should have weighed heavily in risk-averse people's choices.

Researchers have applied the expected utility model in a number of fields. Its axioms underlie the theory of rational choice in economics, for example. Economic analyses frequently assert that consumers' preferences are consistent with the rational choice paradigm (i.e. that behavior does, in fact, conform to the axioms). Furthermore, economists use the theory to predict behavioral changes that will result from changes in the prices of goods and services or in income.

THE LIMITATIONS OF EXPECTED UTILITY THEORY

Does expected utility theory describe how people make decisions?

We might question the assumption that people do maximize expected utility. As noted earlier, people often make poor decisions in risky situations. More specifically, they can make choices inconsistent with each other due to violations of the axioms of expected utility theory or due to differing perceptions of the same problem described in different ways.

Consider the scenario Tversky and Kahneman (1986) presented to students. Imagine that the United States has two alternatives to combat a deadly disease expected to kill 600 people.

> If program A is adopted, 200 people will be saved.
> If program B is adopted, there is a $\frac{1}{3}$ probability that 600 people will be saved and a $\frac{2}{3}$ probability that no one will be saved.

When this choice was presented to a group of students, 72% of them selected alternative A. Tversky and Kahneman then presented the following choice to a second group of students.

> If program C is adopted, 400 people will die.
> If program D is adopted, there is a $\frac{1}{3}$ probability that no one will die and a $\frac{2}{3}$ probability that 600 people will die.

When this question was posed, only 22% chose alternative C, even though it has the same probabilities and outcomes as A.

These choices exemplify irrational or suboptimal behavior because they are inconsistent. People choose differently for the same problem "framed" in different ways (i.e. as a gain or loss).

People also display preferences inconsistent with the axioms. Consider the example in Figure 2.3, also provided by Kahneman and Tversky (1979). In

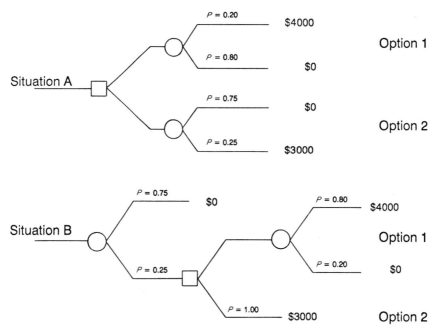

Figure 2.3. Two choice situations. Kahneman and Tversky (1979) found that, when presented with the situations shown here, most people chose Option 1 in Situation A and Option 2 in Situation B, despite the fact that these choices violate expected utility theory.

Situation A, there is a 0.20 chance to win $4000 and a 0.25 chance to win $3000. In Situation B, there is a probability 0.75 to end the game and a probability 0.25 to move into the second stage. In the second stage, there is a choice between winning $3000 for certain or facing a gamble in which there is an 80% chance of winning $4000 and a 20% chance of winning nothing. Note that an individual playing the game in Situation B has a $0.25 \times 0.80 = 0.20$ chance to win $4000 and a $0.25 \times 1.0 = 0.25$ chance to win $3000. Thus, in terms of final outcomes and probabilities (and according to the reducibility axiom), an individual faces the same choices in both situations. Kahneman and Tversky found, however, that most people choose Option 1 in Situation A and Option 2 in Situation B. People seem to ignore the first stage of the game in B and focus on the choice between $3000 and ($4000, 0.80). This violates expected utility theory's reducibility axiom.

Similarly, in one-stage gambles, people often exhibit what has been called the "certainty effect"—valuing certain outcomes more than the theory predicts. For example, most people say they prefer a certain $3000 to the gamble ($4000, 0.8). The independence axiom then implies they should prefer ($3000, 0.25) to (($4000, 0.8), 0.25), which according to reducibility is equivalent to ($4000, 0.2).

Thus, they should prefer ($3000, 0.25) over ($4000, 0.2). However, most have the opposite preference due to the small probability and large monetary differences between two gambles. Therefore, this second preference contradicts the first, wherein a certain $3000 is valued more than the independence and reducibility axioms would allow.

Does expected utility theory prescribe how people should make decisions?

Evidence that behavior often deviates from expected utility theory does not necessarily mean that the theory inadequately prescribes how people *should* make decisions. Some have argued that such evidence merely reinforces the notion that the theory can improve choices. People may simply have poor abilities to make the calculations required by expected utility theory, just as they are not good at multiplying two 3-digit numbers in their heads (Bell & Farquhar, 1986). And they might readily agree to receive help from the theory just as they would accept help from a calculator. Unfortunately, however, they do not always do so. Many times, when asked to revise their inconsistent preferences, and even when paid money to avoid inconsistencies, people still often stick to their original decisions (Slovic & Lichtenstein, 1983).

The pervasiveness and stubborn persistence of these disagreements, not the disagreements themselves, are what raise troubling questions for decision scientists about the normative merit of expected utility theory and the usefulness of applying it. Analysts commonly measure utilities using techniques which presuppose that people conform to expected utility theory's axioms. However, such assessments remain problematic when inconsistent responses persist. For example, in Figure 2.3 most people's responses in Situation A imply $U(3000) < 0.8U(4000)$ (because $0.25U(3000) < 0.20U(4000)$); whereas in B they imply $U(3000) > 0.8U(4000)$. Decision analysts often ask people to reconsider their preferences in order to resolve such inconsistencies. But when people wish to retain their original preferences, ultilities may be difficult to assess. Also, when one does not have a clear preference for how to change one's answers, many of which may be inconsistent, problems arise. Decision analysis provides no guidelines for choosing between alternative methods of resolution (Politser, 1981).

Some experts contend that inconsistencies arise because there is something inherently wrong with the *theory*, not with behavior. Perhaps the theory is not capturing an important element of people's preferences in risky decisions. If so, it may be foolish to "force" people to obey the axioms. It might be wiser to understand why the inconsistencies occur and, if possible, to offer alternative theories that can capture people's preferences without such inconsistencies. In the remainder of the chapter, we explore these issues. In this section, we focus on criticisms of EU theory and on limitations in applying the theory in decision analysis. The following section discusses alternative models and decision aids.

In recent decades, some researchers have questioned whether people *should* obey the principles of expected utility theory. Some of the axioms are uncontroversial. For example, most people agree that transitivity is an important tenet of rational behavior. Researchers often point out that individuals who do *not* obey the transitivity axiom can be made to behave as "money pumps." Suppose, for example, that an individual who owns automobile A displays cyclical preferences such that he prefers A to automobile B and B to C but also C to A. It would be possible to persuade the individual to pay some amount of money to trade A for C (since he prefers C to A). By the same logic, it would be possible to persuade him to pay some amount to trade C for B once he obtained C (because he prefers B to C). But it would also be possible to persuade him to pay to obtain A (which he held in the first place in exchange for B). In theory, one could repeat the cycle over and over again, continually "pumping" money from a stubbornly intransitive person.

Some observers have pointed out that people may violate the transitivity axiom in a seemingly logical or rational manner. A person may base a choice among alternatives on multiple criteria, for example (Tversky, 1969). Imagine an individual who has rated the previous automobiles on several dimensions as follows:

	Price	Appearance	Durability
A:	Good	Fair	Excellent
B:	Fair	Excellent	Good
C:	Excellent	Good	Fair

If the person prefers the car that is better on two of the three dimensions, he will prefer A to B, B to C, and C to A, thus exhibiting intransitive preferences. Another basis for violations of the transitivity axiom is illustrated in the following preferences, where the set of options presented to the person is shown in parentheses:

$$A \underset{p}{>} B \quad (A, B)$$

$$B \underset{p}{>} C \quad (B, C)$$

$$C \underset{p}{>} A \quad (A, C)$$

$$A \underset{p}{>} B \underset{p}{>} C \quad (A, B, C,)$$

Intransitive preferences arise here because different elements are added to or taken away from the decision set (Anand, 1987).

But even if people have intransitive preferences in practice, they might change their behavior if alerted to the inconsistency. Most observers believe that transitivity is one of the least arguable principles. Experimental evidence does not support the notion that people do not want to eliminate intransitivities when made aware of them, although such evidence does exist for the independence axiom (Slovic & Tversky, 1974).

Researchers have more intensely debated the normative foundation of other axioms. For example, some have stated that the completeness principle imposes unrealistic requirements on individuals because it requires that they have precise, well-known preferences. Critics have wondered why it is necessarily rational to possess such preferences or to possess preferences at all. In reality, people often have ambivalent or imprecise preferences, and their attitudes and tastes change (Anand, 1987). And a person's choice between A and B may depend on whether option C is included in the discussion (Shafer, 1986).

Framing and context effects raise questions about whether there really exist basic tastes and preferences that are compatible with expected utility theory (Schoemaker, 1982). Consider an example offered by Savage, who argued that people should make choices that maximize expected utility. A man decides against purchasing a radio costing $93.85 for his car, yet decides to buy the radio for his new car because the extra cost of the radio seems small compared to the cost of the car. Savage argued that such behavior was irrational—that the cost of the radio was the same to the man, regardless of whether or not he bought the car. Savage believed that, if it were pointed out to him, the man would realize his error—that if he already had the new car, he wouldn't purchase the radio—and would decide not to buy the radio. But some have questioned why we should assume that the man's first choice was correct. Perhaps only in the context of buying a new car does the man best face up to the value he is willing to place on the radio (Shafer, 1986). In this case, he might call his feeling that he would not pay for the radio the error. Again, a decision analyst might argue that this is fine so long as we identify the person's "true" preference. However, decision analytic methods seldom can assess preferences in the many contexts that might affect choices. Also, when inconsistencies arise, the "correct" preference may remain unclear.

Other researchers have criticized expected utility theory because it omits many important factors. First, the theory often does not consider cultural attributes, ethical codes, standards of decency, or emotions (Shweder, 1986). Critics charge that such factors cannot be inferred from conventional principles of rational decision making. Also, the standard microeconomic model of expected utility assigns no role to generosity or good will (Kahneman, Knetsch, & Thaler, 1986). In addition, decision analysis usually attempts only to optimize *individual* welfare, and does not account for elements such as fairness, morality, or ethics. Context and culture also affect what people consider fair (Kunreuther, 1986). A Safeway store in Alaska *lowered* the price of orange juice (and rationed it to two per customer) after an earthquake, even though demand was very high. On the other hand, the prices of candles and flashlights increased after a major power failure in New York City in 1965.

But some have argued that the theory could be generalized to accommodate multiple dimensions, including the above factors and others. The utility function could apply to alternatives that have several dimensions rather than just one (e.g. money) but critics note that measuring these other dimensions may be very difficult. Also, they ask whether people can really be expected to assign utilities to all possible alternatives, especially if preferences vary across many contexts. In addition, they raise questions about the feasibility of assigning probabilities to all future events and of exhaustively enumerating the alternatives.

ALTERNATIVE MODELS OF DECISION MAKING

If expected utility theory does not adequately prescribe how people should make decisions, perhaps other models can improve upon it. Many have argued that we must relax some of the standard axioms of the theory. Fishburn (1988), for example, has proposed a method for combining probabilities and utilities that, in its most general form, requires neither transitivity nor independence. And even if one assumes transitivity, the new model allows probabilities to be weighted so that one still can have a preference for certainty more than expected utility theory allows. This then would allow some preference patterns that, according to expected utility, were inconsistent (e.g. violations of the independence axiom due to the certainty effect). In theory, then, even in these previously problematic cases, one could evaluate people's preferences and still provide some decision assistance.

Other researchers have attempted to enrich decision-making models by incorporating psychological factors not included in expected utility theory. Bell, for example, has proposed that utility models include factors such as "regret" and "disappointment" (Bell, 1984, 1985). Bell defines regret as the state resulting from a comparison of the actual outcome with the outcome that would have occurred had the decision maker made the best choice (in retrospect, knowing the outcome of uncertain events). Disappointment, on the other hand, is created by comparing actual outcomes with prior expectations. According to these formulations, you may prefer $900 for sure rather than a 50-50 gamble between $0 and $2000 because doing so removes the possibility of regret (i.e. of knowing that you could have had $900 for sure after you chose the gamble and got nothing) or of disappointment (i.e. of getting $1000 less than the gamble's $1000 expected value). Both regret and disappointment affect people's decisions. For example, a physician or a manager faced with a risky decision may act to minimize regret by making the "safe" decision, thus avoiding the worst possible outcome. A physician may also take a patient's potential disappointment into account when recommending treatment options.

Bell has proposed methods to measure an individual's regret or disappointment. In effect, these might determine how much a decision maker will trade off dollars to gain psychological satisfaction. However, as with Fishburn's non-expected utility model, applications of these methods today remain relatively complex. And while the new models may better conform to people's expressed preferences, the new methods may merely do more to describe behavior and less to improve it in some situations.

Others have taken a different approach. Simon (1979), for example, has long argued that rather than obeying expected utility theory, decisions instead follow concepts of "bounded rationality." In this view, individuals factor problems into a modest number of variables and make decisions which appear "reasonable" rather than "optimal." An individual's search for a solution may terminate when an aspiration level, or "satisfaction" choice, has been achieved. In this way, people "satisfice" rather than optimize.

Simon argues that by giving up assumptions about maximizing expected utility, a more realistic normative theory can be constructed. Instead of assuming that firms set prices to maximize profits, for example, one may assume that they behave according to a simple formula such as cost-plus pricing—establishing prices a fixed amount above actual costs. One might also postulate that people will work a certain number of hours so long as they attain a "target" income or that home sellers will consider alternative bids in turn and accept the first one exceeding some pre-determined cutoff point. Other behavior might result from similar decision rules or rules of thumb. Fishburn (1977) and others have observed that investors frequently associate risks with the failure to attain a target return on their investment. Fishburn has proposed a class of "aspiration" models which incorporate the notion that investors act to do "well enough." That is, they are satisfied as long as they earn the target return.

Some observers have faulted satisficing strategies for not assuring that the chosen solution will exceed the expected value of other potential ones. Payne (1976) has shown that while a satisficing heuristic can reduce the effort involved in choosing between gambles, it often results in poor accuracy (relative to an "optimal" strategy, like expected utility). Some have begun developing decision aids based on research concerning the effort and accuracy of different simplifying techniques in different situations (Politser, 1987).

Some guidelines are based on naturally occurring heuristics such as ways to simplify problems by eliminating certain options. One strategy is to serially eliminate least preferred alternative hypotheses and instruct people to consider attributes distinguishing the remaining alternative pairs. For example, in choosing among apartments one might first reject expensive apartments, then poorly located ones, and so forth until only a few alternatives remain (Payne, 1976). A final decision might be made by asking whether the better location for one apartment compensates for its higher rent. Such combined heuristics can perform nearly as well as optimal strategies, while requiring much less mental effort. Such hybrid strategies have been incororated into computer decision aids (Politser et al., 1987).

FUTURE DIRECTIONS

Over the years, even the most vocal critics of the expected utility model have noted that it deserves praise for its scope, power, and simplicity (Tversky & Kahneman, 1986) and have called it one of the most impressive intellectual achievements of the twentieth century (Simon, 1983). Moreover, despite its critics, the theory has remained surprisingly resilient. In one experiment examining preferences, for example, EU accounted for over 86% of the preference orderings (Coombs & Huang, 1970).

In many ways, critics have found the theory an easy target precisely because of its clarity and simplicity. But alternative models have their own problems and limitations. And as yet, no single model has become widely accepted.

However, even after decades of research, expected utility theory applications remain controversial. Research has revealed that psychological factors play an important role in decision making, and many of these factors are not adequately captured by expected utility theory. Einhorn and Hogarth (1986) have noted that the real world of risk involves factors such as ambiguous probabilities, dependencies between probabilities and utilities, context and framing effects, and regret. They conclude that "given the richness of the phenomena before us, our biggest risk would be to ignore them."

Some researchers argue that we need to move beyond expected utility models. Others question the usefulness of searching for a unifying theory. Tversky and Kahneman (1986) have written that the dream of constructing such a theory is unrealizable. Plott (1986) argues that the issue is not simply whether a choice is "rational" or not but whether the margin of error involved is acceptable. This has led many to begin working on the development of probabilistic sensitivity analyses to quantify the likelihood of analytic error (Doubilet, Begg, Weinstein, et al., 1985; Willard & Crutchfield, 1986). However, such analyses rest upon subjective assessments that may themselves introduce considerable error. So our ability to quantify error and determine its acceptability remains uncertain.

Where does this leave the state of decision analysis today? The crucial questions we must answer are: (a) How can we improve decision analysis? (b) In what situations should we use it?

One area most needing improvement is utility analysis, and some investigators have been attempting to overcome the obstacles it must surmount. For example, we have long known that it is difficult to assess people's utilities for future events never experienced. Recently, however, Llewelyn-Thomas, Thiel, and Clark (in press) have found that patients' evaluations of their current health status depend not only on their evaluations of actual health states but also on the state they had expected to experience and that they believed others their age enjoy. This work eventually may help us better predict individuals' future preferences when making risky choices.

As noted in Chapter 3 by Yates and Stone, numerous researchers have studied people's attitudes toward, and perceptions of, risk. Studies have revealed that factors such as the controllability, voluntariness, and catastrophic potential of the risk as well as media coverage of accidents strongly influence perceptions (Slovic, 1987). Thus, people perceive nuclear power and airplane crashes to be riskier than associated mortality rates would indicate. These studies may suggest how to improve decision analyses. For example, it may not be sufficient to abstractly describe a health state and have people estimate its utility. We may need first to ensure that we have adequately described the relevant risk dimensions (e.g. catastrophic potential, uncontrollability).

Another area needing improvement is probability assessment. Accordingly, some researchers are attempting to better understand how different analytical structures influence probability estimation error. For example, Ravinder, Kleinmuntz, and Dyer (1988) have described conditions under which decomposition of probabilities will or will not increase their reliability and how such decomposition can best be accomplished (e.g. in finding $P(A) = P(A/B_1)P(B_1) + P(A/B_2)P(B_2) + \cdots$). Sometimes we can reduce such error by choosing more nearly equiprobable conditioning events (e.g. $B_1, B_2, \ldots$).

Finally, we must better understand in what situations decision analyses yield the most benefit. Toward this end, Politser (1991) has shown that measures of the gains from medical decision analyses, as they become more complex, generally increase both for physicians and non-physicians. As some other findings also suggest, analyzing more complex problems often may yield more gain than analyzing simpler ones.

The preceding findings remain tentative and most will require further research. Many questions remain concerning how best to select problems for analysis as well as the extent to which, depending on the context, we should increase analytic complexity (by decomposing probability and utility evaluations). However, ongoing research in these areas may eventually help us provide a scientific basis for decision analytic designs, which have heretofore been almost entirely intuitive.

CONCLUSION

Evidence that humans have limited abilities to make risky decisions has not led to the development of unambiguous or universally accepted methods to improve them. We have learned that a model, however elegant, cannot easily capture the nature of risk in human decision making. But we have made important strides toward understanding risk and optimal decision making. We have learned how people violate the expected utility axioms. We have learned how to construct alternative models less susceptible to these violations. And we have begun to learn how to improve traditional decision analyses, either by enhancing their design or by selecting more suitable problems to analyze. Many disagreements and unsolved issues remain. And we still lack a single cure for all the ills that plague our decisions. However, to palliate these ills, we are finding many new remedies and discovering how better to apply them. Equally important, we are learning the dangerous ailments that improperly applied remedies may cause.

SUMMARY

Evidence that humans have limited abilities to make risky decisions has not led to the development of unambiguous or universally accepted methods to improve them. This chapter describes "optimal" decision models and the current debate over their application. The chapter discusses why we need better decision making, expected utility theory as a theoretical foundation for "rational" decision making, and criticism of, and alternatives to this model.

Expected utility theory has remained surprisingly resilient over the years, and as yet, no single alternative model has become widely accepted. Nevertheless, even after decades of research, the use of decision analytic methods resting on expected utility theory remains controversial. Research has revealed that several factors, such as ambiguous probabilities, context and framing effects, and regret, play important roles in decision making under risk, and that many of these factors are not adequately captured by expected utility theory.

Evidence that behavior often deviates from expected utility theory does not necessarily mean that the theory inappropriately prescribes how people *should* make decisions. But the pervasiveness and stubborn persistence of inconsistencies raise troubling questions for decision scientists about the normative merit of the theory and the usefulness of applying it. Where does this leave the state of decision analysis today? The crucial questions we must answer are: (a) How can we improve decision analysis? (b) In what situations should we use it?

We have learned that a model, however elegant, cannot easily capture the role of risk in human decision behavior. But we have made important strides toward understanding risk and optimal decision making. We have learned how people violate the expected utility axioms. We have learned how to construct alternative models less susceptible to these violations. And we have begun to learn how to improve traditional decision analyses, either by enhancing their design or by selecting more suitable problems to analyze.

ACKNOWLEDGMENTS

Preparation of this chapter was supported in part by US National Library of Medicine grant LM-07037 and by grant SES-8822929 from the US National Science Foundation. Dr Politser was the recipient of Research Career Development Award LM-03366 from the US National Library of Medicine.

REFERENCES

Anand, P. (1987). Are the preference axioms really rational? *Theory and Decision*, **23**, 189–214.

Bell, D. E. (1984). Putting a premium on regret. *Management Science*, **31**, 117–120.

Bell, D. E. (1985). Disappointment in decision making. *Operations Research*, **33**, 1–27.

Bell, D. E., & Farquhar, P. (1986). Perspectives on utility theory. *Operations Research*, **34**, 179–183.

Bernoulli, D. (1738). Specimen theoriae novae de mensura sortis. *Commentarii Academiae Scientiarium Imperialis Petropolitanae*, **6**, 175–192. Translated by L. Sommer (1954). Exposition of a new theory on the measurement of risk, *Econometrica*, **22**, 23–36.

Casscells, B. S., Schoenberger, A., & Graboys, T. B. (1978). Interpretation by physicians of clinical laboratory results. *New England Journal of Medicine*, **229**, 999–1000.

Cole, R. B., Balmer, J. P., & Wilson, T. S. (1974). Surveillance of elderly hospital patients for pulmonary tuberculosis. *British Medical Journal*, **1**, 104–106.

Coombs, C. H., Dawes, R., & Tversky, A. (1970). *Mathematical psychology: An elementary introduction*. Englewood Cliffs, NJ: Prentice Hall.

Coombs, C. H., & Huang, L. C. (1970). Tests of a portfolio theory of risk preference. *Journal of Experimental Psychology*, **85**, 23–29.

Craven, R. B., Wenzel, R. P., & Atuk, N. O. (1975). Minimizing tuberculosis risk to hospital personnel and students exposed to unsuspected disease. *Annals of Internal Medicine*, **82**, 628–632.

Dawes, R. M. (1988). *Rational choice in an uncertain world*. San Diego: Harcourt, Brace, Jovanovich.

Detmer, D. E., Fryback, D. G., & Gassner, K. (1978). Heuristics and biases in medical decision-making. *Journal of Medical Education*, **53**, 682–683.

Doubilet, P., Begg, C. B., Weinstein, M. C., *et al.* (1985). Probabilistic sensitivity analysis using Monte-Carlo simulation: A practical approach. *Medical Decision Making*, **5**, 157–177.

Einhorn, H. J., & Hogarth, R. M. (1986). Decision making under ambiguity. *Journal of Business*, **59**, 225–250.

Elstein, A. S., Shulman, L. S., & Sprafka, S. A. (1978). *Medical problem solving: An analysis of clinical reasoning*. Cambridge, MA: Harvard University Press.

Fischhoff, B., Slovic, P., & Lichtenstein, S. (1978). Fault trees: Sensitivity of estimated failure probabilities to problem representation. *Journal of Experimental Psychology: Human Perception and Performance*, **4** 333–344.

Fishburn, P. C. (1977). Mean-risk analysis with risk associated with below-target returns. *American Economic Review*, **67**, 116–126.

Fishburn, P. C. (1988). Normative theories of decision-making under risk and under uncertainty. In D. E. Bell, H. Raiffa, & A. Tversky (Eds.), *Decision making: Descriptive, normative, and prescriptive interactions*. New York: Cambridge University Press.

Gradison, B., & Stark, P. (1989). *The medical quality research and improvement act*. US House Ways and Means Committee, Subcommittee on Health.

Kahneman, D., Knetsch, J. L., & Thaler, R. H. (1986). Fairness and the assumptions of economics. *Journal of Business*, **59**, 285–300.

Kahneman, D., & Tversky, A. (1979). Prospect theory: An analysis of decision under risk. *Econometrica*, **47**, 262–290.

Kunreuther, H. (1986). Comments on Plott and on Kahneman, Knetsch, and Thaler. *Journal of Business*, **59**, 329–336.

Kunreuther, H., Ginsberg, R., Miller, L., *et al.* (1978). *Disaster insurance protection: Public policy lessons*. New York: Wiley.

Llewelyn-Thomas, H. A., Thiel, E. C., & Clark, R. M. (in press). Patients vs surrogates: Whose opinion counts on ethics review panels? *Clinical Research.*

Machina, M. J. (1987). Decision making in the presence of risk. *Science,* **236,** 537–543.

McNeil, B. J. Weichselbaum, R., & Pauker, S. G. (1978). Fallacy of the five-year survival in lung cancer. *New England Journal of Medicine,* **299,** 1397–1401.

Payne, J. (1976). Task complexity and contingent information processing in decision making: An information search and protocol analysis. *Organizational Behavior and Human Performance,* **16,** 366–387.

Plott, C. R. (1986). Rational choice in experimental markets. *Journal of Business,* **59,** 301–354.

Politser, P. E. (1981). Decision analysis and clinical judgment: A re-evaluation. *Medical Decision Making,* **1,** 361–389.

Politser, P. E. (1987). Medical education for a changing future: New concepts for revising texts. *Medical Education,* **21,** 320–333.

Polister, P. E. (1991). Do medical decision analyses' largest gains grow from the smallest trees? *Journal of Behavioral Decision Making,* **4,** 121–138.

Politser, P. E., Gastfriend, D., Bakin, D., & Nguyen, L. (1987). An intelligent display system for psychiatric education in primary care. *Medical Care,* **25,** 123–127.

Ravinder, H. V., Kleinmuntz, D. N., & Dyer, J. S. (1988). The reliability of subjective probabilities obtained through decomposition. *Management Science,* **34,** 186–199.

Savage, L. J. (1954). *The foundations of statistics.* New York: Wiley.

Schoemaker, P. J. H. (1982). The expected utility model: Its variants purposes, evidence, and limitations. *Journal of Economic Literature,* **20,** 529–563.

Shafer, G. (1986). Savage revisited. *Statistical Science,* **1,** 463–501.

Shapiro, S., Slone, D., Lewis, G. P., *et al.* (1971). Fatal drug reactions among medical inpatients. *Journal of the American Medical Association,* **216,** 467–472.

Shweder, R. A. (1986). Comments on Plott and on Kahneman, Knetsch, and Thaler. *Journal of Business,* **39,** 345–354.

Simon, H. A. (1979). Rational decision making in business organizations. *American Economic Review,* **69,** 493–513.

Simon, H. A. (1983). *Reason in human affairs.* Stanford, CA: Stanford University Press.

Slovic, P. (1987). Perceptions of risk. *Science,* **236,** 280–285.

Slovic, P., & Lichtenstein, S. (1983). Preference reversals: A broader perspective. *American Economic Review,* **73,** 596–605.

Slovic, P., & Tversky, A. (1974). Who accepts Savage's axiom? *Behavioral Science,* **19,** 368–373.

Thaler, R. (1980). Toward a positive theory of consumer choice. *Journal of Economic Behavior and Organization,* **1,** 39–60.

Tversky, A. (1969). Intransitivity of preferences. *Psychological Review,* **76,** 31–48.

Tversky, A., & Kahneman, D. (1986). Rational choice and the framing of decisions. *Journal of Business,* **59,** 251–284.

von Neumann, J., & Morgenstern, O. (1947). *Theory of games and economic behavior* (2nd ed.). Princeton University Press.

Weinstein, M. C., & Fineberg, H. V. (1980). *Clinical decision analysis.* Philadelphia: Saunders.

Willard, K., & Crutchfield, G. C. (1986). Probabilistic analysis of decision trees using symbolic algebra. *Medical Decision Making,* **6,** 93–100.

Wortman, P. (1972). Medical diagnosis: An information processing approach. *Computer Biomedical Research,* **5,** 318–328.

Wright, G. (1984). *Behavioral decision theory.* Beverly Hills, CA: Sage.

Chapter 3

Risk appraisal

J. Frank Yates and Eric R. Stone
The University of Michigan

CONTENTS

Risk-taking Behavior. Edited by J. F. Yates
© 1992 John Wiley & Sons Ltd

As indicated in Chapter 1, risk as the possibility of loss is a special negative feature a prospective action might possess. Its essential elements are potential losses and the uncertainty and significance of those losses. The present chapter addresses risk appraisal, how people characterize the riskiness of specific, given alternatives, say, buying the house at 323 Elm Street or approving Allied Industries' proposed waste disposal plan. Risk-taking behavior is driven in part by the risk individuals see in the options available to them. Thus, understanding risk appraisal goes a long way toward achieving an understanding of risk-taking behavior more generally. Some risk-taking activities are more successful than others. It is plausible that at least some ineffective risk-taking behaviors are undertaken because of faulty risk appraisals. For this reason, our discussion focuses not only on how risk appraisals are typically formulated, but also on how they might be improved.

Some risk appraisals apply only to particular risk elements, while others concern overall risk as an entity in itself. The chapter is organized according to this distinction. The first four sections discuss the assessment of risk elements. The opening section considers the existence of loss potential. ("Could anything harmful happen if I took this action?") The second addresses how specific potential losses are identified. ("Exactly what *are* the bad outcomes that could occur here?") The third examines the assignment of likelihoods to possible losses. ("What are the chances of those unfortunate things actually happening?") And the fourth discusses how the significance of losses is assessed. ("Just how serious would it be if those calamities really did occur?") The fifth and final major section considers appraisals of overall risk. ("Taking everything into account, how risky would this action be?")

LOSS POTENTIAL

In order for a situation to be considered risky, the person contemplating that situation—the "risk appraiser"—must believe that it harbors the potential for losses, even if those possible losses cannot be identified. Further, it seems that, the more numerous the suspected losses—even if unspecified—the greater the risk. These observations implicate the establishment of loss potential as one aspect of risk appraisal. Does this kind of appraisal play a major role in risk-taking behavior, or does it have only minor importance? Slovic, Fischhoff, and Lichtenstein (1986) have reviewed numerous psychometric studies, including their own, concerning perceptions of the riskiness of various technologies. A recurrent finding is that people pay close attention to the extent to which the losses that might be caused by a technology are well known; the less that is known, the greater the risk. One interpretation of these results is that risk takers are greatly concerned about establishing loss potential. Moreover, their conclusions about whether losses could occur in given situations strongly affect their actions in those situations.

How good are people at judging the existence and extent of possible losses? Do we tend to suspect that every situation is fraught with prospects of disaster? Or do we proceed on our way, oblivious to the dangers that surround us? Unfortunately, no one can answer these questions definitively, because the issues have not been studied systematically. However, results from other research suggest reasonable hypotheses that should be evaluated rigorously in the future.

Gettys *et al.* (1987) asked subjects to generate proposals for relieving a university parking shortage. Every individual subject suggested only a fraction of the alternatives that were offered by the entire group of subjects. More interestingly, the subjects markedly underestimated the number of high-quality alternatives they had neglected to mention, where quality was evaluated by a panel of experts. This result could well generalize to the present issue (see also Fischhoff, Slovic, & Lichtenstein, 1978). That is, risk takers might routinely think that the situations they face harbor fewer potential losses than could actually occur.

The previous hypothesis is indeed plausible. But it seems inconsistent with Slovic, Fischhoff, & Lichtenstein's (1986) psychometric results indicating a strong preoccupation with knowing about potential losses. A reconciliation might lie in the notion of signals of ignorance. Specifically, perhaps risk takers sometimes underestimate the existence and extent of potential losses, but only for situations that are deceptively familiar to them. Indirect evidence supporting this view comes from the overconfidence literature. There we find that, although novices and laypersons are often overconfident in their opinions, experts and professionals seldom are (Yates, 1990, Chapter 4). Also, circumstances tend to differ in the amount of overconfidence observed in them. Taken as a whole, the available data imply that overconfidence is encouraged when there is nothing in a situation to suggest or "signal" that a person's knowledge might be deficient. Thus, virtually everyone is overconfident about their answers to general knowledge questions, say, whether New York or London is farther north. But experts and professionals working in their specialities are seldom overconfident; they have learned from experience that their knowledge is limited. And we as laypersons definitely are not overconfident when we make judgments concerning things about which we are patently ignorant, for example, medicine or the inner workings of television sets.

LOSS IDENTITY

The goal of professional risk analysis is "the identification and estimation of risks" (Earle & Cvetkovich, 1988, p. 365; also see Crouch & Wilson, 1982; Kaplan & Garrick, 1981; and Slovic, 1987). The identification part of this goal requires, for instance, that risk analysts working in hazardous waste mangement begin by alerting their clients to the varieties of adverse outcomes that might result from their activities, say, genetic abnormalities and legal sanctions. This is an instance of the more general appraisal task whereby risk takers try to identify the specific losses that might result from the actions available to them. How and how well do people perform this task? How could it be done better? These are the questions examined in this section.

Identification accuracy

Risk analysts implicitly assume that, left on their own, their clients would be unable to specify the potential losses entailed by their activities, even when they have the uneasy feeling that losses of some kind are possible. Is this assumption warranted? Are risk takers generally deficient in their identification of losses? There is no direct evidence one way or the other. But because risk analysts' services remain in demand, we might infer that their assumption has at least some validity. Relatedly, in interviews with managers about their risk-taking behavior, March and Shapira (1987) found that those individuals' business decisions were dominated by a surprisingly small number of key concerns, presumably to the neglect of other perhaps more important ones. Also, as indicated previously, a generalization of the results of Gettys *et al.* (1987) is that people tend to overlook significant aspects of any decision problem, including potential losses and gains.

Is there reason to suspect that risk takers are especially likely to neglect *losses*, as opposed to any other kind of decision consideration? A case can be made on either side of the issue. Consistent with the expectation that losses will receive short shrift is evidence for the *Pollyanna effect*, whereby people generally accentuate the positive. This phenomenon is thought to be reflected in the fact that there exist many more positive words than negative ones (Boucher & Osgood, 1969). One proposed explanation is that we find it painful to dwell on bad things and hence avoid talking (and thinking) about them. Thus, we would not devote the effort required to adequately identify the losses that might befall us in risky situations.

Counter to this view, there have been numerous demonstrations that humans and other animals react especially strongly to noxious stimuli (e.g. Fisher & Fisher, 1969). The generalization that people respond more intensely to losses than to equivalent gains is now an established element of many contemporary views of decision making, for instance, Kahneman and Tversky's (1979) prospect theory. Suppose we indeed are hypersensitive to losses whenever those losses actually occur. Then it seems plausible that we would be especially likely to bring such losses to mind, too, since we would want to prevent their occurrence. This hypothesis is a corollary of the proposition that special sensitivity to noxious stimuli is functional for any organism's survival, under the assumption that such stimuli are signals of potential harm.

A definitive conclusion about whether people are or are not especially poor at identifying losses must await further research. It is conceivable, however, that dual mechanisms are at work. For instance, as suggested by the previously discussed Slovic, Fischhoff, and Lichtenstein (1986) studies, perhaps our sensitivity to losses makes us acute sensors of loss potential in given situations, causing us to readily notice that "There's something wrong here." But our aversion to unpleasantness prevents us from analyzing those situations in detail in order to identify the losses that lie in wait. Instead, whenever possible, we simply avoid ominous situations altogether.

Identification mechanisms

The working register (or working memory) within the human cognitive system has limited capacity (see, for example, Anderson, 1985; Glass & Holyoak, 1986). Thus, in everyday terms, we are able to hold in mind and manipulate only a small number of considerations at any given instant. This fact alone would account for some difficulties in identifying potential losses. The priming features of the working register might be another major contributor (Hoch, 1984, 1985; Yates, 1990, Chapter 12). Specifically, suppose that one class of information is presently occupying the working register. Because capacity is limited, little if any other information can be added. Of course, there is always some turnover in the current contents of the working register, with new information from long-term memory and the environment replacing information that drops out. But, for various reasons, there is a tendency for that new information to be related to the current contents; unrelated information is at a decided disadvantage in the competition for working register space.

Risk takers themselves propose or identify some of the actions they consider pursuing; other actions are suggested by other individuals. The above priming aspects of the working register imply that the source of a proposed action could easily influence the risk taker's recognition of potential losses. The argument is as follows: When a person proposes some particular action, it is because one or more of that action's positive features have captured the individual's attention, that is, have gained access to the working register. For instance, when a shopper considers buying a certain suit, she does so because some appealing aspect of the suit catches her eye, say, the fabric. Ideally, as the risk taker's deliberations proceed, appropriate attention is devoted to other, less immediate features of the given action, for instance, the poor stitching of the suit being considered by our shopper. However, as suggested above, features that are unrelated to the advantages of the action should be relatively neglected, including, perhaps, the potential losses it might produce. In our example, the shopper could overlook the poor stitching, a feature she might have noticed more easily if someone else had recommended the suit. In the latter case, the stitching would not be disadvantaged because the working register was not previously occupied by positive features of the suit. So, in general, the accuracy of loss identification should be worse for actions proposed by risk takers themselves than for those suggested by others.

The previous hypothesis needs to be tested directly. However, anecdotal evidence agrees with it. For instance, the public often seems to regard the risks of technologies like nuclear power as more serious than do the officials responsible for those technolgies. Part of this disagreement arises from the tendency of officials to view risk more narrowly than do members of the public, almost exclusively in terms of fatality rates rather than considerations like catastrophic potential as well (Fischhoff, Slovic, & Lichtenstein, 1981). But it is possible that officials judge the risks as less severe partly because they are the ones who propose the technologies and hence have the advantages of those technologies foremost in consciousness. Members of the public also feel that virtually *every* aspect of contemporary life is too risky (Slovic, 1987). This tendency might be another reflection of the proposed mechanisms. When people are asked about the riskiness of some activity, the very question itself should lead respondents to bring losses to mind, to the neglect of the possible benefits of that activity.

Improving loss identification

Suppose that the above propositions about loss identification are shown to be true. What would be the implications for improving identification? Three strategies seem promising:

First is *active search*. That is, for serious decision problems warranting the attention, risk appraisers should actively search for the losses that are capable of occurring. This search should proceed over several sessions separated in time, and the results of the sessions should be recorded.

The second strategy is *simulation*. Some potential losses are unlikely to come to mind in the abstract. Instead, they attract attention only through direct experience. For example, many aggravations of home ownership do not occur to individuals who have always lived in rental apartments because their buildings were maintained by the managers. A prospective first-time home buyer could simulate the actual experience of ownership by taking care of vacationing friends' houses.

The third strategy is *consultation*. Thus, a risk taker could seek the counsel of an expert who, effectively, has compiled a catalog of losses that have occurred in similar risk-taking situations in the past. As indicated at the outset of our discussion, providing such advice is a stock in trade of risk analysts. But consultation need not be so formal. In fact, some people routinely seek counsel from their friends about lots of their decisions, such as making major purchases.

LOSS LIKELIHOOD

The riskiness of an action increases with its chances of producing losses, as long as those chances fall short of certainty. The caveat applies because risk requires uncertainty; if there is no uncertainty, there is no risk. So the judgment of loss likelihoods is clearly a critical element of risk appraisal. Indeed, in many situations such assessments constitute the entire risk appraisal enterprise. For instance, when researchers try to establish the cancer risk of a new food additive, they seek an indication of how much that additive increases the probability that a person will develop cancer. That is why loss likelihood assessment has been studied more extensively than other aspects of risk appraisal. We now consider what has been learned in that work.

Mode of expression

Before examining likelihood judgment *per se*, it is useful to consider how such judgments are reported. There are two basic modes of expression, words and numbers, in particular, probabilities in the latter case. For instance, we could say that the chance of a borrower defaulting on a loan is "substantial," or we could say it is about "30%." Which means of expression is favored? Does it matter which is used, and why?

The preferred mode for describing loss chances depends on the context. Words are more common in some settings and probabilities in others. For example, accountants like to conceptualize audit risk in terms of probabilities. But they pointedly avoid such probabilities in their audit reports (Sullivan *et al.*, 1985). Two reasons appear to underlie this practice. The first is that some accountants feel that reporting probabilities would suggest that auditors arrive at their opinions more rigorously or "scientifically" than they actually do. Perhaps relatedly, the second reason seems to be that stating audit risk in words makes it more difficult to say that an auditor's opinion was wrong; the inherent imprecision of natural language is a comforting means of obfuscation. (When in doubt, mumble?) Erev and Cohen (1990) have found that people in general, not just accountants, prefer to express their own likelihood judgments in words, but to have others communicate to them quantitatively.

In contrast to accounting practice and despite a natural preference for conveying opinions in words, in areas such as epidemiology, engineering, and insurance, loss likelihoods are often expressed probabilistically. In recent years especially, we have all become familiar with epidemiologists' reports that habits like smoking, drinking alcohol, and overeating increase our chances of early death by various percentages (Jeffery, 1989). Although less widely publicized, safety engineers routinely perform *probabilistic risk analyses* (*PRA*) of potentially hazardous facilities such as power plants, pipe lines, and storage dumps (e.g. Cohen, 1983). The end results of these exercises include the probabilities of malfunctions, injuries, and deaths. And in establishing premium costs, insurers routinely attach probabilities to their chances of incurring losses on each policy (Mehr, 1983).

It is not completely clear why probabilistic judgments are acceptable in domains like epidemiology, engineering, and insurance but not in contexts such as auditing. However, one plausible reason is mere tradition, with the former fields being more closely allied with the formalisms of science. Another possibility is that, at least for epidemiology and insurance, those fields involve thousands of repetitions of essentially identical cases (e.g. patients with lung cancer), situations that easily fit the relative frequency paradigm of probability theory.

One argument favoring probabilistic expression has undoubtedly influenced the advocates and practitioners of PRA. When a risk taker must decide whether the chances of various losses are too great to justify pursuing a given action, what does "too great" mean? It is hard to answer this question when the chances are characterized as "kind of high" or "large." The version of decision analysis that amounts to applied expected utility theory provides precise answers to such "too great" questions, and in the form of probabilities (see Chapter 2, by Neumann & Politser, and Chapter 10, by Pitz). Specifically, this methodology can identify *threshold probabilities*. So, if the probability of an adverse outcome from an action exceeds a critical threshold value of $X\%$, the action is not taken. Officials who must decide about major risky projects, such as whether a nuclear power plant is safe enough to put on-line, are now accustomed to having the results of PRAs to assist them.

Another advantage of probabilistic expression is the converse of the argument that verbally expressed judgments are preferable because it is hard to determine how good (or bad) they are. There exist numerous techniques for analyzing the quality of probability judgments (see, for example, Murphy & Daan, 1985; Yates, 1990, Chapter 3), techniques that do not have counterparts that apply to verbal judgments. These tools imply that the potential for improving probabilistically expressed opinions is substantially better than that for verbally reported assessments. Of course, this assumes that individuals have the means for making their judgments better should they find them to be deficient, an assumption that may or may not be valid.

Likelihood judgment accuracy

How good are judgments about loss chances? As indicated, this question is hard to answer when assessments are described verbally. Hence, virtually all research about judgment quality has examined quantitatively expressed opinions. Nevertheless, assuming that verbally and quantitatively reported judgments share common foundations, the conclusions from studies involving quantitative expression should have general validity.

Likelihood judgment quality is normally characterized in two ways, in terms of coherence and accuracy. Coherence pertains to the consistency of an individual's judgments with probability theory, and will not concern us here (cf. Winkler, 1972, Chapter 1; Yates, 1990, Chapter 5). In contrast, judgments are said to be accurate to the extent that events assigned high likelihoods tend to occur and those given low ones do not. There has been little research on the accuracy of judgments about losses in particular. However, there have been many studies about more general judgment accuracy. Some of the implications of that work for the present issues are as follows.

1. *Overall accuracy*: We cannot expect excellent overall accuracy in loss judgments. Even the accuracy of professionals' likelihood judgments is sometimes surpassed by that of artificial "statistical judges" which report the same judgment from one occasion to the next, making no distinctions between individual cases. Not surprisingly, computerized statistical judges that do make such distinctions exhibit even greater superiority (e.g. Levi, 1985).

2. *Variability*: There is likely to be considerable variability in the accuracy of loss judgments from situation to situation and from one individual to the next. For example, although physicians' judgments about pneumonia seem poor, their assessments about heart attacks appear to be quite good (Christensen-Szalanski & Bushyhead, 1981; Tierney et al., 1986). Moreover, whereas some doctors' opinions fall far short of ideal, others' might well be the best allowed by the circumstances (cf. Yates & Curley, 1985).

3. *Calibration*: Calibration is a component of the overall accuracy of probability judgments. Probabilistic assessments are well-calibrated if they match the relative frequencies with which the relevant events actually occur. For instance, suppose that, whenever a loan officer says that each of a group of applicants has a 5% chance of defaulting, exactly 5% of those applicants indeed do default on their loans. Then that officer's judgments are perfectly calibrated. Various forms of miscalibration in loss judgments can be anticipated. For example, some studies have found that physicians tend to overpredict serious illness (Christensen-Szalanski & Bushyhead, 1981). There is at least some evidence that such miscalibration reflects a *value-induced bias*, whereby an individual reports higher probabilities than are actually thought to be appropriate because such diagnoses encourage better patient care (cf. Wallsten, 1981). Another common form of miscalibration is described as *overconfidence* in one's judgments. With overconfidence, the proportion of times an individual's categorical assertions (e.g. "This patient has pneumonia") are correct falls short of his or her average probability judgment that those assertions are correct. As discussed previously, laypersons and novices exhibit more overconfidence than do professionals and experts (e.g. Keren, 1987). This probably happens because the latter individuals have benefited from feedback about the quality of their opinions.

4. *Noise*: We should expect that loss judgments will contain excessive noise

or scatter, that is, variability that is unrelated to the occurrence or nonoccurrence of the focal losses. Such deficiencies are sometimes due to individuals responding to factors they think are predictive of the events in question but which actually are not (Poses *et al.*, 1985). They might also implicate the inherent inconsistency of human cognition (Yates, McDaniel, & Brown, 1991).

5. *Discrimination*: Another component of overall probability judgment accuracy is the ability of those judgments to discriminate instances when the focal event is going to occur from those when it is not. Risk takers' judgments should often surpass those of computer-driven models in their discrimination of occasions when losses will and will not happen. This occurs because human judges typically have access to situation-specific information that cannot be programmed into computerized judgment routines (Centor, Dalton, & Yates, 1984).

Likelihood judgment procedures

How do risk appraisers formulate their judgments about loss chances? We can expect three classes of procedures to be employed, procedures relying on relative frequencies, subjective reasoning, and formal models, respectively. They are described below.

Relative frequency procedures

In the relative frequency approach, the risk appraiser considers the current situation to be essentially similar to large numbers of previous ones. The chance of some particular loss occurring in the current setting is taken to be the same as the relative frequency with which losses like that have been observed in the earlier situations. Life insurance is perhaps the most familiar context in which the relative frequency approach is commonly used. The proportion of similar men who have died before age 75, according to the death tables, is taken as the probability that policy applicant "John Smith" will die by 75.

The accuracy of relative frequencies as loss probabilities is enhanced to the degree that the similarity between the current and prior cases is high with respect to features that are statistically related to the focal loss. In epidemiology and medicine, such contingent features are described as *risk factors* (e.g. see Kahn, 1983). Thus, smoking is a risk factor for heart failure and family history is a risk factor for breast cancer. Ideally, a practitioner of the relative frequency approach seeks a perfect match on all known risk factors between the current case and some large pool of previous ones. For instance, suppose patient "Paula Olsen" is 35, childless, of northern European descent, and has no family history of any cancer. In assessing her chances of developing breast cancer, her physician would prefer knowing the breast cancer rate of a sample of thousands of women who shared all those characteristics of Paula Olsen.

The major limitation of the relative frequency strategy is implicit in the previous remarks: Risk takers often have few if any prior cases that are "essentially similar" to the one of interest. This happens in situations like that of Paula Olsen because, the more specific are the characteristics on which similarity is defined, the fewer are the cases that share those characteristics. (In the extreme, all situations really are unique.) In other cases, the problem arises because the hazard is completely novel (e.g. a new, possibly carcinogenic cleanser) or the class of hazards is inherently uncommon (say, large-scale power plants). Sometimes remote approximations of similarity are considered better than nothing, for example, extrapolating cancer rates for humans from studies of laboratory animals (Russell & Gruber, 1987). Often, however, risk takers have no recourse but to rely on other means of determining loss chances.

Subjective reasoning procedures

In the subjective reasoning strategy, the risk taker uses the particulars of the situation to "argue" that the chance of a given loss occurring is X % rather than Y %. Some subjective reasoning techniques are known as rules of thumb, or *judgmental heuristics*. Examples, including the representativeness, availability, and anchoring-and-adjustment heuristics, have been described well in numerous places (e.g. Kahneman, Slovic, & Tversky, 1982).

Other instances of subjective reasoning are better characterized as applications of individuals' personal *mental models* of the given situations (Jungermann, Schutz, & Thuring, 1988). In some cases these models are the person's conception of how various factors literally bring about the occurrence of a given event. This seems especially common in medicine, where physicians often have readily available biological models of focal diseases. In other cases, individuals' mental models appear to be little more than collections of their beliefs that various factors are statistically associated with the target event. The belief that certain personal characteristics of borrowers are correlated with their credit-worthiness is an illustration.

The *lens model paradigm*, including *social judgment theory* (Brehmer, 1986; Earle & Cvetkovich, 1988), is a valuable means of conceptualizing and studying how people use various factors in arriving at their judgments, including their opinions about loss likelihoods (e.g. Levi, 1985). Properly applied, lens model analysis can establish which situational features a risk appraiser really does rely on in assessing loss chances, and how heavily. Sometimes these indications of cue use can be compared to the "objective" predictiveness of the cues, thereby permitting valuable feedback about the appropriateness of an individual's judgment strategy. Comparisons of how two or more risk appraisers use such cues can also facilitate the resolution of disagreements about loss chances (e.g. Hammond *et al.*, 1984).

Several phenomena that affect subjective reasoning have special relevance for assessing the likelihoods of losses.

1. *Contingency judgment deficiencies*:   As indicated, implicit in people's strategies for anticipating losses are their beliefs about correlations between those losses and various cues, for instance, between disease and putative risk factors. Considerable research suggests that, unfortunately, our ability to evaluate such contingencies properly is limited under certain circumstances (e.g. see Alloy & Tabachnik, 1984).

2. *Value biases*:   Likelihood judgments are not independent of the significance of the focal events to the person making the judgments. Most often, people inflate the chances of events whose occurrence they would prefer seeing and deflate the chances of unappealing events (e.g. Rothbart, 1970; Weinstein, 1984, 1987; Zakay, 1984). However, there is also evidence that for rare events like those relevant to many kinds of risk taking, for instance, preparing for major disasters, the effect is reversed (Yates, Cole, & Rodgers, 1989).

3. *Personal role biases*:   Related to, but distinct from, value biases and overconfidence in one's own judgment, individuals also tend to judge that, if they think their own actions have a role in a situation, the chance of favorable outcomes is improved (e.g. Langer, 1975). There is some evidence that men, as opposed to women, are especially susceptible to personal role biases (Foersterling, 1980).

4. *Perceptually-based biases*: Some risk-taking situations are such that people effectively are overconfident in their ability to avoid calamities because of peculiarities in how the perceptual system operates. For example, each year hundreds of people in the United States die when drivers attempt—and fail—to pass through railroad crossings before on-coming trains reach those crossings. Leibowitz (1985) has argued convincingly that one contributor to these tragedies is drivers' underestimation of train speed. This misperception is a product of an illusion of velocity and size, whereby large objects (e.g. locomotives) are perceived to be moving more slowly than smaller objects (e.g. cars) that are actually moving at the same speed. Other visual misperceptions contribute to the dramatically higher rate of fatalities that occur in night driving (Leibowitz & Owens, 1986).

5. *Mood and individual difference effects*:   Judgments about loss chances are affected by the individual's mood state, such that "down" moods induce opinions that losses are especially probable (e.g. Johnson & Tversky, 1983). There are also indications that people who are generally anxious or depressed have greater expectations of bad outcomes than do other individuals (e.g. Butler & Mathews, 1983; Pietromonaco & Rook, 1987). In Chapter 7, Mann discusses additional connections between risk and affect.

6. *Level effects*:   Fischhoff and MacGregor (1983) asked subjects to estimate the chances of death from a host of causes, using several different response modes. For example, in an illustrative item for the "estimate death rate" mode,

the subject was asked (p. 230):

> In a normal year, for each 100000 people who have influenza, how many people do you think die of influenza?

In the corresponding item for the "estimate survival rate" mode, the question was (p. 230):

> In a normal year, for each person who dies of influenza, how many do you think have influenza but do not die of it during the year?

In principle, the various response modes should have produced equivalent responses. So, if we know the death rate for a particular malady, it is easy to derive the corresponding survival rate. Fischhoff and MacGregor converted subjects' responses to a common implicit response scale, death rates per 100000. In general, subjects' direct or implied death rate judgments were highly similar to one another in terms of their rank orders. However, the absolute magnitudes of the death rates differed dramatically from one response mode to the next. For example, the average direct death rate estimate for the 20 maladies considered by the subjects was 2366 per 100000, whereas the average estimate implied by their survival rate judgments was only 54 per 100000.

We noted in our discussion of probabilistic risk analysis (PRA) that some approaches to deciding about risk entail "thresholds." Thus, a threshold rule might say that a power plant startup should be permitted only if the probability of an accident is less than $X\%$. Suppose that Fischhoff and MacGregor's results generalize. This suggests that, if an individual were asked to judge the probability of a given loss in one way, the judgment is likely to be much higher than if he or she were asked differently. Such response mode "level effects" pose obvious difficulties for threshold methods of risky decision making.

Formal model procedures

For major risky projects, such as applying new technologies and selecting the sites for manufacturing plants, the stakes are large and the circumstances unique. This makes it worthwhile to construct models of the situations. These can then be used to evaluate the chances of losses, such as accidents, fatalities, and bankruptcies. Among the elements or derivatives of risk models are fault and event trees (cf. Pate-Cornell, 1984). These are representations of failures and other events as combinations of other, more elementary events. Probabilities for the larger events of interest can then be derived from probabilities for their constituent events using Boolean algebra and the probability calculus. Likelihood judgments for the constituent events might be obtained by a variety of means, including relative frequency and subjective reasoning techniques.

Modeling, an instance of the more general "divide and conquer" strategy, is thought to be advantageous partly because it is easier to find people who are experts about parts of a complex situation than individuals who are knowledgeable about the situation as a whole. Nevertheless, it is clear that the accuracy of the resulting loss judgments is constrained by the validity of the models that are constructed. Models typically involve numerous assumptions and elaborate, interactive relationships. Such relationships imply that seemingly small variations in assumptions or component judgments can—and often do—cause large changes in the resulting risk assessments. When people see these widely discrepant risk judgments from presumed authorities, their natural tendency is to discredit *all* the experts (cf. Covello, von Winterfeldt, & Slovic, 1986). After all, how can they as laypersons rationally choose whom to believe?

A special evaluation problem: remoteness

In many important risky situations, the chances of the pertinent losses are remote, or at least hopefully so. Moreover, the situations themselves are uncommon, for instance, nuclear power plants and the use of nerve gas. For these situations it is impossible to collect enough cases to reliably evaluate the accuracy of loss judgments. For example, suppose that the judged probability that a reactor core with a certain design will melt down in a given year is 1 in 100000.There are too few nuclear power plants and too few years available to determine if this judgment is, say, well calibrated. This is not the case for many comparably sized judgments about diseases, since there are millions of people in the world who are susceptible to those illnesses.

Clearly, very different approaches must be taken in evaluating the quality of judgments about remote losses as opposed to more middling ones. One strategy is to focus on the procedures by which the judgments are produced. Thus, analysts who report judgments for remote events should be explicit about their derivations, so that their reasoning can be scrutinized thoroughly. A worrisome hazard of this strategy is that people seem limited in their insight about their own cognitive processes (see Nisbett & Wilson, 1977, and Slovic, Fleissner, & Bauman, 1972, but also Ericsson & Simon, 1980, and Reilly & Doherty, 1989).

Improving likelihood judgments

How can risk appraisers improve the accuracy of their loss likelihood judgments? One class of strategies relies on *feedback*. In this approach, the appraiser is told how accurate or inaccurate his or her assessments are. The expectation is that, if the report says that accuracy is deficient, then the appraiser will do whatever is necessary to achieve improvement. Two assumptions are implicit in feedback methods. The first is that appraisers ordinarily are unaware of their deficiencies. The second is that they have the means to effect beneficial changes in their judgment procedures. The first assumption seems valid in many instances. For instance, people are often surprised when they learn how poorly calibrated their probability judgments are. The validity of the second assumption appears to be more limited. On the one hand, people are quite adept at improving their calibration when given feedback about it (e.g. Lichtenstein & Fischhoff, 1980). On the other, there is little evidence that simply telling people that the overall accuracy of their judgments is poor results in their developing better judgments (see, for instance, Staël von Holstein's (1972) study concerning stock price forecasting).

The *alerting* strategy is similar in spirit to the feedback approach. Instead of being told how well he or she has performed in the past, a risk appraiser is told of the tendency of people in general to exhibit various judgmental deficiencies. For instance, a risk appraiser might be alerted to value biases, with the expectation that he or she would then do something to avert such biases. There have been few if any indications that the alerting strategy works (e.g. see Fischhoff, 1982). This implies that significant improvements in individuals' likelihood judgments require very pointed, active interventions. That is, these interventions must effect specific changes in the way a person goes about forming opinions. For example, the lens model literature suggests that the following technique would be beneficial (Balzer, Doherty, & O'Connor, 1989). First, a descriptive model of how a risk appraiser currently arrives at his or her judgments is constructed. The appraiser is then given a comparison between how the model says the appraiser uses various cues and how objective statistical evidence indicates the cues *should* be used.

A third strategy for achieving better loss likelihood judgments is to rely on the opinions of others. Expert consultants would be an obvious source of such opinions. However, even the opinions of individuals no more expert than the risk taker himself or herself should be useful. Using one or more of several group strategies, the risk taker should then be able to synthesize better assessments than could be expected from consulting any one of the individuals exclusively (see, for example, Michaelson, Black, & Watson, 1989; Sniezek & Henry, 1989).

LOSS SIGNIFICANCE

The more severe are the potential losses from an action, the greater is its riskiness. There is at least some objectivity to loss severity or significance. For instance, everyone would agree that being without a job for a year is worse than being unemployed for only a month. But there is considerable subjectivity to loss significance, too. Although one person might feel that having a child with a birth defect would be devastating, another would expect to feel quite differently. As a consequence, the riskiness of childbearing would be seen differently by

these individuals also. This example highlights the importance of loss significance appraisal.

Significance judgment accuracy

Formally, a judgment is an opinion about what the state of some aspect of the
world is or will be (Yates, 1990, Chapter 1). That is why it is legitimate for us to
have referred to loss likelihood assessments as judgments; these are opinions
about whether particular losses will or will not occur. When we evaluate the
significance of a potential loss, we are really answering the question, "How
much would this loss actually hurt?" From this perspective, significance
appraisals are more transparently judgments, too, and thus can be in error.
Consider, for example, an individual who anticipates that having a child with a
birth defect would be extremely painful. In the event that this ultimately
happens, the experience might be less traumatic than that. Then again, however,
the experience could be even worse than expected, in which case the opposite
error has occurred.

Do significance appraisal errors really happen? Are they common? If and
when they do occur, do they tend to be large or small? Unfortunately, there has
been extremely little research on such questions, and so there are no definitive
answers to them. Nevertheless, everyday experience tells us that significance
appraisal errors certainly do occur. A simple example: We have all bought items
of clothing we fully expected to wear with pride for years but soon despised so
much that we buried them in the deep recesses of our closets. As another
example, compare the present feelings any divorcing couple have for each other
to the feelings they anticipated at their wedding. While indeed there has been
little research on significance appraisal errors, such work is beginning to emerge,
and the results are consistent with our expectations. For instance, Kahneman
and Snell (1990) have documented several cases in which subjects' intuitions
about their own and others' reactions to aversive outcomes disagree with what
actually happens.

Significance appraisal mechanisms

How might significance appraisal errors arise? Although the issue has not been
examined systematically, several phenomena that have been studied in isolation
are illuminating for the question. We find that these phenomena are most
readily appreciated within a coordinating conceptual framework. The particular
framework we have adopted focuses on the experience of significance itself. As
we will argue, various aspects of that experience constitute specific means by
which appraisal errors can come about.

What causes a loss to hurt either a little or a lot? In the present analysis, this
question is more usefully formulated as two different ones (cf. Yates, 1990,

p. 271). First, there is the "entailment" issue:

Exactly what is it that happens when a loss occurs?

Then there is the "reactivity" question:

How does the person react to the specific things that happen?

These questions—and their answers—are most easily understood with the aid of examples and schematics.

When a given loss occurs, typically several outcomes are experienced simultaneously, not just the outcome that is explicitly acknowledged as the loss itself. Imagine, for instance, a man whose parents have just died in an auto accident. Most of us would consider the parents' deaths to be the focal loss. However, there are numerous other aspects of the scenario, too. We could describe the entire situation as an "outcome ensemble." Besides the deaths themselves are the attendant circumstances, such as whether the driver who caused the accident was intoxicated, the time of day, the kind of errand the parents were performing, and so on. The protagonist in our scenario is indifferent to most elements of the outcome ensemble. But he does care about some of them. These are the ones that constitute his "subjective outcome ensemble," which includes the outcomes that determine the significance of the focal loss, "My parents' deaths."

As suggested in Figure 3.1, besides the focal loss there are two classes of

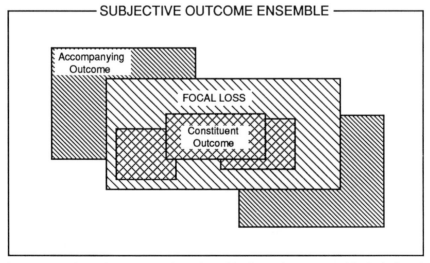

Figure 3.1. Schematic representation of a subjective outcome ensemble, including the focal loss (e.g. death of parents) with its accompanying outcomes (e.g. accidental circumstances) and constituent outcomes (e.g. companionship loss).

important outcomes in the subjective outcome ensemble. First, there are the "constituent outcomes." These are the outcomes that are inherent to the focal loss itself. Then there are the "accompanying outcomes." These are ones that happened at the same time as the focal loss, but whose occurrences were not necessary concomitants of that loss. In our example, the absence of the parents' affection, companionship, and counsel would be constituent outcomes; they would occur regardless of how the parents died. In contrast, the fact that the parents died in an accident would be an accompanying outcome; the parents could have died of some other cause, such as illness. In essence, constituent outcomes actually "constitute" the focal loss. Such things as loss of affection are what it "means" to have one's parents die. But they are not the whole story. The circumstances surrounding a focal loss, say, accidental versus natural causes of death, can either soften or worsen the entire experience.

From the present perspective, we immediately see one reason why appraising loss significance is such a difficult task. Any given loss—more specifically, its subjective outcome ensemble—can entail a very large number of constituent and accompanying outcomes. As we have noted, a risk appraiser's working register has limited capacity. So that individual is capable of taking into account only a subset of the outcomes that will eventually determine the loss experience. Imagine, for instance, a woman with children who is contemplating divorcing her husband. At the moment that she is considering how bad a life with only partial access to her children would be, she can hold in mind only a small number of the potential adverse outcomes, because there are so many of them.

Ideally, the risk appraiser should try to predict which accompanying and constituent outcomes will actually occur if a given loss takes place. Anticipating accompanying outcomes is difficult because, by definition, they differ from one situation to the next. For example, the circumstances surrounding child custody arrangements are almost never exactly the same. But predicting constituent outcomes often should be hard, too, despite the fact that they are necessary features of the focal loss. This is especially the case when such losses are rare. For instance, although divorce is common in society as a whole, any particular mother is unlikely to have extensive first-hand experience with life deprived of her own children.

Suppose a risk appraiser could accurately predict *all* of the outcomes entailed in a given loss. There would still be room for error in anticipating how much that loss would hurt. This is because the appraiser might misjudge his or her reactivity to those outcomes. By "reactivity" we mean the polarity—positive or negative—and the strength of the affective response that outcome elicits, for instance, one's personal anguish over being separated from her children. There is reason to expect that any particular outcome is unlikely to spark the identical reaction in every person who encounters it. Indeed, motivation theories of risk taking are predicated on the notion that there are large and stable individual differences in how people react to losses (e.g. Atkinson, 1964; see also Bromiley & Curley, Chapter 4 this volume, and Lopes, 1987). We should even expect random reactivity changes in a given person from one occasion to the next (see Thurstone, 1927, for a classic discussion of this issue).

Risk appraisal can be complicated by an additional consideration, too. Specifically, a risk taker might have little or no reliable basis for anticipating his or her reaction to novel outcomes, constituent or accompanying. For instance, a breast cancer patient can *guess* what her reaction to having post-mastectomy breast reconstruction would be like, but that guess could well be in error (cf. Hill, 1986).

Improving significance appraisal

Do the previous remarks imply that it is hopeless even to seek improvements in loss significance appraisal? No one can say for sure because no one has seriously tried to achieve such improvements. However, the random elements in significance determination (e.g. the variability of accompanying outcomes) mean that it is impossible to *perfectly* anticipate loss significance. Recognizing this should at least relieve risk takers of the frustration that trying to achieve perfection would induce (see Einhorn, 1986, for related ideas). On the more positive side, though, the previous observations suggest that at least two strategies might hold promise.

The first strategy is entailment search. Interviews with individuals who have made decisions that turned out badly suggest that appraisal errors are often traceable to entailment judgment errors. In particular, the decision makers completely overlooked some of the specific outcomes that constituted the focal outcomes they considered during the decision making process. Those interviews also suggest that the decision makers would have anticipated many of the neglected outcomes if someone had simply asked them to *try* to do so. The implication is that loss significance appraisal should be enhanced by an active search for the outcomes that are associated with the losses that immediately come to mind. Ideally, because of working register limits, this search should be carried out over an extended period of time and with paper and pencil.

The second strategy for improving significance appraisal relies on experience simulation. This approach should be particularly useful for trying to predict reactions to novel losses. An example: Being an undergraduate research assistant has qualitative differences from a career as a professional researcher. But the roles also have important similarities. Hence, if a student responds negatively to the lack of structure in the former role, he or she is likely to feel the same about that in the latter. This might be an indication that a research career is inappropriate, since that individual's reactivity to an essential feature of a research career is negative instead of positive.

OVERALL RISK

When people make overall risk appraisals, they say things like, "That's a very risky proposition" or "I think this proposal is riskier than that one." Extensive research has sought to discover what people mean when they make such statements. In this section we first offer a perspective on this work. Our subsequent summary of major conclusions from the research is divided into two parts, which correspond to a distinction that defines the area. Some research on overall risk appraisals has focused on situations where the risk taker is concerned about a single, quantified outcome, for instance, investments whose financial returns are the sole issue. Other research has emphasized situations with more general outcomes, for example, programs for protecting life and the environment from the hazards of technological development. We therefore begin by discussing single-dimension situations and then proceed to more general, multidimensional ones.

A perspective

The nature of overall risk appraisals

Exactly what *are* overall risks appraisals? As implied previously, a distinction can be made between judgments and decisions (cf. Yates, 1990, Chapter 1). Whereas a judgment is an opinion about what is or will be the state of some aspect of the world, a decision is the selection of an action with the aim of producing outcomes at least as satisfactory as would result from any other available action. An "evaluation" is a special class of decision, a statement of how much an alternative is worth. An example is a bid on a house or an interviewer's report to her boss that a job candidate is "pretty good." The overall evaluation or subjective worth of a decision alternative is a function of its riskiness, along with other considerations, that is,

$$\text{Worth} = f(\text{Risk, Other considerations}) \qquad (3.1)$$

From this point of view, an overall risk appraisal is a type of decision, specifically, a partial evaluation. In a manner that is beyond the scope of the present discussion, this evaluation is combined with evaluations of other aspects of an alternative to arrive at the comprehensive evaluation of that option.

In principle, at least, it is easy to characterize judgment quality. A judgment is good to the degree that it corresponds to the state of the world it is intended to anticipate. Does the classification of overall risk appraisals as partial evaluations imply that the quality concept does not apply to them? No, at least no more than it is impossible to say that a decision is good or poor. In general, a decision procedure has high quality to the extent that it tends to produce favorable outcomes (cf. Vlek *et al.*, 1984). Thus, overall risk appraisals are good if, as critical contributors to risk-taking behavior, the decisions they support tend to yield satisfactory results.

The role of overall risk appraisals

Although the precise role of overall risk appraisals in people's decision behavior is outside our scope, some comment on the issue is warranted. One means by which risky decision making might proceed is depicted in Figure 3.2. There the risk taker is confronted with the given situation. The individual then constructs a representation or personal characterization of that situation. On the basis of that representation, the risk taker makes a decision about what to do. Figure 3.2a suggests that the representation that drives the risk taker's actions does indeed take risk into account. But it does so only on the basis of various risk elements, such as the potential losses that are envisioned, along with their significance and uncertainty; the representation does not include a characterization of overall risk. Interpreted as reflections of what decision makers literally do when they decide, most mainstream theories of risky decision making implicitly assume this scenario. Thus, expected utility theory (Chapter 2) and prospect theory (Kahneman & Tversky, 1979) entail such constructs as utilities, values, and probabilities, but not overall risk.

An alternative possibility is suggested in Figure 3.2b. Notice that here there is an additional representation of the risk-taking situation, "Representation 2." In this second representation, the various risk elements are synthesized into an overall risk appraisal. The claim is thus that an overall risk assessment, along with other considerations, *does* dictate the risk taker's behavior. Risk-taking theories that make such claims are less common than theories that do not. However, they do exist. Examples include Coombs's (1975) portfolio theory and various expected value vs risk rules (Libby & Fishburn, 1977).

Discovering the kinds of representations people really do spontaneously construct and use in their decision making is an important topic of future risk-taking research. At the present time, no one knows which of the scenarios in Figure 3.2 is a more accurate depiction of what actually happens. However, it is plausible that the representation that is adopted depends on the circumstances. In particular, it seems that the overall risk representation might be more common in social rather than strictly personal settings. In the former, people are often provided with other people's characterizations of the pertinent situations. For example, a woman might tell her friend that she thinks it would be "highly risky" for him to take on a certain project. Or a voter might read in the news that an environmental group has pronounced a certain land-use proposal "too risky" for the local water supply. Socially communicated assessments like these undoubtedly affect people's risk-taking behavior. So, on these grounds, if nothing else, understanding how people arrive at overall risk appraisals is more than an exercise in popular semantics.

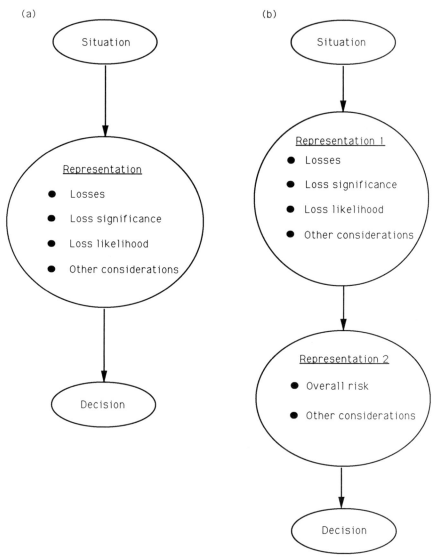

Figure 3.2. Alternative characterizations of risky decision making: (a) approaches that rest on representations of risk elements but not overall risk appraisals; (b) approaches that entail representations of both risk elements and overall risk.

Individual differences in overall risk appraisals

Researchers who study overall risk appraisals often comment that they observe large individual differences. Fischhoff and MacGregor (1983) go as far as to recommend against even asking people to make "risk" appraisals because the term means such different things to different people. Instead, they contend, it makes more sense to ask people about more specific risk elements, such as loss likelihoods. Extensive individual differences in overall risk appraisals are significant for at least two reasons.

Widely discrepant risk appraisals are important, first, because they imply that we should interpret research reports with special care. Thus, when reports say that the typical person appraises risk in a certain manner, there may be few real people who behave like this "typical person." Regrettably, risk researchers have rarely indicated just how large the individual differences in their subjects' responses really are. They have also not described in detail the common, but nondominant, risk appraisal mechanisms that differ from the average mechanism. This neglect of individual differences is, unfortunately, standard practice in cognitive psychology generally. Cognitive psychologists tend to write as if high-level cognitive processes are as uniform and "hard-wired" as those studied in biopsychology, when they are actually far more varied.

The second implication of large individual differences bears directly on risk-taking behavior, and has been discussed by Lopes (1984). When two individuals behave differently in a given risk-taking situation, the differences could arise from two sources. On the one hand, those individuals might see the situation identically, but employ different decision rules. For instance, whereas one person might decide according to rules similar to those in prospect theory (Kahneman & Tversky, 1979), the other might choose via rules like those in portfolio theory (Coombs, 1975). Alternatively, individuals who respond differently to a given situation might use the same decision rules, but see that situation differently. It is in this latter context that individual differences in risk appraisal would matter. For instance, although one person could appraise the situation as highly risky, another might not.

Single-dimension situations

Single-dimension alternatives are often conceptualized as probability distributions over the given quantity. For example, investment options A and B could be represented as:

Option A: (5%, −$400; 25%, −$200; 50%, $500; 20%, $900)

and

Option B: (15%, −$700; 20%, −$300; 40%, $800; 25%, $1100)

where the probability of earning or losing a given sum of money precedes that amount in the list. Imagine that an individual is asked to appraise the overall risk entailed by such options. Investigators have sought to determine whether and how these appraisals can be accounted for in terms of features of the distributions. Weber (1988; Weber & Bottom, 1989) has provided excellent recent reviews of this work. So only a brief summary and commentary is required here.

Early studies focused on the possibility that the variance—alone or in combination with other distributional features—was the basis for people's single-dimension risk appraisals (see Chapter 1, by Yates & Stone). However, this possibility was rejected almost immediately (Coombs & Bowen, 1971; Slovic, 1967). Consistent with the idea that the core of risk is the possibility of loss, those initial studies instead implicated a dominant role for features pertaining to the negative outcomes of alternatives, for example, the probability of losing money.

Over the years, several more detailed and specific proposals for subjective risk appraisal principles have been explored. Current data indicate that one of the most viable is Luce and Weber's (1986) *conjoint expected risk (CER) model.* (But see also Fishburn, 1982, 1984; and Keller, Sarin, & Weber, 1986.) Suppose X denotes the outcome that actually occurs, say, the amount of money an investment yields or the number of lives a public health program saves. As described by Weber (1988), the CER model says that the risk appraisal of a given alternative is

$$\text{Risk} = A(0)P(X = 0) + A(+)P(X > 0) + A(-)P(X < 0)$$
$$+ B(+)E[X^{k(+)}|X > 0]P(X > 0)$$
$$+ B(-)E[|X|^{k(-)}|X < 0]P(X < 0) \tag{3.2}$$

The first three terms in this model imply that the probabilities of breaking even ($X = 0$), coming out ahead ($X > 0$), and losing ($X < 0$) all contribute to the appraised risk. Just how *much* of a contribution they make is reflected in the corresponding coefficients or weights, $A(0)$, $A(+)$, and $A(-)$, which presumably could vary from person to person and could be either positive or negative. The important ingredient in the fourth summand on the right-hand side of Equation 3.2, $E[X^{k(+)}|X > 0]$, is a partial expectation, over positive outcomes. Thus, for alternatives with discrete outcomes, it is the sum of all the positive outcomes X raised to the power $k(+)$ and then multiplied by their probabilities. The essential part of the fifth term is analogous, as applied to negative outcomes. When the exponents are 1.0, these partial expectations are closely akin to expected losses (see Chapter 1, p. 18). When they differ from 1.0, they most closely resemble semivariances or their generalizations, assuming a reference outcome of $X = 0$ (Fishburn, 1977). As in the case of the probability weights $A(0)$, $A(+)$, and $A(-)$, the parameters $B(+)$, $B(-)$, $k(+)$, and $k(-)$ allow for considerable variation in the influence that potential gain and loss magnitudes can have on risk appraisals.

Under the assumption that all the $A(\cdot)$ and $B(\cdot)$ coefficients in Equation 3.2 are nonzero, the most striking feature of the CER model is the role it reserves for values of $X > 0$. That is, it implies that the appraised risk of an alternative is affected not only by losses and nil payoffs, but by gains as well. This runs counter to the notion that risk rests solely on adverse outcomes. What does this say about people's interpretation of the word "risk?" It is possible that, despite their instructions, the subjects whose responses validated the model somehow considered their task to be evaluating the *attractiveness* of the alternatives rather than their riskiness. This seems implausible partly because in a separate task Luce and Weber's (1986) subjects were explicitly asked to indicate their preferences for the options, and the rules describing preferences differed from those accounting for risk appraisals. So, at least tentatively, it appears that the subjective riskiness of an alternative can be moderated by sweetening its potential gains.

Lopes (1984) has suggested that people's conceptions of the riskiness of single-dimension options do not correspond to features of entire first-order outcome distributions, such as the variance or other moments like skewness. Instead, she contends, people most naturally characterize risk according to aspects of cumulative outcome distributions, say, the chance that they will earn at least some amount of money. Her experiments using a special kind of cumulative distribution known as a Lorenz curve are consistent with this conclusion. Her results also agree with those supporting the CER model, emphasizing probabilities of both gains and losses.

General situations

Studies of overall risk appraisal involving more than single-dimension outcomes have focused primarily on two classes of activities, hazards for which injury and death are prominent possibilities and purchases of consumer products. Our discussion is organized accordingly.

Hazards

When people think and converse about hazards such as nuclear power and pollution, several issues seem to recur, for example, the newness and severity of the potential consequences of those hazards. The key assumption guiding the dominant approach to understanding hazard risk appraisal is that people's fundamental notions of risk must be implicit in those recurrent themes. After all, the issues would not arise if they were irrelevant to the topic of discourse, risk. Thus, discovering how particular hazards are viewed in terms of these related issues provides a window on the underlying risk conception.

The implied strategy is made concrete in the tack taken by Slovic, Fischhoff, and Lichtenstein (1985). Subjects were asked to consider a large number of activities that might threaten life and limb, for instance, nuclear power, pesticides, railroads, mountain climbing, and power mowers. Initially, the subjects were asked to rate each activity on nine different scales, which corresponded to the kinds of recurrent risk themes suggested above. In subsequent studies, this list was extended to include 18 scales. The nine themes (or "risk characteristics," as they were described) that were used in all the studies, along with the corresponding scale stems, were (Slovic, Fischhoff, & Lichtenstein, 1985, from Table 5):

Voluntariness   "Do people face this risk voluntarily?"
Immediacy of Effect
                       "To what extent is the risk of death immediate—or is death likely to occur at some other time?"
Knowledge By Exposed
                       "To what extent are the risks known precisely by the persons who are exposed to the risks?"
Knowledge By Science
                       "To what extent are the risks known to science?"
Control   "If you are exposed to the risk, to what extent can you, by personal skill or diligence, avoid death?"
Newness   "Is this risk new and novel or old and familiar?"
Chronic-Catastrophic Character
                       "Is this a risk that kills people one at a time (chronic risk) or a risk that kills large numbers of people at once (catastrophic risk)?"
Common-Dread Character
                       "Is this a risk that people have learned to live with and can think about reasonably calmly, or is it one that people have a great dread for—on the level of a gut reaction?"
Severity of Consequences
                       "When the risk from the activity is realized in the form of a mishap or illness, how likely is it that the consequence will be fatal?"

The remaining nine issues and scales were similar in spirit.

The ratings were then factor analyzed, using the principal components technique (Morrison, 1976). The goal of this analysis can be understood *roughly* as follows: To the degree that the 18 scales embody everything people mean by "risk" and that the hazards under consideration run the gamut from minimum to maximum risk, then the variability in scale ratings is due to variations in whatever risk is, as suggested in Figure 3.3a. At one level, we could say that risk "is" every one of the 18 scales along which an individual varies his or her ratings of the hazards. But this characterization would be unsatisfactory on at least two counts.

First, *a priori*, it seems unlikely that all the scales would vary by the same amount; the properties they reflect would not all be equal contributors to the perceived riskiness of the hazards under consideration. Second, and perhaps more importantly, it also seems improbable that each of the reflected properties is unrelated to all the others. Instead, as suggested by the curved arcs in Figure 3.3a, we could expect some redundancy. Thus, the 18-scale characterization would be both imprecise and unparsimonious. Now suppose that variations in

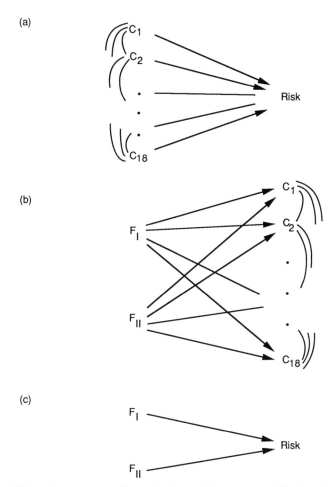

Figure 3.3 Schematic representation of relationships between (a) risk characteristics (the Cs) and subjective risk (Risk), (b) risk appraisal factors (the Fs) and risk characteristics, and (c) risk appraisal factors and subjective risk.

the 18 scale ratings were actually due to variations in two other variables or "factors" F_I and F_{II} that are independent of each other, as suggested in Figure 3.3b by the fact that F_I and F_{II} are unlinked. Then, ultimately, the variations in risk are the result of variations in those factors, too, as depicted in Figure 3.3c. We could then say that risk "is" whatever those factors happen to be, a much more suitable account. The factor analysis of Slovic, Fischhoff, and Lichtenstein (1985) sought to discover if such factors might exist and, if so, to identify them.

As has occurred in numerous studies, two major factors did emerge. They are defined by the scales that statistically are highly correlated with the factors and are identified by what is common to those scales. Factor I, the one that explained most of the variability in ratings, was labeled "Dread Risk." Factor II, which was independent of Factor I and accounted for the second largest amount of rating variance, was called "Unknown Risk." The rationale for these names is suggested by the scale values associated with the positive directions of the respective factors:

Factor I: Dread Risk
Uncontrollable, Dreaded, Catastrophic, Globally Catastrophic, Fatally Consequential, Inequitably Consequential, Affects Future Generations, Not Easily Reduced, Increasing Over Time, Involuntary, Affects Me Personally

Factor II: Unknown Risk
Not Observable, Unknown To Those Exposed, Effects Delayed, New, Unknown To Science

Figure 3.4 is a geometric depiction of the factors. The interpretation of the factors is even further enhanced by the locations of selected specific hazards at their factor score coordinates in one of the Slovic, Fischhoff, and Lichtenstein (1985) studies. So, for instance, we see that nerve gas is an extremely dreaded risk, but is moderate with respect to unknown risk.

What is most interesting about Factors I (Dread Risk) and II (Unknown Risk) is that they correspond quite well with the two basic constituents of the theoretical risk concept, loss significance and loss uncertainty, respectively. The analysis implies that, when people think and communicate about the riskiness of a given hazard, they really do have in mind those two constructs. Besides a confirmation of this idea, the present work highlights the psychological richness of the constructs as revealed in the scales. Thus, in the context of life-threatening hazards, there are surprisingly broad ranges of horror encompassed by the dread dimension. Similarly, there are multiple aspects to the uncertainty that can surround such a threat, aspects that extend beyond something as simple as mere probability of injury or death.

How universally valid are the above conclusions about how people appraise the overall risk of hazards? Similar factor structures have been found in studies using the same approach in other countries besides the United States, for example, Hungary and Norway (Teigen, Brun, & Slovic, 1988). However, the perceived status of particular hazards within that structure varies. This seems to make sense, given local differences in the severity of various hazards and the publicity given to them, for instance, industrial pollution in eastern Europe vs the West.

When the basic research strategy is altered, conclusions have tended to differ somewhat, too, though not dramatically. One difference in approach concerns the appraisal task subjects are requested to perform. Instead of asking individu-

Figure 3.4. Factors characterizing the riskiness of hazards. Adapted from Figure 2, Slovic, Fischhoff, and Lichtenstein (1985), and reproduced by permission of Clark University.

als to rate hazards on specified scales, other methods have required them to do such things as evaluate the similarity of the riskiness of pairs of hazards, to sort hazards into risk categories, and to simply describe the riskiness of hazards in any manner they like (Arabie & Maschmeyer, 1988; Johnson & Tversky, 1984; Vlek & Stallen, 1981). When researchers have used different tasks, they have also tended to ask subjects to consider different hazards. So it is difficult to make proper attribution for the differences in conclusions. However, the differing results have highlighted one potential drawback of the previously described scale-rating approach. Explicitly asking a person to rate a particular risk characteristic forces that individual to pay attention to that characteristic. In more naturalistic settings, that consideration might completely escape an individual's notice. There is at least some evidence that this is the case for concern about the effects of hazards on future generations (Earle & Lindell, 1984; Slovic, Fischhoff, & Lichtenstein, 1986).

One universality limitation is reliable and especially important. The above characterization of hazard risk appraisal applies to laypersons. Risk experts' appraisals are, interestingly, much simpler. Rather than conceptualizing risk in terms of multiple considerations like dread, reducibility, and observability, experts' appraisals of hazards seem to be dictated almost solely by the numbers of fatalities due to those hazards (Slovic, Fischhoff, & Lichtenstein, 1985; von Winterfeldt, John, & Borcherding, 1981). This difference in and of itself portends difficulties in communications between experts and the public in debates about hazard management.

Consumer purchases

For some time, marketing researchers have suspected (and actually demonstrated) that the risk a potential customer sees in a product dampens enthusiasm for buying that product (Bauer, 1960; Dowling, 1986). If a seller can understand how customers arrive at such overall risk appraisals, then avenues for productive changes are opened. The seller could alter the aspects of the product that heighten its "actual" risk. Or the seller could merely present the original product differently, attempting to change how those risk-relevant features are perceived.

The typical approach applied to investigating overall risk appraisals for consumer products has been straightforward. The researcher begins with a conceptual analysis which suggests that consumers make distinctions among products with respect to various aspects of risk. Subjects are then asked to rate products according to the implied distinctions or risk components. Next, the subjects indicate either the overall riskiness of the products or how much they would be inclined to buy those products. The original conception is considered validated to the extent that the component ratings are predictive of the overall risk appraisals or purchase intentions.

Early work in the area focused on the broad distinction between the significance and uncertainty elements of product risk and how they are combined into overall risk appraisals (e.g. Bettman, 1973, 1975). Since then, however, most research has emphasized distinct classes of adverse outcomes a purchase might produce and, to a lesser extent, the different kinds of uncertainty such purchases might entail. For example, the most widely used classification of outcomes is that due to Jacoby and Kaplan (1972; Kaplan, Szybillo, & Jacoby, 1974). According to that system, the major classes of outcomes that contribute to risk in consumer purchasing are: (a) financial, (b) performance, (c) physical, (d) psychological, (e) social, and (f) time loss (see Chapter 1). Variability along these dimensions has been found to account for 40–70% of the variability in subjects' ratings of overall product risk.

Additionally, two notable distinctions have been made about different *types* of consumer risk. The first is that between inherent and handled risk (Bettman, 1973). "Inherent risk" is the risk endemic to a certain product class, that is, the risk that is "inherent" within the class. "Handled risk," on the other hand, is the risk associated with choosing a certain brand within the buyer's typical purchase situation. Thus, handled risk refers to the amount of risk that remains with the product after the buyer has had access to information which should serve to reduce the amount of risk. As a concrete example, Bettman (1973) found that toothpaste has a much higher perceived inherent risk than handled risk, while dry spaghetti receives similar ratings for both types of risk. An explanation is that the type of toothpaste a person uses matters considerably (hence the relatively high inherent risk), but that typically the consumer has access to enough information about the different brands of toothpaste to significantly reduce the risk (hence the relatively low handled risk). Conversely, for dry spaghetti, there is little risk involved at either level, leading to similar ratings on both types or risk. Bettman (1973) has further demonstrated that inherent risk is affected largely by the importance of the purchase decision (positively) and the percentage of brands that are acceptable (negatively), and that the handled risk of a product increases with inherent risk and decreases with the amount of information held about the product class.

The second consumer risk typology distinguishes "search goods" and "experience goods" (Derbaix, 1983). The distinction concerns the locus of the uncertainty about how the consumer would feel about a product if it were purchased. Search goods, for example, dinner plates in Derbaix's (1983) study, are such that this uncertainty can be resolved by simply inspecting the products. In contrast, the uncertainty in experience goods, for instance, shampoos, must be resolved through the actual use of the product.

SUMMARY

Risk appraisals are indications of how risky specific actions or situations are. Some appraisals apply to basic risk elements: the existence, identity, likelihood, and significance of potential losses. Other appraisals concern overall risk.

Little is known about how and how well people judge whether a given situation contains many potential losses or only a few. However, indirect evidence suggests that risk takers are greatly concerned about this issue. Similar remarks apply to the task of identifying the specific losses that might occur in a risky enterprise. That is why loss identification is a major part of formal risk analyses. Research suggests several reasons to expect deficiencies in loss identification. Perhaps the most plausible concern the limited capacity and priming features of the working register in the human cognitive system.

More is known about how people judge the likelihoods of losses than about any other aspect of risk appraisal. One major conclusion suggested by available results is that people make their loss likelihood judgments according to three classes of procedures, which rely on relative frequencies, subjective reasoning, and formal models, respectively. Further, several aspects of likelihood judgment have special relevance to risk appraisal. It has been shown, for example, that likelihood judgments for events are not independent of how much people want those events to happen (or not happen); that moods influence the apparent chances of an event; and that judgments are highly sensitive to how they are elicited. These effects are consistent with evidence implying that we should not expect loss likelihood judgments to be highly accurate.

Systematic research on the quality and foundations of loss significance appraisals is only just beginning. Nevertheless, theoretical arguments as well as indirect empirical evidence imply numerous difficulties. Thus, errors in significance appraisal, for instance, cases where losses affect a risk taker less than was expected, should be common. These errors can be expected to arise from either or both of two sources. The first is a failure to consider or anticipate the specific outcomes that are entailed in a given loss, implying "entailment errors." The other is a misjudgment of how a person would react to those specific outcomes, leading to "reactivity errors."

Overall risk appraisals, for instance, "this is a very risky deal," can be seen as special kinds of decisions, as partial evaluations of the alternatives considered by an individual. As such, their quality is more difficult to determine; they are good to the extent that they contribute to the selection of actions that tend to turn out well for the risk taker. A large body of research on overall risk appraisal has focused on alternatives that yield outcomes along a single valued dimension, for example, business opportunities for which the sole concern is the amount of money they earn. One of the most interesting results from such work is that subjective risk appraisals are affected not only by losses, but also by gains. Other overall risk research has explored appraisals of more general situations, including life-threatening hazards and consumer purchases. The most consistently supported conclusion about the perceived riskiness of hazards is that people characterize hazards according to two factors, "dread risk" and "unknown risk." Consumer behavior research has documented that buyers recognize and respond to the potential for several different kinds of losses, for example, losses of money and social esteem. Moreover, concerns about these losses collectively increase the riskiness of buying a product, and hence reduce the chance of a purchase.

ACKNOWLEDGMENTS

We are grateful to the following colleagues for their helpful comments and suggestions: Nancy Johnson, Ju-Whei Lee, Gordon Pitz, Paul Price, Karen Siegel-Jacobs, and Carolynn Young. Preparation of this chapter was supported in part by the Arthur F. Thurnau Endowment at the University of Michigan.

REFERENCES

Alloy, L. B., & Tabachnik, N. (1984). Assessment of covariation by humans and animals: The joint influence of prior expectations and current situational information. *Psychological Review*, **91**, 112–149.

Anderson, J. R. (1985). *Cognitive psychology and its implications* (2nd ed.). San Francisco: Freeman.

Arabie, P., & Maschmeyer, C. (1988). Some current models for the perception and judgment of risk. *Organizational Behavior and Human Decision Processes*, **41**, 300–329.

Atkinson, J. W. (1964). *An introduction to motivation*. Princeton, NJ: Van Nostrand.

Balzer, W. K., Doherty, M. E., & O'Connor, R., Jr (1989). Effects of cognitive feedback on performance. *Psychological Bulletin*, **106**, 410–433.

Bauer, R. A. (1960). Consumer behavior as risk taking. In R. S. Hancock (Ed.), *Dynamic marketing for a changing world* (pp. 389–398). Chicago: American Marketing Association.

Bettman, J. R. (1973). Perceived risk and its components: A model and empirical test. *Journal of Marketing Research*, **10**, 184–190,

Bettman, J. R. (1975). Information integration in consumer risk perception: A comparison of two models of component conceptualization. *Journal of Applied Psychology*, **60**, 381–385.

Boucher, J., & Osgood, C. E. (1969). The Pollyanna hypothesis. *Journal of Verbal Learning and Verbal Behavior*, **8**, 1–8.

Brehmer, B. (1986). The psychology of risk. In W. T. Singleton & J. Hovden (Eds.), *Risk and decisions* (pp. 25–39). Chichester, England: Wiley.

Butler, G., & Mathews, A. (1983). Cognitive processes in anxiety. *Advances in Behavioral Research and Therapy*, **5**, 51–62.

Centor, R. M., Dalton, H. P., & Yates, J. F. (1984, November). *Are physicians' probability estimates better or worse than regression model estimates?* Paper presented at the Sixth Annual Meeting of the Society for Medical Decision Making, Bethesda, MD.

Christensen-Szalanski, J. J. J., & Bushyhead, J. B. (1981). Physicians' use of probabilistic information in a real clinical setting. *Journal of Experimental Psychology: Human Perception and Performance*, **7**, 928–935.

Cohen, B. L. (1983). Probabilistic risk assessment of wastes buried in the ground. *Risk Analysis*, **3**, 237–243.

Coombs, C. H. (1975). Portfolio theory and the measurement of risk. In M. F. Kaplan & S. Schwartz (Eds.), *Human judgment and decision processes* (pp. 63–85). New York: Academic Press.

Coombs, C. H., & Bowen, J. N. (1971). A test of VE-theories of risk and the effect of the central limit theorem. *Acta Psychologica*, **35**, 15–28.

Covello, V. T., von Winterfeldt, D., & Slovic, P. (1986). Risk communication: A review of the literature. *Risk Abstracts*, **3**, 171–182.

Crouch, E. A. C., & Wilson, R. (1982). *Risk/benefit analysis*. Cambridge, MA: Ballinger.

Derbaix, C. (1983). Perceived risk and risk relievers: An empirical investigation. *Journal of Economic Psychology*, **3**, 19–38.

Dowling, G. R. (1986). Perceived risk: The concept and its measurement. *Psychology & Marketing*, **3**, 193–210.

Earle, T. C., & Cvetkovich, G. (1988). Risk judgment, risk communication and conflict management. In B. Brehmer & C. R. B. Joyce (Eds.), *Human judgment: The SJT view* (pp. 361–400). New York: Elsevier.

Earle, T. C., & Lindell, M. K. (1984). Public perception of industrial risks: A free-response approach. In R. A. Waller & V. T. Covello (Eds.), *Low-probability/high-consequence risk analysis* (pp. 531–550). New York: Plenum.

Einhorn, H. J. (1986). Accepting error to make less error. *Journal of Personality Assessment*, **50**, 387–395.

Erev, I., & Cohen, B. L. (1990). Verbal versus numerical probabilities: Efficiency, biases, and the preference paradox. *Organizational Behavior and Human Decision Processes*, **45**, 1–18.

Ericsson, K. A., & Simon, H. A. (1980). Verbal reports as data. *Psychological Review*, **87**, 215–251.

Fischhoff, B. (1982). Debiasing. In D. Kahneman, P. Slovic, & A. Tversky (Eds.), *Judgment under uncertainty: Heuristics and biases* (pp. 422–444). New York: Cambridge University Press.

Fischhoff, B., & MacGregor, D. (1983). Judged lethality: How much people seem to know depends on how they are asked. *Risk Analysis*, **3**, 229–236.

Fischhoff, B., Slovic, P., & Lichtenstein, S. (1978). Fault trees: Sensitivity of estimated failure probabilities to problem representation. *Journal of Experimental Psychology: Human Perception and Performance*, **4**, 330–344.

Fischhoff, B., Slovic, P., & Lichtenstein, S. (1981). "The public" vs "the experts": Perceived vs actual disagreements about risks of nuclear power. In V. T. Covello, W. G. Flamm, J. V. Rodricks, & R. G. Tardiff (Eds.), *The analysis of actual versus perceived risks* (pp. 235–249). New York: Plenum.

Fishburn, P. C. (1977). Mean-risk analysis with risk associated with below-target returns. *American Economic Review*, **67**, 116–126.

Fishburn, P. C. (1982). Foundations of risk measurement. II. Effects of gains on risk. *Journal of Mathematical Psychology*, **25**, 226–242.

Fishburn, P. C. (1984). Foundations of risk measurement. I. Risk as probable loss. *Management Sciences*, **30**, 396–406.

Fisher, G. L., & Fisher, B. E. (1969). Differential rates of GSR habituation to pleasant and unpleasant sapid stimuli. *Journal of Experimental Psychology*, **82**, 339–342.

Foersterling, F. (1980). Sex differences in risk taking: Effects of subjective and objective probability of success. *Personality and Social Psychology Bulletin*, **6**, 149–152.

Gettys, C. F., Pliske, R. M., Manning, C., & Casey, J. T. (1987). An evaluation of human act generation performance. *Organizational Behavior and Human Decision Processes*, **39**, 23–51.

Glass, A. L., & Holyoak, K. J. (1986). *Cognition* (2nd ed.). New York: Random House.

Hammond, K. R., Anderson, B. F., Sutherland, J., & Marvin, B. (1984). Improving scientists' judgments of risk. *Risk Analysis*, **4**, 69–78.

Hill, H. L. (1986). Radiation or mastectomy: A choice for living. *Journal of Psychosocial Oncology*, **4**, 77–90.

Hoch, S. J. (1984). Availability and interference in predictive judgment. *Journal of Experimental Psychology: Learning, Memory, and Cognition*, **10**, 649–662.

Hoch, S. J. (1985). Counterfactual reasoning and accuracy in predicting personal events. *Journal of Experimental Psychology: Learning, Memory, and Cognition*, **11**, 719–731.

Jacoby, J., & Kaplan, L. B. (1972). The components of perceived risk. In M. Venkatesan (Ed.), *Proceedings of the Third Annual Conference of the Association for Consumer Research* (pp. 382–393). Chicago: Association for Consumer Research.

Jeffery, R. W. (1989). Risk behaviors and health: Contrasting individual and population perspectives. *American Psychologist*, **44**, 1194–1202.

Johnson, E. J., & Tversky, A. (1983). Affect, generalization, and the perception of risk. *Journal of Personality and Social Psychology*, **45**, 20–31.

Johnson, E. J., & Tversky, A. (1984). Representations of perceptions of risks. *Journal of Experimental Psychology: General*, **113**, 55–70.

Jungerman, H., Schutz, H., & Thuring, M. (1988). Mental models in risk assessment:

Informing people about drugs. *Risk Analysis*, **8**, 147–155.

Kahn, H. A. (1983). *An introduction to epidemiologic methods*. New York: Oxford University Press.

Kahneman, D., Slovic, P., & Tversky, A. (Eds.). (1982). *Judgment under uncertainty: Heuristics and biases*. New York: Cambridge University Press.

Kahneman, D., & Snell, J. (1990). Predicting utility. In R. M. Hogarth (Ed.), *Insights in decision making* (pp. 295–310). Chicago: University of Chicago Press.

Kahneman, D. & Tversky, A. (1979). Prospect theory: An analysis of decision under risk. *Econometrica*, **47**, 263–291.

Kaplan, S., & Garrick, B. J. (1981). On the quantitative definition of risk. *Risk Analysis*, **1**, 11–27.

Kaplan, L. B., Szybillo, G. J., & Jacoby, J. (1974). Components of perceived risk in product purchase: A cross-validation. *Journal of Applied Psychology*, **59**, 287–291.

Keller, L. R., Sarin, R. K., & Weber, M. (1986). Empirical investigation of some properties of the perceived riskiness of gambles. *Organizational Behavior and Human Decision Processes*, **38**, 114–130.

Keren, G. (1987). Facing uncertainty in the game of bridge: A calibration study. *Organizational Behavior and Human Decision Processes*, **39**, 98–114.

Langer, E. (1975). The illusion of control. *Journal of Personality and Social Psychology*, **32**, 311–328.

Leibowitz, H. W. (1985). Grade crossing accidents and human factors engineering. *American Scientist*, **73**, 558–562.

Leibowitz, H. W., & Owens, D. A. (1986). We drive by night. *Psychology Today*, **20** (1), 54–58.

Levi, K. R. (1985). *Numerical likelihood estimates from physicians and linear models*. Unpublished doctoral dissertation, University of Michigan, Ann Arbor.

Libby, R., & Fishburn, P. C. (1977). Behavioral models of risk taking in business decisions: A survey and evaluation. *Journal of Accounting Research*, **15**, 272–292.

Lichtenstein, S., & Fischhoff, B. (1980). Training for calibration. *Organizational Behavior and Human Performance*, **26**, 149–171.

Lopes, L. L. (1984). Risk and distributional inequality. *Journal of Experimental Psychology: Human Perception and Performance*, **10**, 465–485.

Lopes, L. L. (1987). Between hope and fear: The psychology of risk. In L. Berkowitz (Ed.), *Advances in experimental social psychology, Vol. 20* (pp. 255–295). New York: Academic Press.

Luce, R. D., & Weber, E. O. (1986). An axiomatic theory of conjoint, expected risk. *Journal of Mathematical Psychology*, **30**, 188–205.

March, J. G., & Shapira, Z. (1987). Managerial perspectives on risk and risk taking. *Management Science*, **33**, 1404–1418.

Mehr, R. I. (1983). *Fundamentals of insurance*. Homewood, IL: Irwin.

Michaelson, L. K., Black, R. H., & Watson, W. E. (1989). A realistic test of individual versus group consensus decision making. *Journal of Applied Psychology*, **74**, 834–839.

Morrison, D. F. (1976). *Multivariate statistical methods* (2nd ed.). New York: McGraw-Hill.

Murphy, A. H., & Daan, H. (1985). Forecast evaluation. In A. H. Murphy & R. W. Katz (Eds.), *Probability, statistics, and decision making in the atmospheric sciences* (pp. 379–437). Boulder, CO: Westview Press.

Nisbett, R. E., & Wilson, T. D. (1977). Telling more than we can know: Verbal reports on mental processes. *Psychological Review*, **84**, 231–259.

Paté-Cornell, M. E. (1984). Fault trees vs event trees in reliability analysis. *Risk Analysis*, **4**, 177–186.

Pietromonaco, P. R., & Rook, K. S. (1987). Decison style in depression: The contribution of perceived risks versus benefits. *Journal of Personality and Social Psychology*, **52**, 399-408.

Poses, R. M., Cebul, R. D., Collins, M., & Fager, S. (1985). The accuracy of experienced physicians' probability estimates for patients with sore throats: Implications for decision making. *Journal of the American Medical Association*, **254**, 925-929.

Reilly, B. A., & Doherty, M. E. (1989). A note on the assessment of self-insight in judgment research. *Organizational Behavior and Human Decision Processes*, **44**, 123-131.

Rothbart, M. (1970). Assessing the likelihood of a threatening event. *Journal of Personality and Social Psychology*, **15**, 109-117.

Russell, M., & Gruber, H. (1987). Risk assessment in environmental policy-making. *Science*, **236**, 286-290.

Slovic, P. (1967). The relative influence of probabilities and payoffs upon perceived risk of a gamble. *Psychonomic Science*, **9**, 223-224.

Slovic, P. (1987). Perception of risk. *Science*, **236**, 280-285.

Slovic, P., Fischhoff, B., & Lichtenstein, S. (1985). Characterizing perceived risk. In R. Kates, C. Hohenemser, & J. Kasperson (Eds.), *Perilous progress: Managing the hazards of technology* (pp. 91-125). Boulder, CO: Westview Press.

Slovic, P., Fischhoff, B., & Lichtenstein, S. (1986). The psychometric study of risk perception. In V. T. Covello, J. Menkes, & J. Mumpower (Eds.), *Risk evaluation and management* (pp. 3-24). New York: Plenum.

Slovic, P., Fleissner, D., & Bauman, W. S. (1972). Analyzing the use of information in investment decision making. *Journal of Business*, **45**, 283-301.

Sniezek, J. A., & Henry, R. A. (1989). Accuracy and confidence in group judgment. *Organizational Behavior and Human Decision Processes*, **43**, 1-28.

Staël von Holstein, C.-A. (1972). Probabilistic forecasting: An experiment related to the stock market. *Organizational Behavior and Human Performance*, **8**, 139-158.

Sullivan, J. D., Gnospelius, R. A., DeFliese, P. L., & Jaenicke, H. R. (1985). *Montgomery's accounting* (10th ed.). New York: Wiley.

Teigen, K. H., Brun, W., & Slovic, P. (1988). Societal risks as seen by a Norwegian public. *Journal of Behavioral Decision Making*, **1**, 111-130.

Thurstone, L. L. (1927). A law of comparative judgment. *Psychological Review*, **34**, 273-286.

Tierney, W. M., Fitzgerald, J., McHenry, R., Roth, B. J., Psaty, B., Stump, D. L., & Anderson, F. K. (1986). Physicians' estimates of the probability of myocardial infarction in emergency room patients with chest pain. *Medical Decision Making*, **6**, 12-17.

Vlek, C., Edwards, W., Kiss, I., Majone, G., & Toda, M. (1984). What constitutes a "good decision?" *Acta Psychologica*, **56**, 5-27.

Vlek, C., & Stallen, P.-J. (1981). Judging risks and benefits in the small and in the large. *Organizational Behavior and Human Performance*, **28**, 235-271.

von Winterfeldt, D., & Edwards, W. (1986). *Decision analysis and behavioral research*. New York: Cambridge University Press.

von Winterfeldt, D., John, R. S., & Borcherding, K. (1981). Cognitive components of risk ratings. *Risk Analysis*, **1**, 277-287.

Wallsten, T. S. (1981). Physician and medical student bias in evaluating diagnostic information. *Medical Decision Making*, **1**, 145-164.

Weber, E. U. (1988). A descriptive measure of risk. *Acta Psychologica*, **69**, 185-203.

Weber, E. U., & Bottom, W. P. (1989). Axiomatic measures of perceived risk: Some tests and extensions. *Journal of Behavioral Decision Making*, **2**, 113-131.

Weinstein, N. D. (1984). Why it won't happen to me: Perceptions of risk factors and susceptibility. *Health Psychology*, **3**, 431–457.

Weinstein, N. D. (1987). Unrealistic optimism about illness susceptibility: Conclusions from a community-wide sample. *Journal of Behavioral Medicine*, **10**, 481–500.

Winkler, R. L. (1972). *Introduction to Bayesian inference and decision*. New York: Holt, Rinehart, and Winston.

Yates, J. F. (1990). *Judgment and decision making*. Englewood Cliffs, NJ: Prentice Hall.

Yates, J. F., Cole, L. G., & Rodgers, W. (1989, November). *Value biasing in probability judgment*. Paper presented at the Annual Meeting of the Psychonomic Society, Atlanta.

Yates, J. F., & Curley, S. P. (1985). Conditional distribution analyses of probabilistic forecasts. *Journal of Forecasting*, **4**, 61–73.

Yates, J. F., McDaniel, L. S., & Brown, E. S. (1991). Probabilistic forecasts of stock prices and earnings: The hazards of nascent expertise. *Organizational Behavior and Human Decision Processes*, **48**, 60–79.

Zakay, D. (1984). The influence of perceived event's controllability on its subjective occurrence probability. *Psychological Record*, **34**, 233–240.

Chapter 4

Individual differences in risk taking

Philip Bromiley and Shawn P. Curley
Carlson School of Management, University of Minnesota

CONTENTS

Risk-taking Behavior. Edited by J. F. Yates
© 1992 John Wiley & Sons Ltd

The casual observer knows that individuals differ in their attitudes toward risk. Some individuals seek certain kinds of risks that others desperately avoid. Consequently, it would seem straightforward to differentiate individuals according to their tendencies toward risk. Such is not the case. An extremely diverse set of research examines individual differences in risk taking with equally diverse results. Research on individual differences addresses several questions:

1. Do specific individuals demonstrate consistent risk-taking tendencies across differing kinds of risks? Do individuals differ in risk-taking behaviors for a given kind of risk? That is, do individuals show a consistent "risk-taking propensity" across different kinds of risk (or situations), and do individuals differ in such a propensity?
2. If individual differences exist, can we describe, explain, or predict them, recognizing that the differences may not be stable across different kinds of risks? What frameworks are available for doing so, and how well do they perform?
3. Finally, what do the results of these research efforts imply for further research and practical decision making under risk?

This chapter examines efforts to understand how individuals differ in risk taking. We begin by outlining six conceptual approaches to studying risk taking. Our review of research using these approaches finds evidence of both individual and situational differences in risk taking, i.e. understanding risk taking requires understanding both individual traits and risk-taking situations. Consequently, we organize our survey of individual differences in risk taking by situational categories, follow this with a look at several intersituational studies and what they find, and end with a general discussion and summary of these efforts.

APPROACHES TO STUDYING RISK TAKING

Studies of individual differences in risk taking highlight the diversity of conceptualizations and measures of risk. Figure 4.1 provides a structure to help us explain different research approaches.

Since risk behavior may vary across people and situations, we would like to characterize situations and individuals in some general ways to allow for theory development. For example, we might want to differentiate between lotteries and physical risks and between young and old individuals. Thus, down the side of

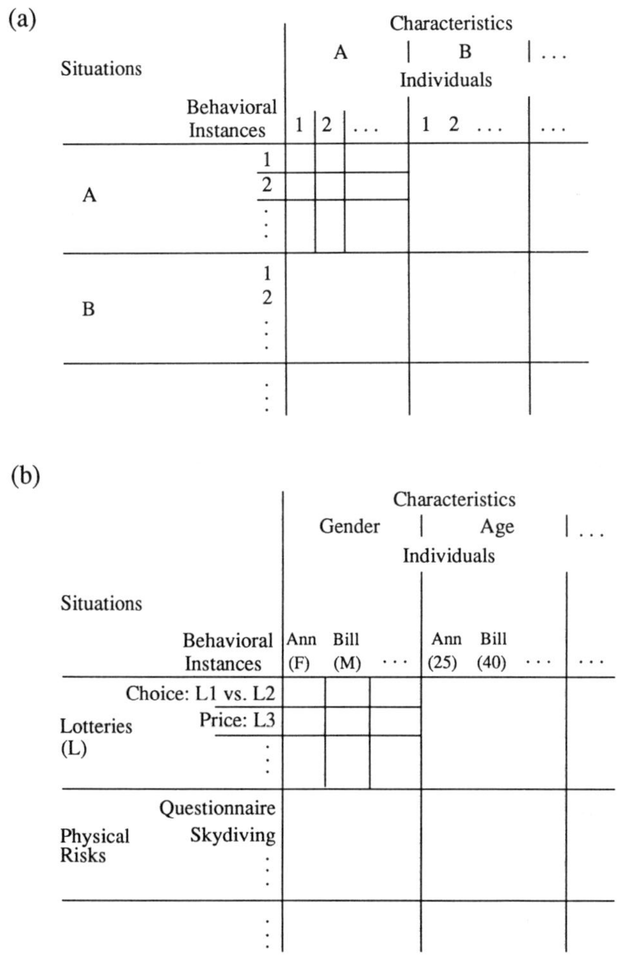

Figure 4.1. Behavioral instance (situation) by individual (characteristic) matrix for demonstration of research designs. (a) The generic framework is given along with (b) a matrix with exemplars.

the matrices appear different kinds of risky situations and across the top of the matrices appear different characteristics of people. The kinds of risky situations can be further defined by specific behavioral instances. For example, physical risks might be divided into skydiving, sports car driving, etc., and lotteries might be divided by specific lottery formats. Individual characteristics are reflected by specific individuals who fall into different categories (gender, age, education, etc.). Thus, across the top of the matrices appear a number of variables researchers have used to explain interindividual differences in risk taking.

Researchers chiefly have used six approaches to studying behavior within Figure 4.1, with two approaches historically characterizing most of the risk research. In the first, researchers assume that average behavior is of interest and risk-taking propensity is generalizable within a situation. Thus, they ignore interpersonal differences and study average behaviors within a given situation where the instances of the situation vary in the parameters or values involved, but not substantially in structure. This corresponds to focusing on a situation row of the matrix and averaging across the columns of individuals (Figure 4.2a). No characteristics are used. This is the dominant approach within decision theory, where a single kind of choice situation is used with varying parameters (for example, choosing between lotteries that vary in amounts and probabilities to win/lose) and the emphasis is on how subjects respond on average. Such an approach presumes that risk taking is consistent across individuals; individual differences are minor.

The second approach rotates the argument by assuming that risk-taking behavior is generalizable across situations and that it varies with one or a very

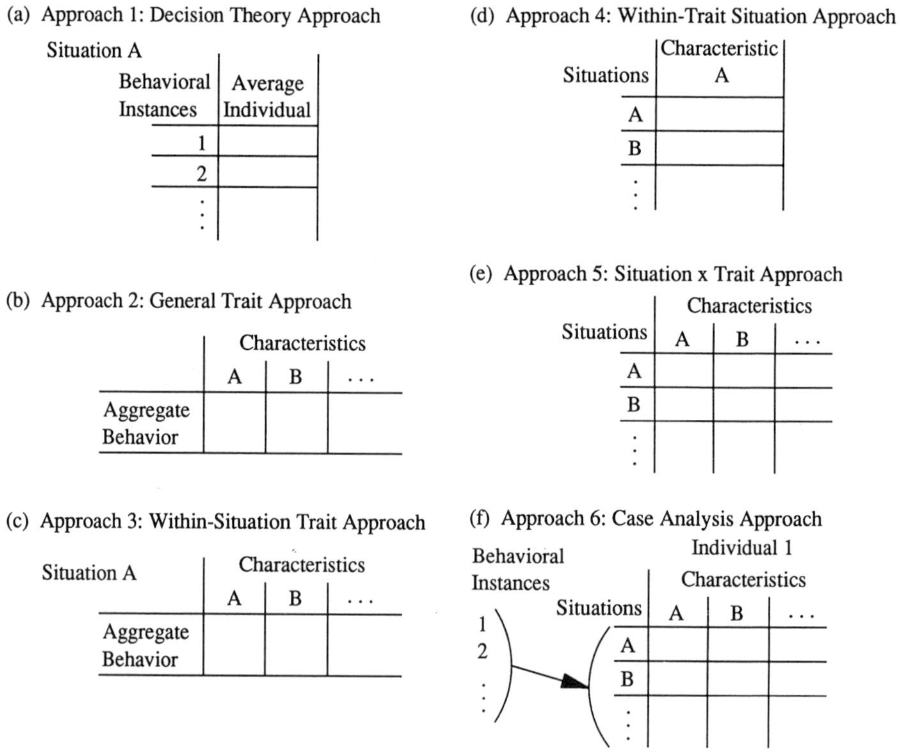

Figure 4.2. Six approaches to the study of risk taking following the structure of Figure 4.1.

few individual characteristics. Researchers in this tradition examine the connections between a small number of personality traits and risk taking across situations (for example, describing males as greater risk takers in general). This corresponds to aggregating over individuals within characteristics, focusing on a few columns of the matrix and underplaying differences across the rows, in the extreme collapsing the rows completely as shown in Figure 4.2b. Early personality trait theorists used this approach. It presumes that risk taking is fairly consistent across behavioral instances; there is little situational influence. However, in fact, the evidence indicates substantial differences when a given trait is examined across situations. This suggests three additional approaches.

In Approach 3, one tries to identify multiple individual differences within particular situations. For example, how do age, gender, and extroversion influence financial investments? Whereas Approaches 1 and 2 looked at a given situation or characteristic and then collapsed differences in the other dimension, this approach looks at individual differences within a given situation, recognizing that situations differ (Figure 4.2c). In Approach 4, one focuses on the situational differences, forming the transpose of Figure 4.2c. The personality characteristic remains constant and we look across situations (Figure 4.2d). For example, does extroversion influence gambling differently than it influences investment decisions? Fifth and most complicated, one can allow both personality characteristics and situations to vary: examining a number of individual differences across a number of situations, forming a characteristic × situation matrix (Figure 4.2e). This approach is more general than the other approaches, encompassing them as special cases.

The final approach is a case analysis. This approach inverts Figure 4.1; each individual is a focus of study (Figure 4.2f). In the risk domain, case analysis tries to identify characteristics of the individual that might differentiate risk-taking propensities of other individuals and/or to identify situations that would allow a categorization of instances. Primarily, this approach can be viewed as an exploratory approach preliminary to one of the other five approaches to risk taking.

All but the first of these six approaches describe individuals by characteristics. Researchers have explored both demographic variables such as age or gender, and personality-based characteristics. In particular, risk taking *per se* might be a personality characteristic. To explain the issues involved, we will consider the concept of a personality "trait" in general and then the prospects of isolating risk taking as a stable trait. We conclude that situation interacts with personality traits like risk taking in influencing behavior. Thus, research designs should allow for both situational and individual variation as do Approaches 3 to 6. (Although Approach 1 is still left open at this point, its limitations will be apparent in the next sections.) Subsequent sections look at research on different kinds of situations and then some important studies which have looked across situations.

PERSONALITY CHARACTERISTIC OR SITUATION?

The General Trait Approach to research in risk taking (Figure 4.2b) assumes that personality characteristics can be identified which explain behavior across a variety of situations. Is this possible?

The nature of personality traits

Personality trait research has its foundations in the development of measures of intelligence through factor analysis (Anastasi, 1983). Factor analysis continues to be a primary tool in personality psychology (Briggs & Cheek, 1986). As such, traits are not to be considered as causal factors in the strong sense of implying behavior. As Buss (1989) described:

> In personality trait psychology, the impact of experimental manipulations typically is not investigated, although there are exceptions, of course. More attention is paid to the content of behavior than to the psychological processes underlying the behavior, although there are exceptions. (p. 1379)

Thus, traits are to be treated as descriptive, rather than explanatory, categories. This descriptive orientation of trait research implies a scarcity of explanatory investigations.

It is instructive to contrast the trait construct with the related constructs of state and attitude. A *state* is time-specific, it describes a condition at a point in time; a trait applies across instances and times (Allport, 1937; Cattell, 1972). An *attitude* is an evaluative condition with reference to some thing; one has an attitude about something. Traits are not so constrained, nor do they entail any evaluative connotation (Sherman & Fazio, 1983). Thus, a trait implies temporal and cross-instance stability. It describes a general orientation, rather than a specific stance.

Cattell (1950, p. 2) defined personality as "that which permits a prediction of what a person will do in a given situation," or as a relatively enduring disposition to behave consistently across situations (Cattell, 1972). This is perhaps the strongest version of stability as applied to individual characteristics and drives the general trait approach in Figure 4.2b. At the other extreme is the position that behavior is completely situationally determined. The latter position has been attributed to Mischel (1968) through his conclusion that only 5–10% of the variance in behavior is attributable to individual differences. However, Mischel clearly espoused a more moderate view involving the interaction of situational factors and cognitive expectancies; the crux of his argument was that behavior is highly situation-specific. Some version of interactional theory prevails among current personality theorists (Fiske, 1988; Kenrick & Funder, 1988). Buss (1989) argued that it is useless to debate whether situations or traits capture more variation, since the researcher can design the study to favor one or the other: Novel situations, restrictions on subjects' responses due to task demands, detailed instructions, or task brevity, all favor nonhabitual behavior leading to the promotion of situational influences upon behavior; whereas, the contrary conditions promote typical behavior and the impact of stable traits.

Taking a situational perspective

Acknowledging that personality traits interact with situations in determining behavior attacks the viability of traits in the strongest sense of cross-situational behavioral consistencies (Mischel, 1977). Behavior will not necessarily generalize across situations. This conclusion has broad support beyond consideration of risk taking as a trait; cross-situational behavioral consistency is typically low (Zuckerman, 1979b), particularly for the prediction of single behaviors (Jaccard, 1974). Studies of risk taking as a characteristic agree with this general result (Slovic, 1964) as do the cross-situational studies of risk taking described later in the chapter.

Although trait constructs may not predict across situations, they can have consistent ties to behavior within a particular kind of situation. Zuckerman (1979a) identified a trait's regularity as characterizing average behavior over many occasions, not necessarily being accurate for a particular instance and time. Supporting this is the observation that personality measures can correlate well with multiple criteria (Epstein, 1979, 1980, 1982; Jaccard, 1974). For example, Weigel and Newman (1976) found low correlations between measured attitudes toward environmental issues and each of 14 behavioral observations made several months later (e.g. signing petitions, volunteering in programs); however, the attitudes correlated well (0.62) with a measure based on all behaviors.

Fishbein and Ajzen (1974; Ajzen & Fishbein, 1977; Ajzen, 1982) explained the phenomenon via a specificity hypothesis, whereby attitudes and behaviors must match in level of specificity for accurate prediction. Consequently, general risk-taking measures, and a general risk-taking construct, can be expected to poorly predict specific behavioral instances, but better predict more general aggregates of similar behaviors. The key is to appropriately categorize instances into situational categories which are cohesive, i.e. for which variability is low, regularity is high (Buss & Craik, 1980, 1981). Thus, the goal is to identify moderately parsimonious sets of individual characteristics and to develop categories of situations that would reduce the dimensionality of the matrix in Figure 4.1a to the matrix described by Figure 4.2e. Particularly lacking in this effort is the analysis of instances into situations. For the most part, this has only been done intuitively (a practice we follow below). Personality psychologists have rarely applied the technology which they use to cluster behaviors into traits to similarly cluster occasions into situations (Buss, 1989).

The next four sections address four broad situations involving risk: activities that involve physical sensation, games and lotteries, everyday life choices, and business settings. Research in these categories not only exemplifies the identification of characteristics that apply to risk taking, but also typifies the different approaches to the study of individual differences in risk taking. We use these categories to organize this chapter, but do not presume that they constitute a good taxonomy of situations for further theory or research. In each category, we attempt to illustrate the variety of methods used to study individual differences in risk taking, to present exemplar descriptive results, and to comment on the status and promise of different avenues of research.

RISK AS PHYSICAL SENSATION

A substantial research tradition has looked at situations involving physical risk, i.e. possible physical injury or death. The research often explores the possibility that some individuals have a "sensation seeking" trait which inclines them to activities that include some perceived possibility of death, for example, skydiving, mountain climbing, and scuba diving.

Sensation Seeking Scale and subscales

Given the multiple manifestations of risk taking in different situations, it is perhaps fortunate that the alternate term "sensation seeking" has been adopted recently by personality theorists to specify physical risk taking. However, perhaps unfortunately, the term has narrowed to be almost synonymous with measures of the Sensation Seeking Scale; the fifth version (SSS V) of which is currently in use. Zuckerman (1979a) chronicles the scale's development which typifies the personality approach. Scale items were selected by intuition and historical tradition, retained on the basis of statistical validation, and partitioned to form subscales as identified through factor analysis.

SSS V has four subscales (Zuckerman, 1978, 1979a): (a) Thrill and Adventure Seeking which measures the desire to engage in physically adventurous activities (e.g. skydiving); (b) Experience Seeking which measures a desire for experiential variety through a nonconforming lifestyle (e.g. counterculture groups); (c) Disinhibition which measures traditional nonconformity through release and social disinhibition (e.g. through social drinking); and (d) Boredom Susceptibility which measures an aversion to repetition and routine (e.g. restlessness). Although interpreted as different expressions of sensation seeking which can differentiate individuals, the subscales correlate from 0.06 to 0.48 in English and American samples (Zuckerman, Eysenck, & Eysenck, 1978). (Table 4.4 includes some items from this scale.)

Use of the Sensation Seeking Scales

Aside from continuing development of the trait scale (SSS VI is underway, Zuckerman, 1983), researchers have applied Sensation Seeking Scales in two different kinds of individual differences studies. First, researchers have compared the responses of different groups of people to the scale. In terms of Figure 4.2, such studies examine differences in a trait for a given situation, i.e. the within-situation trait approach (Figure 4.2c). Second, to validate the measure, researchers have examined the correlation of sensation-seeking scores with measures of other constructs. In the approximately 25 years since the first SSS was developed (Zuckerman *et al.*, 1964), studies using the scale have flourished.

Recent studies examining sensation seeking across groups used subjects from different countries (Birenbaum & Montag, 1987; Zuckerman, Eysenck, & Eysenck, 1978), compared injured and uninjured skiers (Bouter *et al.*, 1988), and compared males and females on the relations between sensation seeking and forced-choice questionnaires (Franken, Gibson, & Rowland, 1989). Some recent studies of the second type examined correlations between sensation seeking (and/or its subcomponents) and food preferences (Terasaki & Imada, 1988), decisiveness and a desire for individual responsibility (Franken, 1988), components of humor appreciation (Ruch, 1988), and time used in taking the SSS itself (Rogers, 1987).

Zuckerman, Buchsbaum, and Murphy (1980) summarized the established behavioral correlates of sensation seeking. Researchers have reported that high sensation seeking correlated with greater sexual activity, multidrug use, cigarette smoking, volunteering for unusual experiments, participation in physically dangerous activities, the Hypomania (Ma) and Psychopathic Deviate (Pd) scales of the Minnesota Multiphasic Personality Inventory (MMPI, a set of questionnaire item scales purported to measure types of pathology), gender (males tend to score higher), and younger age.

In addressing the promise of the research, three motivations underlying the studies need to be differentiated. The first motivation is scale validation. To validate the scale, the researcher measures the sensation seeking of groups of people whom the researcher hypothesizes differ in sensation seeking. Alternatively, variables or scales which theoretically relate to sensation seeking are correlated with the scale. Validation studies attempt to improve the scale, its reliability, and correspondence with measures of conceptually related constructs. A strict focus on validation alone has limited promise because it can lead to a scattered approach, not necessarily guided by a well-developed theoretical account.

A second motivation is that identifying high and low sensation-seeking groups or finding a correlation between the scale and some behavior may have practical applications. For example, an established correlation between sensation seeking and cigarette smoking may assist individuals to quit smoking by redirecting their sensation seeking to other avenues. One such effort involved former drug users who successfully turned to skydiving to supplant drugs as their source of excitement (Zuckerman, 1978). Most such practical applications of the scale are narrowly focused.

The third motivation is theoretically-based hypothesis testing. This motivation may support the first motivation as well, providing a cohesiveness to the eclectic findings listed above. Zuckerman has presented the most concrete theory of this sort (Zuckerman, 1979a, 1983; Zuckerman, Simons, & Como, 1988) in postulating and testing a biological mechanism for sensation-seeking behavior, whereby individual differences in sensation seeking are in part attributable to brain chemistry differences. This is a potentially promising avenue of research into physical risk taking, with some supportive findings to date (Zuckerman, Simons, & Como, 1988).

A number of other scales have been tied to risk taking as a trait, though not always as directly as the SSS. Many of these have been correlated against the SSS. Typically, modest correlations have been obtained, but the scales differ in their underlying constructs. Researchers have proposed that the Torrance–Ziller scale of risk-taking tendencies (Himelstein & Thorne, 1985; Jobe, Holgate, & Scapansky, 1983), Eysenck's impulsivity, extraversion, and neuroticism scales (Eysenck, 1983; Zuckerman et al., 1983), and the Myers–Briggs scales (Campbell & Heller, 1987) each capture some aspect of risk taking. All of these are self-report questionnaire measures, as is the SSS V. Another scale of this type is the measure of Constraint from the Multidimensional Personality Questionnaire (MPQ); Low MPQ Constraint is described as associated with impulsiveness, sensation seeking, and the rejection of conventional confines on behavior. An elaborate twins study of the genetic basis of this and other traits estimated that 58% of the variance in this factor was genetically determined (Tellegen et al., 1988). The finding tends to buttress Zuckerman and colleagues' efforts at determining a biological basis for sensation seeking, supporting the promise of that avenue of research.

RISK IN GAMES AND LOTTERIES

Several major research streams have looked at choice behavior in experimental situations using games as tasks or lotteries as stimuli. Many researchers use lotteries as models of the decision situation under uncertainty—subjects choosing between alternatives with uncertain outcomes. Similarly, games are used as metaphors of strategic decision making, decisions involving chance and skill elements. Although some question the validity of these representations (cf. Wagenaar, 1988), they underlie a large body of risk-taking research. Even if they do not adequately represent decision making in naturalistic situations, they are choice situations in the sense of Figure 4.1 where individual differences in risk taking have been studied. Most of this section looks at risk-taking behavior in these experimental situations.

Alternatively, one can look at risk taking in situations for which games and lotteries *are* the reality of interest. Gambling behavior connects to a real-world class of such situations. We begin there.

Gambling

Devereux (1968) evaluated the research on gambling as follows:

> In these many different approaches that have touched on the subject, the interest in gambling has often been peripheral to some other, central interest, with the result that the coverage is piece-meal and fragmentary. While there are scattered bits of useful knowledge and theory, systematic treatises on gambling are sadly lacking. Moreover, many of the treatments that do exist are speculative, impressionistic, and moralistic, and many are also without adequate data. (p. 53)

Regarding individual differences in risk taking as observed in gambling, this statement needs little amendment. Gambling as pathology and the legal aspects of gambling have been extensively researched; however, risk taking has not been. Apparently, researchers assume that the experimental games and lotteries described below adequately model actual gambles. However, based on observations and studies of gamblers, Wagenaar (1988) has questioned the correspondence between gambling in naturalistic settings and subjects' behavior in laboratory games. Gamblers may be influenced by factors, for example, the perception of luck as a causal agent in games of chance (Wagenaar & Keren, 1988), that have not arisen in laboratory research.

Using a utility-based measure (described below), Goodman *et al.* (1979) found casino gamblers were risk neutral when offered laboratory-type lotteries. In contrast, Wagenaar (1988) and colleagues (Wagenaar, Keren, & Pleit-Kuiper, 1984) have observed individual differences in risk taking among gamblers in a naturalistic setting. Still, almost no research addresses how individual characteristics differentiate risk-takers within the naturalistic gambling context. We turn, then, to laboratory settings.

Experimental games of skill

In an oft-cited series of studies, Atkinson and colleagues related risk taking in games of skill and chance to motivational needs for achievement and failure. They characterized needs for achievement and failure as relatively stable dispositions of individuals, and associated risk primarily with low expectancy or probability of success. Atkinson (1957) argued that the motivation to perform an act combines one's motivations to approach and to avoid the situation. More specifically, the appeal of an alternative depends on the subject's dispositions toward achieving success and avoiding failure. (This approach/avoidance conflict is prominent in many decision situations, note Coombs & Avrunin, 1977.)

Most tests of the theory present subjects with games that involve differing levels of chance and skill and allow the subjects to choose among conditions that differ in level of difficulty. The theory predicts that subjects whose achievement motive is higher than their motive to avoid failure will prefer intermediate risks: They desire challenging tasks at which success is possible. Subjects with a higher failure-avoidance motive relative to the achievement motive tend to prefer either high- or low-risk tasks. They want either success or failure to be ensured, removing the onus of failure from themselves. Empirical results have been consistent with the theory in skill situations, and less consistent in chance tasks.

In these game-based situations, researchers use a personality perspective similar in methodology to that used in the sensation-seeking studies discussed earlier. The achievement and failure-avoiding motives are dispositional; the studies examine individual differences in them and the resultant behaviors. The studies measure achievement need using McClelland's n Ach scale which derives from subjects' responses to a projective test, e.g. the Thematic Apperception Test (TAT). The test requires subjects to respond to pictures with stories which are coded for themes indicative of achievement motives (Atkinson, 1964).

An early study had young children toss rings at a peg, allowing them to select the distance. McClelland (1958) observed that children high in achievement motive tended to take more tosses at intermediate distances than children low in achievement motive. Atkinson et al. (1960) replicated the basic result both with another skill task of a shuffleboard game in which subjects tried to hit a circular target and with a chance task of choosing among monetary gambles. The results fit the theory better in the skill than in the chance tasks, indicating the difference between the two situation types.

To illustrate the theory's use, consider Atkinson and Litwin's (1960) study employing a ring toss game. The subjects chose the distance from which they attempted to toss a ring onto a peg. Atkinson and Litwin used French's (1958) Test of Insight (a projective test similar to the TAT) to classify subjects as high or low in achievement motive, and they used the Mandler and Sarason (1952) Test Anxiety Questionnaire (a self-report instrument) to measure failure avoidance. Figure 4.3 presents their results. Subjects with high achievement and low failure-avoidance scores strongly favored tossing the ring from intermediate distances, indicating a preference for intermediate levels of risk taking. Subjects with low achievement and high failure-avoidance scores chose short or long distances more frequently than other subjects, indicating less preference for intermediate levels of risk taking. Hamilton (1974) generally replicated their findings (for reservations, see Hamilton, p. 860).

These studies are part of a broader research agenda in motivational determinants of behavior that has proven quite generative (Atkinson, 1983). As predicted

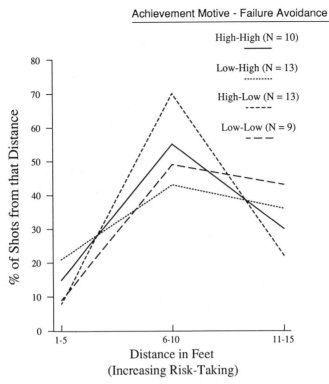

Figure 4.3.   The percentage of subjects who elected to shoot from each of three distances in a ring toss game for each of four groups of subjects (developed from Atkinson & Litwin, 1960, Table 1, p. 56, by permission of the American Psychological Association). Subjects were classified as High or Low in achievement motive and as High or Low in failure avoidance. For example, the Low-High group consisted of subjects Low in achievement motive and High in failure avoidance.

by the theory, these studies found that individual differences in risk taking relate to different dispositions to achievement and avoiding failure, particularly in skill settings. Like the physiological explanation of sensation seeking in settings involving physical risks, this research uses an explanatory theory for observed risk-taking differences, and empirical results exhibit support for the theory.

Skill versus chance

The distinction between chance and skill gaming situations has been supported in other studies but raises some empirical difficulties. Littig (1962) found different preferences in the two types of situation, as have others (see the cross-situational studies described below). However, the skill/chance distinction is not always clear-cut. Langer (1975) found an "illusion of control" whereby subjects behaved in chance situations as if skill were involved when the situation contained cues associated with skill tasks. Similarly, subjects have difficulty in detecting covariations between variables, or the lack thereof (cf. Alloy & Tabachnik, 1984; Beyth-Marom, 1982; Crocker, 1981). In a most illustrative study, Gilovich, Vallone, and Tversky (1985) obtained evidence that streak shooting in basketball (the tendency for hits and misses to cluster in runs) did not exceed what would be expected by chance despite widespread beliefs that such clustering occurs at a greater than chance rate. This suggests that subjects may not differentiate between tasks which experimenters distinguish as chance or skill tasks, consequently showing similar behaviors in the tasks. In particular, people find it very hard to accept the probabilistic, chance nature of events, and are reluctant to perceive situations as completely devoid of skill (Wagenaar, 1988). With this caveat, we consider a prototypical chance stimulus, a lottery.

Experimental lotteries

A different tradition in psychology, the experimental tradition, has predominated in studies of behavior using lottery stimuli. The most influential theory for this research has been expected utility (EU) theory and its variants, as discussed in Chapter 2, by Neumann and Politser. Partly due to its use in decision analysis, it has had a widespread influence both theoretically and in its practical applications, e.g. in medicine, public policy, and economics (cf. Beach, 1975; Krischer, 1980; Watson & Buede, 1987). We look at several approaches to risk taking in lotteries, with the intent of evaluating their promise for individual differences research.

Basis in utility theory

Expected utility (EU) theory and related models use the lottery as a metaphor for the decision situation; a choice among lotteries forms the prototypical decision behavior. The theory assumes that an individual consistently chooses the alternative with the highest expected utility, where utility represents an individual's preferences over outcomes (e.g. money). Thus, the utility function represents mathematically the individual's preferences over outcomes and simple lotteries, and EU theory captures choice as the maximization of the expected utility associated with different alternatives. For example, consider a lottery in which you have a 50% chance of winning $10; otherwise you win nothing. We summarize the lottery as ($10, 0.50; $0). The expected utility of the lottery would be 0.50 times the utility of $10 plus 0.50 times the utility of $0, the utility function being defined over dollar amounts.

The treatment of risk taking within this paradigm stands in sharp contrast to the personality approach. Personality researchers treat risk as a specific construct which individuals directly value and they argue that a specific personality trait associates with such valuation. In contrast, expected utility defines risk preference in terms of the curvature of the utility function, i.e. as implicit in the individual's overall valuation of certain (i.e. non-random) quantities of a particular good.

In utility theory, risk taking, typically labelled *risk seeking*, is defined as convexity of the utility function, often over monetary outcomes of a lottery (Keeney & Raiffa, 1976). To motivate this definition, consider the task of pricing the lottery ($10, 0.50; $0). (See also Chapter 1, p. 12) What is the smallest amount for which you would sell the chance to play this lottery? Suppose your *minimum selling price* is $6. You are expressing an equivalence between the lottery and the amount $6. The lottery's expected value is 0.50($10) + 0.50($0) = $5. You value the lottery at greater than its mathematical expected value, purportedly favoring the lottery's riskiness relative to the sure amount: an expression of risk seeking. The *risk premium* (RP), the difference between your your price and the lottery's expectation, indicates your risk seeking; in this example it equals $5 − $6 = −$1 (the negative sign indicates risk seeking as opposed to risk aversion).

In expected utility theory, your indifference between a lottery and a sure price implies their expected utilities are equal: Expected U(lottery) = $0.50 * U(\$10) + 0.50 * U(\$0) = U(\$6)$ where $U(x)$ stands for the utility of x. Anchoring the utility function by setting $U(\$10) = 1$ and $U(\$0) = 0$, we obtain U($6) = 0.50. As shown by the bold arc in Figure 4.4, a convex curve connects the three utility values, indicating risk seeking. If the subject offered even more for the lottery, the risk premium would be more negative and the resultant utility curve would be more convex, as illustrated by the lower arc in Figure 4.4. Conversely, if one priced the lottery at less than its expectation (less than $5), the risk premium would be positive and the resultant utility function would be concave (the upper arc in Figure 4.4).

Although the theory clearly accommodates differences in risk seeking across individuals, individual differences have largely been ignored in EU research for at least three reasons. First, in the economic application of EU, utility theory often operates as a postdictive theory, i.e. its truth is accepted and the model is used to identify behavioral coherency (Schoemaker, 1982). Risk seeking as a feature within the model is similarly neither descriptive nor predictive, and issues of risk seeking as a personality construct are moot. (This chapter's second author can still freshly recall the incredulity of one audience to his discussion of the psychological validity of utility-based measures of risk attitudes. Members of the audience argued that the curvature of the utility function defined risk attitude; to speak of its validity was at best irrelevant and at worst a sure sign of premature senility: a valid conclusion under a postdictive interpretation of risk seeking.)

Second, as Lopes (1987) argued, lottery studies derive from an experimental

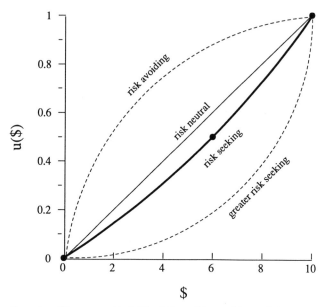

Figure 4.4. Sample utility curve (bold line) for subject with a minimum selling price of $6 for the lottery ($10, 0.50; $0). The thin solid line shows a utility curve for a risk-neutral subject who maximizes expected value, and the dashed curves describe risk-avoiding and risk-seeking subjects.

tradition and experimentalists focus on commonalities rather than differences. Experimentalists normally look at average responses, rather than individual differences, along the lines of the Decision Theory Approach to risk taking (Figure 4.2a).

Third, the study of individual differences may be hampered by confounding in the definition of risk seeking. Empirical estimates of utility curves, which EU theorists use to calculate risk measures, reflect at least two factors in their curvature: decreasing marginal value of the commodity in question (e.g. money: the first $5 is worth more than the second $5, and so forth), and the individual's attitude toward risk (since the curve is derived from an individual's choices among lotteries). Arguably, estimating the attitude toward risk is confounded by the simultaneous effect of marginal utility.

Empirical findings

Despite these reasons, some research relevant to individual differences in risk seeking has appeared. Some of the research is described later when discussing cross-situational studies. Another group of studies parallels those studies described above involving methods and motivations similar to those employed by personality theorists. For example, using a self-report questionnaire designed to measure an internal/external personality disposition, Liverant and Scodel (1960) found that externals took more long shots. Internal versus external refers to the extent to which an individual attributes rewards to personal behavior or to external forces and luck, as based on responses to a self-report internal-external (I-E) control scale. Similarly, Weinstein and Martin (1969) found small but statistically significant correlations ($r < 0.20$) between risk seeking with monetary bets and two self-report questionnaire scales of interpersonal risk: Machiavellianism and extraversion. We discuss potential overlap among measures of risk taking further in a later section.

In other results, Scodel, Ratoosh, and Minas (1959) demonstrated different patterns of betting preferences between Air Force enlisted men and college students, with the military subjects showing greater preference for high dollar/ low probability options. Dillon and Scandizzo (1978) posed hypothetical gambles to sharecroppers and small farmers in Brazil. They found owners more risk-averse than sharecroppers, much more so if subsistence was at risk. They concluded that income and perhaps other socioeconomic factors influence risk. These studies point to possible cultural and subcultural differences which are identifiable as aggregate trends. Such studies suggest the use of culture as a promising individual characteristic. However, as with similar studies relative to sensation seeking as a personality trait, such findings are more descriptive than explanatory.

Slovic (1972) reports findings that question simple explanations of individual differences in risk behaviors. Using gambles, he found only modest correlations between prices (How much would you sell this game for?) and strength of preference ratings (How strongly do you prefer this game to that?). The paper concluded: "In light of the efforts that were made in order to increase generality, the modest size of these correlations must be viewed more as support for the importance of situational factors than support for the notion of risk-taking propensity as a stable trait" (p. 133). Not only does the exact representation of the lottery (situation) matter, but little is known on exactly how it matters.

Despite these few exceptions, research using monetary lotteries has predominately ignored individual differences. Still, two general efforts have offered a promise of extending beyond the Decision Theory Approach to risk taking (Figure 4.2a) and the limitations of the EU theory's conceptualization of risk seeking. One effort works within utility theory, attempting to identify a better or more reliable measure of risk seeking than those typically used. The second works outside utility theory, adopting a different conceptualization of choice among lotteries.

Decompositions of risk seeking

As pointed out previously, assessed utility curves confound two possibilities: They can reflect a changing marginal value and an individual's attitude toward risk. The first effort is an attempt to decontaminate utility-based measures of risk seeking, by removing the first of these factors. This is accomplished with a *value function* derived from choices without uncertainty (Keeney & Raiffa, 1976), which presumably reflects only the marginal value component. The difference between the value function (elicited using only certain outcomes) and the utility function (elicited using uncertain options) is then interpreted as reflecting the individual's attitude toward risk in a purer fashion. Several researchers have explored this approach (Bell, 1983; Dyer & Sarin, 1982; Fishburn, 1980; Karmarkar, 1978; Krzysztofowicz, 1983).

Continuing our prior example will clarify how this is done. Figure 4.5 contains the utility curve for our exemplar subject with minimum selling price of $6 for the lottery ($10, 0.50; $0). This utility curve was obtained through an implicit comparison of a risky lottery with a non-risky amount. A similar *value* curve can be obtained using a riskless procedure. In one such technique, the subject specifies an amount of money (value equivalent, VE) such that the subject is equally willing to exchange $0 for VE as exchange VE for $10 (Dyer & Sarin, 1979). In Figure 4.5, we suppose VE = $4.50. Since this "exchange

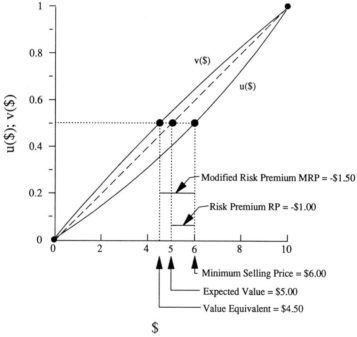

Figure 4.5. Sample utility (u) and value (v) curves for subject with minimum selling price of $6 for the lottery ($10, 0.50; $0) and value equivalent of $4.50 for the amounts $10 and $0. The dashed line describes the risk-neutral, expected value-maximizing subject. The risk premium and modified risk premium are indicated.

method" involves no risk, researchers hypothesize that any nonlinearity in this curve derives solely from the subject's marginal value for money (in this example, it is decreasing). The difference between an individual's value and utility functions provides a purer measure of attitude toward risk than the difference between mathematical expected value and utility. Numerically, the *modified risk premium* (MRP) equals the difference between the prices in the two value and utility procedures: MRP = $4.50 − $6 = − $1.50 (again, the negative sign indicates risk seeking as opposed to risk aversion).

This approach faces two major problems. First, the resulting measure, and other utility-based measures, have some undesirable properties which argue against their use as measures of a behavioral risk-taking trait. For example, the asymmetry of the MRP scale is illustrated by Figure 4.6, which shows the range of MRP values for various values of RP obtained for the lottery ($10, 0.50; $0). Note, for instance, that for RP = − $1, the MRP can range from [− $6, $4]. A value in the interval [− $6, $0) indicates risk seeking; a value in the interval ($0, $4] indicates risk aversion. The differing ranges demonstrate that the scale can be asymmetric and may reflect a nonlinear metric which presents substantial interpretation difficulties. Curley (1983) detailed this and other difficulties with utility-based risk-seeking measures.

Second, subjects really may not interpret the riskless and risky assessment situations differently. Even using different risky assessment procedures, different

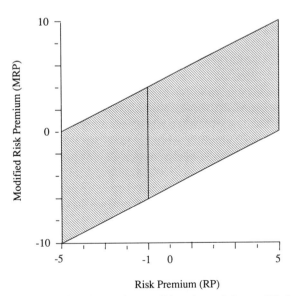

Figure 4.6. The shaded region shows the possible values of the modified risk premium as a function of the risk premium. The solid vertical line indicates possible modified risk premium values for the exemplar subject with risk premium = − $1.

utilities result. For example, instead of assessing minimum selling prices as described above, one could assess indifference probabilities: What is the probability p in the lottery ($10, p; $0) for which you are indifferent between playing the lottery and taking $5 for certain? Selling price and indifference probability procedures typically do not give the same utility curves even for the same subjects in the same time period (Schoemaker, 1982). This is problematic since the disagreement between value and utility functions is not reliably greater than the difference among utility functions obtained by different methods. The result questions the validity of risk-seeking measures like the modified risk premium (von Winterfeldt & Edwards, 1986).

Basis in choice theories using a risk construct

The second attempt to broaden risk-taking research with lotteries abandons utility theory, adopting instead a conceptualization which includes risk as an explicit parameter (see Lopes, 1984, 1987, 1988). A similar account can be derived using alternative risk characterizations, e.g. the conjoint expected risk model discussed in Chapter 3, pp. 72–73.

The stability of individual risk preferences found by Schneider and Lopes (1986) recommends the possibilities of this approach. Schneider and Lopes presented five decisions to 1382 undergraduates. In each decision, the subject chose between a chance at some positive amount or zero versus a sure gain of some smaller amount. The expected values of the two options were the same for each decision. Subjects were classified based on their responses. The risk-averse (RA) group included 30 subjects who always preferred the sure amount and the risk-seeking (RS) group included 30 subjects who preferred the gamble for at least four of five decisions. These 60 subjects then gave their preferences, in pairwise fashion, for nine multioutcome lottery options and a sure-thing option. The ten options varied in their skewness and variance, but all options had equal expected value. The ten options appeared in a gain condition as well as in a loss condition in which all amounts were preceded with a minus sign.

To demonstrate the main findings, Figure 4.7 illustrates three of the multioutcome lotteries. Each lottery involved drawing a ticket from 100 tickets; the figure shows the distribution of the tickets relative to their payoffs. Schneider and Lopes presented a motivational theory to account for subjects' choices among risky options. In the theory, risk-taking differences derived from weighings of two motivations: a desire for security (avoiding bad outcomes) and a desire for high return (approaching good outcomes). The desire-for-security motivation dominates RA subjects whereas the desire for high return most heavily influences RS subjects. The theory's motivational underpinnings relate to Atkinson and colleagues' theories relating risk taking to achievement motives, as discussed previously, and have the resulting benefit of potentially both describing and explaining individual differences.

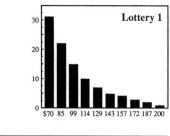

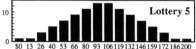

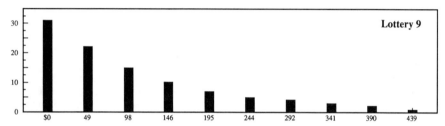

Figure 4.7. Three lotteries used by Schneider and Lopes. Each lottery involved drawing one ticket from 100 tickets. The distributions of prizes are plotted. Adapted from Figure 4, p. 539, Schneider and Lopes (1986). Copyright © 1986 by the American Psychological Association. Adapted by permission of the American Psychological Association and the authors.

Schneider and Lopes presented the ten options in pairs to subjects who chose one from each pair. They presented each pair three times, so that an option could be chosen up to 27 times (three repetitions × nine other lotteries to which an option is compared). Figure 4.8 presents the mean number of times that the three lotteries in Figure 4.7 were chosen, using one graph for the gain condition and one for the loss condition. As the figure indicates, the responses of RA and RS subjects were mirror images. Schneider and Lopes argued that for gains a desire for security leads to high weighting of the low end of the scale, so that Lottery 1 is preferable to Lottery 5 which is preferable to Lottery 9. That is, for gains subjects concern themselves strongly with the lowest returns produced by an option. The RA subjects (those with high security motivation) largely evidenced this pattern by preferring Lottery 1 to 5 to 9. A desire for return focuses attention on the upper ends of the scale where Lottery 9 is best and Lotteries 1 and 5 are similar. However, Lottery 1 appeals to both motives, offering equivalent high-level returns and higher security than Lottery 5. Thus, the U-shaped preference pattern observed for RS subjects arises. For losses,

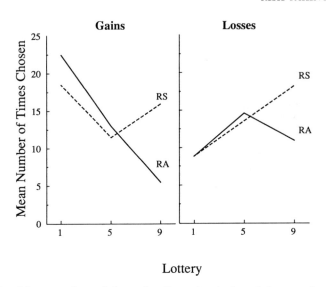

Lottery

Figure 4.8. Mean number of times that Lotteries 1, 5, and 9 were chosen by Risk-Seeking (RS) and Risk-Avoiding (RA) groups when outcomes were gains and when outcomes were losses. N = 30 for both subject groups. Adapted from Figures 5 and 6, p. 541, Schneider and Lopes (1986). Copyright © 1986 by the American Psychological Association. Adapted by permission of the American Psychological Association and the authors.

these same motivations explain the directly opposite preference patterns found (see Figure 4.8). The other lotteries in the design gave similarly consistent results.

Several positive aspects of the conceptualization and methodology warrant mention. First, using multiple lotteries with very different distributions of outcomes provides a more heterogeneous and richer set of stimuli than conventional designs. Second, identifying risk-avoiding and risk-seeking subjects in one stage of a study and then examining their responses to subsequent experiments increases intersubject differences within the subsample used for subsequent experiments and so improves the ability to discriminate the effects of individual differences. Finally, the motivational theory provides an underlying explanation for the behaviors observed. On the other hand, these models propose that individuals assess risk and then make choices. The adequacy of such two-stage decision models has yet to be established, although, as noted in Chapter 3 above by Yates and Stone, they seem reasonable in certain contexts. Overall, this approach to studying individual differences in risk taking appears promising and warrants extension. (For example, what does the model predict when both losses and gains are involved in the same lottery?)

RISK IN EVERYDAY LIFE EXPERIENCES

Kogan–Wallach Choice Dilemmas

Several experimental studies have used the Kogan–Wallach Choice Dilemmas Questionnaire (CDQ) to examine risk-taking behavior using paragraph descriptions of everyday life problems, each with an identified course of action. The subject indicates the minimum odds of success that are required before recommending that course of action. Table 4.1 presents one of the dilemmas from the CDQ. The CDQ has been employed chiefly by social psychologists, and many of the studies do not examine individual differences. Instead, researchers often average across individuals to isolate situational or social differences. In this respect, the approach parallels that used by experimental psychologists using lotteries as stimuli (pp. 100–108). An important research stream in this area has studied the effects of groups on risk-taking behavior. The original result was that group interaction influenced individuals to greater risk taking, the "risky shift" (Wallach, Kogan, & Bem, 1962). Subsequently, as discussed in some detail in Chapter 6 by Davis, Kameda, and Stasson, this phenomenon was relabelled as the *choice shift*, since it was determined that for

Table 4.1. Sample item from the Choice Dilemmas Questionnaire (Kogan & Wallach, 1964).

Mr A, an electrical engineer, who is married and has one child, has been working for a large electronics corporation since graduating from college five years ago. He is assured of a lifetime job with a modest, though adequate, salary, and liberal pension benefits on retirement. On the other hand, it is very unlikely that his salary will increase much before he retires. While attending a convention, Mr A is offered a job with a small, newly founded company which has a highly uncertain future. The new job would pay more to start and would offer the possibility of a share in the ownership if the company survived the competition of the larger firms.

Imagine that you are advising Mr A. Listed below are several probabilities or odds of the new company's proving financially sound.

Please check the lowest *probability that you would consider acceptable to make it worthwhile for Mr A to take the new job.*

——The chances are 1 in 10 that the company will prove financially sound.
——The chances are 3 in 10 that the company will prove financially sound.
——The chances are 5 in 10 that the company will prove financially sound.
——The chances are 7 in 10 that the company will prove financially sound.
——The chances are 9 in 10 that the company will prove financially sound.
——Place a check here if you think Mr A should *not* take the new job no matter what the probabilities.

Source. Reproduced from Kogan and Wallach (1964) by permission of Holt, Rinehart, and Winston and the authors.

some choice dilemma items, group interaction effected greater caution in individuals (a situational difference) (cf. Cartwright, 1971; Myers & Lamm, 1976; Pruitt, 1971). In terms of Figure 4.1, the risky shift and choice shift studies examined differences in situations (group versus individual) in average risk taking, a general form of the Decision Theory Approach (Figure 4.2a).

Aside from these studies with situational emphasis, the CDQ has been used to examine personality differences. Gender differences have obtained. For example, Higbee and Lafferty (1972) found that males took more risks in less important choices but no such differences obtained for females. Coet and McDermott's (1979) male groups took far more risks than female or mixed gender groups. Bonoma and Schlenker (1978) modified the CDQ to examine how subjects' behavior differed from utility maximization. They found no differences across gender, training, age, or race in one experiment and found males to be more conservative in another experiment. The mixed results on gender effects suggest that such effects may be situation specific or even spurious. Gender effects, in general, are further addressed in the general discussion below. Objections to the CDQ appear in the section on cross-situational studies; the investigations described there bear directly upon the CDQ and similar instruments.

Simulations

In addition to the CDQ, a number of psychologists have examined more complex simulations. Higbee and Streufert (1969) argued that more realistic risk experiences may provide substantively different results than the CDQ. In a military simulation with undergraduates, Higbee (1971) attempted to correlate CDQ measures of risk-taking tendencies with both subjects' expectations concerning their risk taking and their actual risk taking within the simulation. He found high CDQ scores associated with subjects' anticipating that they will take risks but not with actual risks taken.

In a similar simulation, Higbee and Streufert (1969) assessed whether perceived environmental control within the simulation increased or decreased risk taking. Their scale measured perception of perceived control over specific facets of the environment in contrast to the I-E scale's more generalized control beliefs. They found that teams that perceived they had control over their environment took fewer risks at first than teams that perceived that they did not control their environment. The differences diminished sharply over time. They observed that in many risky situations individuals retain some degree of control and concluded that if degree of control influences behavior as their results indicated, then gambling experiments using random devices may have extremely limited generality. This corroborates Wagenaar's (1988) claim of laboratory versus naturalistic setting differences based on observations of casino gamblers. Again, the results suggest the need for a better situational analysis.

RISK IN BUSINESS AND FINANCE

Investments

Numerous studies examine investment decision making, but the studies are difficult to coalesce since they vary considerably across situations and subject populations with no explanatory basis driving the variations. The studies mix professional investment advisors, serious amateur investors, the general population, and students as well as mixing hypothetical securities choices, actual holdings of investors, and other investment settings.

In addition, although studying the actual risk choices made by individuals in the conduct of their own lives appears most desirable, these choices are substantially confounded. For example, if one wants to test whether age influences riskiness of actual holdings, it is hard to factor out the influences of other age-related circumstances. Middle-aged, middle-class families tend to have a highly leveraged house purchase, whereas older people tend to have paid off some of the mortgage (reducing the leverage on the house) and are more likely to have assets to invest for retirement. Rather than a choice among competing financial instruments or investments, some of the data reflect differing consumption needs and other extraneous factors. Such confounding factors are important in understanding studies of risk taking in the investment context.

Hypothetical investments

Several demographic characteristics have been examined using hypothetical investments. Blum (1976) asked a mixed sample of 181 adults to invest a windfall equal to one year's salary in investments of differing specified risk. No gender or age effects were found, but teachers and civil servants chose less risky investments. Gooding (1975) asked investment professors, portfolio managers, and individual investors to assess the similarity of differing stocks. Using a multidimensional scaling technique, he found significant differences among professional fund managers, investment professors, and individual investors in the dimensions they used to evaluate stocks. Due to the technique, the details of the results are difficult to interpret, but it appeared that portfolio managers and professors used two dimensions (related to price-earnings ratios and downside risk) whereas individual investors used three dimensions (related to dividend yield, past returns from holding the stock, and past growth). Baker and Haslem (1974) surveyed investors on the "relative influence on common stock purchase decisions" of a number of factors. Based on a univariate analysis, younger investors valued price appreciation while dividend yield and marketability were more important to older investors. Females valued dividend yield and price stability more than males, and dividend yield was more important to investors who were separated, divorced, or widowed. Income influenced the importance of dividend yield, but occupation and portfolio size were not related to any of the variables. There is a caveat concerning this study, however, in that the investigators examined many outcome variables and many personal characteristics pairwise rather than within a more comprehensive multivariate analysis. A single factor might cause statistical associations between several variables and risk. Furthermore, examining so many correlations raises the likelihood of spurious associations. Together, the studies suggest that demographic characteristics (age, gender, and marital status) are weakly and occupation more strongly associated with differences in choices among hypothetical investments.

Actual investments

In a more naturalistic setting, Blume and Friend (1975) ascertained the degree of diversification of the asset holdings of a large sample of wealthy households. Diversification is an important and proper technique for reducing risk in financial investments, so much so that finance theorists often assume that all stockholders are fully diversified (i.e. their portfolios are sufficiently large and diversified that they have eliminated any idiosyncratic risks associated with any given stock and are only sensitive to risks that influence all stocks). Overall, Blume and Friend found very low levels of diversification. The only strong explanatory variable was wealth, which had a positive influence on diversification. Weaker results indicated that families with more dependents, a male household head, a self-employed household head, and nonretired persons had more diversified portfolios.

Watts and Tobin (1967) examined a survey of approximately 4000 households and attempted to explain holdings of various kinds of assets (furniture, kitchen appliances, installment debt, mortage debt, etc.). Although a number of explanatory variables attained statistical significance, they explained almost none of the variance in family holdings of these asset categories (generally, $R^2 < 0.05$). As in the Blume and Friend study, weak support was observed for a number of influences: higher education resulted in more assets and less debt; occupation, family size, region of country, and income all appeared to have some influence on holdings. Older householders differed from younger in having older durable goods and less debt, which was consistent with the confounding life cycle effect noted above.

Insurance purchases form a negative risk investment. Hammond, Houston, and Melander (1967) examined a cross-sectional survey of expenditures on life insurance premiums. Income, wealth, education, occupation (professional, managerial), and being married with children increased premiums. Overall, it appeared that increased income, net worth, education, family size, and employment as a manager or professional increased expenditures on insurance. Some of the results differed across income classes, for example, within low- and middle-income classes, Caucasians appeared to spend less on insurance.

Cohn *et al.* (1975) surveyed 588 brokerage firm customers. They categorized assets as risky or risk-free, and then attempted to explain the percentage of assets held in risky assets. They found higher income (or wealth which in their data were extremely highly correlated), age, and being single all increased the proportion of assets in risky assets.

The studies, therefore, substantiate the existence of differences in risk taking across demographic categories but these demographic variables explain little of the variance in these investment studies. The demographic variables' correlations with risk taking may be spurious or not useful. Of the four studies, Cohn *et al.*'s probably reflected most clearly "risk-taking propensity" rather than life cycle or total income effects. In their study, the median and mean participant had substantially greater dollar value of stock holdings than personal residence (median stock holdings of $43 000 compared to personal residence of $36 000, mean stock holdings without outliers of $76 436 and personal residence of $40 071). Excluding pension values, personal residences constituted only 37% of the median subject's total assets and the mean value of personal residences constituted 17% of the average total assets (with outliers removed). The subjects allocated relatively large amounts of funds to competing financial investments and so the results may be less driven by life cycle or consumption needs than investment choices *per se*. Thus, it seems reasonable to believe that within this group, which was more affluent and older than the general population as well as being predominantly male, increasing wealth, age, and being single were associated with making riskier investments.

Managers

A variety of methods have been used to study risk taking by managers; indeed most of the techniques outlined above have been applied to managers. The diversity of techniques reflects the diversity of training among those who have studied risk taking in this population.

Harnett and Cummings (1980) studied approximately 550 managers from Europe and the USA. They measured risk attitudes with Yes-No answers to items like: "Do you like to invest money in a promising invention?" They also measured conciliation/belligerence, internal/external control, and suspiciousness/trust using self-report instruments. In their sample, Scandinavian, Central European and Greek managers were risk-averse, Spanish managers less so, and American managers most risk-taking. The business function in which managers worked (e.g. marketing, production, etc.) weakly influenced risk attitudes. In a subsample of the data using Belgian managers, private employees seemed less risk-averse than public employees. Factor analyses of personality and risk measures indicated some, although small, intergroup differences in risk factor structures obtained among American and European managers taking the instrument in English and European managers taking the instrument in their native languages (Danish, Finnish, etc.), and between US military officers and private sector managers. Furthermore, risks involving personal danger and monetary risks appeared as separate factors, suggesting a distinction between these risk categories.

In another cross-cultural study, Tse *et al.* (1988) presented Canadian, Hong Kong, and mainland Chinese managers (PRC) with risky choices having equivalent expected values displayed as hypothetical business problems. They found very different responses across the three groups with a particularly large difference between the PRC managers and the other two groups. The PRC managers were more inclined to recall a bad product than to send out a warning of the defect to buyers, to force an adoption of an alternative chosen by the leader rather than develop consensus among subordinates, to repay a friend rather than destroy an enemy. Both the PRC and Hong Kong executives were more likely to continue unprofitable product lines rather than admit failure compared to the Canadians.

Laughhunn, Payne, and Crum (1980) presented each of 237 managers with hypothetical gambles that offered expected returns below the manager's aspiration level. The gambles were phrased in both business and personal investment terms. For nonruinous losses, 77% of the choices made by managers took on more risk than would have been prescribed by maximizing expected value; they were risk seeking in these below target return gambles. On the other hand, 23% of the managers were consistently risk-averse and 26% not consistently risk-seeking or risk-averse. When facing potential losses large enough to cause bankruptcy, the managers were less risk-seeking. For 77 of the managers (all either from Germany or the Netherlands), the measure of risk seeking was regressed against a variety of individual characteristics. Using nonruinous potential losses, being from the Netherlands rather than Germany tended to reduce risk seeking but being from an airline company and being junior tended to increase risk seeking. When potentially ruinous losses were included in estimating risk seeking, country and organizational level again were significant. A number of additional firm types appeared to have strong influences on risk seeking. Airlines were the most risk-seeking, with food chains next, then buildings and chemicals, then banks. These findings are consistent with the existence of cultural and occupational differences in investment risk taking.

Trying to isolate risk experience, Diskson (1982) presented a set of 15 risk managers (corporate employees with responsibility for insurance and related activities) and 14 other managers with hypothetical business decisions. Risk managers primarily concern themselves professionally with the difficulties presented by losses. The risk managers were more risk-averse than the others in loss situations and had lower variability in answers. Both groups were about the same in gain situations.

Miller, Kets de Vries, and Toulouse (1982) surveyed senior managers (primarily chief executive officers) from 33 businesses spanning a wide range of sizes and industries in the Montreal area. Risk taking was measured by two scales with end points as follows: (a) Is there a proclivity toward (i) low-risk projects or (ii) high-risk projects; and (b) (i) it is best to explore by timid behavior or (ii) bold wide-ranging acts are viewed as useful. Within this sample, risk taking was associated with internal rather than external control. Small firm CEOs appeared more inclined toward risk taking. The tenure of a CEO did not have a significant influence on risk taking.

Grey and Gordon (1978) defined managers as risk-taking if they responded that they wanted to "make decisions on own, have personal responsibility, have broad freedom to act" vs wanting "security, solid company, stable income." They found that "risk takers" were promoted faster, evaluated as more effective (higher profit and lower employee turnover) and were "seen as (having) high potential for future advancement." Risk takers said they wanted employees who were risk takers, saw corporate demands as less challenging, saw authority limits as less clear, and preferred individual incentive programs over group or nonincentive pay. The indication is that risk taking is favored in this managerial environment; however, the measure leaves open whether risk taking is confounded here with decisiveness or responsibility.

Several studies have examined a particular kind of managers, entrepreneurs. Despite the intuition that entrepreneurs are risk takers, research has not upheld this viewpoint (Brockhaus, 1980, 1982). Shapero (1975) summarized research concerning the correlates of entrepreneurship by describing the entrepreneur as tending to be: (a) a displaced person (those who have fallen on hard times, e.g. political refugees, persons who are fired or whose corporate advancement has been blocked), (b) with internal locus of control, (c) with examples of others similar to oneself who were successful entrepreneurs, and (d) with the resources. Aside from the consistent correlation with internal locus of control, no particular personality characteristics appear common to entrepreneurs; and successful managers in general tend to have an internal locus of control.

Overall, these studies of managers' behaviors indicate influences of cultural, organizational, occupational, and personal differences on risk taking. Further, the differing choices need to be understood within the context of both the nationality and the situation, rather than being ascribed simply to a more broadly-based risk-taking trait.

CROSS-SITUATIONAL STUDIES

In addition to work that focused primarily on behavior in a particular setting, some key research efforts looked explicitly across situations. This section describes several of these important efforts.

Slovic (1962)

Using a group of college fraternity seniors, Slovic examined the convergence among four types of risk-taking measures. The first type of measures indexed styles of responding to questionnaire tasks ("response set" measures) including: (a) a speed/accuracy set, which measures a tendency to respond rapidly on a timed test thus achieving speed at the expense of accuracy; (b) an inclusiveness set which measures a tendency to include many items as belonging in an ambiguous, stated category; and (c) a gambling set which measures a tendency to guess in a multiple-choice test which includes a penalty for wrong answers. The second type of measures consisted of a pair of self-report personality questionnaires: the Torrance–Ziller Inventory which encompasses a variety of risk settings (physical sensation, financial and life experiences) and the Job Preference Inventory (risk taking as a preference for jobs with independence, responsibility, and high variance outcomes). The third type of measures employed games and lotteries. Two of these described betting behavior in chance situations and one described risk taking in a skill task—the amount bet on vocabulary questions. The fourth type consisted of a rating measure. Fellow fraternity brothers rated one another on a Likert-type scale with endpoints labelled as, "Loves to take risks. A daredevil" and "Cautious. Does not like to take chances. Avoids risky situations."

Of 36 intercorrelations among individual measures used in the study, three statistically differed from zero at $p < 0.01$, and an additional six differed at $p < 0.05$ (see Table 4.2). However, three of the latter six had signs opposite to the predicted direction, and of the six significant correlations in the expected direction, none of these was between measures of the same type. Thus, little correspondence was indicated among the various measures of risk taking in different situations, or among different measures of risk taking within a particular type of situation (as grouped by Slovic). The study strongly supports the need for a situational analysis of risk taking.

Kogan and Wallach (1964)

Kogan and Wallach studied the effects of motivational determinants on a number of psychological measurements, including risk taking. In this regard, the study paralleled those of Atkinson and his colleagues (pp. 97–99). However, Kogan and Wallach incorporated a larger number of instruments within a single study and used a different underlying motivational model in which individual differences were moderated by other variables. Kogan and Wallach analyzed the responses by gender and within joint levels of two moderator variables: defensiveness (high/low) and test anxiety (high/low). Thus, for each measure, a $2 \times 2 \times 2$ correlation table was determined and presented; this design and the sample sizes are illustrated by Table 4.3. Defensiveness was measured using

Table 4.2. Intercorrelations among measures of risk taking of four general types.

	Response set measures			Personality questionnaires		Gaming tasks		
	1	2	3	4	5	6	7	8
Response set measures								
1. Speed/Accuracy								
2. Inclusiveness	−0.17							
3. Gambling	0.16	0.05						
Personality questionnaires								
4. Torrance–Ziller	0.05	0.27**	−0.04					
5. Job Preference[a]	0.07	−0.14	−0.19	−0.06				
Gaming tasks								
6. Chance 1	0.32**	0.03	−0.07	0.23*	0.07			
7. Chance 2	0.16	−0.03	−0.07	−0.03	−0.35*	−0.17		
8. Skill	−0.08	0.19*	−0.24*	0.05	0.09	0.04	−0.20	
Risk rating	0.05	0.00	−0.24*	0.34**	0.10	0.02	0.18*	−0.02

Note. N = 82; *p*-values are one-tailed, except with measure 7.
[a]N = 55.
*p < 0.05, **p < 0.01.
Source. Adapted from Slovic (1962), Table 1, p. 70. Reproduced by permission of the author.

Table 4.3. Moderator variable table illustrating the correlational analyses employed by Kogan and Wallach (1964).

Test anxiety	Defensiveness	
	Males	
	Low	High
Low	$r_{LL,m}$	$r_{LH,m}$
	N = 30	N = 35
High	$r_{HL,m}$	$r_{HH,m}$
	N = 27	N = 22
	Females	
Low	$r_{LL,f}$	$r_{LH,f}$
	N = 28	N = 22
High	$r_{HL,f}$	$r_{HH,f}$
	N = 24	N = 29

Source. Reproduced from Kogan and Wallach (1964) by permission of Holt, Rinehart and Winston and the authors.

Crowne and Marlowe's (1960) 33-item scale of need for social approval. Test anxiety was measured using Alpert and Haber's (1960) 19-item anxiety scale.

Within the context of these moderators, the authors investigated intercorrelations among a variety of instruments: response set measures (similar to those employed by Slovic, 1962, and described above), personality inventory measures (e.g. self-sufficiency and impulsiveness scales), intellectual aptitude tests (e.g. Scholastic Aptitude Test scores), the Choice Dilemmas Questionnaire, and betting measures for skill and chance tasks. The authors presented the intercorrelations in detailed fashion using the format in Table 4.3. For the overall set of subjects (stratified by gender, but not stratified by test anxiety and defensiveness), the correlations between the personality measures and various gaming-based indicators were uniformly low. Of 196 correlations (cf. Kogan & Wallach, 1964, pp. 160–161), only 17 attained statistical signficance at $p < 0.05$. However, the authors concluded that the moderator variable design was justified in that correlations among different measures varied with levels of the moderating variables. In particular, subjects high on both defensiveness and anxiety tended to show greater regularity of risk taking across situations. Females also showed greater consistency than males.

A limitation of the procedure was its exploratory nature. Numerous statistically significant results obtained, but no prior hypotheses guided the findings. The authors instead attempted to characterize the results *post hoc*. Perhaps a tighter theory could usefully apply the moderator analysis employed. Still, the results do corroborate sizeable situation specificity of risk taking and once again find some personality and gender differences.

Keyes (1985)

This readable, interesting work by Keyes is noteworthy for the distinctiveness of the approach compared to the other research cited in this chapter. In particular, Keyes employed a case approach (Figure 4.2f), a methodology which, in the study of human behavior, has been widely used in clinical psychology. He presents case analyses of several types of risk takers, including gamblers, a wire walker, a skydiver, entrepreneurs, and individuals choosing drastic life and career changes.

The case analyses supported many of the points made by other research methodologies. Risk taking did not appear to generalize across risk situations, supporting an individual-by-situation analysis. Interestingly, many of the individuals in the cases who were high risk takers often did not perceive themselves as such. For example Philippe Petit, a wire walker, was quoted as saying: "I have no room in my life for risk. You can't be both a risk taker and a wire walker. I take absolutely no risks" (p. 10). This may be due to an association of risk with loss. Keyes observed that "venturesome" individuals (his term for high risk taking) are more intent on winning than losing; they focus on controlling the situation. This agrees with Atkinson and colleagues' theorized connection between achievement motivation and risk taking and with the numerous studies on internal locus of control. To take risks with reasonable probability of massive losses would be consistent with an achievement motivation that greatly exceeds motivation to avoid failure. In addition, belief in personal control of outcomes (internal locus of control) agrees with taking large risks but not perceiving them as such. The analyses corroborated individual differences in perceived risk.

Also, Keyes noted the apparently physiological aspects particularly of sensation seeking. For example, he described the case of a man who was acquitted on four counts of drug smuggling by reason of temporary insanity in the form of an addiction for action. The man described his reaction to action as a soldier in Vietnam: "In the end, . . . I craved it—I was like a zombie when I went without it. You know, I felt really alive when I got back from a mission. I had risked my life and made it back. I needed the stimulation and became listless without it" (p. 131). This coincides with the direction of Zuckerman and colleagues' efforts in theorizing a physiological basis for sensation seeking.

MacCrimmon and Wehrung (1986, 1990)

MacCrimmon and Wehrung examined risk taking by 300 American and Canadian executives using a number of measures. A factor analysis of a portion of the measures yielded six factors which correspond almost identically to the forms in which risk was measured: (a) pricing gambles in a business investment context, (b) pricing gambles in a personal investment context, (c) measures derived from a ranking of gambles in a personal investment context, (d) "in-basket" problems (the subject assumes the role of an executive reacting to a situation similar to a CDQ item, but more detailed, involving possible financial loss or involving possible financial gain), (e) personal actual behaviors (personal debt, wealth held in risky assets, personal gambling), and (f) self-ratings (sensation-seeking scale, using a subset of the SSS items, and a personal rating of risk propensity). The initial risk measures were almost completely uncorrelated across measurement techniques and so yielded factors that were uncorrelated. A factor analysis of the socioeconomic characteristics of the respondents yielded four factors: (a) success (authority over hiring and firing people of given salaries, income, wealth, position in organization), (b) maturity (age, seniority in organization, number of dependents), (c) nationality and education (Canadian managers had substantially less education than American managers in the sample), and (d) size and industry of employing firm (most of the large firms were banks, so this distinguishes between large banks and other firms).

MacCrimmon and Wehrung transformed the subjects' factor scores into three levels of risk taking (low, medium, high), and attempted to distinguish between the levels using stepwise discriminant analysis. For three of the six risk factors, success had a significant positive influence on risk taking. For three of the risk factors, being from a large bank had a significant negative influence on risk taking. Maturity reduced risk taking for both personal actual behaviors and self-ratings, and being Canadian increased risk taking for personal gambles. Even though the multiple-risk measures were collected at the same time from the same managers, the risk measures were largely uncorrelated and none of the socioeconomic factors had statistically significant associations with more than half of the risk factors.

Still, the situational differences and the effect of age and culture upon risk taking corroborate other findings described in this chapter. Further, as Mac-Crimmon and Wehrung highlight, this situational specificity has important implications for use of the CDQ instrument. This and similar instruments (e.g. the Torrance–Ziller Inventory investigated by Slovic, 1962) request responses to a variety of different risky situations. In addition to life situations (such as whether to take a new job or get married), the CDQ also contains items that may involve sensation seeking (whether to attempt a risky escape from a POW camp), financial risk (a choice between personal stock investments, and a president selecting between business ventures), and gaming risk (a choice between moves in a game of chess) (Kogan & Wallach, 1964). The definition of a risk-taking measure across such diverse situations is questionable given the clear situation specificity of risk taking as demonstrated by MacCrimmon and Wehrung.

DISCUSSION

Beyond the specific indications already presented, some general issues are noteworthy. Underlying a great deal of research on risk taking is a desire to develop better tools for managing risk or to validate particular models of risk taking for use as building blocks in other models. For example, behavioral decision theorists and others have discussed the problems generated by average characteristics such as risk avoiding in the realm of possible gains vs risk seeking in the loss domain (e.g. McNeil *et al.*, 1982; Thaler, 1980; Tversky & Kahneman, 1981). Finance theorists have used similar findings as the basis for models that explain levels of corporate dividends and the use of options (Shefrin & Statman, 1985, 1988). Strategic management researchers have used such explanations to explain patterns for corporate performance and variation in performance (Bowman, 1982; Fiegenbaum, 1990; Fiegenbaum & Thomas, 1986, 1988; Miller & Bromiley, 1990). Substantial portions of economics rest on expected utility theory.

These general applications assume two very different generalization patterns. Many assume that individual differences are of little interest, and many assume that situations do not differ substantially. Both assumptions are suspect. If risk-taking behavior varies across individual characteristics and situations, these enterprises are compromised. For example, if risk seeking on below average returns does not hold in the population of interest, even though it is generally found with experimental subjects, then efforts to alleviate risk seeking may in fact worsen outcomes. The evidence strongly supports a conclusion that risk taking varies across populations and situations, but as yet does not give us strong guides as to how it varies.

In addition, studies of individual characteristics usually measure only a small number of characteristics. If, as MacCrimmon and Wehrung demonstrated, many individual characteristics associate strongly with other individual characteristics, then serious research efforts should be directed toward testing multiple characteristics at once, with some theoretical and empirical attempt to delineate the causal or empirical structure of the relations. If individual characteristics correlate even moderately, naïve research that examines small sets of characteristics may find statistically significant relations but have a very low probability of discriminating underlying causal variables.

For example, this problem arises in studies of relations between risk taking and demographic variables, particularly gender and age. Most typically, though not universally, studies find males take greater risks and risk taking decreases with age. Such results are primarily descriptive; at best, they provide only a very low level of explanation for the individual differences observed.

Consider the case of gender effects. That men and women differ in their risk taking provides little understanding of the difference between them. Continued persistence in the search for gender effects may be attributable to the variable's dichotomous character which lends itself to a contrast orientation on the part of researchers, despite the typically small effects generally associated with gender (Belle, 1985). That is, it is an easy variable to obtain and correlate with any measure of interest, regardless of any underlying theory supporting its consideration. In fact, gender differences may be spurious, that is they can be attributed to situational variables which are gender-linked (Deaux, 1984; Wallsten & O'Leary, 1981). Consequently, researchers justifiably question the value of using gender as an experimental subject variable (Deaux, 1984; Gaeddert, 1987). For example, Wallach and Kogan (1959), using the Choice Dilemmas Questionnaire (CDQ), observed that male subjects were more risk taking on items involving death, income, and a football game, whereas females were more risk taking on items involving career and marriage choices. Understanding what underlies gender differences such as these may provide explanatory power and further our understanding of characteristics associated with differences in risk taking.

A similar lesson can be learned from age effects. As Fischhoff notes in Chapter 5 in his discussion of a developmental perspective on risk taking, risk taking itself can be a misleading term. To the extent that age correlates with other behavioral variables that influence risk taking, a focus on age differences can obfuscate more fundamental explanations. For example, older individuals on average simply may value monetary and nonmonetary outcomes differently than younger individuals. Fischhoff offers a number of possibilities along these lines.

The findings suggest a pronounced situational specificity. Clearly, we need theoretically and empirically based situational analyses to understand the features which differentiate situations (Sherman & Fazio, 1983). The rough taxonomy used in this chapter—physical sensation, games and lotteries, life experiences, financial—represents only a shadow of what is needed.

The problem promises to be difficult because individuals handle tasks that are extremely similar in very different ways. In lotteries, pricing (how much would you sell this for?) and choice (how much do you prefer this one to that?) responses to the same gambles often have little correlation. And, for personality inventories, what interconsistency occurs is at least partly due to the use of equivalent questionnaire items (Zuckerman, 1979b). Table 4.4 demonstrates this observation for three scales that we have discussed in this chapter: scales of sensation seeking (Zuckerman, 1979a), sociability, and impulsivity (Eysenck, 1983). Given items with very similar wordings, it would be surprising indeed to find no intercorrelation among them, even if they were designed to measure independent constructs.

Table 4.4 Some sample items from the Sensation Seeking, Sociability, and Impulsivity Scales

(SS)	1.	A.	I like "wild" uninhibited parties.
		B.	I prefer quiet parties with a good conversation.
(S)	75.		Do you find it hard to really enjoy yourself at a lively party?
(SS)	5.	A.	I get bored seeing the same old faces.
		B.	I like the comfortable familiarity of every day friends.
(S)	30.		Do you prefer to have a few but special friends?
(SS)	18.	A.	I would like to take off on a trip with no pre-planned or definite routes, or timetable.
		B.	When I go on a trip I like to plan my route and timetable fairly carefully.
(I)	8.		Do you stop and think things over before doing anything?
(I)	20.		Do you often do things on the spur of the moment?
(SS)	25.	A.	I am not interested in experience for its own sake.
		B.	I like to have new and exciting experiences and sensations even if they are a little frightening, unconventional or illegal.
(I)	1.		Do you often long for excitement?
(SS)	27.	A.	I enjoy spending time in the familiar surroundings of home.
		B.	I get very restless if I have to stay around home for any length of time.
(S)	27.		Do you like going out a lot?

Note. Sources of items are: scale of sensation seeking (SS) (Zuckerman, 1979a, pp. 397–400), and scales of sociability (S) and impulsivity (I) (Eysenck, 1983, p. 9.). The SS scale requires subjects to select A or B. The S and I scales require a Yes or No response.

More troublesome, however, is a disconnectedness of the various efforts, partly due to the different disciplinary backgrounds of researchers studying risk-taking propensity. Theory-driven research may help to connect the pieces, providing the explanation that is currently sparse. Several promising research streams have been identified in this chapter which address this multisituation, multicharacteristic problem. Atkinson and colleagues' theory of need achievement as underlying risk taking in skill situations, Lopes and her colleagues' related motivational theory of risk taking, and Zuckerman and his colleagues' physiological theory of sensation seeking exemplify the potential of theory in guiding an analysis of risk-taking differences.

Researchers may also want to reduce the dimensionality of risk situations and of personality measures relevant to risk. Given a subject population, and drawing on previous exploratory research on dimensions of risky situations, empirical inquiry might identify either categories or dimensions of risk situations (see Baird & Thomas, 1985; Baird, 1986). For example, dangerous sports may comprise a category of situations within which risk taking generalizes; similar categories might also be explored. Likewise, a statistical effort to identify the dimensionality of the plethora of personality measures related to risk might reduce redundancy in that area. Basically, these efforts involve making the structure implied by Figure 4.1b more concrete, filling in the situations and characteristics that have meaning for the representation of risk taking.

This situational analysis would, in turn, benefit from a better understanding of what people mean by risk in various situations, an issue explored in Chapter 1 by Yates and Stone. Differences in what people perceive as risky is not the same as differences in their reactions to perceived risk. This distinction has not been adequately sorted out. At a descriptive level, the same individual differences arise. However, at the level of explanation, identifying differing perceptions of risk may offer a promising perspective toward understanding individual differences in risk taking. Clearly, individual differences in risk perception exist (see Chapter 3, by Yates and Stone). How much of the observed variance in risk taking might be explained by analyzing these perceptual differences is an open question.

Perhaps differing perceptions of the roles of chance and skill in risky situations affect perceived risk, in turn affecting behavior. March and Shapira (1987) found that managers think of risky situations in ways that differ substantially from decision theorists. Managers distinguish between risk taking and gambling; they say that they should take risks but should not gamble. Schoemaker (1989) observed that so-called risk takers may not perceive themselves as such, instead focusing on the control, or skill, aspects of the risky situation. Designers also largely engage in risk management, rather than risk taking (see Chapter 10, by Pitz), opting for skill over chance. Keyes (1985), on the basis of case study data, suggested that some differences in risk taking appear driven by differences in risk perception. In the extreme, the chance element may be completely ignored. For example, Wagenaar, in Chapter 9, has observed that people involved in accidents perceived to be due to excessive risk taking, in fact, sometimes never considered that risk was present.

Finally, having a population of manageable dimensions of both situations and individual characteristics, an explicitly exploratory approach might help to identify ties between individual characteristics and risk-taking situations. Whether exploratory or theoretically driven research is more productive at this juncture depends on the quality of the theory available. We do not perceive strong theories that address the critical situational and individual factors. Exploratory research might resemble the multisituation, multicharacteristic work of MacCrimmon and Wehrung (1986, 1990). Such an approach would allow early rejection of potential individual characteristics and also provide a sensible backdrop for the development of theory.

SUMMARY

Despite the observation that individuals clearly differ in risk taking, differentiation of individuals' risk-taking propensities has not been a straightforward matter. Perhaps as a consequence, a number of different approaches have been adopted to study individual differences. Trait theory currently recognizes the joint influence of situation and personality characteristics in generally determining behavior, and, presumably, in specifically determining risk taking. The key is to identify cohesive sets of instances which form situational categories and parsimonious sets of characteristics that identify individual differences. The study of risk taking greatly lacks situational analysis. This is supported throughout the available research, particularly in the cross-situational studies of risk taking.

To organize the material for presentation, we separated situations into four categories and discussed research in each: activities that involve physical sensation, games and lotteries, everyday life choices, and business settings. The categories served to organize the chapter, but we did not presume that they constitute good categories for theory development. The chapter looked at the methodologies employed and the results achieved toward the study of individual differences in risk taking.

Various research methodologies have been employed in the study of risk taking. The traditional personality approach to the study of risk taking is exemplified by the use of the Sensation Seeking Scale, mainly involving scale construction through factor analysis and correlational scale validation. A more experimental personality approach is also observed, for example, in the study of risk taking in games. In contrast, the related study of risk taking in lotteries has been dominated by an experimental approach wherein attention to individual differences has been minimized. Case studies have also been used to analyze risk taking in a variety of settings.

In terms of results, numerous demographic and behavioral correlates of risk taking in different situations have been obtained. For example, measures of risk taking often correlate with age, gender, occupational, and cultural differences, as well as other personality trait scales. These results describe individual differences in risk taking but few studies present explanatory theories for individual differences. Consequently, such efforts, when they arise, are noteworthy. For example, the theories of Zuckerman and colleagues, Atkinson and colleagues, and Lopes and colleagues were highlighted in the chapter as attempts to go beyond description and to address the underlying nature of individual differences.

Also particularly noted were several studies employing cross-situational analyses. Given the importance of situational features for the study of individual differences, these efforts make major contributions. Greater attention to and analysis of situational factors would provide a valuable addition to our understanding of the role of individual differences in risk-taking behavior.

REFERENCES

Ajzen, I. (1982). On behaving in accordance with one's attitude. In M. P. Zanna, E. T. Higgins, & C. P. Herman (Eds.), *Consistency in social behavior: The Ontario symposium* (Vol. 2; pp. 3-15). Hillsdale, NJ: Erlbaum.

Ajzen, I., & Fishbein, M. (1977). Attitude-behavior relations: A theoretical analysis and review of empirical research. *Psychological Bulletin*, **84**, 888-918.

Alloy, L. B., & Tabachnik, N. (1984). Assessment of covariation by humans and animals: The joint influence of prior expectations and current situational information. *Psychological Review* **91**, 112-149.

Allport, G. W. (1937). *Personality: A psychological interpretation.* New York: Holt.

Alpert, R., & Haber, R. N. (1960). Anxiety in academic achievement situations. *Journal of Abnormal and Social Psychology*, **61**, 207-215.

Anastasi, A. (1983). Evolving trait concepts. *American Psychologist*, **38**, 175-184.

Atkinson, J. W. (1957). Motivational determinants of risk-taking behavior. *Psychological Review*, **64**, 359-372.

Atkinson, J. W. (1964). *An introduction to motivation.* Princeton, NJ: Van Nostrand.

Atkinson, J. W. (1983). *Personality, motivation and action.* New York: Praeger.

Atkinson, J. W., Bastian, J. R., Earl, R. W., & Litwin, G. H. (1960). The achievement motive, goal setting, and probability preferences. *Journal of Abnormal and Social Psychology*, **60**, 27-36.

Atkinson, J. W., & Litwin, G. H. (1960). Achievement motive and test anxiety conceived as motive to approach success and motive to avoid failure. *Journal of Abnormal and Social Psychology*, **60**, 52-63.

Baird, I. S. (1986). *Defining and predicting corporate strategic risk: An application in the telecommunications industry.* Unpublished doctoral dissertation, University of Illinois, Champaign-Urbana, IL.

Baird, I. S., & Thomas, H. (1985). Toward a contingency model of strategic risk-taking. *Academy of Management Review*, **10**, 230-244.

Baker, H. K., & Haslem, J. A. (1974). The impact of investor socioeonomic characteristics on risk and return preferences. *Journal of Business Research*, **2**, 469-476.

Beach, B. H. (1975). Expert judgement about uncertainty: Bayesian decision making in realistic settings. *Organizational Behavior and Human Performance*, **14**, 10-59.

Bell, D. E. (1983). Risk premiums for decision regret. *Management Science*, **29**, 1156-1166.

Belle, D. (1985). Ironies in the contemporary study of gender. *Journal of Personality*, **53**, 400-405.

Beyth-Marom, R. (1982). Perception of correlation reexamined. *Memory and Cognition*, **10**, 511-519.

Birnbaum, M., & Montag, I. (1987). On the replicability of the factorial structure of the sensation seeking scale. *Personality and Individual Differences*, **8**, 403–408.

Blum, S. H. (1976). Investment preferences and the desire for security: A comparison of men and women. *Journal of Psychology*, **99**, 87–91.

Blume, M. E., & Friend, I. (1975). The asset structure of individual portfolios and some implications for utility functions. *Journal of Finance*, **30**, 585–603.

Bonoma, T. V., & Schlenker, B. R. (1978). The SEU calculus: Effects of response mode, sex and sex role on uncertain decisions. *Decision Sciences*, **9**, 206–227.

Bouter, L. M., Knipschild, P. C., Feij, J. A., & Volovics, A. (1988). Sensation seeking and injury risk in downhill skiing. *Personality and Individual Differences*, **9**, 667–673.

Bowman, E. H. (1982). Risk seeking by troubled firms. *Sloan Management Review*, **23**(4), 17–31.

Briggs, S. R., & Cheek, J. M. (1986). The role of factor analysis in the development and evaluation of personality scales. *Journal of Personality*, **54**, 106–148.

Brockhaus, R. H., Sr (1980). Risk taking propensity of entrepreneurs. *Academy of Management Journal*, **23**, 509–520.

Brockhaus, R. H., Sr. (1982). The psychology of the entrepreneur. In C. A. Kent, D. L. Sexton, & K. H. Vesper (Eds.), *Encyclopedia of entrepreneurship* (pp. 39–57). Englewood Cliffs, NJ.: Prentice Hall.

Buss, A. H. (1989). Personality as traits. *American Psychologist*, **44**, 1378–1388.

Buss, D. M., & Craik, K. H., (1980). The frequency concept of disposition: Dominance and prototypically dominant acts. *Journal of Personality*, **48**, 379–392.

Buss, D. M., & Craik, K. H. (1981). The act-frequency analysis of interpersonal dispositions: Aloofness, gregariousness, dominance, and submissiveness. *Journal of Personality*, **48**, 175–192.

Campbell, J. B., & Heller, J. F. (1987). Correlations of extraversion, impulsivity and sociability with sensation seeking and MBTI-introversion. *Personality and Individual Differences*, **8**, 133–136.

Cartwright, D. (1971). Risk taking by individuals and groups: An assessment of research employing choice dilemmas. *Journal of Personality and Social Psychology*, **20**, 361–378.

Cattell, R. B. (1950). *Personality: A systematic, theoretical and factual study.* New York: McGraw-Hill.

Cattell, R. B. (1972). The nature and genesis of mood states: A theoretical model with experimental measurements concerning anxiety, depression, arousal and other mood states. In C. D. Spielberger (Ed.), *Anxiety: Current trends in theory and research* (Vol. 1; pp. 115–183). New York: Academic Press.

Coet, L. J., & McDermott, P. J. (1979). Sex, instructional set, and group make-up: Organismic and situational factors influencing risk-taking. *Psychological Reports*, **44**, 1283–1294.

Cohn, R. A., Lewellen, W. G., Lease, R. C., & Schlarbaum, G. G. (1975). Individual investor risk aversion and investment portfolio composition. *Journal of Finance*, **30**, 605–620.

Coombs, C. H., & Avrunin, G. S. (1977). Single-peaked functions and the theory of preference. *Psychological Review*, **84**, 216–230.

Crocker, J. (1981). Judgment of covariation by social perceivers. *Psychological Bulletin*, **90**, 272–292.

Crowne, D. P., & Marlowe, D. (1960). A new scale of social desirability independent of psychopathology. *Journal of Consulting Psychology*, **24**, 349–354.

Curley, S. P. (1983). *The structural validity of measures of risk aversion.* Unpublished manuscript, University of Michigan, Ann Arbor, MI.

Deaux, K. (1984). From individual differences to social categories: Analysis of a decade's research on gender. *American Psychologist*, **39**, 105–116.

Devereux, E. C., Jr. (1968). Gambling. *International Encylopedia of the Social Sciences*, **6**, 53-62.

Dillon, J. L., & Scandizzo, P. L. (1978). Risk attitudes of subsistence farmers in northeast Brazil: A sampling approach. *American Journal of Agricultural Economics*, **60**, 425-435.

Diskson, G. C. A. (1982). A comparison of attitudes towards risk among business managers. *Geneva Papers on Risk and Insurance*, **7**, 89-97.

Dyer, J. S., & Sarin, R. K. (1979). Measurable multiattribute value functions. *Operations Research*, **27**, 810-822.

Dyer, J. S., & Sarin, R. K. (1982). Relative risk aversion. *Management Science*, **28**, 875-886.

Epstein, S. (1979). The stability of behavior: I. On predicting most of the people much of the time. *Journal of Personality and Social Psychology*, **37**, 1097-1126.

Epstein, S. (1980). The stability of behavior: II. Implications for psychological research. *American Psychologist*, **35**, 790-806.

Epstein, S. (1982). The stability of behavior across time and situations. In A. I. Rabin, J. Aranoff, A. M. Barclay, & R. Zucker (Eds.), *Further explorations in personality* (Vol. 2; pp. 209-268). New York: Wiley.

Eysenck, H. J. (1983). A biometrical-genetical analysis of impulsive and sensation seeking behavior. In M. Zuckerman (Ed.), *Biological bases of sensation seeking, impulsivity, and anxiety* (pp. 1-36). Hillsdale, NJ: Erlbaum.

Fiegenbaum, A. (1990). Prospect theory and the risk-return association: An empirical examination in 85 industries. *Journal of Economic Behavior and Organization*. **14**(2) 187-204.

Fiegenbaum, A., & Thomas, H. (1986). Dynamic and risk measurement perspectives on Bowman's risk-return paradox for strategic management: An empirical study. *Strategic Management Journal*, **7**(5), 395-408.

Fiegenbaum, A., & Thomas, H. (1988). Attitudes toward risk and the risk-return paradox: Prospect theory explanations. *Academy of Management Journal*, **31**(1), 85-106.

Fishbein, M., & Ajzen, I. (1974). Attitudes toward objects as predictors of single and multiple behavioral criteria. *Psychological Review*, **81**, 59-74.

Fishburn, P. C. (1980). A simple model for the utility for gambling. *Psychometrika*, **45**, 435-448.

Fiske, D. W. (1988). From inferred personalities toward personality in action. *Journal of Personality*, **56**, 815-833.

Franken, R. E. (1988). Sensation seeking, decision making styles, and preference for individual responsibility. *Personality and Individual Differences*, **9**, 139-146.

Franken, R. E., Gibson, K., & Rowland, G. L. (1989). Sensation seeking and feelings about the forced-choice format. *Personality and Individual Differences*, **10**, 337-339.

French, E. G. (1958). Development of a measure of complex motivation. In J. W. Atkinson (Ed.), *Motives in fantasy, action, and society* (pp. 242-248). Princeton, NJ: Van Nostrand.

Gaeddert, W. P. (1987). The relationship of gender, gender-related traits, and achievement orientation to achievement attributions: A study of subject-selected accomplishments. *Journal of Personality*, **55**, 687-710.

Gilovich, T., Vallone, R., & Tversky, A. (1985). The hot hand in basketball: On the misperception of random sequences. *Cognitive Psychology*, **17**, 295-314.

Gooding, A. E. (1975). Quantification of investors' perceptions of common stocks: Risk and return dimensions. *Journal of Finance*, **30**, 1301-1316.

Goodman, B., Saltzman, M., Edwards, W., & Krantz, D. H. (1979). Prediction of bids for two-outcome gambles in a casino setting. *Organizational Behavior and Human*

Performance, **24**, 382–399.

Grey, R. J., & Gordon, G. G. (1978). Risk-taking managers: Who gets the top jobs? *Management Review*, **67**, 8–13.

Hamilton, J. O. (1974). Motivation and risk taking behavior. *Journal of Personality and Social Psychology*, **29**, 856–864.

Hammond, J. D., Houston, D. B., & Melander, E. R. (1967). Determinants of houshold life insurance premium expenditures: An emprical investigation. *Journal of Risk and Insurance*, **34**, 397–408.

Harnett, D. L., & Cummings, L. L. (1980). *Bargaining behavior: An international study.* Houston: Dame Publications.

Higbee, K. L. (1971). Expression of "Walter Mitty-ness" in actual behavior. *Journal of Personality and Social Psychology*, **20**, 416–422.

Higbee, K. L., & Lafferty, T. (1972). Relationships among preferences, importance, and control. *Journal of Psychology*, **81**, 249–251.

Higbee, K. L., & Streufert, S. (1969). Perceived control and riskiness. *Psychonomic Science*, **17**, 105–106.

Himelstein, P., & Thorne, S. B. (1985). Relationship between the sensation seeking scale and a biographical inventory designed to predict risk-taking behavior. *Personality and Individual Differences*, **6**, 121–122.

Jaccard, J. J. (1974). Predicting social behavior from personality traits. *Journal of Research in Personality*, **7**, 358–367.

Jobe, J. B., Holgate, S. H., & Scrapansky, T. A. (1983). Risk taking as motivation for volunteering for a hazardous experiment. *Journal of Personality*, **51**, 95–107.

Karmarkar, U. S. (1978). Subjectively weighted utility: A descriptive extension of the expected utility model. *Organizational Behavior and Human Performance*, **21**, 61–72.

Keeney, R. L., & Raiffa, H. (1976). *Decisions with multiple objectives: Preferences and value tradeoffs.* New York: Wiley.

Kenrick, D. T., & Funder, D. C. (1988). Profiting from controversy: Lessons from the person-situation debate. *American Psychologist*, **43**, 23–34.

Keyes, R. (1985). *Chancing it: Why we take risks.* Boston, MA: Little, Brown and Company.

Kogan, N., & Wallach, M. A. (1964). *Risk taking: A study in cognition and personality.* New York: Holt, Rinehart and Winston.

Krischer, J. P. (1980). An annotated bibliography of decision analytic applications to health care. *Operations Research*, **28**, 97–113.

Krzysztofowicz, R. (1983). Strength of preference and risk attitude in utility measurement. *Organizational Behavior and Human Performance*, **31**, 88–113.

Langer, E. J. (1975). The illusion of control. *Journal of Personality and Social Psychology*, **32**, 311–328.

Laughhunn, D. J., Payne, J. W., & Crum, R. (1980). Managerial risk preferences for below-target returns. *Management Science*, **26**, 1238–1249.

Littig, L. W. (1962). Effects of skill and chance orientations on probability preferences. *Psychological Reports* **10**, 67–70.

Liverant, S., & Scodel, A. (1960). Internal and external control as determinants of decision making under conditions of risk. *Psychological Reports*, **7**, 59–67.

Lopes, L. L. (1984). Risk and distributional inequality. *Journal of Experimental Psychology: Human Perception and Performance*, **10**, 465–485.

Lopes, L. L. (1987). Between hope and fear: The psychology of risk. *Advances in Experimental Social Psychology*, **20**, 255–295.

Lopes, L. L. (1988). Economics as psychology: A cognitive assay of the French and American schools of risk theory, In B. R. Munier (Ed.), *Risk, decision, and rationality* (pp. 405–416). Dordrecht, Holland: Reidel.

MacCrimmon, K. R., & Wehrung, D. A. (1986). *Taking risks: The management of uncertainty*, New York: The Free Press.

MacCrimmon, K. R., & Wehrung, D. A. (1990). Characteristics of risk taking executives. *Management Science*, **36**, 422-435.

Mandler, G., & Sarason, S. B. (1952). A study of anxiety and learning. *Journal of Abnormal and Social Psychology*, **47**, 166-173.

March, J. G., & Shapira, Z. (1987). Managerial perspectives on risk and risk taking. *Management Science*, **33**, 1404-1418.

McClelland, D. C. (1958). Risk taking in children with high and low need for achievement. In J. W. Atkinson (Ed.), *Motives in fantasy, action, and society* (pp. 306-321). Princeton, NJ: Van Nostrand.

McNeil, B. J., Pauker, S. G., Sox, H. C., Jr, & Tversky, A. (1982). On the elicitation of preferences for alternative therapies. *New England Journal of Medicine*, **306**, 1259-1262.

Miller, D., Kets de Vries, M. F. R., & Toulouse, J. (1982) Top executive locus of control and its relationship to strategy-making, structure, and environment. *Academy of Management Journal*, **25**, 237-253.

Miller, K. D., & Bromiley, P. (1990). Strategic risk and corporate performance: An analysis of alternative risk measures. *Academy of Management Journal*, **33**, 756-779.

Mischel, W. (1968). *Personality and assessment*. New York: Wiley.

Mischel, W. (1977). The interaction of person and situation. In D. Magnusson, & N. S. Endler (Eds.), *Personality at the crossroads: Current issues in interactional psychology* (pp. 333-352). Hillsdale, NJ: Erlbaum.

Myers, D. G., & Lamm, H. (1976). The group polarization phenomenon. *Psychological Bulletin*, **83**, 602-627.

Pruitt, D. G. (1971). Conclusions: Toward an understanding of choice shifts in group discussion. *Journal of Personality and Social Psychology*, **20**, 495-510.

Rogers, T. B. (1987). Evidence for sensation seeking behavior during assessment of the trait: A note on the construct validity of the measurement operation. *Personality and Individual Differences*, **6**, 957-959.

Ruch, W. (1988). Sensation seeking and the enjoyment of structure and content of humor: Stability of findings across four samples. *Personality and Individual Differences*, **9**, 861-871.

Schneider, S. L., & Lopes, L. L. (1986). Reflection in preferences under risk: Who and when may suggest why. *Journal of Experimental Psychology: Human Perception and Performance*, **12**, 535-548.

Schoemaker, P. J. H. (1982). The expected utility model: Its variants, purposes, evidence and limitations. *Journal of Economic Literature*, **20**, 529-563.

Schoemaker, P. J. H. (1989). *Conceptions of risk-taking: Do intrinsic risk-attitudes matter?* Working paper, Center for Decision Research, University of Chicago, Chicago, IL.

Scodel, A., Ratoosh, P., & Minas, J. S. (1959). Some personality correlates of decision making under conditions of risk. *Behavioral Science*, **4**, 19-28.

Shapero, A. (1975). The displaced, uncomfortable entrepreneur. *Psychology Today*, **9**(6), 83-88, 133.

Shefrin, H., & Statman, M. (1985). The disposition to sell winners too early and ride losers too long: Theory and evidence. *Journal of Finance*, **40**, 777-790.

Shefrin, H., & Statman, M. (1988). *Applying behavioral finance to the use of options*. Working paper, Santa Clara University, Santa Clara, CA.

Sherman, S. J., & Fazio, R. H. (1983). Parallels between attitudes and traits as predictors of behavior. *Journal of Personality*, **51**, 308-345.

Slovic, P. (1962). Convergent validation of risk taking measures. *Journal of Abnormal and Social Psychology*, **65**, 68–71.

Slovic, P. (1964) Assessment of risk-taking behavior. *Psychological Bulletin*, **61**, 220–233.

Slovic, P. (1972). Information processing, situation specificity, and the generality of risk-taking behavior. *Journal of Personality and Social Psychology*, **22**, 128–134.

Tellegen, A., Lykken, D. T., Bouchard, T. J., Jr, Wilcox, K. J., Segal, N. L., & Rich, S. (1988). Personality similarity in twins reared apart and together. *Journal of Personality and Social Psychology*, **54**, 1031–1039.

Terasaki, M., & Imada, S. (1988). Sensation seeking and food preferences. *Personality and Individual Differences*, **9**, 87–93.

Thaler, R. (1980). Toward a positive theory of consumer choice. *Journal of Economic Behavior and Organization*, **1**, 39–60.

Tse, D. K., Lee, K., Vertinsky, I., & Wehrung, D. A. (1988). Does culture matter? A cross-cultural study of executives' choice, decisiveness, and risk adjustment in international marketing. *Journal of Marketing*, **52**, 81–95.

Tversky, A., & Kahneman, D. (1981). The framing of decisions and the psychology of choice. *Science*, **211**, 453–458.

von Winterfeldt, D., & Edwards, W. (1986). *Decision analysis and behavioral research*. Cambridge: Cambridge University Press.

Wagenaar, W. A. (1988). *Paradoxes of gambling behavior*. Hove and London, England: Erlbaum.

Wagenaar, W. A., & Keren, G. B. (1988). Chance and luck are not the same. *Journal of Behavioral Decision Making*, **1**, 65–75.

Wagenaar. W. A., Keren, G. B., & Pleit-Kuiper, A. (1984). The multiple objectives of gamblers. *Acta Psychological*, **56**, 167–178.

Wallach, M. A., & Kogan, N. (1959). Sex differences and judgment processes. *Journal of Personality*, **27**, 555–564.

Wallach, M. A., Kogan, N., & Bem, D. J. (1962). Group influence on individual risk taking. *Journal of Abnormal and Social Psychology*, **65**, 75–86.

Wallsten, B. S., & O'Leary, V. E. (1981). Sex makes a difference: Differential perceptions of women and men. *Review of Personality and Social Psychology*, **2**, 9–41.

Watson, S. R. & Buede, D. M. (1987). *Decision synthesis: The principles and practice of decision analysis*. New York: Cambridge University Press.

Watts, H. W., & Tobin, J. (1967). Consumer expenditures and the capital account. In D. D. Hester, & J. Tobin (Eds.), *Studies of portfolio behavior* (pp. 1–39). New York: Wiley.

Weigel, R. H., & Newman, L. S. (1976). Increasing attitude-behavior correspondence by broadening the scope of the behavioral measure. *Journal of Personality and Social Psychology*, **33**, 793–802.

Weinstein, E., & Martin, J. (1969). Generality of willingness to take risks. *Psychological Reports*, **24**, 499–501.

Zuckerman, M. (1978). The search for high sensation. *Psychology Today*, **11**(9), 38–46, 96–99.

Zuckerman, M. (1979a). *Sensation seeking: Beyond the optimal level of arousal*. Hillsdale, NJ: Erlbaum.

Zuckerman, M. (1979b). Traits, states, situations, and uncertainty. *Journal of Behavioral Assessment*, **1**, 43–54.

Zuckerman, M. (Ed.) (1983). *Biological bases of sensation seeking, impulsivity and anxiety*. Hillsdale, NJ: Erlbaum.

Zuckerman, M., Ballenger, J. C., Jimerson, D. C., Murphy, D. L., & Post, R. M. (1983). A correlational test in humans of the biological models of sensation seeking, impulsivity, and anxiety. In M. Zuckerman, (Ed.), *Biological bases of sensation seeking, impulsivity and anxiety* (pp. 229-248). Hillsdale, NJ: Erlbaum.

Zuckerman, M., Buchsbaum, M. S., & Murphy, D. L. (1980) Sensation seeking and its biological correlates. *Psychological Bulletin*, **88**, 187-214.

Zuckerman, M., Eysenck, S., & Eysenck, H. J. (1978). Sensation seeking in England and America: Cross-cultural, age and sex comparisons. *Journal of Consulting and Clinical Psychology*, **46**, 139-149.

Zuckerman, M., Kolin, E. A., Price, L., & Zoob, I. (1964). Development of a sensation-seeking scale. *Journal of Consulting Psychology*, **28**, 477-482.

Zuckerman, M., Simons, R. F., & Como, P. G. (1988). Sensation seeking and stimulus intensity as modulators of cortical, cardiovascular, and electrodermal response: A cross-modality study. *Personality and Individual Differences*, **9**, 361-372.

Chapter 5

Risk taking: A developmental perspective

Baruch Fischhoff
Carnegie Mellon University

CONTENTS

Developmental changes in risk taking are an established bit of folk wisdom. Probably the most common claim is that the rate of risk taking decreases as

Risk-taking Behavior. Edited by J. F. Yates
© 1992 John Wiley & Sons Ltd

people age. Thus, the news media are full of stories about the risks that today's adolescents are taking. Conversations among parents often echo a similar theme. For their part, adolescents grumble about their parents' unwillingness to try anything new (or to let their kids do so). Those parents may tussle with their own parents over the need to take the risks associated with moving out of the family home, meeting new people, or letting their children risk raising their grandchildren differently. Like most general patterns, this one has its exceptions. Parents also complain about the difficulty of getting their kids to try different foods or vacation spots. Senior executives may lament the loss of entrepreneurial spirit among their subordinates.

The familiarity of these claims carries, of course, no guarantee of their accuracy. Empirical evidence would be needed to establish, say, that adolescents really are more likely than adults to use drugs or to smoke or to drink and drive, or that investment patterns really vary with executives' age. Such studies could be surprising. It is not hard to think of reasons why appearances might be deceiving. For example, adolescents' lack of privacy may make their risky acts disproportionately visible; their lack of legal and financial resources may increase the chances that their risky acts will become known; their lack of respect for adult conventions may encourage them to flaunt risk-taking acts that adults perform more discretely. Once collected, such evidence on the rate of risk behaviors would be but a starting point for determinining why people of different ages behave differently (or similarly). People can take different risks for similar reasons and similar risks for different reasons.

The present chapter offers a general framework for studying and characterizing developmental changes in risk taking. That framework has two components, a way of thinking about individual acts of risk taking and a way of thinking about the individuals taking (or avoiding) those acts. The first component adopts the perspective of decision theory, viewing risk taking as the result of more or less deliberate choices among alternative courses of action. The second component adopts the perspective of life-span developmental psychology, viewing the individuals facing risk situations in terms of where they are in their life cycle.

Both components of the framework draw on familiar material. As such, it is not a theory, but more of a task analysis, laying out the issues that need to be considered in a systematic developmental approach to risk taking. Its intended contribution is stating each component in a way that facilitates exploring their interface. That means asking, on the one hand, how people's general cognitive, affective, and social development affects their exposure and approach to specific risk situations (e.g. increasing their sophistication, reducing their resilience). And it means asking, on the other hand, how people's experience with specific risk situations enhances or restricts their general development (e.g. increasing their sophistication, reducing their resilience).

Unfortunately, it is easier to raise these questions than to provide full, empirically substantiated answers to them. Few risk topics have been studied in comparable terms across any significant portion of the life cycle. Those studies that have been conducted often provide relatively little insight into the social or psychological processes accounting for behavioral differences or similarities. Thus, there are detailed statistics on the rates at which people of different ages suffer from various injuries and diseases (Jeffrey, 1989; National Safety Council, 1987; *Statistical Abstract of the United States*, 1988). By themselves, such statistics can serve the important public health purpose of identifying situations demanding attention. However, they can direct that attention in only the most general way.

For example, adolescent males die from traffic accidents at a higher rate than any other population group. That well-established result could, however, mean many things, each suggesting different explanations and different interventions. Objective factors contributing to these higher death rates could include tendencies for adolescent males to drive more miles, at greater speed, in less safe cars, after drinking more, or at more dangerous times of the day. Subjective factors might include being less attuned to these risk factors and gaining more benefit from incurring them, relative to other drivers (Brown & Groeger, 1988; Colbourn, 1978; Robertson, 1981).

Whether these (or other) risk factors are differentially present for adolescent males is an empirical question. If they are, then concurrent developmental changes offer possible explanations. For example, one might explore whether adolescent males generally enjoy particularly high levels of stimulation, or are particularly likely to get into situations with unfamiliar risks, or particularly exaggerate their control over situations. Similarly, one could look for sociological and economic factors that are correlated with age and gender. For example, adolescent males' financial resources may direct them toward certain leisure activities. Conversely, knowledge of general developmental differences can direct the search for risk factors in specific situations (e.g. knowing how psychomotor skills, or the ability to concentrate, change with age).

The framework advanced here is a complicating, rather than a simplifying, approach to understanding the development of risk-taking behavior. Rather than offering sweeping generalizations, it calls for a detailed look at people and situations. It does not preclude bold hypotheses, but assumes that they are identified most productively through analyses that recognize the diversity of risks and risk takers. That attention to detail applies both to identifying hypotheses that make sense from different disciplinary perspectives and to designing studies that include the measures needed by each.

The decision-making perspective focuses attention initially on those factors that an objective analysis would identify as being relevant to an individual's choices among risky alternatives. These include the options that are available, the consequences that might follow from the choice of those options, and the effect of those consequences on the individual's well-being. The perspective then proceeds to consider the gaps between this objective analysis of an individual's situation and its subjective representation. For example, do people overlook self-protective options, underestimate long-term health risks, exaggerate the benefit that they will get from additional income, or act impulsively, thereby failing to take advantage of their knowledge? In this context, a developmental perspective looks at changes with age that could affect either the objective risk situations that individuals face or their subjective representation. It can also ask (more speculatively) how experience with risky decisions might affect general developmental processes.

The reason for adopting a programmatic approach in this chapter is that there are so few studies to cite that would satisfy both disciplines (i.e. students of development and of risk taking). What one typically finds, instead, are incomplete, although often tantalizing pieces. These are studies that document age differences in how frequently risks are realized (e.g. auto accidents), but leave open the set of possible causes. There are studies of age differences in risk behaviors (e.g. unprotected sex) that ignore the cognitions that might motivate those behaviors, or use unsatisfactory measurement procedures (e.g. vague "probability" scales applied to ill-specified events). And there are carefully measured risk judgments elicited from respondents whose social and developmental status is poorly characterized, or which hardly varies at all. All such studies are, of course, better than rank speculation. As a result, there is more to say on *how* to think about developmental aspects of risk taking than on *what* to think about them.

Task analyses can be boring. In effect, they "just" put into some logical order factors that are already more or less well known. My hope is to provide an encompassing framework, some conceptual clarification, access to several literatures, and a few potentially interesting hypotheses. It would be nice to have a theory. It may be some solace to have a plan.

A DECISION-MAKING PERSPECTIVE

The most general definition of *risk taking* is any action having at least one uncertain outcome (cf. Chapter 1, by Yates & Stone). That outcome might be positive (e.g. winning a lottery) or negative (e.g. contraceptive failure). By this definition, everyone takes risks, all the time. Often, the term is used more restrictively, referring to particular uncertain outcomes. For example, educators may worry about unplanned pregnancies and the *risk behaviors* that sometimes produce them.

From a decision-making perspective, risk taking is the deliberate choice of a risky behavior. That choice may produce a single behavior (and its stream of consequences) or a sequence of behaviors (e.g. repeatedly driving a car for which the airbag option has been declined). There should, however, be a voluntary choice somewhere along the line if an individual is to be described as taking risks, rather than just bearing them.

In this light, alternative actions are characterized by the consequences associated with them. Thus, apparently similar behaviors (e.g. one act of unprotected sex) can present very different risks for individuals in different circumstances (e.g. married and unmarried couples). On the other hand, similar risks may result from rather different behaviors (e.g. driving more slowly to compensate for poorer sight or slower reaction time). Thus, risk behaviors are an imperfect indicator of the risks that people are taking. A full characterization of those risks would include a probability distribution over each outcome dimension (showing, for example, the likelihood of injuries of varying severity). The more detailed these characterizations become, the less likelihood there is of lumping together behaviors having significantly different consequences (frustrating the search for common causes).

People's risk behaviors are even more imperfect indicators of the risks that they believe themselves to be taking. For example, investors may not realize that they are boarding an emotional rollercoaster when they assign half of their pension to an equity fund. Nor is there any guarantee that the impact of acknowledged consequences will be perceived accurately. People who have never suffered a physiological addiction may not be able to imagine what such a loss of control is like.

When making risky choices, people may consider more than the uncertain and negative consequences of their actions. Indeed, they presumably would not voluntarily expose themselves to a risk if there were not some compensating benefit. That benefit may "just" be avoiding a more serious risk (or a certain negative consequence). Or, it may be bundled with the risk itself, such as the exhilaration of driving fast.

Thus, a full account of a risky decision would have to consider the entire range of outcomes that it entails, both positive and negative, both certain and uncertain. In this respect, "risk taking" can be a misleading, or at least unproductive, term. It focuses attention on a limited portion of people's choices, typically, the risky outcomes that interest investigators, educators, public health officials, and the like. In the eye of the "behavers," on the other hand, these risks are the price paid to achieve (or at least have a chance at) some benefits. Their behavior cannot be understood without considering all dimensions of their choices. Doing so means looking equally hard at the costs and benefits of the alternatives to the risk behavior. The problems (indeed, risks) with an overly restrictive view of risk taking might be seen in the growing discussion of the possibility that some teens view pregnancy as a benefit, rather than a risk (Dryfoos, 1990; Kalmus, Lawton, & Namerow, 1987; Morrison, 1985). These young women see it as providing access to social services and status which alternative "nonrisky" behaviors do not.

As mentioned, a full account of a risky decision would also have to characterize it from both an objective and a subjective perspective. The former is essential for estimating the rate of (positive and negative) outcomes that would follow from particular patterns of behavior. The latter is needed for predicting the rate of such behaviors. Their combination is needed for designing interventions intended to change the rates of risky behaviors (or outcomes) by changing either people's circumstances or their perceptions.

Recognizing the possibility of human imperfection, decision theory has developed three interrelated branches. The *normative* theory develops logically defensible procedures for making decisions. The *descriptive* theory examines how people actually make decisions. The *prescriptive* theory explores methods for bridging gaps between the prescriptive and the normative, thereby helping people to make better decisions. Points of access to these literatures include Fischhoff (1988), Kahneman, Slovic, and Tversky (1982), Raiffa (1968), Russo and Schoemaker (1989), von Winterfeldt and Edwards (1986), Watson and Buede (1987), and Yates (1990), as well as Chapter 2 above, by Neuman and Politser.

The prescriptive interest of behavioral decision theory has prompted many descriptive studies to be cast in terms of deviations between actual and desired behavior. That normative theory specifies the rules to be followed when formulating beliefs and when integrating those beliefs in order to identify preferred courses of action. This emphasis on rule manipulation means that the descriptive theory of decision making has a distinctly cognitive bent. Thus, there are many studies of how people assess the probabilities of individual events, combine information from various sources, evaluate different outcomes, and integrate assessments of value and probability in order to reach conclusions (Fischhoff, 1989; Slovic, 1987).

From a cognitive perspective, people's shortcomings can be attributed to the lack of general intellectual skills, to a lack of specific substantive knowledge, or to a failure to exploit their skills and knowledge adequately. Thus, people may not know how to perform the tasks that experimenters (or life's risks) impose on them (Kahneman & Tversky, 1982). Or they may not have the information upon which those skills should be exercised. (They may also lack the skills needed to acquire needed information.) Or they may execute a task sloppily, perhaps because it is too complex or because they are too rushed (Reason, 1990).

Given this conceptualization, the most directly applicable chapters in developmental psychology are those on cognitive development. All other things being equal, people should become more proficient at risk taking as their cognitive skills and knowledge improve over their life span. One "thing" that might not remain equal is the difficulty of the risk situations that people face (e.g. just when we have learned when to risk raising our hands in class, we have to learn when to risk raising our voices in staff meetings). As a result, any discussion of the effect of cognitive development on risk taking must consider the cognitive challenges to effective decision making.

The normative theory is mute regarding the affective and social skills and knowledge needed for effective decision making. It assumes, rather, that people have mastered these aspects of their lives well enough to allow exploiting their cognitive skills and knowledge. Necessary affective skills include the ability to muster the mental resources needed for concentrated decision making, the ability to suppress distracting emotional pressures, and the ability to translate feelings into goals (subject to cognitive analysis). Necessary social skills include the ability to use other people as sources of information with known biases, the ability to explain one's choices to others, and the ability to treat the desire for social acceptance as a goal (and, hence, subject to cognitive analysis).

Here, too, the adequacy of people's abilities must be judged in the context of the situations that they face. Ideally, our resources for coping with risky decisions would keep pace with the demands placed on us. We should not have responsibility for complex, high-stakes decisions until we are ready for them. Indeed, a critical "meta" decision-making skill is knowing what decisions we have no business making.

The existence of multiple concurrent changes in people's abilities and circumstances creates the possibility of radically different accounts for any changes in risk behavior over the life span. For example, if the rate of trying new street drugs decreases with age after late adolescence, that might mean many things:

- As they age, people may acquire the cognitive skills needed to understand and weigh the consequences of drug use. On the other hand, the relevant skills may be as consolidated as they are going to get by mid-adolescence.
- Younger people may lack the knowledge and experience upon which to exercise their thinking skills. On the other hand, between health classes and street talk, young people may be relatively well informed.
- Younger people may have less of the emotional control needed to stick to the task of thinking their way through difficult decisions. On the other hand, they may be affectively predisposed to obsessing about decisions, continuing to think beyond the point of diminishing returns. (Emotionality may, in fact, follow from thinking too much and experiencing frustration at the lack of resolution.)
- Younger people may not have inculcated the social norms proscribing drug use. On the other hand, they may be particularly aware of behavioral norms of substance abuse (i.e. usage rates among their peers and elders) that give the lie to these espoused norms.

And so on. It is difficult enough to determine the sources of any specific decision or to discern the common elements in a set of decisions made by a single individual. It is more daunting still to seek broad development patterns that will account for significant portions of the variance in the risk behaviors of diverse people over diverse decisions. The remainder of this chapter is offered as a step in this direction. It views complication as a precondition for simplification. The set of potentially relevant factors must first be identified, before the really important factors can be sought.

The following sections consider, in turn, the processes of cognitive, affective, and social development, as those relate to risk taking. They ask what might develop in each domain and how those changes might affect people's risk taking, focusing particularly on the four critical components of: (a) identifying possible options, (b) assessing the likelihood of possible consequences, (c) evaluating the attractiveness of those consequences, and (d) integrating these considerations in order to reach a decision. More weakly, each section asks how these general developmental processes might be shaped by people's experience with decision making. The concluding section considers the implications of these (necessarily speculative) analyses for three practical pursuits: research, education, and public policy.

A DEVELOPMENTAL PERSPECTIVE

In what follows, "cognitive development" will include changes in what and how people *think* about the world. "Affective development" will include changes in what and how people *feel* about the world. "Social development" will include changes in the roles that others play in people's choices. Although common, this trichotomy (perhaps like most in social sciences) breaks down under close examination, For example, how people feel may be represented cognitively as explicit values, as well as experienced directly. How those values are manipulated may depend, in turn, on people's emotional maturity which, itself, may depend on their mastery of social situations. In all cases, "development" will refer to changes over the life span, without any evaluative connotation (implying that what develops later is better).

Cognitive development

Cognitive functioning is often divided into three components: capacity, knowledge, and skills (Keating, 1990). Developments in each domain might be expected to influence, and be influenced by, risk-taking behavior.

Capacity

Capacity is the ability to muster cognitive resources for thinking through problems. It involves such fundamental processes as being able to focus attention, to keep several facts in mind, and to consider abstract as well as concrete issues. Any growth in cognitive capacity would clearly increase the intellectual resources that are potentially available for decision making. It should allow people to consider more options, to think more deeply about them, and to bring more relevant experiences to bear on a problem.

If these changes occurred in isolation, they might justify a variety of predictions. For example, individuals with greater capacity might spend more time on decision-making tasks, because they can get further into a task before it becomes overwhelmingly complex. Or, they might do more simultaneous evaluation of options, because they can bear more considerations in mind. Or, they might be better attuned to recognizing risks, because they are better at considering multiple possible futures.

Although these are intriguing possibilities, capacity considerations seem to offer little predictive power. Capacity seems to asymptote fairly early in an individual's life and to stay at the level until threatened by organic factors associated with aging (e.g. strokes, Alzheimer's Disease) (Institute of Medicine, 1990). Whatever its level, the effects of capacity are moderated by other factors. People may seem to have less capacity when they actually just have less motivation. They may exploit knowledge and skills in order to compensate for capacity limits (e.g. by knowing what to do in advance, by having greater facility to integrate information). They may avoid situations where their capacity is stretched or rely on guardians to keep them from such challenges. In part for these reasons, it has proven notoriously difficult to measure capacity in all but the most controlled situations (e.g. laboratory studies of "mental workload").

Perhaps the clearest links between risk taking and cognitive capacity may actually lie in the opposite direction. People who make ill-advised decisions about drugs and drink may diminish their cognitive capacity. People who view themselves as having been successful risk takers may be more likely to use what capacity they have. That propensity might even emerge as a personality characteristic, such as internal locus of control (Baumrind, 1968, 1988; Langer, 1989).

Knowledge

As people age, they acquire beliefs, based on what they have heard, observed, inferred, and been told. Not all of these beliefs will be accurate. As time goes on, however, there is the opportunity for beliefs to be based on increasingly large sets of information and to have been refined through confrontation with reality. These developments should have different implications for different elements of risky decision-making processes:

Identifying alternatives   The easiest kind of learning ought to be the acquisition of options. As life goes, people should expand the repertoire of actions that they have observed someone taking. Those actions should, in turn, suggest additional responses that could be created within the "option space" that they define. Other things being equal, this is one aspect of risky decision making where people should improve with age *per se*. Some of the wisdom associated with age may reflect the ability to retrieve and create options worth evaluating.

One thing that might not be equal is the nature of the risky situations being faced. To the extent that options are situation specific, experience will provide less guidance in novel situations. Indeed, a core activity in "life skills training programs" is teaching "refusal strategies," possible ways to "say 'No'" from which adolescents might choose when thrust into risk-taking situations (Botvin, 1983; Schinke & Gilchrist, 1984; Spirak & Shure, 1974). Although easily understood, these options are not spontaneously generated.

In time, the sheer volume of experience may limit its value. One part of coming of age is realizing just how many different things one could do. That can be both liberating and intimidating, even paralyzing. In a study of possible strategies for dealing with the threat of sexual assault, we identified a set of over 1100 options—each of which could reasonably be supposed to have a different profile of possible consequences. In openended interviews, lay respondents listed about 25 of these, on average, while experts produced some 45 (Furby, Fischhoff, & Morgan, 1990). The sheer number of possibilities would frustrate any systematic evaluation, especially under crisis conditions. We were hard pressed to review them in the light of empirical studies of effectiveness (Furby & Fischhoff, in press).

Estimating consequences   Once options have been generated, the consequences of adopting them must be estimated. That estimation process may involve anything from a rough screening procedure to creating explicit probability distributions, showing the likelihood of all possible consequences. Whether people know the answers to these estimation questions depends on the learning opportunities that they have had. Other things being equal, people should know the most about the risks that they have been dealing with the longest. Thus, experienced drivers should know more about what can happen when a particular maneuver fails, and how likely that is. Teens should know more about how drugs are used in their subculture than do more distant adults (Dickson & Hutchinson, 1988: Jonah, 1986; Namerow, Lawton, & Philliber, 1987).

One thing that may not be equal is the opportunity for direct instruction regarding a risk. Effective opportunities require exposure to relevant facts provided by trustworthy sources in a comprehensible form. Often, there are deliberate efforts to create such exposures for the people who need them the most. Thus, teens are forced to attend health classes and driver's education, women's magazines write about osteoporosis and sexual assault, hunters are invited to National Rifle Association safety courses, and older people get lectures from physicians and pharmacists.

Unfortunately, the kinds of facts needed for risk decisions have often proven particularly difficult to learn. They force individuals to deal with: (a) potentially biased information sources (e.g. can one trust parents, peers, politicians?), (b) great uncertainty (i.e. no one knows, or even claims to know, how large a risk is), (c) unfamiliar units (e.g. annual failure rates, concentrations per billion parts), (d) unfamiliar numbers (either very large or very small), (e) lack of background information (e.g. the physiology needed to make sense out of confusing and conflicting messages regarding drugs, sex, or diet), and (f) consequences that unfold over time, making their effects hard to observe or integrate (diSessa, in press; Fischhoff, 1989; Gentner & Stevens, 1983).

The realization of these potential difficulties can be found in a variety of studies documenting the lacunae in lay risk perceptions. These include misconceptions regarding the magnitude of risks, the processes that produce them, and the effectiveness of strategies to ameliorate them (Fischhoff, 1989; Slovic, 1987; Weinstein, 1987). Although such problems have been found with individuals of varying ages, there are few explicit cross-age comparisons in knowledge. Generating predictions requires anticipating the developmental course of these barriers to understanding the facts to which one has been exposed. For example, with time, people may become more proficient at reinterpreting messages from questionable sources. On the other hand, without direct training, people may never make sense of very small numbers or technical units.

Evaluating consequences Estimating what will happen is a precursor to estimating what it will mean. People need knowledge about their own preferences, just as they need knowledge about their possibilities (see also Chapter 3, pp. 63–67). An extreme state of knowing what one wants is having a fully specified (multiattribute) utility function spanning the space of possible consequences. One could then "read off" the attractiveness of any option's expected consequences.

Such articulated preferences are a useful abstraction for formal analyses. More realistically, the precision of an individual's values vary widely across consequences. Table 5.1 describes some circumstances that should encourage clear likes and dislikes. For any fixed set of consequences, older respondents should have a better understanding of relative values. That understanding need not make decision making easier. Indeed, the realization of sharp and conflicting tastes is a price of maturation. The potential benefit of such increased self-knowledge is, of course, a better chance at identifying (and maximizing) those consequences that really are important. Thus, age should reduce the frequency of feeling that, "I got what I was looking for, but it turned out not to be what I wanted."

One complication to such a simple prediction of competence increasing with age is that the set of potentially relevant consequences may increase as well. Age

Table 5.1.   Conditions favorable to articulated values.

Personally familiar (time to think)
Personally consequential (motivation to think)
Publicly discussed (opportunity to hear, share views)
Uncontroversial (stable tastes, no need to justify)

Few consequences (simplicity)
Similar consequences (commensurability)
Experienced consequences (meaningful)
Certain consequences (comprehensibility)

Single or compatible roles (absence of conflict)
Diverse appearances (multiple perspectives)
Direct relation to action (concreteness)
Unbundled topic (considered in isolation)

Familiar formulation

Source. Fischhoff (1990). Copyright © 1991 the American Psychological Association. Reprinted by permission.

typically brings opportunities to affect additional aspects of one's own and others' worlds. As these consequences arise, they reduce one's decision-making competence, at least until their relative importance has been understood. Competence may be particularly compromised in periods where consequences have become objective possibilities, but are not yet subjective realities. For example, teens may shoplift "knowing" that being caught could compromise their career chances, but not realizing how big a deal that is.

A second complication arises when the set of consequences is fixed, but the valuations change. Those changes may reflect physiology (e.g. puberty, senescence), life circumstances (e.g. impoverishment), or even satiation. Here, too, the threats to effective risk taking may be greatest at times of transition, when changes have occurred, but not been recognized. For example, mid-life crises can arise from achieving security only to discover that one now needs adventure.

Integrating considerations   In order to produce a decision, these estimates and evaluations must be integrated into a summary recommendation. Decision theory does, of course, provide procedures for this task. They are, however, an unlikely bit of knowledge (and, as discussed below, not a very useful one). Indeed, little attempt is made to teach these procedures in the many programs designed to teach decision making to adolescents (Beyth-Marom *et al.*, 1991). Nor are guides for adults likely to go beyond simple (although potentially useful) rules, such as "count the number of reasons for and against an action." If the normative rules of decision theory are really so unintuitive (Lichtenstein, Slovic, & Zink, 1969), a developmental change in people's familiarity seems unlikely.

A more likely kind of knowledge concerns what to do in specific situations. Such solutions may summarize the experiences of an individual or group with using different strategies, showing what seems to have worked in the past. Or, they may reflect norms, specifying how one should resolve value conflicts or deal with risks, as a matter of principle, not efficacy. Although they can resolve decision problems, such rules shortcircuit the decision-making process. In effect, they convert it into a problem-solving process, attempting to diagnose situations precisely enough to reveal the right response to them.

Age should mean familiarity with more of these prepared solutions (Berg, 1989). With time, people develop more habits, hear more advice, learn more social norms. In order to improve the quality of people's risk-taking decisions, these solutions must reflect their circumstances and preferences (i.e. their consequence estimates and evaluations). As a result, "knowing" a solution means being able to determine its suitability. Unless it also confers that ability, age need not improve risk taking merely by increasing the repertoire of possibilities.

Recognizing that there are conflicting solutions is a first step toward sophistication. That can, however, be a troubling step as well as a liberating one. On the one hand, one is more likely to hedge one's bets, be alert to things going awry and to try new things, when one realizes that there are challenges to the advice offered by one's parents, peers, professors, or financial advisors. On the other hand, it can be debilitating when the sources of conflict are obscure. For example, how is a woman to deal with the sharply divided advice over whether to resist sexual assaults physically (Furby & Fischhoff, in press; Morgan, 1986)?

In addition to demonstrating their substantive expertise, advisors adopt various strategies to show sensitivity to advisees' values. For example, some stockbrokers' come-on in cold calls includes a "test" of potential clients' risk-return preferences. Many public service announcements (e.g. regarding drugs, sex) attempt to evoke particular elements in recipients' set of conflicting values. "Life skills" training programs may reduce risk-taking behavior, in part, because they emphasize the sovereignty of participants' values in decision making–before leading them all to the same conclusions. Age should improve people's ability to use risk-related advice if it either teaches them whom to trust in specific circumstances or provides some general evaluative skill.

Skills

Task analysis   When people do not know, in advance, the answer to all or part of a risk-taking problem, then they must infer it. That is, they must identify

alternatives, estimate and evaluate consequences, or integrate these considerations. Table 5.2 offers one characterization of the cognitive tasks involved in
decision making, as well as some of the problems possible if people lack the
requisite skills. Related cognitive task analyses can be found in Adams (1989),
Beyth-Marom, Novick, and Sloan (1987), Mann, Harmoni, and Power (1987),
Ross (1981), and in the introduction to many teaching programs (reviewed in
Beyth-Marom *et al.*, 1991; Hamburg, 1989). They could be supplemented by
consideration of the skills needed to produce the substantive knowledge to
which these skills are applied (e.g. discerning cause-effect relationships, generalizing experiences).

Table 5.2. Potential sources of bias in Bayesian hypothesis evaluation & decision
making.

Task	Potential bias	Special cases
Hypothesis formation	Untestable	Ambiguity, complexity, evidence unobservable
	Nonpartition	Nonexclusive, nonexhaustive
Assessing component probabilities	Misrepresentation	Strategic responses, nonproper scoring rules
	Incoherence	Noncomplementarity, disorganized knowledge
	Miscalibration	Overconfidence
	Nonconformity	Reliance on availability or representativeness
	Objectivism	—
Assessing prior odds	Poor survey of background	Incomplete, selective
	Failure to assess	Base-rate fallacy
Assessing likelihood ratio	Failure to assess	Noncausal, "knew-it-all-along"
	Distortion by prior beliefs	Preconceptions, lack of convergence
	Neglect of alternative hypotheses	Pseudodiagnosticity, inertia, cold readings
Aggregation	Wrong rule	Averaging, conservatism?
	Misapplying right rule	Computational error, conservatism?
Information search	Failure to search	Premature conviction
	Nondiagnostic questions	Tradition, habit
	Inefficient search	Failure to ask potentially falsifying questions
	Unrepresentative sampling	—
Action	Incomplete analysis	Neglecting consequences, unstable values
	Forgetting critical value	Confusing actual and effective certitude

A full developmental account of risk taking would chart the acquisition of each of these skills. This already daunting task is complicated further by the possibility that the applicability of whatever skills people have is task-dependent. For example, people's deductive reasoning seems different with concrete, familiar topics than with abstract, unfamiliar ones (Evans, 1982). Their failure to make logical inferences has sometimes been traced to confusion about the underlying premises (Siegler, 1981).

Such an account is beyond the scope of the present essay. Given the paucity of directly relevant studies, it would have the same speculative flavor as the previous section on the development of decision-related knowledge. An indicator of the likely complexity might be the current state of research on the acquisition of basic cognitive skills through childhood. There, the once-tidy Piagetian scheme of sequentially acquired cognitive structures has given way to a more complex picture, with multiple skills mastered to varying, but generally increasing degrees as people age (Byrnes, 1988; Case, 1987; Gelman & Baillargeon, 1983; Sinnott & Guttman, 1978).

Confidence assessment As an example of what might be found in such studies, consider the intellectual skill of evaluating the extent of one's own knowledge. Implicitly or explicitly, one makes many statements of the form, "I am X% certain that Statement Y is true." Y might be, "The bus will come on time," "Tonight's sexual partner does not have a transmissible disease," or "The writer of that article knows what she's talking about." Comparing a set of such predictions with the truth of the various Ys (as that is revealed) makes it possible to determine the appropriateness of one's confidence (Lichtenstein, Fischhoff, & Phillips, 1982; Yates, 1990).

Most studies making this comparison have found that people still have something to learn about themselves. Individuals' chances of being correct increase with their confidence, but the correlation is weak. That is, people are only partially sensitive to how much they know. The most commonly observed overall bias is overconfidence (e.g. being correct only 80% of the time when they are 100% confident). Studies have also found that people's performance improves if they receive such feedback in a concentrated, comprehensible way. Unfortunately, real life seldom provides such learning opportunities. The truth may be revealed too late to be useful, if it can be determined at all. And how many people even think to look at how often they were right in all cases where they were 80% confident? Moreover, many decisions are relatively insensitive to even moderate errors of probability assessment (Henrion, 1982; von Winterfeldt & Edwards, 1982). As a result, even if the outcome of a risky decision depended on just a single probability assessment, and one could see immediately what consequences arose, that feedback need not provide a very sharp message regarding one's skills.

People's risk decisions may be particularly vulnerable to situations where they generally know a lot, but include some bits of misinformation among their beliefs (Nussbaum & Novick, 1982). For example, Bostrom, Fischhoff, and Morgan (in press) found that people who were generally knowledgeable about the risks of radon typically believed, with equal confidence, that it was a permanent contaminant (not realizing that a radioactive substance could have a short half life.). Or, Jacobs-Quadrel (1990) found that youths who knew much about what determined the risks of pregnancy did not realize that the risk depended on the amount of exposure.

One might ask whether some of teens' problems with risks can be traced to their having even poorer calibration than adults. Investigators studying meta-cognition have found that children as young as three have beliefs regarding the workings of their own minds (e.g. Cavanaugh & Perlmutter, 1982; Furnham, 1988; Suzuki-Slakter, 1988; Wellman, 1990). Although they allow some assessment of the accuracy of these beliefs, such studies do not provide the performance standard of calibration studies.

Jacobs-Quadrel (1990) administered calibration tests to several groups of teens and adults. She found that each group performed similarly on tests dealing with general knowledge and risk knowledge, suggesting that there is nothing special in thinking about risks. She also found that adults and youths drawn from the same middle-class population had very similar performance, suggesting that this skill may asymptote quite early. A group of at-risk youths (drawn from half-way houses and rehabilitation centers), however, performed much more poorly. On the risk questions, in particular, they demonstrated less knowledge and expressed greater confidence than the middle-class youths, resulting in considerably greater overconfidence. At the moment, one can only speculate about the contribution of this bias to their predicament.

Summary

A full treatment of the role of development in risk taking would pursue studies like Jacobs-Quadrel's (1990) for every decision-relevant change in cognitive skill, knowlege, and capacity. Given the current lack of directly relevant data, that treatment would quickly tail off into speculation. It might, however, be supported by detailed consideration of research into correlated cognitive skills (e.g. the ability to retrieve memories when applying the availability heuristic, the capacity for hypothetical thinking when envisioning alternative futures).

Filling in the missing details here is relatively straightforward, insofar as the necessary studies could be conducted using standard (or even proven) research methods. Understanding the role of risk taking in development is much more difficult. Risk taking can be a source of knowledge and skills. In a sense, every decision is an exercise in hypothesis evaluation, seeing how the world responds to various actions (and how one responds to their consequences). Extracting lessons from these exercises is, however, far from trivial. The world being manipulated is often sufficiently complex that it cannot yield a clear signal (Einhorn, 1980; Fischhoff, 1980). Even if it does, that message may come after such long a delay that it cannot be connected with the beliefs that motivated it. When consequences are irreversible, the message may come too late to be of any immediate good. This may be particularly true for risky decisions (e.g. regarding sex, drugs, drinking, driving), where experience is a harsh tutor.

Affective development

Over time, how people feel can change along with how they think. To a first approximation, those feelings might be arranged along a "hot-cold" dimension (Ainslie, 1975; Clark & Fiske, 1982). At the former extreme lie the deep states of arousal (fear, anger, passion) that can drive people to action or inaction, that can focus or diffuse their thought processes. At the other extreme lie the cognitive representations of these desires. Some investigators have proposed "dual process" models, incorporating both cognitive and affective aspects of how people regulate their risk-taking behavior (Averill, 1987; Leventhal, 1980, 1984).

Cold affect

When they evaluate specific consequences, people can sometimes draw on direct knowledge of how much they would like (or dislike) their occurrence. In other cases, though, they must derive their evaluations from more basic values. The development of those values might be expected to parallel that of people's other cognitions. For example, with age, people might be expected to acquire more complex and abstract basic values, with better understood realms of applicability.

There are many possible changes in these values over the life span. The most encompassing accounts can be seen in claims that there are developmental sequences for moral values analogous to Piagetian schemes for cognitive structures (Kohlberg, 1984). Such claims have generated enormous controversy. Some reflect measurement concerns, like those that have plagued Piagetian attempts to classify behavior in stages (e.g. Brainerd, 1975). Others reflect the strong normative connotations of "development," implying that later stages are better stages. Yet other criticisms concern the neglect of values that have no place in the posited orderly progression (e.g. Colby et al., 1983; Gilligan, 1982). Even changes that are clear advances when thinking about facts may be more ambiguous when thinking about values. For example, unduly abstract thinking may anesthetize people's moral thinking. Thus, one might hope to balance young people's concrete, situation-specific feelings of justice with the more abstract, generalized values of their elders.

In principle, one could point to any age-related change in personal circumstances, ego development, social situation, or physiology as potentially changing what people value. For those changes to affect overall patterns of risk-taking behavior, they would have to have some systematic expression in the decisions that people face. Predicting such linkages requires high-order speculation. For example, as discussed in Chapter 4 by Bromiley and Curley, some investigators (Zuckerman, 1979, 1983) have claimed that some people prefer higher levels of stimulation than others. Such a preference could increase exposure to risk where it is satisfied by activities like fast driving and sky diving. It could reduce exposure where it is satisfied by activities like reading gothic novels, watching horror movies, or working too hard. It might also reduce exposure to risk behaviors that are seen as numbing, such as excessive drinking. It might have no effect on the exposures of people suffering from addictions that override other values.

Thus, a given basic value can be realized in quite different ways. The chances of linking any single value with particular behaviors is complicated further by differences in other values and in beliefs. For example, consider the possiblility that adolescents tend to prefer higher levels of stimulation. That preference should encourage risk behaviors because the uncertainty about their outcomes would be stimulating. That tendency would be enhanced if adolescents saw uncertain situations as offering chances to learn something about the world or about themselves. On the other hand, adolescents might avoid risk behaviors if they had a particularly high fear of failure, always a possibility with uncertain events.

Of course, what adolescents do depends on the uncertainty that they perceive. As mentioned, Jacobs-Quadrel (1990) found particularly great overconfidence in the risk beliefs of at-risk youths. Given such confidence they would be engaging in risk behaviors not so much to see what would happen as to incur expected consequences.

Thus, even if one knew the distinctive features of an age group's basic values, it would be hard to predict its distinctive patterns of risk taking. These difficulties mirror those that have bedeviled the search for attitude-behavior relationships (Ajzen & Fishbein, 1977; Schuman & Johnson, 1976). Prediction improves as attitudes become more specific and, hence, more distant from basic values. Thus, the best predictions of whether people will engage in Behavior X follow from "attitude" statements of the form, "I really like doing X."

It is natural (and tempting) to develop theories of the form, "Kids (senior citizens, middle-aged men,...) find (basic value) X very important, as a result they are particularly likely to do (risk behavior) Y." However, there is too much going on in people's lives for such theories to be very productive, in terms of prediction or explanation. Even the hormonal changes at puberty (Brooks-

Gunn & Reiter, 1990; Udry, 1988), which clearly create new desires, still find enormously varied expression. Here, too, we need multifactor accounts that consider the complexity of people's perceptions and motivations.

Hot affect

In decisions dominated by cold affect, people calculatedly derive choices from their basic values, using skills like those discussed in the section on cognitive development. When hot affect dominates, these thought processes are short-circuited, so that choices reflect the most salient feelings, rather than a balanced appraisal.

A developmental account of hot affect would consider both the role it plays in decision-making processes and the choices that it encourages. "Hot" decisions (in this sense) could avoid risks as well as incur them, depending on what people's most salient feelings are. They might be fear of failure and embarrassment in some cases, the desire for excitement and sexual gratification in others.

Other things being equal, hot affect decisions do require simpler behavioral accounts. By definition, they involve a smaller number of basic values and a reduced role for factual deliberations. Nonetheless, one still must identify those focal values and when they come into play. In the absence of independent evidence upon which to build, it is a daunting task to build a developmental account of risk taking in even this restricted and simpler domain. It is complicated enough to discern the role of affect in even controlled experimental settings (Fiske & Taylor, 1990).

Consider, for example, the common claim that decision making becomes colder as people age (Botwinick, 1966; Wallach & Kogan, 1961). Speculatively, it is easy enough to think of processes that might contribute to such a trend. For example, as life's surprises mount up, people may be more likely to look before they leap, considering competing goals and not just the first objective that comes to mind. Experience may also increase older people's confidence in their decision-making abilities, encouraging them to think longer about a problem before throwing up their hands and relying on habit or intuition. Older people may live in a more stable world, where they have already solved most problems, allowing them time for reflection on the relatively few novel decisions that they encounter. Unfortunately, quite opposite speculations are also possible. For example, so many choices may become automatic with time that older people are less likely to stop and think. Feelings of powerlessness might also discourage deliberation (Harter, 1990; Hauser & Bowlds, 1990; Langer, 1989), as might the discovery that the world tolerates mistakes or least obscures their consequences (Fischhoff, 1980; von Winterfeldt & Edwards, 1982).

The content and structure of decisions may shape their affective component, as well as vice versa. For example, some topics may be too hot to handle, provoking quick decisions. Other topics may signal the need to act coolly, so as to demonstrate competence. Indeed, much professional training is aimed at creating emotional control, as a necessary condition for thinking effectively. Recently, we conducted 100-plus interviews with adolescents who described the decisions occupying them. A strong impression from preliminary analyses of these interviews is that such youths find it very frustrating when hard thought does not produce clear-cut answers to important decision problems. One hard lesson of life is that important decisions are often gambles, regardless of how much one worries about them. Until younger people learn that lesson, they may often be both deliberate and impulsive in their risk decisions. That is, they may think long and hard, but then allow transient emotional states to resolve residual uncertainties because they know no more orderly procedure. Those emotional states might encourage particular choices. For example, frustration might induce fatalism or the desire for immediate gratification. That desire could, in turn, increase anything from casual sex to snacking to movie going, depending on the context.

Overall, these plausible processes seem to frustrate any general developmental account of the relationship between affect and risk taking. The decisions facing people at different ages are sufficiently different that it would be meaningless to try to say that one age shows greater cool than another. Some particularly emotional topics seem more common for the young (e.g. separation from parents, volatile social situations, sexuality), whereas others seem more com mon for the old (e.g. separation from children, illness, approaching death). Young people may exaggerate the catastrophic potential of their decisions because they have not been through many storms (e.g. "I'll die if I don't make the team" or "if she doesn't ask me out"). Or, they may understate it because they see themselves as having the time and strength to recover from big setbacks (Hauser & Bowlds, 1990). Affect and risk taking are doubtless related in specific situations. However, we know too little about each for any serious developmental theorizing.

Social development

A continuing challenge of life is living with other people. These interactions can affect both the contents and processes of people's decision making. Other people are also a source of beliefs and values, as well as of consequences; acting contrary to their expectations and desires can be both costly and beneficial. Other people are also a source of both options and restrictions; their involvement can make actions both more and less feasible.

One way to characterize social development is in terms of opposing processes of socialization and individuation. At the same time as they are integrating themselves with society, people are also distancing themselves from it (Harter, 1990), as they create a personal identity with some degree of social acceptability. Individuation creates, in effect, the individual who needs to be integrated. These are obviously complex processes. Nonetheless, considering their most general directions may help to complete the present broad outline of a comprehensive developmental account of risk taking.

Socialization

As they age, people learn what their society as a whole believes, values, and chooses. In time, society's perspective may become one's own. At that point, they assume the status of personal values, beliefs, and ways of integrating considerations in order to make choices. As such, they become subject to the developmental processes discussed in earlier sections.

If socialization is effective, then it should reduce the rate of risk behaviors. Societies devalue the benefits of such behaviors, publicize their dangers, and proscribe their selection. Thus, to a first approximation, risk taking might be interpreted as a failure of socialization. That could, in turn, be traced to several processes which might be differentially prevalent at different points in the developmental process.

One possible failure of socialization is not getting the message. Much schooling assumes that young people do not know what society thinks about risk issues. Educators point, for example, to youths' ignorance of behavioral norms even among their own peers. Youths have been found to exaggerate the prevalence of risk behaviors such as smoking, sex, and drug experimentation (Sussman et al., 1988)—at least relative to the rates reported to risk researchers. Estimating the rates of risk behaviors is complicated for youths (and for investigators) by their illicit status, which makes both reports and observations suspect. Whatever its exact source, such a bias would make risk behaviors seem more appropriate than they would be to individuals who subscribe to accepted social wisdom about the normalcy of those behaviors.

Analogous complications should frustrate estimating the effects of risk behaviors. People must reconcile what they are told (as accepted wisdom) with what they see and hear, accommodating whatever they believe about the biases in each source. Those processes allow for a second general failure of socialization, rejecting social conventions because they lack credibility—seeming to be either ill-informed or deliberate misrepresentations (e.g. what adults tell kids).

That rejection may be in favor of personal beliefs or those of a nonmajority group. For example, youths may feel that their own subculture offers better guidance on risky subjects—regarding what will happen, how things feel, what is important, and what to do (Savin-Williams & Berndt, 1990). In that case, they have been successfully socialized, to a unit outside their immediate family. However, that unit is not society as a whole. The possibility of conflicting socialization pressures has been detailed in schemes such as control theory, subculture theory, strain theory, and integrated social control theory. Empirical studies have shown, among other things, that the common notion of an all-controlling teen culture is a considerable oversimplification (Brown, in press).

Without greater understanding of socialization processes *per se*, it is hard to imagine a satisfying account of their effect on risk taking. Younger people have, presumably, internalized fewer of the general society's perspectives. However, that does not say what perspectives come in their stead.

Individuation

Individuation is a basic human need (Harter, 1990). It is obviously also a necessity. All people are at the juncture of different social units with conflicting pressures. People who fail to resolve these conflicts in a reasonably stable way suffer from identity confusion (or even crises). Even within a single social unit, few beliefs, values, or rules are sufficiently well-specified to require no adaptation to individual circumstances. Establishing oneself as an individual involves several interrelated processes. One is acquiring the right to make one's own choices. A second is dealing with others' direct intrusions into one's decision-making processes (e.g. their advice and remonstrations). A third is managing others' impact on the consequences of decisions.

A necessary condition for exercising such judgment is the right to choose one's own actions. Ideally, life would pose a series of graded exercises, each stretching people to make slightly more complicated decisions, followed by useful feedback. Anxious parents of toddlers seek this goal when they engineer the architecture of their homes to regulate the risks of locomotion. They hope to bring down the barriers at a rate that will produce few close calls, as their children learn to gamble about walking, running, and jumping. If this plan works, then their children will not only acquire these risk-taking skills at a reasonable price, but also a sense of self-efficacy.

In the short run, children (or teens or adults) who get in too deep too fast risk painful experiences. In the long run, these failures can cause self-doubt that can, in turn, lead them to surrender autonomy to others (parents, peers, superiors, fashions) or just to reduce their cognitive commitment altogether (Steinberg, 1990; Torney-Purta, 1990). Of course, moving too slowly, under too great constraints, can produce the same lack of autonomy, leaving people insecure and inexperienced when they are able to take risks.

One possible symptom of imbalance is the radical relativism sometimes attributed to teens (Chandler, 1987). According to this account, adolescents can be destabilized by the realization that adult authority can be challenged. Without a clear sense of how to sort out conflicting claims, it may seem as though anything goes, or "my guess is as good as theirs." In some ways, this parallels the frustration and skepticism of (adult) citizens who are confused by controversies among experts over the risks of hazardous technologies (Fischhoff, 1989; Krimsky & Plough, 1988; Pitz, Chapter 10 below). At times, if people appear to lack competence, they may find their autonomy restricted, legally as well as psychologically (Gardner, Scherer, & Tester, 1989; Starr & Whipple, 1980). Unfortunately for the theoretician, there is no simple pattern to the risks that people take when they are in over their heads. Critics of public behavior often accuse laypeople of both undue caution and undue capriciousness (e.g. Lewis, 1990).

In this light, the clearest developmental trend in risk taking is the increasing range of situations in which people are allowed to exercise sovereignty and, hence, to develop a distinct identity. In doing so, people must cope intellectually with the expectations to which they have been socialized. Those perspectives are represented most visibly in the individuals who are present when decisions are made. Those individuals might be bosses, teachers, parents, friends, foes, or physicians.

Research has shown fairly complex patterns in how youths seek advice (East, 1989; Foxman, Tansuhaj, & Ekstrom, 1988; Steinberg, 1990). For example, parents are relied upon more heavily than images of rebellious teens would suggest (Smetana, 1988). Consulting successfully with other people requires some nontrivial social skills. One such skill is being able to make one's situation clear enough to elicit useful comments. A second is being able to understand others well enough to see how their perspectives and interests differ from one's own (Keating & Clark, 1980; Shantz, 1983). A third is soliciting comments without getting committed to following them (or feeling compelled to resist). For the accomplished consultant, other people can serve as "peripheral processors," working through a decision from alternative points of view.

Implicit in many such consultations is a process of negotiation, whereby people recruit support for their choices. If others can be induced to accept a decision, then one blunts any reprobation for the act itself or for adverse consequences that follow. There are also more direct forms of complicity. Some risk behaviors require other people's participation (e.g. wild parties, sex), as do some forms of risk avoidance (e.g. abstinence). Until they master these skills, people have not individuated themselves,

Recognizing this interdependence, many substance-abuse programs teach such skills directly. For example, they may show participants how to support one another's risk-avoidance decisions, to avoid situations where risk behaviors are options, to offer socially acceptable reasons for nonrisk behaviors (e.g. "I'm allergic to marijuana"), to feign conformity, and even to organize nonrisk social groups where the need for individuation is less (e.g. SADD—Students Against Drunk Driving).

Evaluations of these programs suggest fairly dramatic reductions in risk behaviors (Best et al., 1988; Ellickson & Bell, 1990; Hamburg, 1989). Thus, these skills may be quite powerful determinants of risk behaviors, which ordinary life cannot be entrusted to teach. Unfortunately for scientific purposes, so much goes on in these programs that it is hard to identify just which elements make the difference (Beyth-Marom et al., 1991).

CONCLUSION

Understanding even a single decision can be a complicated business. The observer needs to grasp its cognitive, affective, and social dimensions—as must the effective decision maker. The choice being made can depend on what the decision maker thinks and feels, as well as on which other people are involved. Decision makers' thinking may depend on their cognitive capacity, their beliefs, and their skills (for manipulating those beliefs within the constraints imposed by their capacity). This thinking goes on against the backdrop of affective and social pressures whose management requires additional skills.

People's decision-making capabilities should improve as they age. That is, they should be better able to identify the courses of action in their own best interest, and to execute those choices. The extent of this improvement should depend on the quality of the feedback that their world provides. That feedback may be good for some risk-related skills (e.g. knowing what one enjoys) and poor for others (e.g. assessing the quality of one's own knowledge). New feedback may be needed whenever their world changes, either endogenously (e.g. new tastes) or exogenously (e.g. new risks). Indeed, the pace of change could undo whatever secular improvements come with age.

Decisions involving risk behaviors may constitute a distinct category for investigators or educators. However, for the people facing them, they are just another set of problems, within which any of their cognitive, affective, and social resources are fair game. The development of risk decisions must be seen against the background of the general development of these resources. Although this complicates risk researchers' task, it also means that a wide variety of other studies conducted by other disciplines become potentially relevant.

After locating the decisions that interest them in this broader context, risk investigators can begin studying risk-specific aspects of decisions. These include perceptions of the likelihood and attractiveness of particular outcomes (e.g. pain, excitement), the affect that particular options and outcomes evoke, and the social environment within which they are made. Only with such a detailed analysis is it possible to distinguish differences in people's behavior from differences in their situations.

Failure to take such care can be socially destructive, as well as scientifically unproductive. For example, one may mistake a conscious, willful rejection of social values as an ill-considered choice. Such misunderstanding can blur social discourse by obscuring value conflicts. It can misdirect educational efforts into emphasizing information that is already well known (e.g. that crack cocaine can kill), while neglecting value issues that need clarification (e.g. the possibility that future gains justify postponing current pleasure). Recipients of these risk communications will appear even more stupid for apparently misunderstanding a message that they actually reject.

At the other extreme, people may avoid risks out of habit or conformity, rather than as the result of reasoned deliberation. Their choices may become more erratic and risky if they must face new situations. Taking socially accepted behavior as evidence of risk-taking skill may mean depriving people of needed guidance or structural protection (for cases where they are not competent to choose).

More generally, incomplete diagnoses will underestimate the complexity of people and the situations that they face (Nisbett & Ross, 1980). As mentioned, the most common general speculation is probably that risk taking declines from adolescence to old age. Even if this claim is true regarding the relative prevalence of some risk behaviors, it does not capture the cognitive, emotional, and social processes prompting those actions. As a result, not only will the opportunity to address specific problems be missed, but the tenor of social discourse will be poisoned by reducing other groups to caricatures. One result may be a general policy of controlling youths, rather than valuing (and even creating) opportunities for them to take manageable, instructive risks (Wallerstein & Bernstein, 1988).

The study of decision making might aid these social processes in several ways, drawing on the variety of approaches discussed in the chapters of this volume. Descriptive analyses can characterize how participants and observers view risk situations. Normative analyses can clarify the conditions under which various options are advised (e.g. which risks are worth worrying about, how far should one "test the envelope," how should uncertainty about tastes be accommodated). Prescriptive analyses can craft (and test) methods of improving decision making. Finally, a decision-making perspective *per se* can remind one how misleading the term "risk taking" can be, if it obscures the fact that the risk that someone takes is only one feature of an option that is chosen from among other options, each with its own risks.

SUMMARY

Opportunities to take—or avoid—risks occur for every person at every age. How they respond depends in part on who they are, in terms of their cognitive, affective, and social development. Conversely, the risks that people take—and avoid—provide experiences which can enhance or constrain their development. This chapter examines the complex interactions between risk taking and development based on the research literatures in these respective areas. Although it raises many speculative hypotheses, its main message is cautionary. Unduly simplistic accounts of risk taking or of development can produce bad science and bad public policy—whenever a group (e.g. teen males, older women) is treated according to some undocumented image of its risk taking.

ACKNOWLEDGMENTS

Support for the preparation of this chapter was provided by the Carnegie Council on Adolescent Development and the National Science Foundation. It is gratefully acknowledged, as are the thoughtful comments offered on earlier drafts by John Coley, Lita Furby, Grant Gutheil, Daniel Keating, George Loewenstein, and J. Frank Yates. The views expressed are those of the author.

REFERENCES

Adams, M. J. (1989). Thinking skills curricula: Their promise and progress. *Educational Psychologist*, **24**(1), 25–77.

Ainslie, G. (1975). Specious reward: A behavioral theory of impulsiveness and impulse control. *Psychological Bulletin*, **82**, 463–496.

Ajzen, I., & Fishbein, M. (1977). Attitude-behavior relations: A theoretical analysis and review of empirical research. *Psychological Bulletin*, **84**, 888–918.

Averill, J. R. (1987). The role of emotion and psychological defense in self-protective behavior. In N. D. Weinstein (Ed.), *Taking care: Understanding and encouraging self-protective behavior* (pp. 54–78). New York: Cambridge University Press.

Baumrind, D. (1968). Authoritarian vs authoritative control. *Adolescence*, **3**, 255–272.

Baumrind, D. (1988). Rearing competent children. In W. Damon (Ed.), *Child development today and tomorrow: New directions for child development* (pp. 349–378). San Francisco: Jossey-Bass.

Berg, C. (1989). Knowledge of strategies for dealing with everyday problems from childhood through adolescence. *Developmental Psychology*, **25**, 607–618.

Best, J. A., Thomson, S. J., Santi, S. M., Smith, E. A., & Brown, K. S. (1988). Preventing cigarette smoking among school children. *Annual Review of Public Health*, **9**, 161–201.

Beyth-Marom, R., Fischhoff, B., Jacobs, M., & Furby, L. (1991). Teaching adolescents decision making. In J. Baron & R. Brown (Eds.), *Teaching decision making* (pp. 19–60). Hillsdale, NJ: Erlbaum.

Beyth-Marom, R., Novick, R., & Sloan, M. (1987). Enhancing children's thinking skills: An instructional model for decision-making under certainty. *Instructional Science*, **16**, 215–231.

Bostrom, A., Fischhoff, B., & Morgan, G. M. (in press). Characterizing mental models of hazardous processes: A methodology and an application to radon. *Journal of Social Issues*.

Botvin, G. J. (1983). *Life skills training.* New York: Smithfield Press.

Botwinick, J. (1966). Cautiousness in advanced age. *Journal of Gerontology*, **21**, 347–353.

Brainerd, C. J. (1975). The stage question in cognitive-developmental theory. *Behavioral and Brain Sciences*, **2**, 173–213.

Brooks-Gunn, J., & Reiter, E. O. (in press). The role of pubertal processes in the early adolescent transition. In S. S. Feldman & G. R. Elliott (Eds.), *At the threshold: The developing adolescent* (pp. 16–53). Cambridge, MA: Harvard University Press.

Brown, B. B. (1990). Peer groups and peer cultures. In S. S. Feldman & G. R. Elliott (Eds.), *At the threshold: The developing adolescent* (pp. 171–196). Cambridge, MA: Harvard University Press.

Brown, I. D., & Groeger, J. A. (1988). Risk perception and decision making during the transition between novice and experienced driver status. *Ergonomics*, **31**, 585–597.

Byrnes, J. (1988). Formal operations: A systematic reformulation. *Developmental Review*, **8**, 66–87.

Case, R. (1987). The structure and process of intellectual development. *International Journal of Psychology*, **22**, 571–607.

Cavanaugh, J. L., & Perlmutter, M. (1982). Metamemory: A critical examination. *Child Development*, **53**, 11–28.

Chandler, M. (1987). The Othello effect: Essay on the emergence and eclipse of skeptical doubt. *Human Development*, **30**, 137–159.

Clark, M. S., & Fiske, S. T. (Eds.) (1982). *Cognition and affect*. Hillsdale, NJ: Erlbaum.

Colbourn, C. J. (1978). Perceived risk as a determinant of driver behavior. *Accident Analysis and Prevention*, **10**, 131–141.

Colby, A., Kohlberg, L., Gibbs, J., & Lieberman, M. A. (1983). A longitudinal study of moral judgment. *Monographs of the Society for Research in Child Development* (Serial No. 200).

Dickson, G. C. A., & Hutchinson, G. E. (1988). Children's perception of and anticipated responses to risk. *British Journal of Education Psychology*, **58**, 147–151.

diSessa, A. A. (in press). Knowledge in pieces. In G. Forman & P. Pufall (Eds.), *Constructivism in the computer age*. Hillsdale, NJ: Erlbaum.

Dryfoos, J. G. (1990). *Adolescents at risk: Prevalence and prevention*. New York: Oxford University Press.

East, P. L. (1989). Early adolescents' perceived interpersonal risks and benefits: Relations to social support and psychological functioning. *Journal of Early Adolescence*, **9**(4), 374–395.

Einhorn, H. J. (1980). Learning from experience and suboptimal rules in decision making. In T. S. Wallsten (Ed.), *Cogntive processes in choice and decision behavior* (pp. 1–20). Hillsdale, NJ: Erlbaum.

Ellickson, P. L., & Bell, R. M. (1990). Drug prevention in junior high: A multisite longitudinal test. *Science*, **247**, 1299–1305.

Evans, J. St. B. T. (1982). *The psychology of deductive reasoning*. London: Routledge & Kegan Paul.

Fischhoff, B. (1980). For those condemned to study the past: Reflections on historical judgment. In R. A. Shweder & D. W. Fiske (Eds.), *New directions for methodology of behavioral science: Fallible judgment in behavioral research* (pp. 79–93). San Francisco: Jossey-Bass.

Fischhoff, B. (1988). Judgment and decision making. In R. J. Sternberg & E. E. Smith (Eds.), *The psychology of human thought* (pp. 153–187). New York: Cambridge University Press.

Fischhoff, B. (1989) Risk: A guide to controversy. Appendix to National Research Council, *Improving risk communications*. Washington, DC: National Academy Press.

Fischhoff, B. (1991). Value elicitation: Is there anything in there? *American Psychologist*, **46**, 835–847.

Fischhoff, B., & Beyth-Marom, R. (1983). Hypothesis evaluation from a Bayesian perspective. *Psychological Review*, **90**, 239–260.

Fiske, S. T., & Taylor, S. (1990). *Social cognition* (2nd edition). Reading, MA: Addison-Wesley.

Foxman, E. R., Tansuhaj, P. S., & Ekstrom, K. M. (1988). Family members' perceptions of adolescents' influence in family decision making. *Journal of Consumer Research*, **15**, 482–491.

Furby, L., & Fischhoff, B. (in press). Rape self-defense strategies: A review of their effectiveness. *Victimology*.

Furby, L., Fischhoff, B., & Morgan, M. (1990). Preventing rape: How people perceive the options for assault prevention. In E. Viano (Ed.), *The victimology research handbook* (pp. 227–259). New York: Garland Publishing.

Furnham, A. F. (1988). *Lay theories*. London: Pergamon Press.

Gardner, W., Scherer, D., & Tester, M. (1989). Asserting scientific authority: Cognitive development and adolescent legal rights. *American Psychologist*, **44**, 895–902.

Gelman, R., & Ballargeon, R. (1983). A review of some Piagetian concepts. In J. H. Flavell & E. M. Markman (Eds.), *Handbook of child psychology* (Vol. III, pp. 167–230). New York: Wiley.

Gentner, D., & Stevens, A. L. (1983). *Mental models*. Hillsdale, NJ: Erlbaum.

Gilligan, C. (1982). *In a different voice*. Cambridge, MA: Harvard University Press.

Hamburg, B. (1989). *Life skills training: Preventive interventions for early adolescents*. Washington, DC: The Carnegie Council on Adolescent Development.

Harter, S. (1990). Adolescent self and identity development. In S. S. Feldman & G. R. Elliot (Eds.), *At the threshold: The developing adolescent* (pp. 352–387). Cambridge, MA: Harvard University Press.

Hauser, S. T., & Bowlds, M. K. (1990). Stress, coping and adaptation within adolescence: Diversity and resilience. In S. S. Feldman & G. R. Elliott (Eds.), *At the threshold: The developing adolescent* (pp. 388–413). Cambridge, MA: Harvard University Press.

Henrion, M. (1982). *The value of knowing how little you know: The advantages of a probabilistic approach to uncertainty in policy analysis*. Unpublished doctoral dissertation. Carnegie Mellon University, Pittsburgh, PA.

Institute of Medicine. (1990). *The second fifty years: Promoting health and preventing disability*. Washington, DC: National Academy Press.

Jacobs-Quadrel, M. (1990). *Elicitation of adolescents' risk perceptions: Qualitative and quantitative dimensions*. Unpublished doctoral dissertation. Carnegie Mellon University, Pittsburgh, PA.

Jeffrey, R. W. (1989). Risk behaviors and health: Contrasting individual and population perspectives. *American Psychologist*, **44**, 1194–1202.

Jonah, B. (Ed.) (1986). Youth and traffic accident risk. *Accident Analysis & Prevention*, **18**(4).

Kahneman, D., Slovic, P., & Tversky, A. (Eds) (1982). *Judgment under uncertainty: Heuristics and biases*. New York: Cambridge University Press.

Kahneman, D., & Tversky, A. (1982). On the study of statistical intuitions. *Cognition*, **11**, 123–141.

Kalmus, D., Lawton, A. I., & Namerow, P. B. (1987). Advantages and disadvantages of pregnancy and contraception: Teenagers' perceptions. *Population & Environment*, **9**(1), 23–40.

Keating, D. P. (1990). Adolescent thinking. In S. S. Feldman & G. R. Elliott (Eds.), *At the threshold: The developing adolescent* (pp. 54–89). Cambridge, MA: Harvard University Press.

Keating, D. P., & Clark, L. V. (1980). Development of physical and social reasoning in adolescence. *Developmental Psychology*, **16**, 23–30.

Kohlberg, L. (1984). *The psychology of moral development*. New York: Harper & Row.

Krimsky S., & Plough, A. (1988). *Environmental hazards*. Dover, MA: Auburn House.

Langer, E. J. (1989). Minding matters: The consequences of mindlessness-mindfulness. In L. Berkowitz (Ed.), *Advances in experimental social psychology* (Vol. 22, pp. 137–173). New York: Academic Press.

Leventhal, H. (1980). Toward a comprehensive theory of emotion. In L. Berkowitz (Ed.), *Advances in experimental social psychology* (Vol. 13, pp. 139–209) New York: Academic Press.

Leventhal, H. (1984). A perceptual-motor theory of emotion. In L. Berkowitz (Ed.), *Advances in experimental social psychology* (Vol. 17, pp. 117–182). New York: Academic Press.

Lewis, H. W. (1990). *Technological risk*. New York: Norton.

Lichtenstein, S., Fischhoff, B., & Phillips, L. D. (1982). Calibration of probabilities: State of the art to 1980. In D. Kahneman, P. Slovic, & A. Tversky (Eds.), *Judgment under uncertainty: Heuristics and biases* (pp. 306–334). New York: Cambridge University Press.

Lichtenstein, S., Slovic, P., & Zink, D. (1969). Effect of instruction in expected value on optimality on gambling decisions. *Journal of Experimental Psychology, 79*, 236–240.

Mann, L., Harmoni, R., & Power, C. (1989). Adolescent decision making: The development of competence. *Journal of Adolescence, 12*, 265–278.

Morgan, M. (1986). Conflict and confusion: What rape prevention experts are telling women. *Sexual Coercion and Assault, 1*(5), 160–168.

Morrison, D. M. (1985). Adolescent contraceptive behavior: A review. *Psychological Bulletin, 98*, 538–568.

Namerow, P. B., Lawton, A. I., & Philliber, S. G. (1987). Teenagers' perceived and actual probabilities of pregnancy. *Adolescence, 22*, 475–485.

National Safety Council (1987). *Accident facts.* Chicago, IL: National Safety Council.

Nisbett, R., & Ross, L. (1980). *Human inference: Strategies and shortcomings of social judgment.* Englewood Cliffs, NJ: Prentice Hall.

Nussbaum, J., & Novick, S. (1982). Alternative frameworks, conceptual conflict and accommodation: Toward a principled teaching strategy. *Instructional Science, 11*, 183–200.

Raiffa, H. (1968). *Decision analysis.* Reading, MA: Addision-Wesley.

Reason, J. (1990). *Human error.* New York: Cambridge University Press.

Robertson, L. S. (1981). Patterns of teenaged driver involvement in fatal motor vehicle crashes: Implications for policy change. *Journal of Health Policy Politics & Law, 6*, 303–314.

Ross, J. A. (1981). Improving adolescent decision-making skills. *Curriculum Inquiry, 11*(3), 279–295.

Russo, J. F., & Schoemaker, P. J. H. (1989). *Decision traps.* New York: Doubleday.

Savin-Williams, R., & Berndt, T. J. (1990). Peer relations during adolescence. In S. S. Feldman & G. R. Elliott (Eds.), *At the threshold: The developing adolescent* (pp. 277–307). Cambridge, MA: Harvard University Press.

Schinke, S. P., & Gilchrist, L. D. (1984). *Life skills counseling with adolescents.* Austin, TX: Pro-ed Publishers.

Schuman, H., & Johnson, M. P. (1976). Attitudes and behavior. *Annual Review of Sociology, 2*, 161–207.

Shantz, C. U. (1983). Social cognition. In J. H. Flavell & E. M. Markman (Eds.), *Handbook of child psychology, III* (pp. 495–555). New York: Wiley.

Siegler, R. (1981). Developmental sequences within and between concepts. *Monographs of the Society for Research in Child Development, 46* (Serial No. 189).

Sinnott, J. D., & Guttmann, D. (1978). Dialectics of decision making in older adults. *Human Development, 21*, 190–200.

Slovic, P. (1987). Perception of risk. *Science, 236*, 280–285.

Smetana, J. (1988). Adolescents' and parents' conceptions of parental authority. *Child Development, 59*, 321–335.

Spivak, G., & Shure, M. B. (1974). *Social adjustment of young children: A cognitive approach to solving real-life problems.* San Francisco: Jossey-Bass.

Starr, C., & Whipple, C. (1980). Risks of risk decisions. *Science, 208*, 114–119.

Statistical Abstract of the United States (1988). Washington, DC: Department of Commerce.

Steinberg, L. (1990). Autonomy, conflict, and harmony in the parent-adolescent relationship. In S. S. Feldman & G. R. Elliott (Eds.), *At the threshold: The developing adolescent* (pp. 255–276). Cambridge, MA: Harvard University Press.

Sussman, S., Dent, C. W., Mestel-Rauch, J., Johnson, C. A., Hansen, W. B., & Flay, B. R.

(1988). Adolescent nonsmokers, triers, and regular smokers' estimates of cigarette smoking prevalence: When do overestimations occur and by whom? *Journal of Applied Social Psychology*, **18**, 537–551.

Suzuki-Slakter, N. S. (1988). Elaboration and metamemory during adolescence. *Contemporary Educational Psychology*, **13**, 206–220.

Torney-Purta, J. (1990). The adolescent in relation to social institutions: Polity, society, and community. In S. S. Feldman & G. R. Elliot (Eds.), *At the threshold: The developing adolescent* (pp. 457–478). Cambridge, MA: Harvard University Press.

Udry, J. R. (1988). Biological predispositions and social control in adolescent sexual behavior. *American Sociological Review*, **53**, 709–722.

von Winterfeldt, D., & Edwards, W. (1982). Cost and payoffs in perceptual research. *Psychological Bulletin*, **91**, 609–622.

von Winterfeldt, D., & Edwards, W. (1986). *Decision analysis and behavioral research.* New York: Cambridge University Press.

Wallach, M. A., & Kogan, N. (1961). Aspects of judgment and decision making: Interrelationships and changes with age. *Behavioral Science*, **6**, 23–36.

Wallerstein, N., & Bernstein, E. (1988). Empowerment education: Freire's ideas adapted to health education. *Health Education Quarterly*, **15**, 379–394.

Watson, S., & Buede, D. (1987). *Decision synthesis.* New York: Cambridge University Press.

Weinstein, N. (Ed.) (1987). *Taking care: Understanding and encouraging self-protective behavior.* New York: Cambridge University Press.

Wellman, H. M. (1990). *The child's theory of mind.* Cambridge, MA: MIT Press.

Yates, J. F. (1990). *Judgment and decision making.* Englewood Clifts, NJ: Prentice Hall.

Zuckermann, M. (Ed.) (1979). *Sensation seeking: Beyond the optimal level of arousal.* Hillsdale, NJ: Erlbaum.

Zuckerman, M. (Ed.) (1983) *Biological bases of sensation seeking, impulsivity, and anxiety.* Hillsdale, NJ: Erlbaum.

Chapter 6

Group risk taking: Selected topics

James H. Davis, Tatsuya Kameda, and Mark F. Stasson
University of Illinois, Urbana-Champaign, University of Tokyo, and Virginia Commonwealth University

CONTENTS

Risk-taking Behavior. Edited by J. F. Yates
© 1992 John Wiley & Sons Ltd

INTRODUCTION

Making decisions involving risk is prominent among the many chores task-oriented small groups are assigned to perform. The idea of risk taking generally implies a choice among alternative courses of action, the presence of some uncertainty, and that something can be lost—or at least not gained (cf. Chapter 1). Some group decisions are advisory (e.g. to organizational or institutional officers), while others are themselves decisive (e.g. petit juries). Boards, panels, committees, and commissions charged with arriving at a single decision, report, solution, etc., are widespread, and it is perhaps instructive to ask why this might be so, when so many actions could in principle have been taken by an "individual-in-charge." In short, what functions do decision-making groups serve, and how well do they serve them?

We will restrict our attention here to groups required to reach a consensus on a single collective action. (The term "consensus" is a widely used label for mere agreement on what the group-level decision is to be. As used here, it does not imply anything about the extent of members' current personal preferences, level of agreement or acquiescence, or the nature of the rules, procedures, or processes for producing the collective response.) Thus, not only is the preference of the individual member an important ingredient, but so also is the interpersonal process responsible for pooling, combining, concatenating, or otherwise aggregating these preferences into a collective response. We will also confine our attention to groups ranging from two to a dozen or so members, the typical size range of committees and panels. The similar study of larger assemblies (e.g. town meetings and legislative bodies) represents a rather different social decision environment, and consideration of that general topic lies well outside our focus. Finally, we should observe that a comprehensive review of group risk taking would be roughly comparable to a similar summary of individual risk taking. Neither task could be accomplished in a single chapter. Rather, we address a few topics that have been largely overlooked, or their nature not widely understood (e.g. consensus decisions and the role of aggregation processes in producing the final output).

Why a group rather than an individual?

Conventional wisdom and popular lore suggest that there are at least three categories of reason for assigning a decision task to a group rather than to an individual:

1. Increased resources (people) imply potential improvement in task performance that can include such things as increasing the probability of a correct response, maximizing some return, reducing error, minimizing loss, and so on. In general, the idea is to enhance the output in one way or another.
2. Group interaction permits "social value enhancement" that can include a variety of extra-decisional considerations, ranging from a respectful recognition of abstract democratic values to very practical aims. Prominent among the latter are subsequent increases in acceptability of the group's decision and likely implementation through the heightened commitment of members or interested constituents. Observe that group decision performance itself is not the primary issue.
3. A group member has the potential to diffuse the risk on those tasks that are subject to some kind of loss, in that "we lose" can be substituted for "I lose;" the example of insurance is widely appreciated, and anecdotes abound about the difficulties in fixing the blame for group decisions gone bad.

The first category above, *task performance considerations*, represents the major thrust of this chapter, and those topics will occupy most of the discussion to follow. The second category above, *social value considerations*, has been studied less, and less systematically, than its apparent importance would imply. The third category above, *risk diffusion considerations*, is virtually uninvestigated. The payoff/loss structure of small decision-making groups is in principle an interesting object of study, and numerous questions stimulated by a variety of actual contexts come easily to mind. Normative models of risk sharing and group decision making not only have valuable potential applications, but imply some fascinating questions for empirical research and eventually descriptive theory of actual group decision behavior (e.g. see Eliashberg & Winkler, 1981). Unfortunately, the sketchy literature on relevant *empirical* research does not constitute a systematic body of knowledge. Aside from occasional studies of "equity theory" (e.g. see Bierhoff, Cohen, & Greenberg, 1986) that do not actually address the behavior of intact groups making risky decisions, and research on coalition behavior and *n*-person games (e.g. see Komorita, 1984; and Kahan & Rapoport, 1984) that does not generally address the decision environment of the consensus-seeking committee or panel at issue here, the most closely relevant research is the study of attributions of responsibility of collective endeavors that generally do not explicitly involve risk management (e.g. see

Leary & Forsyth, 1987). Consequently, this chapter will address only the first two topics above.

The individual-group discontinuity in decision research

The emergence of behavioral decision making as a coherent research area during the last 30 years has been a major development. This close relationship with other disciplines, indeed an earlier developmental association with them, is evident in vocabulary, concepts, and even research problems addressed. For example, while human decision processes are more general than can be accommodated by gambling and economic metaphors that are so widely familiar, such notions as expected value, utility, risk, and so on are essential to a comprehensive understanding of what is known about individual judgment and choice. Research on *group* decision making, on the other hand, has its origins largely within social psychology, and developed primarily out of a century-long research tradition that was generally concerned more with interpersonal processes and social relations within small task-oriented groups than with performance of the task *per se*. Even research that closely focused on the group decision did not often follow the conceptual paths familiar from individual judgment and decision research (cf. Kameda & Davis, 1990, for a similar argument).

One consequence of the discontinuity imposed by different origins is a degree of conceptual confusion; some theoretical notions (e.g. "risk") are used rather differently in individual and group decision-making research. In general, much of the accumulated empirical knowledge about small group performance, including risk taking, does not quite seem to match the questions decision researchers studying individuals have tended to ask. These themes will recur during later discussions, but it is instructive now to summarize two categories of "discontinuity problems."

Decision task structure

Decision problems used in small group research are likely to be poorly defined in comparison to those used in individual decision research. For example, decision alternatives are often not clearly distinguished, and the explicit nature of uncertainty or risk is often not well characterized, even in principle. (See Weber, 1988, for a concise discussion of risk conceptions and risk perception characteristic of various approaches to traditional decision research problems.) This problem may have arisen as a side-effect of attempts to mimic natural decision-making group environments, especially when attention was largely confined to interpersonal relations. Moreover, actual groups in existing organizations and institutions are often assigned the job of studying, formulating, and attacking problems precisely *because* they are ill-defined and ambiguous. In other words, high-fidelity group decision environments are understandably attractive objects of study, but sufficiently refined research paradigms are often lacking.

Interpersonal payoff-loss structure

As noted earlier, individuals are interlinked to some degree as recognized members of a group, and the nature of a shared responsibility for the outcome may itself be an important influence on group actions and interaction. Generally, this has no counterpart in individual decision research, although individuals may also have social, organizational, or institutional responsibilities and constraints implied by the setting. Also, like some individual decision environments, the group decision may be advisory, and consequent payoffs/losses for members may be remote, deferred, or indirect (e.g. petit juries, granting agency advisory panels, etc.). Clearly, research on individual behavior in the face of a decision task entailing risk may not be an accurate guide to group behavior in a similar context.

Overview

We will first discuss selected topics in research on *ad hoc* groups, teams, or committees that have been temporarily formed to address a particular goal or task. Then we will discuss the "mere aggregation" techniques that have sometimes been proposed to engineer more efficient, higher quality, more accurate, or somehow better group performance in the face of risk. Finally, we will summarize the small literature of empirical research on long-term groups facing risky decisions.

RISKY DECISIONS AND *AD HOC* GROUPS

Task-oriented groups that have been assembled solely or largely for the purpose of reaching a consensus decision on a particular task are surprisingly ubiquitous in society. Juries are carefully sampled aggregations that have a particular, and uniquely important, task and are then disbanded. Campus promotion and tenure committees decide a sequence of cases, and have no further function. Granting agency panels have a brief life; groups of experts who may be only marginally acquainted recommend disbursements of large monetary sums to peers after discussions lasting minutes to hours over the course of only a few days. Such decisions, whether decisive or advisory, may not immediately put the members themselves directly at risk; only derivatively and in the long run, perhaps, is there potentially some kind of personal loss, in one kind of coin or another. The important point is that *ad hoc* groups are pervasive and make some of the most important of society's decisions. Sometimes composed of experts (e.g. some judgmental forecasting groups) and sometimes composed of amateurs (e.g. petit juries) these consensus-seeking groups are widely thought to represent superior decision making mechanisms, as discussed earlier.

Task performance considerations

Conventional wisdom and the case of the "risky shift"

While conventional wisdom has long suggested that groups produce "better" decisions than individuals, there has also existed the notion that groups produce prudent but unexceptional decisions, relative to individuals. Consensus action generally requires compromise among disparate preferences of individuals or factions, and this leads to the search for some common denominator, or middle-ground. The compelling intuition, then, has been that decision-making groups unlike individuals reluctantly "take chances," and generally avoid extremes. Thus, a group decision inclines to some kind of central tendency of member preferences; individuals, not groups, strike out in bold new directions.

The discovery that groups were on the average *more* willing than individuals to "take a risk" was thus surprisingly counterintuitive, and perhaps disturbing as well (Stoner, 1961; Wallach, Kogan, & Bem, 1962). A flurry of studies replicated the basic effect, which came to receive the engaging label "risky shift,' and extended the research effort to a variety of different settings (see the review by Dion, Baron, & Miller, 1970). The prototypical experimental setup was deceptively simple. A small set of subjects privately completed a questionnaire composed of "choice dilemma items." A choice dilemma is a familiar social situation in which a central figure is confronted with two behavioral alterna-tives, one of which (the "riskier" choice) has a highly but apparently unlikely desirable outcome. Subjects indicate privately the *minimum* probabilities (1 in 10; 3 in 10;...; 10 in 10) that can prevail for them to be willing to advise the central character in the dilemma to choose the more desirable but apparently riskier alternative. (Choice dilemma examples are given in Table 6.1; Wallach, Kogan, & Bem, 1962; also see the discussion in Chapter 4, pp. 109–110, by Bromiley & Curley.) The set of subjects is then required to act as a group; they are to discuss each item freely and thoroughly, and reach a consensus decision.

For a decade and a half, empirical studies generally demonstrated a risky shift with a variety of subject populations and in a number of different contexts. Perhaps unsurprisingly, ex-members' personal inclinations to risk taking (as defined by lower probability endorsement) had also been increased by the group action, although they were generally less extreme than the preceding group-level consensus endorsement. (See Kerr *et al.*, 1975, for a discussion of the average individual-group-individual relationship.) Between-subjects designs typically produced somewhat reduced shifts, and discussion without consensus somewhat

Table 6.1.   Examples of choice dilemma items. The first two tend to result in "cautious shifts."

---

1. A captain of a college football team, in the final seconds of a game with the college's traditional rival, may choose a play that is almost certain to produce a tie score, or a more risky play that would lead to sure victory if successful, sure defeat if not.

2. A low ranked participant in a national chess tournament, playing an early match with the top-favored man, has the choice of attempting or not trying a deceptive but risky maneuver which might lead to quick victory if successful or almost certain defeat if it fails.

3. The president of an American corporation which is about to expand may build a new plant in the United States where returns on the investment would be moderate, or may decide to build in a foreign country with an unstable political history where, however, returns on the investment would be very high.

4. An engaged couple must decide, in the face of recent arguments suggesting some sharp differences of opinion, whether or not to get married. Discussions with a marriage counselor indicate that a happy marriage, while possible, would not be assured.

Source: From Wallach, Kogan, & Bem (1962). Copyright © 1962 by the American Psychological Association. Reproduced with permission.

further reduced the effects among ex-members. (See Dion, Baron, & Miller, 1970, and Myers & Lamm, 1976, for relevant reviews of this voluminous literature.) Attention was largely confined to risk-taking proclivities of individuals, and explanations of the risky shift focused likewise on risk perception and individual opinion change. Indeed, Kogan and Wallach's (1964) preliminary research had addressed the relationship between individual risk-taking behavior, and cognitive and personality factors.

Initial explanations emphasized the *diffusion of responsibility* for the decision that was possible in groups. Such an explanation has considerable intuitive appeal, and easily meshes with the idea of spreading the risk after the fashion of "insurance," a potential asset of groups discussed earlier. However, Nordhoy (1962) and Stoner (1968) reported observing *cautious* shifts on some other choice dilemma items. That is, average group decisions could shift in the opposite (cautious) direction, relative to individuals, in that *higher* probability of success endorsements characterized group decisions on these items. Indeed, it turned out that choice dilemma items existed that routinely produced risky, cautious, or even no significant directional shifts. (In Table 6.1, items 1 & 2 tend to risky shifts, and 3 & 4 tend to cautious shifts.)

We will not take the space here to relate the details of the empirical literature, or the ups and downs of the race to explain risky/cautious shifts—ultimately labeled *choice shifts* in order to accommodate changes toward either risky or cautious extremes. Rather, we shall focus on later theoretical developments. In the end, a textbook summary (Brown, 1965, 1986) offered an explanation in passing that there exists a cultural value for "taking a risk;" when members of a group discover during discussion that others are on the average just as risk-prone (extreme) as they, there is a tendency to revise ratings of personal risk preferences in the valued direction. Thus, when the group consensus is reached it is based on the members' revised probability inclinations—new positions that are riskier. The explanation quickly gained popularity, perhaps because it was lodged at the individual level; engaged familiar social comparison notions (Festinger, 1954); and, most of all, could be revised to accommodate shifts in the opposite (cautious) direction with the simple amendment that the content of some items engaged social values promoting risk, some items engaged caution, and some items did neither. And there the theoretical matter rested as empirical research interest in the choice shift waned. Parenthetically, we should note that, at about the same time, French university students were discovered to express, on the average, more extreme attitudinal judgments following group discussion then they had expressed previously (Moscovici & Zavalloni, 1969; also see Nemeth, 1986). Rather awkwardly labeled "attitude polarization," this surprising finding also had important implications for risky decision making by individuals. For some (e.g. Lamm & Myers, 1978; Myers & Lamm, 1976), the attitude polarization phenomenon associated with individual members seemed to "explain" shifts in risk taking at the group level. Yet, the question remained unanswered as to why discussion changes individuals toward one extreme, toward the other, or toward neither. Thus, it is not clear what has been explained, and it is not clear which of the two "effects" (choice shifts and polarizations) is cause and which is consequence—or some of both. We will not pursue further the notion of member polarization as an explanation of group-level choice shifts.

The decline of interest in investigating the parameters of group risk taking was unfortunate in at least three respects:

First, in practice, small groups continue to make important decisions—albeit not always for reasons having to do with decision quality—ranging from cabinets and parole boards (where any associated risk involves others besides the decision makers) to investment clubs and air crews (where the risk is quite personal). Decision moderation through group interaction *per se* is still intuitively compelling, and few procedural safeguards have been developed to control interaction, voting, agenda construction, and so on that might influence the magnitude of any immoderate (extremity) shifts. Procedure-targeted research would have considerable practical appeal, especially in heavily rule-guided settings—petit juries, military courts, tenure committees, and the like. In short, the conventional wisdom persists that group decisions are generally moderate rather than extreme, despite such contrary evidence as we have discussed above.

Second, there are theoretical approaches that, while not necessarily in conflict with theoretical notions described above, are generally somewhat more explicit, parsimonious, and general, but which do not assign risk the same theoretical role. These models tend to emphasize interpersonal information pooling or aggregation (e.g. Davis, 1982; Grofman & Owen, 1986; Penrod & Hastie, 1979, and Stasser, 1988). A number of research questions follow from these notions, but have yet to be addressed.

Third, in general, group risk-taking research focused heavily on the structurally ambiguous "choice dilemma" task. However, there exist a variety of experimental tasks after the fashion of individual decision research that permit greater experimental control, and potentially allow exploration of richer decision environments. The latter two points (information-pooling models and various kinds of research tasks) will be considered in the course of the following discussion.

Uncertain events, choices, and bets   The choice dilemma item has the virtue of mundane realism in that the choice presented is imbedded within an engaging social puzzle. A choice must be made between two alternatives. One alternative contains an apparently more desirable outcome than the outcomes associated with the other alternative, which has as well at least one outcome of very low desirability. The probability of the highly desirable outcome of the first alternative is implied to be naturally very low, whereas the lower valued outcome of the second alternative has a very high probability. It is the subject's "probability-setting" in order to choose the first alternative that is the measure of risk taking. Comparisons with other decision studies are impeded because there is no clear means of evaluating the worth or utility of outcomes, or the probabilities of outcomes (aside from the unusual odds-setting response). Moreover, the number and structure of outcomes per decision alternative is often unclear—and apparently variable across items.

Not surprisingly, several studies of group risk taking undertook to remedy these ambiguities of task and setting with decision problems that may have lacked the appeal of the well-turned story, but offered a more controlled task and setting (e.g. Davis, Hoppe, & Hornseth, 1968; Johnson & Davis, 1972; Zajonc *et al.*, 1968). These investigations employed a variety of tasks, but the primary feature was that they were devoid of overt social content, explicitly controlled the probability (relative frequencies) of events, and quantified the outcome in money, points, successes, or the like. The important finding overall was that group decisions under risk or uncertainty could indeed become more extreme on the average than individual decisions, essentially supporting the choice shift results observed with choice dilemma items. Again, even without social content to engage "cultural values," there was an increased extremity of the group response, relative to individuals' responses. Such a result not only enhances the practical importance of the empirical phenomenon but weakens the likely role of norm-value explanations that depend on social content in the task.

Information pooling, aggregation, and consensus   Although the content of some decision tasks offered no apparent social content for discussion, social values *could* guide discussion—exemplified perhaps by norms about how groups should arrive at consensus, defining a "fair" scheme, or by prescribing an appropriate procedural rule. Zajonc (1966; Smoke & Zajonc, 1962) discussed, for the two-alterantive case, how mere aggregation processes could produce individual-group differences—the discrepancy that after all lies at the heart of the choice shift. Highly versatile pooling/aggregation models have been generalized to the *n*-alternative case (Davis, 1973, 1982; Stasser, Kerr, & Davis, 1989; Thomas & Fink, 1961), and form the basis for an illustrative analysis of the choice shift in individual-group risk taking discussed below.

An illustrative example   A duplex bet is a compound event; the probability and amount to be won (first element) is separate from and independent of the probability and amount to be lost (second element). A typical display contains two pie graphs. One of these shows an area representing the probability to win some amount of money, while the remaining area represents the probability of winning nothing; the second pie similarly portrays an area proportional to the probability of losing some fixed amount and the remainder the probability of losing nothing. (See Slovic, 1969, for a more detailed description and statistical properties.) Davis *et al.* (1974) instructed independent samples of individuals and four-person groups to make decisions about the attractiveness of each of a set of duplex bets, having a range of expected values (in money) from low negative amounts to large positive values. (See Chapters 1 and 2 for discussions of expected value.) Not only were individual subjects' mean attractiveness ratings highly correlated with expected value ($r = 0.93$), but the frequency distributions of individual ratings were consistently skewed—the bulk of the ratings were in the more attractive direction (negatively skewed) for large (positive) expected values, and toward the unattractive end of the scale (positively skewed) for small (negative) expected values. Rating distributions for bets with expected values near zero tended to be symmetric around the middle of the scale. Group distributions tended to be more extreme; individual level perturbations tended to be exaggerated at the group level. That is to say, the group decision distributions were more skewed than the individual distributions; symmetric distributions (bets with near zero expected values) were more leptokurtic for groups than individuals. (See Ono *et al.*, 1988, for a more extensive simulation illustrating how distributional perturbations at a lower level can be exaggerated at a higher level by familiar preference aggregation processes.)

Suppose that deciding collectively under risk or uncertainty depends upon achieving a majority or a plurality of some sort. Such dominant factions not only possess normative influence in democratic societies, but simple coercion, force, or information can underwrite their power to determine the group decision. Thus, a majority or plurality, if it exists, is likely to determine with high probability the group consensus in the *ad hoc*, freely interacting groups we are considering. In this application, the group is hypothesized to choose, with probability near one, that rating alternative favored by a majority, otherwise alternatives are chosen in proportion to the faction size favoring them.

Predictions and observed group decision distributions from the article by Davis *et al.* (1974) are given in Figures 6.1 and 6.2 in cumulative form. Clearly, predictions are consistent with data from groups rating duplex bets. Groups "shifted" in direction and degree roughly in keeping with the skewness of individual-level response distributions, themselves dependent on the EVs of the bets. A majority process implies a strong role for faction size in achieving the final consensus. It thus seems that as important as task parameters (EV, cultural values, etc.) may be in influencing individual preferences, a majority social consensus process may at the least be a sufficient rule to predict consensus decisions. Of course, the subjects in this and most such experiments cannot report with complete accuracy the precise social decision scheme used to determine consensus—such as the required order of majority (3/4, 2/3, simple, etc.). However, ex-member self-reports containing such phrases as "majority," "strong majority," "everyone had to agree" (unanimity), or "anybody's idea was ok" (equiprobability) tend to approximate the consensus process inferred through the social decision scheme model.

A parallel example (Davis & Hinsz, 1982) can be constructed by composing a sample of groups with members arrayed in known factions, and counting the group decision as established by majorities, etc. See Table 6.2. In this simulation example, group members were assumed to obey a majority rule, by simply acquiescing to a majority, if one existed. A shift in mean responses from individual to group judgments is the result. Whether members truly change their personal preferences before or after consensus, or never, is irrelevant to the demonstration of this effect.

Concluding remarks

It is perhaps ironic that the major line of research to address specifically group risk taking may have overemphasized the notion of risk in the social consensus process at the expense of routine normative notions guiding members to agreement. But the implications of plurality/majority processes for aggregate risk taking (or risk reduction) are considerable. In retrospect, the heavy use of the choice dilemma scenario with its structural impediments to sharp experimental control may have contributed to this emphasis on risk rather than social consensus process. However, the subsequent experiments, with decision tasks devoid of social content, also showed group shifts, suggesting at least the sufficiency of the social combination process to produce the counterintuitive

174

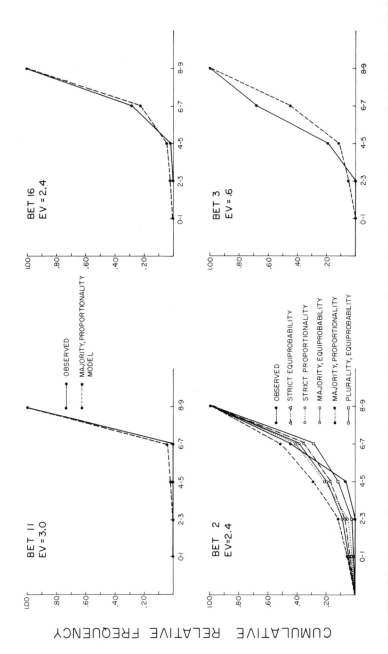

175

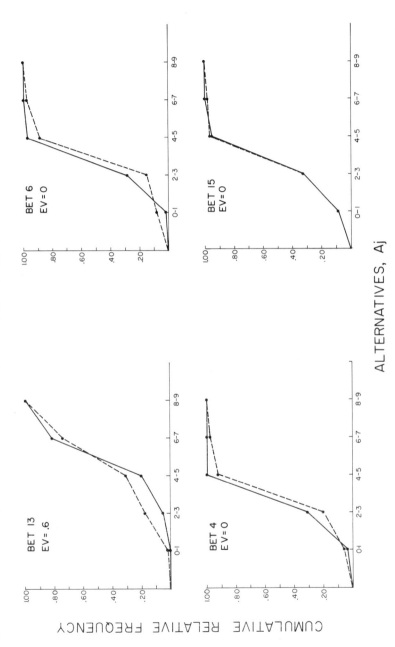

Figure 6.1. Cumulative relative frequency observed at Period 2 for male group preferences (solid curve) for the alternatives, A_j, on each bet and predictions (broken curve) under the majority-proportionality model. (Predictions under several other social decision scheme models are illustrated for Bet 2.) (From Davis *et al.*, 1974. Copyright © 1974 the American Psychological Association. Reproduced by permission of the authors and the American Psychological Association.)

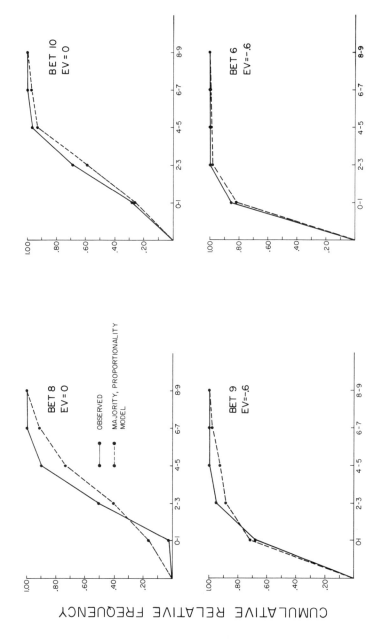

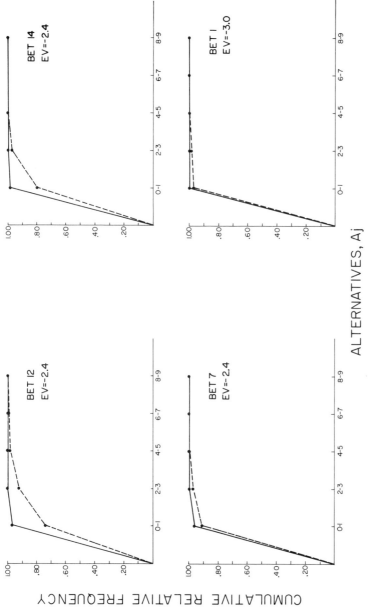

Figure 6.2. Cumulative relative frequency observed at Period 2 for male group preferences (solid curve) for the alternatives, A_j, on each bet and predictions (broken curve) under the majority-proportionality model. (From Davis *et al.*, 1974. Copyright © 1974 the American Psychological Association. Reproduced by permission of the authors and the American Psychological Association.)

Table 6.2. An example of how a sample of four-person groups, acting on a plurality principle, could produce a "shift" (upward) along a ten-category scale.

Group no.	Prediscussion preference	X, Response category value	X, Members' prediscussion average	$Pl(X)$ Plurality rule choice	$[X_I - Pl(X)]$ Ind.-Gp difference
	1	9			
1	2	8	7.50	8	−0.50
	1	5			
	1	8			
2	2	7	6.25	7	−0.75
	1	3			
	3	6			
3	1	5	5.75	6	−0.25
	2	8			
4	1	6	6.50	8	−1.50
	1	4			
	1	9			
5	2	7	6.50	7	−0.50
	1	3			
	3	7			
6	1	4	6.25	7	−0.75
	2	9			
7	1	7	7.00	9	−2.00
	1	3			
	2	6			
8	1	4	4.75	6	−1.25
	1	3			
	2	7			
9	1	6	6.25	7	−0.75
	1	5			
10	3	8	6.50	8	−1.50
	1	2			
Total/ Average	40		6.325	7.30	−0.975

Source: From Davis & Hinsz (1982). Reproduced by permission of the authors and Academic Press Inc.

individual-group difference familiar to researchers as choice shifts. The important role for personal risk perception of the decision *at the individual level* was demonstrated by the Davis *et al.* experiment in which the necessary skewness in the individual preference distribution (input) was found to be closely dependent on the expected value of the duplex bet.

Finally, it is worth emphasizing again that the choice shift is after all only a group-individual difference on some decision task. (Mere extremity does not imply either more nearly optimal or less than optimal decisions; optimality, as discussed in Chapter 2 by Neumann and Politser, is a separate issue.) Although the formerly intense research effort on what controls the magnitude of this difference (e.g. personal values about risk, attitudes about the decision environment, the group consensus process, etc.) has largely waned, *group* decision making is and is likely to remain popular in organizations and institutions of all kinds. The foregoing discussion implies that group "shifts" and "polarizations" are ubiquitous consequences of familiar consensus processes that routinely aggregate or combine member preferences into a group decision. Unfortunately, the preceding message has sometimes been misread. For example, a recent historical summary (Jones, 1985) viewed the choice shift literature with some suspicion, implying (erroneously) that an "artifact" lay at the root of it. Such a conclusion leads one to anticipate that conventional wisdom may persist in our thinking about group risk taking.

There is not space here to sample further current research emphasizing risk in the performance of task-oriented, *ad hoc* groups. (See the recent literature review of group performance by Levine and Moreland, 1990.) We consider next the social and personal reactions of group members involved in a consensus decision with which some risk is associated.

Social value considerations

Earlier we remarked that a second important feature of groups making decisions was the potential enhancement of members' confidence, satisfaction, and other personal, task-related reactions that may be useful in the later implementation or wider acceptance of the decision. Of course, the value of the increased commitment hinges upon the ultimate wisdom of the decision itself. For example, the past two decades have seen a large growth in the literature documenting a variety of "biases" and systematic errors in individual decisions involving risk (e.g. see Zeckhauser & Viscusi, 1990). We have just seen that freely interacting groups tend to be described by consensus processes that can exaggerate individual inclinations, at least when these inclinations constitute a trend at the individual level (e.g. a skewed individual preference distribution). It is not yet clear that the cognitive illusions, apparently due to faulty heuristics (e.g. see Kahneman, Slovic, & Tversky, 1982) employed by the individual, also mark group decisions in a similar way. The apparently low rate of some decision biases may mean that these effects do not survive group discussion and consensus procedures that, as we have discussed above, tend to exaggerate majority and suppress minority positions. Some scattered studies with groups (e.g. Argote, Devadas, & Melone, 1990; Argote, Seabright, & Dyer, 1986; Stasson *et al.*, 1988) suggest that individual level cognitive biases also exist in group judgments, but the research record is not yet sufficiently convincing.

However, our concern here is with the personal reactions of group members that would contribute to the probability of individuals adhering to the decision in which they had participated. Does group-level action contribute to personal feelings of decision confidence, satisfaction, "correctness," or the like? Again, the relevant research literature is surprisingly small, but the consistent answer over a variety of decision environments and tasks is "yes."

For example, Sniezek and Henry (1989) have found group members on the average to have more confidence in their group's decision than do individuals in their own similar responses. Even in quite different settings, where the risk to the decision maker is indirect at best, ex-members of a mock jury have generally been observed (e.g. Davis *et al.*, 1990) to be more satisfied with the proceedings (mock trial and verdict) and judge it fairer than subjects who similarly contemplated a mock trial and made a personal decision without an opportunity to reach a consensus verdict with others. Finally, McGuire, Kiesler, and Siegel (1987), using a task that emphasized risk in a more unambiguous fashion than the research just cited, observed that post-group members' confidence ratings about the decision were higher on the average than pre-group individuals' ratings; results were essentially the same, whether the decision problem was formulated in terms of gains or losses.

Information about subsequent implementation of a decision by ex-members relative to individuals who were never in groups is less direct, at least in the sense of clearly associated risk. However, perhaps the most dramatic finding from Lewin's (1958) classic studies directed at changing attitudes about unpopular cuts of meat during wartime was not that subjects from "group discussion" conditions reacted more favorably than passive individuals hearing a lecture, but that the former actually served the meats subsequently at a higher rate. It is now sometimes forgotten that the group did not reach a consensus decision, in contrast to the format we have been considering, although many other features were largely present during discussion. Although some of the early explanations were later modified (e.g. Pelz, 1958), and experimental procedures were "loose" by current standards, there can be little doubt of strong group-induced commitment effects. (See Kiesler, 1971, for a more comprehensive discussion of socially-induced commitment.) Unfortunately, subsequent research did not address the *group* basis of these early findings, and turned to individual-centered questions; the lack of group decision research that directly addresses risk and risk taking is among the many conceptual casualities of that change in direction. It seems likely that on the average the group making decisions in the face of risk may bind members to a subsequent course of action more strongly than when the decision is made by isolated individuals. The basic mechanisms responsible for commitment as discussed here have never been thoroughly explored, and the parameters controlling duration, strength, etc., of the effort remain largely unmapped.

Concluding remarks

A group decision among risky alternatives may not necessarily be "best." Just as that consensus outcome must be evaluated against applicable criteria, so must the value of the apparent increase in member commitment, confidence, satisfaction, etc., be judged against relevant criteria. The ex-member commitment, satisfaction, and the like that are associated with group decision making relative to individuals can sometimes be an asset, but can also serve as an impediment, depending upon circumstances. For example, confidence in a group-based decision may discourage subsequent reevaluation, even when subsequent events would call for it—e.g. new information that the potential cost is greater, a moderate hazard becomes a more serious one, etc. In general, it would be useful to exploit the virtues of a group (e.g. greater resources, kinds of information, and redundancy than the individual), while minimizing the difficulties.

MERE AGGREGATION OF INDIVIDUAL PREFERENCES AND CHOICES, AND THE ENGINEERING OF GROUP DECISIONS

It is evident from the foregoing discussion that group decisions are not necessarily optimal. In fact, decision making by small groups, such as we are considering, is generally suboptimal or inefficient, relative to plausible normative base lines (e.g. see Brown, 1988; Davis, 1982; Hastie, 1986; McGrath, 1984; Steiner, 1972). In addition to the side-effects of the consensus process such as we have already discussed, there are a number of other "process loss" factors (Steiner, 1972) that potentially can contribute to deviations from optimality in face-to-face discussion. Conformity pressures (e.g. Asch, 1956; Kiesler & Kiesler, 1969; Sherif, 1935, 1958), social loafing (Harkins & Szymanski, 1989; Latané, Williams, & Harkins, 1977), and (inappropriate) facilitation/inhibition effects (Zajonc, 1965, 1980) are among the more salient of such factors catalogued to date. However, groups are likely to remain popular decision-making instruments for a variety of reasons, ranging from their capacity to represent different constituencies to their capacity to instill confidence, commitment, etc., discussed in the preceding section. Finally, in the face of risk, groups are particularly appealing as a means of diffusing responsibility and a source of social support to allay discomfort.

In some decision environments, corrective procedures might involve the "engineering" of the group interaction process, or even eliminating regular social interaction altogether, while retaining multiple sources of input. Inasmuch as the study of group risk taking spans many disciplines, including social psychology, welfare economics, political science, operations research, and management science, it is important to note that the term "group" or "collective" seems to have different meanings and operationalizations across these different disciplines. The focus of this section is on research in a "group" which has no or only a limited amount of interaction among its members. In other words, the group we address here is "nominal" in the sense that behavioral interdependence among group members is either absent or artificially structured according to a format designed to promote good decisions.

Aggregation methods

As Ferrell (1985) has pointed out, there appear to be two basic aggregation methods falling in the "nominal" group category—mathematical and quasi-behavioral. Mathematical aggregation refers to arithmetic (e.g. averaging) or formal (e.g. voting) summarization of individual opinions, a major concern in areas such as social choice (e.g. Fishburn, 1973) and expert judgmental forecasting (e.g. Bates & Granger, 1969). In this tradition, a group is literally nominal, a mere collection of individual choices; its members typically do not interact, and the focus is on developing a system that best aggregates the opinions of these "isolated" independent individuals. In contrast, quasi-behavioral aggregation procedures such as the Delphi method (Dalkey, 1969, 1972a) or the nominal group technique (Delbecq, Van de Ven, & Gustafson, 1975), involve controlled group interaction; these methods attempt to structure or engineer group interaction so that a consensus is reached without undesirable social byproducts (e.g. conformity pressures). The essential idea is that such engineered groups, relative to unstructured groups, offer a means of managing risk and reaching a decision that more closely approaches the normatively optimal, while retaining a collective character that may have been mandated by extra-task considerations (e.g. members represent constituencies).

Mathematical aggregation

Social choice theory   One of the most important mathematical aggregation approaches has been studied in the framework of *social choice* (e.g. Arrow, 1951, 1963; Black, 1958; Fishburn, 1973). Although social choice research is not strictly concerned with risky choices, the approach is applicable to a variety of group decisions under risk.

Social choice theory deals with evaluations of formal decision mechanisms (e.g. voting rules, aggregation procedures) from the perspective of various democratic values. Arrow's famous "Impossibility Theorem" shows that given a set of individually ordered preferences (more than two alternatives), there is no decision function mapping the individual preferences to a group decision that satisfies a set of seemingly reasonably "democratic" assumptions. (For detailed summaries of social choice theory, see Fishburn, 1973; Sen, 1979; see also Brams & Fishburn, 1982, for a discussion of "approval voting," as a novel voting scheme with interesting properties.) In other words, familiar decision schemes that are commonly used in group decision situations involving uncertainty, such as a summing of ranks or majority rule, are not in general consistent with these assumptions, and have the potential to yield paradoxical outcomes in some cases.

Notice that Arrow's theorem considers only the order of individual preferences for a set of alternatives (i.e. *ordinal* utility). Harsanyi (1955) expanded the approach by introducing the notion of *cardinal* utility (i.e. individual preferences are assumed to be measurable on interval scales; thus strength of preferences is considered). Given cardinal utility functions, Keeney (1976) showed that only the weighted linear combination of individual utilities provides an optimal group decision under uncertainty. The weights are determined by the importance of each individual in the group and a scaling factor (cf. Brock, 1980), and the linear combination of individual utilities by these weights is consistent with a set of assumptions comparable to Arrow's. In practice, the definition and estimation of individual importance weights have yet to be worked out. Thus, if we can accept the notion of cardinal utility, the weighted linear combination is satisfactory as a democratic social decision scheme (see Harsanyi, 1977, for discussions related to ordinal vs cardinal utilities).

It should be evident from the foregoing discussion that the criterion for an optimal group decision here includes *democratic values* that the decision process represents to the group/collective. Of course, what is democratic is to some extent an open question, and emphases differ across theoreticians. In Arrow's framework, the major emphasis is placed on a criterion of Pareto optimality. (The Pareto principle implies that if at least one member of the group prefers x to y, with the others being indifferent between them, then the group should prefer x to y in its corporate judgment.) In contrast, other researchers (e.g. Keeney & Kirkwood, 1975; Keeney & Raiffa, 1976) have pointed out that consideration of Pareto optimality alone fails to consider the notion of "equity" or "fairness" in group decisions. For example, suppose that there are two alternatives, one yielding totally unequitable allocations of outcomes among members and the other fairly equitable allocations. On these occasions, it is sometimes the case that the Pareto principle alone does not provide a group decision, even though our ordinary inclination is toward the choice of the latter. Thus, Keeney and others emphasize the necessity of considering equity as one of the criteria for democratic group decision making (see Kirkwood, 1979, for detailed discussion of conflicts between Pareto optimality and equity; see also Eliashberg & Winkler, 1981, for a recent attempt to integrate these two criteria).

In summary, social choice theory is normative theory and addresses the combination or aggregation of individual preferences into a group decision. A social decision function here is a "single-step" function which directly connects the distribution of individual preferences to a group choice. In contrast, Bayesian group decision theory, which is to be examined below, assumes a two-step aggregation processes.

Bayesian group decision theory Recall that traditional individual decision theory has two major components: (a) the subjective probabilities that represent the individual's assessment of the likelihood of uncertain outcomes and (b) the von Neumann–Morgenstern (1947) utility functions expressing the individual's risk attitudes and preferences for various outcomes. The theory prescribes that individuals should choose an alternative that maximizes individual expected utility (cf. Chapter 2). Likewise, Bayesian *group* decision theory assumes two corresponding aggregation processes before rendering a final group choice—aggregation of individual probability assessments into group probability estimates and aggregation of individual utility functions into a group utility function. These two components are then combined to choose the best alternative for the group, one that maximizes the group's expected utility (cf. Bordley, 1982a, 1982b; Keeney & Kirkwood, 1975).

The issue of how to combine individual utility functions to a group utility function was discussed above (e.g. Harsanyi, 1955, 1977; Keeney, 1976; Keeney & Raiffa, 1976). Therefore, we now focus on the combination of individual probability assessments into group probability estimates. This problem of how to aggregate several quantitative estimates into a single quantity has also been a major concern in research on expert judgmental forecasting. (See the recent reviews by Ferrell, 1985; and Lock, 1987). However, the introduction of probability carries with it the constraints imposed by the laws of probability (e.g. the joint probability of two independent events is the product of probabilites for each event). Dalkey (1972b) showed that there is no nontrivial function to be used universally to aggregate a set of probability estimates into a single quantity that is itself consistent with the laws of probability.

One approach to avoiding the problem of introducing inconsistencies through aggregation is to assume that each individual assessing probabilities is essentially a Bayesian. That is, the group members are assumed to have revised their prior beliefs into their probability estimates based on evidence in a way suggested by Bayes's theorem. Now the task is to pool the pieces of evidence in order to arrive at the collective posterior probability estimate.

Bordley (1982a, 1982b, 1986) treated this aggregation process as a task for a "benevolent dictator" who is given a set of probability estimates to combine (see Morris, 1974, 1977, 1983, for similar conceptualizations). The dictator weighs each individual estimate differently depending on the member's expertise, calibration (cf. Lichtenstein, Fischhoff, & Phillips, 1982), and degree of interdependence of the judgment with those of other members. In other words, these weights accommodate various kinds of nonprobabilistic information. Bordley suggests that individual probability estimates for a focal event should be combined *multiplicatively*, adjusted by the weight assigned to each member, to yield a group probability estimate. (See Bordley for explicit expressions.) This notion assumes perfect mutual independence of individual judgments. However, this is a rather unrealistic case in most judgmental situations; information each member receives occasionally overlaps and background knowledge of members is often similar. Thus, member judgments are likely to be interrelated (cf. Hogarth, 1978).

Another common approach to aggregation is the weighted linear combination. In other words, the group probability estimate is the *weighted* average of individual probability estimates. Somewhat related to this method, Nitzan and Paroush (1982) and Shapley and Groman (1984) showed that the optimal group decision in a dichotomous choice situation is obtained by a weighted majority rule with the weights proportional to $\log p_i/(1 - p_i)$, where p_i is the judgmental competence/skill of member i. Notice that this result has implications for many important decision situations in actual settings—such as committee decisions concerning investments, where risk is direct; jury decisions, where questions of risk are indirect, etc. A variety of weighting methods have been proposed besides the two procedures just described (e.g. DeGroot, 1974; Makridakis & Winkler, 1983; Newbold & Granger, 1974; Winkler, 1981). However, studies which have compared the various weighting methods have found little difference in their performance, and improvement over the simple average is not large (cf. Staël von Holstein, 1970; Winkler, 1971; Winkler & Makridakis, 1983). Therefore, in practical situations, it would seem that some sort of cost/benefit analysis is useful, prior to implementing a particular weighting scheme.

In summary, a prime interest of Bayesian group decision theory is the optimal aggregation of individual probability judgments into group probability estimates. Of course, optimality here concerns the *accuracy* of the resulting estimates. These estimates are then to be combined with the group utility functions to choose the alternative maximizing group expected utility.

Quasi-behavioral aggregation

In contrast to mathematical methods, the aggregation schemes to be explained below assume actual interaction and communication among group members. However, the interaction here is not completely free but rather is organized or engineered by a predetermined format. As Steiner (1972) concluded, freely interacting groups are rarely observed to achieve their full potential in task performance. Similarly, factors such as over-directive leadership and conformity pressures have also been linked to suboptimal group performance (Janis, 1972). The motivation behind the development of quasi-behavioral aggregation methods was to improve group performance by controlling interaction processes and thereby to eliminate or reduce the effect of various detrimental social factors.

In passing, we should note that both (formal) forecasting and *judgmental* forecasting aim to predict future events, phenomena, etc. While the former generally involves the use of past data (e.g. product market information) as input to a model (e.g. a time-dependent stochastic model), along with other factors (e.g. political/social climate indices) to predict future conditions (e.g future product market share), the latter is based on human judgment. Poor data, lack of good models, instability of conditions, or time pressures are among the many reasons that judgments, perhaps of experts to be sure, are used to predict future conditions. (In practice, decision making involving forecasting is likely to make use of a mixture of statistical model results and human inferences.) Empirical research on judgmental forecasting generally has been rather sporadic until recent years, and then typically associated with very limited practical aims. Random errors and biases associated with human information processing in the face of high uncertainty and potentially substantial losses/gains have made judgmental forecasting a particularly attractive task for small groups (perhaps a mixture of experts), for all the reasons noted at the outset of this chapter.

Delphi technique   The Delphi technique was developed by Dalkey, Helmer, and their colleagues at the Rand Corporation (Dalkey, 1969, 1975). Its original purpose was to improve judgmental forecasting by providing practical procedures for eliciting expert opinions.

A Delphi exercise is composed of multiple iterations. First, the participants are asked to provide individual estimates for the focal quantity (e.g. amounts or probabilities of longitudinal costs/benefits expected by implementing a certain investment plan), and their opinions are collected and summarized in a way that assures the anonymity of each participant. Then a summary of the participants' opinions is circulated among the individuals. The participants are next provided an opportunity to revise their earlier forecasts. This procedure is repeated several times until individual opinions stabilize; that is, members change no more. The median or mean of the set of individual estimates is taken as the final group forecast. (There have, of course, been a great many variations of this basic procedure. See Linstone and Turoff, 1975, for details.)

Dalkey (1969) claimed that the structured interaction described above avoids the "biasing effects of dominant individuals, of irrelevant communications and of group pressure toward conformity" (p. 408). This method has been quite popular in long-range forecasting, and recent applications include forecasts of future economic trends (Cicarelli, 1984), and fringe benefits (Baldwin, 1982), to name a few.

Nominal group technique   Notice that the Delphi technique provides no real opportunity for face-to-face interaction among participants; "group" members exchange only their opinions in a condensed format summarized by another person, and revision of individual opinions takes place without any discussion. (Obviously, the precise nature of the responses to be pooled depends on the decision task—preferences, estimates, solutions, and the like. "Opinion" is often used as a general term in judgmental forecasting, perhaps to capture the uncertain nature of the response environment.) The "nominal group technique" or NGT (Delbecq, Van de Ven, & Gustafson, 1975) aims to provide an enriched communication opportunity.

An NGT meeting begins with individual assessments of the focal problem; individuals first generate ideas concerning the issue without any discussion. Each participant then presents personal ideas in a face-to-face group meeting, and these ideas are recorded. After all the ideas have been recorded, group discussion begins, and is primarily focused on clarifying the stated ideas. Finally, each individual evaluates the priorities of these ideas (e.g. ranks them), and these evaluations are combined mathematically to yield a group judgment (cf. Delbecq, Van de Ven, & Gustafson, 1975; Van de Ven & Delbecq, 1971).

In the context of probability estimation, Gustafson et al. (1973) compared the accuracy of subjective likelihood ratio estimates made under four different conditions: an estimate made by an isolated individual, a Talk-then-Estimate group method (approximating a freely interacting, conventional group), an Estimate-Feedback-Estimate method (Delphi), and an Estimate-Talk-Estimate method (NGT). Results indicated that NGT was superior to the other three techniques in terms of mean errors and variability of estimates. Fischer (1981) reexamined the effectiveness of Gustafson et al.'s four methods using a forecasting task (prediction of students' GPA scores in their freshman year based on personal profiles). He found no significant difference in judgmental accuracy among the conventional, Delphi, and NGT groups. Furthermore, Fischer converted Gustafson et al.'s results from likelihood ratios to probabilities and found that the largest difference between NGT and Delphi was only 0.038—which he concluded was essentially a negligible difference (see also Gough, 1975; Rohrbaugh, 1979, for related findings).

Given these empirical evaluations, it would seem that the claimed superiority of these techniques over conventional groups is yet to be demonstrated. McGrath (1984) has even remarked, "neither one does any better than the freely interacting groups, whose 'deficient' processes these techniques were intended to improve" (p. 75). Other criticisms center on the statistical foundation of the methods (e.g. Sackman, 1975), and their psychological foundations (e.g. Bardecki, 1984; Stewart, 1987). Of course, most of the empirical evaluations available to date have been conducted with a short-term forecasting task judged by nonexpert subjects (college students). Although there is no specific reason to doubt the generality of the research to date, Stewart (1987) has remarked that the usefulness of these studies for evaluating the same methods applied to long-range forecasting by experts may be limited. Further empirical evaluations are certainly needed, based on research that directly delineates assets and liabilities of these "group engineering" techniques for both short- and long-range, and for both novice and expert forecasting.

Concluding remarks

This section has reviewed normative models of group risky decision making in which member interaction is either absent or artificially structured. Of course, the "normative models" discussed here are not prescriptive in the usual sense. Rather, the aim is to circumvent the inefficiencies and errors ascribable to the interpersonal interactions and consensus procedures typical of decision-making groups, and perhaps the individual biases and errors of their members as well. That such efforts and inefficiencies can exist, depending on task and decision environment, is well documented by empirical research. (Recall that the preceding section of this chapter addressed this problem in part, and emphasized the consequences of the members themselves combining their preferences to reach consensus.)

Unfortunately, empirical research addressing the engineering of group risky decision making has been sparse and largely, but not exclusively, limited to judgmental forecasting environments. Although efforts for engineering optimality have to date not been especially encouraging, it seems intuitively compelling that substantial improvements are possible, relative to randomly composed, unorganized, and untrained groups. To be sure, *ad hoc* and minimally organized groups are surprisingly ubiquitous among societal decision makers (e.g. campus tenure committees, petit and grand juries, government panels, etc.). Yet, even enduring groups (e.g. corporate boards, department executive committees, planning commissions) would seem to be particularly good candidates for procedural engineering. Unfortunately, such groups are not easily accessible for study or for testing new procedures and, worst of all, they are distinctive or even unique. Without replicates, the power of statistical analyses of data is greatly constrained, to say the least. Thus, studies of long-term groups tend to be in-depth observations of unique groups, descriptive and intuitive in nature.

LONG-TERM GROUPS

The previous sections summarized research that focused on groups with little "history" or in which there was limited interaction among group members. This section addresses risk taking in "long-term groups," groups that are characterized by a considerable amount of interaction among members over an extended period of time. Unfortunately, there exist few experimental studies of long-term group risky decision making; the expense and practical difficulties involved in studying laboratory groups over long periods of time discourage such an approach. Consequently, most research projects involving long-term groups take place in the field, and usually consist of a case study of a single group's behavior or surveys of institutions and organizations within which smaller units (groups) function.

Groupthink

The best known research involving decision making by enduring groups is probably the series of case studies conducted by Janis (1972, 1982, 1989; Janis & Mann, 1977). These case studies focused on various groups making policy decisions about which there is strong retrospective agreement that the decisions are either very "good" or very "bad." By comparing groups that made poor decisions ("unsuccessful" groups) to groups that made good decisions ("successful" groups), Janis identified several characteristics unique to the "unsuccessful" groups; labeling this state *groupthink*, he concluded it was composed of "a deterioration of mental efficiency, reality testing, and moral judgment that results from in-group pressures." Largely a descriptive notion, according "to the groupthink hypothesis, members of any small cohesive group tend to maintain esprit de corps by unconsciously developing a number of shared illusions and related norms that interfere with critical thinking and reality testing" (Janis, 1982, p. 35). Conclusions that are particularly relevant to group risk taking emphasized that the symptoms of "defensive decision making" can, in part, be traced to inadequate risk assessment and the group's failure to consider all of the risks associated with the chosen plan of action. For example, Janis has argued that the US naval commander and his advisors seriously underestimated the likelihood of an attack on Pearl Harbor prior to WWII, as a result of "groupthink."

The poor risk-management techniques associated with groupthink are not entirely unavoidable, and Janis (1982) has outlined a number of "antecedent conditions" that are assumed to increase the likelihood of a group's suboptimal treatment of risk. Many of these precursors to groupthink involve structural faults or procedural shortcomings in the group decision-making process. For example, groups in which highly cohesive members are combined with a powerful, opinionated leader in a setting that lacks norms specifying explicit decision-making procedures are especially prone to develop "illusions of invulnerability" and a belief in the "inherent morality of the group" (Janis, 1982), conditions that often result in poor risk-management strategies. In addition to deficiencies in group structure and process, Janis further concluded that "situational contexts" such as pressures and stressors from external threats as well as low group esteem resulting from difficulties in reaching consensus or from recent group failure also serve as precursors to faulty risk management.

Fortunately, in addition to studying cases of faulty group decision making, Janis also studied cases in which groups tended to avoid the groupthink syndrome and to make decisions generally thought to be of high quality. These "successful" groups seemed to follow what Janis (1989) called a "vigilant problem-solving" procedure. The first step in this effective decision-making procedure involves a group formulation of the problem or decision task, and in particular one that provides for accurate assessments of possible gains to be attained and of costs and dangers that should be avoided. The second step is to use all the information available for estimating the risks involved in given courses of action. Subsequent steps include evaluating alternative courses of action, attempting to minimize the risk of costly outcomes, and reformulating alternatives to yield a choice with a high probability of success (Janis, 1989).

This vigilant problem-solving procedure is a descriptive model of what groups are capable of doing, but Janis notes that one should be cautious in using this as a prescriptive model. One limitation of the model focuses on the fact that his findings are based exclusively on retrospective studies of particular groups, albeit where the analyst's perceptions are informed by a larger research literature. While the case study yields an abundance of observational information about group decision making, the method is limited in the extent to which the behavior of any one group can be generalized to other groups. Morever, the danger of elevating hindsight to something more is a constant danger.

The case study method often relies on archival data and second- or third-hand accounts of behavior from parties highly involved in the group, data sources that may be far less accurate than direct observations made by an unbiased investigator if that had been possible. Although Janis attempts to overcome these possible criticisms by selecting a number of different types of groups, and by attempting to obtain transcripts or recordings of as many group discussion sessions as possible, one should keep in mind that Janis studied mainly government policy-making groups and that the accounts of group activities obtained may not be as unbiased as researchers would like. Finally, it is worth pointing out that despite their heuristic value, one cannot really draw cause-and-effect inferences from the types of data collected in these case studies, since many other variables remain uncontrolled.

Organizational risk management

In contrast to case-study approaches, Gladstein and Reilly (1985) studied "long term" groups experimentally. Gladstein and Reilly created long-term groups by having second-year MBA students participate in groups that managed companies in a simulated business game lasting six days. Thus, while these groups did not have as much history as most of the groups studied by Janis, the groups did interact for a much longer period of time than the one- or two-hour session typically allotted for *ad hoc* group decision-making experiments. Especially pertinent to the topic at hand, Gladstein and Reilly examined "group decision making under *threat*," in which the level of threat depended, in part, on the probability and costliness of possible losses— features usually associated with definitions of risk. These researchers also examined a second aspect of threat, namely pressures to make decisions within a short period of time.

Gladstein and Reilly hypothesized that the presence of external threats would decrease the chances that groups would follow what Janis (1989) described as a "vigilant problem-solving procedure," because the likelihood of costly losses, as well as time pressures, is likely to cause groups to restrict information processing and concentrate decision control and power within a core faction or subset of group members as suggested by the "threat-rigidity hypothesis" (Staw, Sandelands, & Dutton, 1981). In short, Gladstein and Reilly predicted that the presence of risks or threats would hamper effective group processes.

Gladstein and Reilly's groups were instructed to make decisions for their "company" in a variety of different situations, some of which involved making choices under risky circumstances (impending labor strikes, possible natural disasters) while other situations involved little risk (notification that a payment was due). All groups went through the same series of events in the same order, and dependent variables were assessed following each decision situation period by asking group members to fill out questionnaires designed to measure their perceptions of their group's functioning in that decision period. The results showed that risk level significantly affected the reported amounts of discussion in the groups and information used by the groups in reaching their decisions. Consistent with some of Janis's observations, when operating in riskier decision situations group members felt they had used less of the available information and spent a shorter amount of time discussing the decision to be made. Although these results imply that such groups do not function optimally in risky decision situations, it is important to note that these were the retrospective perceptions of the group members and that the independent variables in this study were confounded with the level of a group's "development," since all groups went through various events in the same order. Despite these shortcomings, it is useful to note that several of Gladstein and Reilly's results seem to coincide with observations made by Janis with regard to the functioning of policy-making groups.

Another example of research on risk management in long-term groups is due to Singh (1986). Although Singh developed and tested a model of organizational decision making somewhat outside the range of the small group under consideration here, it is important to realize that most organizational decisions (or the critical input to decision makers) are made by committees, panels, or boards. Indeed, a significant portion of Singh's data consists of questionnaire responses collected from the members of "top management groups" in 64 US and Canadian organizations. He combined these questionnaire responses with archival data on each organization's size and performance (e.g. after-tax return on net worth). Although Singh formulated and tested a rather extensive model of organization performance, we shall focus here on the results pertinent to organizational risk taking, as reported by members of the organizations' top executive committees.

The most straightforward result is that poorer performing organizations engaged in more risk taking; the managers of poorly performing organizations reported that their management groups were more likely to choose "risky" courses of action (i.e. those that entertain a larger range of possible outcomes, both very positive and very negative outcomes, or involve a relative low probability of success). This finding is consistent with theories of individual decision making, such as prospect theory, which predicts that people experiencing loss (poor performance) become risk-seeking (Kahneman & Tversky, 1979; for an application of this idea to group decision making, see Kameda and Davis, 1990).

However, Singh also found that performance has a *positive*, indirect effect on risk taking. This positive effect of performance on risk taking is mediated by "absorbed slack," the ratio of organizational expenses to sales. Although Singh does not provide a very thorough explanation of this indirect effect, one possible interpretation is that successful performance leads to a variety of increases in expenses and overheads (salary increase, bonuses, better working conditions, more support staff, etc.), and that these increased expenses spur risk taking, perhaps because higher profits are required as a means of justifying or "covering" the increased expenditures. However, we should point out that the model proposed and tested by Singh is a *static* theory, examining correlational data at only one point in time, and that it is not clear how to use the results in a causal interpretation of the *dynamics* of organizations through cycles of adequate and inadequate performance.

In summary, the study by Singh (1986) illustrates that poorly performing organizations may be risk seeking (as one might expect based on individual decision theory), but there is also the possibility that good performance might increase risk taking. While it is not possible to assess directly whether or not the executive groups in poorly performing organizations employed suboptimal risk-management techniques, Singh did find that members of poorly performing organizations reported highly centralized decision-making procedures, something akin to a group "insulating" itself from outside input and opinion, a condition that was cited earlier as contributing to groupthink (Janis, 1982). Thus, it is possible that organizational executive committees may be prone to groupthink during periods of poor performance, but this has not been thoroughly studied.

Concluding remarks

In this section, we have examined risk taking in long-term groups. The research literature is sparse, but generally suggests that group cohesiveness; overly directive leadership; lack of explicit, systematic group decision procedures;

external threats; and a poor performance history may foster either poor risk management or greater risk taking in groups. However, we must emphasize again the small number of empirical studies of long-term groups. Moreover, we have elected not to consider several theoretical models (e.g. Smart & Vertinsky, 1977) that address group risk taking but have not been thoroughly tested empirically.

SUMMARY

This chapter has reviewed several aspects of small group risky decision making. Although we have necessarily been selective in our coverage due to space limitations, we must also acknowledge that the empirical research rate in the general area is not commensurate with the importance and ubiquitousness of the decision-making group. Even small groups are difficult to manage experimentally, and sample size requirements strain available subject pools. Existing panels, boards, and committees rarely welcome observers, and are without replication in any event. Thus, the empirical research rate is not likely to increase in the near future.

Our survey focused primarily upon group decision-making performance, although the social consequences of group discussion and participation were also noted—viz., the increased member commitment and satisfaction that are potentially of value in spurring acceptance and implementation of the group action. Counterintuitive effects of familiar procedures are often especially notable; for example, the discovery of "choice shifts." That the observed distribution of group decisions tends under certain conditions to be more extreme than that observed for individual decisions was both surprising and fraught with practical implications: A group is not necessarily the "protection" against extreme actions that had been anticipated by conventional wisdom. Moreover, the demonstration that familiar and frequently-occurring consensus processes (viz., plurality and majority rules) can produce just such shifts was perhaps even more surprising.

The foregoing survey leads to a somewhat pessimistic view of social process losses and procedure-induced biases that are not confined to *ad hoc* groups. Long-term groups also can be prone to biases (e.g. groupthink). While some corrective engineering efforts have been undertaken (e.g. Delphi or nominal group techniques), these approaches, and their many variations, have not yet been thoroughly evaluated by systematic empirical study; available results to date, however, are not encouraging. On the other hand, one should not lose sight of the many positive features of group decision making, such as heightened satisfaction, implementation-commitment effects, representation of constituents, and the like cited in our review. In addition, however inefficient, when faced with complete ignorance, and no experimenter to calculate predictions from a relevant normative model, a group can offer more information and more (social) information processing than the individual judge or decision maker working alone—something of a "two (or more) heads are better than one" principle. The key would seem to be continued efforts to engineer group procedures for managing interaction, agenda setting, voting/consensus, and the like in order to prevent emergence of a "too many cooks spoil the broth" phenomenon.

ACKNOWLEDGMENTS

The authors are grateful to Reid Hastie, Craig Parks, and Lorne Hulbert for valuable comments on earlier versions of this chapter.

REFERENCES

Argote, L., Devadas, R., & Melone, N. (1990). The base-rate fallacy: Contrasting processes and outcomes of group and individual judgment. *Organizational Behavior and Human Decision Processes*, **16**, 296–310.

Argote, L., Seabright, M. A., & Dyer, L. (1986). Individual versus group use of base-rate and individuating information. *Organizational Performance and Human Decision Processes*, **38**, 65–75.

Arrow, K. J. (1951). *Social choice and individual values.* New York: Wiley.

Arrow, K. J. (1963). *Social choice and individual values.* (2nd ed.). New Haven, CN: Yale University Press.

Asch, S. E. (1956). Studies of independence and conformity: A minority of one against a unanimous majority. *Psychological Monographs*, **70** (Whole No 416).

Baldwin, G. H. (1982). The Delphi technique and the forecasting of specific fringe benefits. *Futures*, **14**, 319–325.

Bardecki, M. J. (1984). Participants' responses to the Delphi method: An attitudinal perspective. *Technological Forecasting and Social Change*, **5**, 281–292.

Bates, J. M., & Granger, C. W. J. (1969). The combination of forecasts. *Operational Research Quarterly*, **20**, 451–468.

Bierhoff, H. W., Cohen, R. L., & Greenberg, J. (Eds.) (1986). *Justice in social relations.* New York: Plenum.

Black, D. (1958). *The theory of committees and elections.* Cambridge: Cambridge University Press, UK.

Bordley, R. F. (1982a). The combination of forecasts: A Bayesian approach. *Journal of the Operations Research Society*, **33**, 171–174.

Bordley, R. F. (1982b). A multiplicative formula for aggregating probability assessments. *Management Science*, **28**, 1137–1148.

Bordley, R. F. (1986). Bayesian group decision theory. In B. Grofman & G. Owen (Eds.), *Information pooling and group decision making* (pp. 49–68). Greenwich, CN: JAI Press.

Brams, S., & Fishburn, P. C. (1982). *Approval voting.* Cambridge, MA: Birkhauser Boston.

Brock, H.W. (1980). The problem of "utility weights" in group preference aggregation. *Operations Research*, **28**, 176–187.

Brown, R. (1965). *Social psychology.* New York: The Free Press.

Brown, R. (1986). *Social psychology: The second edition.* New York: The Free Press.

Brown, R. (1988). *Group processes: Dynamics within and between groups.* Oxford, England: Basil Blackwell.

Cicarelli, J. (1984). The future of economics: A Delphi study. *Forecasting and Social Change,* **25,** 139–157.

Dalkey, N. C. (1969). Analyses from a group opinion study. *Futures,* **1,** 541–551.

Dalkey, N. C. (1972a). *Studies in the quality of life: Delphi and decision making.* Lexington, MA: Lexington Books.

Dalkey, N. C. (1972b). *An impossibility theorem for group probability functions.* Rand Paper P-5683, Santa Monica, CA: Rand Corporation.

Dalkey, N. C. (1975). Toward a theory of group estimation. In H. A. Linstone, & M. Turoff (Eds.), *The Delphi method: Techniques and applications* (pp. 236–257). Reading, MA: Addison-Wesley.

Davis, J. H. (1973). Group decision and social interaction: A theory of social decision schemes. *Psychological Review,* **80,** 97–125.

Davis, J. H. (1982). Social interaction as a combinatorial process in group decision. In H. Brandstatter, J. H. Davis, & G. Stocker-Kreichgauer (Eds.), *Group decision making* (pp. 27–58). London: Academic Press.

Davis, J. H., & Hinsz, V. B. (1982). Current research problems in group performance and group dynamics. In H. Brandstatter, J. Davis & G. Stocker-Kreichgauer (Eds.), *Group decision making* (pp. 1–22). London: Academic Press.

Davis, J. H., Hoppe, R., & Hornseth, J. P. (1968). Risk-taking: Task response patterns and grouping. *Organizational Behavior and Human Performance,* **3,** 124–142.

Davis, J. H., Kerr, N. L., Sussmann, M., & Rissmann, A. K. (1974). Social decision schemes under risk. *Journal of Personality and Social Psychology,* **30,** 248–271.

Davis, J. H., Stasson, M., Zimmerman, S., & Ono, K. (1990). *Periodic polling and group decision along the continuum: An illustration with mock juries and a civil trial.* Unpublished manuscript, Department of Psychology, University of Illinois, Urbana-Champaign.

DeGroot, M. H. (1974). Reaching a consensus. *Journal of the American Statistical Association,* **69,** 118–121.

Delbecq, A. L., Van de Ven, A. H., & Gustafson, D. H. (1975). *Group techniques for program planning.* Glenview, IL: Scott, Foresman.

Dion, D. L., Baron, R. S., & Miller, N. (1970). Why do groups make riskier decisions than individuals? In L. Berkowitz (Ed.), *Advances in experimental social psychology* (pp. 306–378). New York: Academic Press.

Eliashberg, J., & Winkler, R. (1981). Risk-sharing and group decision making. *Management Science,* **27,** 1221–1235.

Ferrell, W R. (1985). Combining individual judgments. In G. Wright (Ed.), *Behavioral decision making* (pp. 111–145). New York and London: Plenum Press.

Festinger, L. (1954). A theory of social comparison processes. *Human Relations,* **7,** 117–140.

Fischer, G. W. (1981). When oracles fail—A comparison of four procedures for aggregating subjective probability forecasts. *Organizational Behavior and Human Performance,* **28,** 96–110.

Fishburn, P. C. (1973). *The theory of social choice.* Princeton, NJ: Princeton University Press.

Gladstein, D. L., & Reilly, N. P. (1985). Group decision making under threat: The tycoon game. *Academy of Management Journal,* **328,** 613–627.

Gough, R. (1975). The effect of group format on aggregate subjective probability distributions. In D. Wendt & C. Vlek (Eds.), *Utility, probability, and human decision making* (pp. 194–234). Dordrecht, Holland: Reidel.

Grofman, B., & Owen, G. (1986). *Information pooling and group decision making.* Greenwich, CN: JAI Press.

Gustafson, D. H., Shukla, R. K., Delbecq, A., & Walster, G. W. (1973). A comparative study of differences in subjective likelihood judgments made by individuals, interacting groups, Delphi groups, and nominal groups. *Organizational Behavior and Human Performance, 9,* 280–291.

Harkins, S. G., & Syzmanski, K. (1989). Social loafing and group evaluation. *Journal of Personality and Social Psychology, 56,* 934–941.

Harsanyi, J. C. (1955). Cardinal welfare, individualistic ethics, and interpersonal comparison of utility. *Journal of Political Economy, 63,* 309–321.

Harsanyi, J. C. (1977). *Rational behavior and bargaining equilibrium in games and social situations.* Cambridge, UK: Cambridge University Press.

Hastie, R. (1986). Review essay: Experimental evidence on group accuracy. In B. Grofman and G. Owen (Eds.), *Information pooling and group decision making* (pp. 129–158). Greenwich, CN: JAI Press.

Hogarth, R. M. (1978). A note on aggregating opinions. *Organizational Behavior and Human Performance, 21,* 40–46.

Janis, I. L. (1972). *Victims of groupthink.* Boston: Houghton Mifflin.

Janis, I. L. (1982). *Groupthink: Psychological studies of policy decisions and fiascoes.* Boston: Houghton Mifflin.

Janis, I. L. (1989). *Crucial decisions: Leadership in policy making and crisis management.* New York: The Free Press.

Janis, I. L., & Mann, L. (1977). *Decision making: A psychological analysis of conflict, choice, and commitment.* New York: The Free Press.

Johnson, C. E., & Davis, J. H. (1972). An equiprobability model of risk taking. *Organizational Behavior and Human Performance, 8,* 159–175.

Jones, E. E. (1985). Major developments in social psychology during the past five decades. In G. Lindzey & E. Aronson (Eds.), *The handbook of social psychology* (pp. 47–107). New York: Random House.

Kahan, J. P., & Rapoport, A. (1984). *Theories of coalition formation.* Hillsdale, NJ: Erlbaum.

Kahneman, D., Slovic, P., & Tversky, A. (Eds.) (1982). *Judgment under uncertainty: Heuristics and biases.* New York: Cambridge University Press.

Kahneman, D., & Tversky, A. (1979). Prospect theory: An analysis of decision under risk. *Econometrica, 47,* 263–291.

Kameda, T., & Davis, J. H. (1990). The function of the reference point in individual and group risk decision making. *Organizational Behavior and Human Decision Processes, 46,* 55–76.

Keeney, R. L. (1976). A group preference axiomatization with cardinal utility. *Management Science, 23,* 140–145.

Keeney, R. L., & Kirkwood, C. W. (1975). Group decision making using cardinal social welfare functions. *Management Science, 22,* 430–437.

Keeney, R. L., & Raiffa, H. (1976). *Decisions with multiple objects: Preferences and value tradeoffs.* New York: Wiley.

Kerr, N. L., Davis, J. H., Meek, D., & Rissman, A. K. (1975). Group position as a function of member attitudes: Choice shift effects from the perspective of social decision scheme theory. *Journal of Personality and Social Psychology, 31,* 574–593.

Kiesler, C. A. (1971). *The psychology of commitment.* New York: Academic Press.

Kiesler, C. A., & Kiesler, S. B. (1969). *Conformity.* Reading, MA: Addison-Wesley.

Kirkwood, C. W. (1979). Pareto optimality and equity in social decision analysis. *IEEE Transactions on Systems, Man, and Cybernetics, 9,* 89–91.

Kogan, N., & Wallach, M. A. (1964). *Risk-taking: A study in cognition and personality.* New York: Holt.

Komorita, S. S. (1984). Coalition bargaining. In L. Berkowitz (Ed.), *Advances in experimental social psychology* (pp. 183–245). New York: Academic Press.

Lamm, H., & Myers, D. G. (1978). Group-induced polarization of attitudes and behavior. In L. Berkowitz (Ed.), *Advances in experimental social psychology* (pp. 147–195). New York: Academic Press.

Latané, B., Williams, K., & Harkins, S. (1977). Many hands make light the work: The causes and consequences of social loafing. *Journal of Personality and Social Psychology*, **37**, 822–832.

Leary, M. R., & Forsyth, D. R. (1987). Attributions of responsibility for collective endeavors. In C. Hendrick (Ed.), *Review of personality and social psychology: Group processes* (Vol. 8, pp. 167–188). Beverly Hills, CA: Sage.

Levine, J. M., & Moreland, R. L. (1990). Progress in small group research. *Annual Review of Psychology*, **41**, 585–634.

Lewin, K. (1958). Group decision and social change. In E. E. Maccoby, T. M. Newcomb, & E. L. Hartley (Eds.), *Readings in social psychology* (3rd ed.) (pp. 197–211). New York: Holt.

Lichtenstein, S., Fischhoff, B., & Phillips, L. D. (1982). Calibration of probabilities: The state of the art to 1980. In D. Kahneman, P. Slovic, & A. Tversky (Eds.). *Judgment under uncertainty: Heuristics and biases.* (pp. 306–334). Cambridge, UK: Cambridge University Press.

Linstone, H. A., & Turoff, M. (1975). *The Delphi method: Techniques and applications.* Reading, MA: Addison-Wesley.

Lock, A. (1987). Integrating group judgments in subjective forecasts. In G. Wright, & P. Ayton (Eds.), *Judgmental forecasting* (pp. 109–128). Chichester, England: Wiley.

Makridakis, S., & Winkler, R. L. (1983). Averages of forecasts: Some empirical results. *Management Science*, **29**, 987–996.

McGrath, J. E. (1984). *Groups: Interaction and performance.* Englewood Cliffs, NJ: Prentice Hall.

McGuire, T. W., Kiesler, S., & Siegel, J. (1987). Group and computer-mediated discussion effects in risk decision making. *Journal of Personality and Social Psychology*, **52**, 917–930.

Morris, P. A. (1974). Decision analysis expert use. *Management Science*, **20**, 1233–1241.

Morris, P. A. (1977). Combining expert opinion: A Bayesian approach. *Management Science*, **23**, 679–693.

Morris, P. A. (1983). An axiomatic approach to expert resolution. *Management Science*, **29**, 24–32.

Moscovici, S., & Zavalloni, M. (1969). The group as a polarizer of attitudes. *Journal of Personality and Social Psychology*, **12**, 125–135.

Myers, D. G., & Lamm, H. (1976). The group polarization phenomenon. *Psychological Bulletin*, **83**, 602–627.

Nemeth, C. J. (1986). Differential contributions of majority and minority influence. *Psychological Review*, **93**, 23–32.

Newbold, P., & Granger, C. W. J. (1974). Experience with forecasting univariate time series and combination of forecasts. *Journal of the Royal Statistical Society (Series A)*, **137**, 131–165.

Nitzan, S., & Paroush, J. (1982). Optimal decision rules in uncertain dichotomous choice situations. *International Economic Review*, **23**, 289–297.

Nordhoy, F. (1962). *Group interaction in decision making under risk.* Unpublished master's thesis, Massachusetts Institute of Technology, Cambridge, MA.

Ono, K., Tindale, R. S., Hulin, C. L., & Davis, J. H. (1988). Intuition vs deduction: Some thought experiments concerning Likert's linking-pin theory of organizations. *Organizational Behavior and Human Decision Processes*, **42**, 135–154.

Pelz, E. B. (1958). Some factors in "group decision." In E. E. Maccoby, T. M. Newcomb, & E. L. Hartley (Eds.), *Readings in social psychology* (3rd ed.) (pp. 212–218). New York: Holt.

Penrod, S., & Hastie, R. (1979). Models of jury decision-making: A critical review. *Psychological Bulletin*, **86**, 462–492.

Rohrbaugh, J. (1979). Improving the quality of group judgment: Social judgment analysis and the Delphi technique. *Organizational Behavior and Human Performance*, **24**, 73–92.

Sackman, H. (1975). *Delphi critique.* Lexington, MA: Lexington Books.

Sen, A. K. (1970). *Collective choice and individual values.* San Francisco: Holden-Day.

Shapley, L S., & Grofman, B. (1984). Optimizing group judgmental accuracy in the presence of inter-dependencies. *Public Choice*, **43**, 329–343.

Sherif, M. (1935). A study of some social factors in perception. *Archives of Psychology*, **27**, No. 187.

Sherif, M. (1958). Group influences upon the formation of norms and attitudes. In E. E. Maccoby, T. M. Newcomb, & E. L. Hartley (Eds.), *Readings in social psychology* (3rd ed.) (pp. 219–232). New York: Holt.

Singh, J. V. (1986). Performance, slack, and risk taking in organizational decision making. *Academy of Management Journal*, **29**, 562–585.

Slovic, P. (1969). Manipulating the attractiveness of a gamble without changing its expected value. *Journal of Experimental Psychology*, **79**, 139–145.

Smart, C., & Vertinsky, I. (1977). Designs for crisis decision units. *Administrative Science Quarterly*, **22**, 640–657.

Smoke, W. H., & Zajonc, R. B. (1962). On the reliability of group judgments and decision. In J. H. Crisswell, H. Solomon, & P. Suppes (Eds.), *Mathematical methods in small group processes* (pp. 322–333). Stanford CA: Stanford University Press.

Sniezek, J. A., & Henry, R. A. (1989). Accuracy and confidence in group judgment. *Organizational Behavior and Human Decision Processes*, **43**, 1–28.

Staël von Holstein, C.-A. S. (1970). *Assessment and evaluation of subjective probability distributions.* Stockholm: The Economic Research Institute at the Stockholm School of Economics.

Stasser, G. (198). Computer simulation as a research tool: The DISCUSS model of group decision making. *Journal of Experimental Social Psychology*, **24**, 393–422.

Stasser, G., Kerr, N. L., & Davis, J. H. (1989). Influence processes and consensus models in decision-making groups. In P. Paulus (Ed.), *Psychology of group influence* (2nd ed.) (pp. 279–326). Hillsdale, NJ: Erlbaum.

Stasson, M. F., Ono, K., Zimmerman, S. K., & Davis, J. H. (1988). Group consensus processes on cognitive bias tasks: A social decision scheme approach. *Japanese Psychological Research*, **30**, 68–77.

Staw, B. M., Sandelands, L. E., & Dutton, J. E., (1981). Threat-rigidity effects in organizational behavior. A multi-level analysis. *Administrative Science Quarterly*, **26**, 510–524.

Steiner, I. D. (1972). *Group process and productivity.* New York: Academic Press.

Stewart, T. R. (1987). The Delphi technique and judgmental forecasting. *Climatic Change*, **11**, 97–113.

Stoner, J. A. F. (1961). *A comparison of individual and group decisions involving risk*, Unpublished master's thesis, Massachusetts Institute of Technology, Cambridge, MA.

Stoner, J. A. F. (1968). Risky and cautious shifts in group decisions: The influence of widely held values. *Journal of Experimental Social Psychology,* **4**, 420–459.

Thomas, E. J., & Fink, C. F. (1961). Models of group problem solving. *Journal of Abnormal and Social Psychology,* **68**, 53–63.

Van De Ven, A. H., & Delbecq, A. L. (1971). Nominal versus interacting group processes for committee decision-making effectiveness. *Academy of Management Journal,* **14**, 203–212.

von Neumann, J., & Morgenstern, O. (1947). *Theory of games and economic behavior* (2nd ed.). Princeton, NJ: Princeton University Press.

Wallach, M. A., Kogan, N., & Bem, D. J. (1962). Group influence on individual risk taking. *Journal of Abnormal and Social Psychology,* **65**, 75–86.

Weber, E. U. (1988). A descriptive measure of risk. *Acta Psychologica,* **39**, 185–203.

Winkler, R. L. (1971). Probabilistic prediction: Some experimental results. *Journal of the American Statistical Association,* **66**, 675–685.

Winkler, R. L. (1981). Combining probability distributions from dependent information sources. *Management Sciences,* **27**, 479–488.

Winkler, R. L., & Makridakis, S. (1983). The combination of forecasts. *Journal of The Royal Statistical Society (Series A),* **146**, 150–157.

Zajonc, R. B. (1965). Social facilitation. *Science,* **149**, 269–274.

Zajonc, R. B. (1966). *Social psychology: An experimental approach.* Belmont, CA: Brooks/Cole.

Zajonc, R. B. (1980). Compresence. In P. B. Paulus (Ed.)., *Psychology of group influence* (pp. 35–60.) Hillsdale, NJ: Erlbaum.

Zajonc, R. B., Wolosin, R. J., Wolosin, M. A. ., & Sherman, S. J. (1968). Individual and group risk taking in a two-choice situation. *Journal of Experimenal Social Psychology,* **4**, 89–106.

Zeckhauser, R. J., & Viscusi, W. K. (1990). Risk within reason. *Science,* **248**, 559–564.

Chapter 7

Stress, affect, and risk taking

Leon Mann
University of Melbourne

CONTENTS

INTRODUCTION

We begin with several examples to illustrate the need for distinctions in the analysis of the influence of stress, emotional arousal, and mood state on decision making and risk taking.

1. Kimmel, anxiety, and Pearl Harbor

In the summer of 1941, Admiral H. E. Kimmel, Chief Naval Commander of the US fleet stationed at Pearl Harbor, Hawaii, received many warnings of a possible Japanese attack. Kimmel and his staff were conflicted about the best policy for dealing with the threat. They perceived two alternatives: to institute a

Risk-taking Behavior. Edited by J. F. Yates
© 1992 John Wiley & Sons Ltd

full-scale alert that would give priority to defending Pearl Harbor in case an enemy attack eventuated *or* to give priority to continuing Pearl Harbor's main activity as a training and supply base. Kimmel's dilemma constitutes a classic decisional conflict in which both choice alternatives carry the risk of massive costs and losses. The standing policy of continuing normal training and supply activity rather than instituting a full alert could be very costly if the Japanese attacked Pearl Harbor. The alternative policy of instituting and maintaining a full alert for an indefinite period at the expense of urgent training and supply activity could be very costly if the Japanese failed to attack Pearl Harbor but attacked US bases elsewhere.

Kimmel decided to maintain a limited alert condition, which kept the Pacific fleet anchored at Pearl Harbor and provided weekend leave to most service personnel. Although Kimmel may have seemed complacent about the possibility of a Japanese attack, he was, in fact, deeply worried. On 6 December he met with his staff officers who provided reassurance that a policy of limited alert was appropriate. The rest is history. On 7 December the Japanese air force attacked Pearl Harbor, sinking or badly damaging 19 vessels with a loss of 2340 lives. Admiral Kimmel was courtmartialled and stripped of his position.

It is possible that Kimmel's deep-seated anxiety in the face of repeated warnings about a Japanese threat blinded him to several compromise options, such as a stepped-up alert involving round-the-clock radar surveillance, partial air surveillance, some dispersal of warships, and maintenance of anti-aircraft batteries at full strength.

The Kimmel case is an example of how strong, unpleasant emotional states (such as anxiety, guilt, and shame) generated by severe decisional conflict may impair normal patterns of information processing, leading in turn to unnecessarily risky decisions. In this case, the actual or anticipated losses inherent in the decision problem itself—threats to national security, potential loss of numerous lives, massive material losses, threats to the leader's standing and authority—all contributed to the high level of psychological stress, which, according to Janis and Mann (1977), is a major factor in maladaptive decision making.

A question to be addressed in this chapter is how psychological stress, due to strong, unpleasant emotional states, exerts an effect on the risk-taking perceptions and propensities of decision makers.

2. Truman, elation, and Hiroshima/Nagasaki

In August 1945, President Truman ordered the dropping of an atomic bomb on Hiroshima. Japan was on its knees militarily and on the verge of surrender. "Truman was aboard the USS Augusta steaming across the Atlantic on his way home from the Potsdam conference when he received the word that the atomic bomb had been successfully detonated over Hiroshima. Excitedly, Truman rushed to the officer's wardroom and told them the news. The navy men burst into cheers" (*New York Times*, 7 August 1945).

Three days after Hiroshima, Truman ordered the dropping of a second atomic bomb, on the city of Nagasaki. The second bomb brought unnecessary death and misery to many thousands of Japanese civilians and apparently had no effect on the imminent end of the war.

Many commentators have been critical of the haste with which the second bomb was dropped (e.g. Pemberton, 1989). There is speculation that Truman's emotional state may have contributed to his decision to issue an order to General Spaatz "to continue operations as planned" to drop the second bomb (Janis, 1959).

Truman's excitement about the success of the first bomb may have induced him to ignore or overlook information from intelligence sources about the likelihood of a rapid end to the war and the risk of "overkill." This example raises several points about the effect of mood, aroused by the outcome of one decision, on the tendency to act riskily or cautiously in dealing with another related decision. Did Truman's euphoria lead him to press ahead with the second A-bomb? How, if at all, did Truman's elation influence his thinking about the second bomb? Does the Truman example suggest that decision makers who are buoyed by the success of a policy decision become more adventurous in handling subsequent related decisions? Or is it the case, as some writers point out, that positive mood may sometimes promote caution (cf. Isen, 1987)?

3. Eisenhower, anger, and Suez

In 1956 Britain, France, and Israel, without alerting the US, invaded Egypt in response to President Gamal Nasser's seizure of the Suez Canal and illegal closure of it to Israeli ships. President Eisenhower, ordinarily calm in the face of crisis, was furious. According to sources close to the President he "was in a mood of someone betrayed." He personally took the lead in ordering harsh, punitive actions against America's closest allies. Extreme pressure was put on Britain and France to drop their plan to take over the Suez Canal, forcing them to withdraw from Egypt immediately. America's allies were given no opportunity to save face and the governments in London and Paris soon fell. Urgently needed supplies of oil to Britain and France were delayed; relations with Britain and France deteriorated rapidly. France subsequently withdrew from NATO. Here is an example of the influence of a negative mood, in this case anger, on presidential decision making. Eisenhower's hurt feelings may have induced him to choose a course of action which in the long term harmed America's interests. This example raises several questions. Did Eisenhower's anger lead him to respond differently to the crisis? Or would he have been less likely to risk rupturing long-standing relations with America's closest allies if his emotions had been more positive? And, if it appears that Eisenhower's anger contributed to the harshness of his response, how exactly did his mood influence his thinking and judgment?

4. Psychology undergraduates, movie goers, and mood manipulation

In psychology laboratories in many countries, unsuspecting undergraduates are having their moods manipulated into experiencing positive and negative feeling states. At the University of Maryland, students are induced into a positive mood by giving them a coupon for a free hamburger (Isen & Patrick, 1983) or by offering them a gift of a small bag of candy (Isen & Geva, 1987). At Oregon, the University of California at Berkeley, and Carnegie-Mellon, students are plunged into a gloomy mood by having them read a brief newspaper report of the death of a normal, young male undergraduate unknown to them, or lifted into a happy mood by reading an account of a medical student who achieves success (Johnson & Tversky, 1983). At Flinders University, high school students are put into happy or sad moods by having them listen to heart-warming stories such as *The original warm, fuzzy tale* or tearjerkers such as *Sadako and the thousand paper cranes* (Simpson, 1989). Researchers at the University of New South Wales allow Hollywood to conduct the mood manipulation. Filmgoers are stopped as they leave city cinemas and their mood states measured following exposure to such happy films as *Beverly Hills Cop* and *Back to the Future* or to such sad films as *Dance with a Stranger* and *Birdy* (Forgas & Moylan, 1987). The reason for these various attempts to manipulate or capture mood states is to examine how the arousal of different types of mood influences subsequent judgments and decisions. For example, Isen and Patrick (1983) found that the happy recipients of a free hamburger coupon bet *more* than the controls on a low-risk bet (83% chance of winning) but wagered *less* than the controls on a high-risk bet (17% chance of winning). Johnson and Tversky (1983), for their part, found that their gloom-induced students, having read about the murder of an undergraduate, showed a significant increase in their estimates of the frequency of all kinds of hazards. The world now seemed a more dangerous place. However, the happy-induced students showed a decrease in their estimates of the same risks and hazards. What do these studies have in common? They all demonstrate that people who have been infused with a temporary mood or affective state are influenced in their subsequent perceptions of risk and their choices involving risk. We shall endeavor to explain why in this chapter.

5. Chronic mood states

Various forms of mental illness are associated with characteristic displays of mood and emotion. For example, some psychotic disorders have as their major feature extreme distortions of mood—such as deep depression on the one hand and manic reactions of high excitement and elation on the other. Clinical psychologists have studied the effects of depression on risk perception and decision making. Costello (1983) found that depressed people are more conservative in their choices than non-depressives.

Similarly, Pietromonaco and Rook (1987) found that depressed, compared to nondepressed students, assign greater weight to risks and accordingly are more reluctant to make positive decisions. The availability of clinical and nonclinical samples that exhibit intense mood states over a sustained period of time enables the researcher to investigate the prolonged effects of intense mood on risk taking and decision making and, in particular, to answer the question of consistency of response. The clinical evidence, moreover, provides another source of data for explaining how mood affects risk taking and decision making.

To summarize: We have briefly described five different examples of possible linkages between emotional arousal, affect, and decision making/risk taking.

In Kimmel and Pearl Harbor, the decision maker's emotional arousal is an intrinsic part of the decision matrix. The very nature of the dilemma arouses strong emotions which in turn may have had deleterious effects on the decision maker's capability to gauge the best options for resolving the problem.

In Truman and Hiroshima/Nagasaki, the success of a recent decision or action may have created a mood state which infused the decision maker's way of dealing with a new, related problem. The sequence of *decision–mood arousal–decision* is an interesting phenomenon deserving separate analysis.

In Eisenhower and Suez, we have an example of how a decision taken by others elicits a strong emotional reaction which sparks the decision to retaliate strongly and perhaps excessively. Irving Janis (1989) refers to this as the "angry retaliation" rule, an example of how emotive decision rules interfere with vigilant problem solving.

In the mood manipulation of psychology undergraduates (and others), moods are aroused by a variety of ingenious techniques, none of them related to the decision tasks to be performed. This line of research captures the question of how feelings aroused by watching one's team lose a close match, finding a quarter in a telephone box, or reading a tear-jerking novel, spill over to influence and sometimes cloud our immediate judgment on totally unrelated matters. Research following this tradition is typically confined to the effects of temporary, low-level mood states on everyday decision problems (cf. Isen, 1987), although there are exceptions (cf. Forgas, 1989). A frequently forgotten source of evidence is the control group of subjects who face the decision task without their moods manipulated. These subjects carry with them a variety of ambient mood states, whose effects on decision-making performance constitute another source of data.

Finally, in the study of clinically depressed subjects, the effects of persistent, intense mood states are examined for their influence on risk perception and decision making. This research, conducted in the clinic and the laboratory, examines how strong, affective states flood all aspects of the patient's capacity to make decisions. The study of psychopathology often provides rich clues to important factors underlying a phenomenon in normal life.

We have described five different examples of the links between stress, affect, and risk taking. We could have included several more—for example, the link which posits risk-taking behavior such as gambling and shop-lifting as an attempt to attain emotional arousal.

The following points emerge from these distinctions:

1. We will approach risk taking as a form of decision making from an information-processing perspective (cf. Janis & Mann, 1977; Payne, 1985).
2. We will analyze the effect of strong emotional arousal, such as was illustrated in the cases of Kimmel/Pearl Harbor, Truman and Hiroshima/ Nagasaki, and Eisenhower/Suez, separately from the more mundane mood states typically captured in the laboratory. The conflict theory of decision making (Janis & Mann, 1977) and the constraints model of policy making (Janis, 1989) will be used as conceptual frameworks to analyze the effects of strong emotions, including psychological stress, on risk taking. Other theories and models, such as the affect-maintenance principle (Isen, 1987) and the mood-memory model (Bower, 1981), will be used to examine the effects of transient mood states on risk perception and judgment.
3. A clear distinction will be made between findings due to the effects of emotions and mood on personal, consequential decisions, and findings derived from studies of hypothetical decisions involving responses to scenarios and vignettes. This is consistent with our basic assumption that the psychology of consequential, real-life decisions follows a different set of principles from the psychology of hypothetical and make-believe decisions.
4. Wherever possible, we will draw firm generalizations about the effects of affect and mood across a wide range of decision phenomena. However, as is evident from our five examples, the relationships between mood, emotion, and risk taking in decision making take many forms and may not be reducible to one or two sovereign principles.

Several questions will guide our discussion:

1. Is the increase (or decrease) in risk taking produced by mood changes indicative of poor or ill-advised decisions? We make no assumption that risk taking *per se* or different levels of risk-taking constitute poor decisions. Quite clearly, an overly-cautious response may be as inappropriate a response as an overly adventurous one. A clue to answering the question is whether the increase (or decrease) in risk taken corresponds to an increase (or decrease) in the quality of information processing involved in the making of the decision. If, for example, a particular mood state leads to a substantial increase in riskiness, accompanied by a deterioration of informa- tion-processing performance, we would consider the heightened riskiness as symptomatic of poor decision making.
2. Are the effects of negative and positive emotions on risk taking/decision

making symmetrical? Are the expression of, say, anxiety on the one hand and euphoria on the other similar in their effects on decision making (in which case we only need to invoke the concept of arousal) or are they different (in which case, we must account for the specificity of emotions)? The same question can also be asked of negative and positive mood states. Do the various mood states have equally potent effects on risk taking and do they follow similar, or different, mechanisms? It is possible that strong emotions follow different principles from mild transient feeling states in their effect on decision making. For example, the arousal of a strong emotion may itself be informative to the decision maker and may itself be taken into account when choosing an option, whereas a transient mood state may have only an indirect effect on the decision, perhaps influencing the tempo of information recalled and taken into account. (I am grateful to Joseph Forgas for this suggestion.)

3. Which kinds of risk taking are most susceptible to emotional and mood-induced effects? In Chapter 4 above, Bromiley and Curley make a useful distinction between kinds of risk-taking situations—for example, gaming and gambling, health-related risks, risks to life and limb, risks of social rejection and ostracism. They argue that risk taking tends to be situation-specific. If so, to what extent does affect/mood contribute to the situation-specificity of risk taking? In addition, are decisions made by groups more susceptible to riskiness induced by mood than decisions made by individuals (see Chapter 6, by Davis, Kameda, & Stasson)? There is some suggestion that groups are particularly vulnerable to adventurous decisions stemming from the warm glow of camaraderie and the members' feeling that their group is "Number 1" (cf. Janis, 1982).

4. How much of the variance in risk taking can be attributed to affect and mood? Is the influence of emotion and feeling on decision making powerful? Do we observe substantial qualitative effects that alter the nature of decisions, or are we dealing with essentially modest effects?

A final note before we begin. It will be seen that only a few studies directly address the interrelationships of affect, mood, and risk taking. The bulk of the research literature deals with general processes of judgment, problem solving, and decision making. We believe, however, that it is possible to derive some insights from this general literature that will provide answers to at least some of the many questions raised in this introduction.

THE EFFECT OF PSYCHOLOGICAL STRESS ON DECISION MAKING

Janis and Mann's (1977) conflict theory is a detailed model of how stress and affective reactions engendered by decisional conflict can facilitate or interfere with effective decision making. The heart of the theory is an analysis of five basic coping patterns which are used to deal with conflict and stress. The five patterns are unconflicted inertia, unconflicted change to a new course of action, defensive avoidance (which takes three forms: procrastination, shifting decision responsibility to others, and rationalization), hypervigilance (rapid and impulsive choice) and vigilance (careful evaluation of alternatives and deliberate choice). Each of the five patterns is identified with a distinctive set of antecedent conditions, a particular level of psychological stress experienced by the person, and a separate style of information processing in searching and evaluating alternative courses of action.

The conflict theory is a general model of decision making that is highly relevant to the analysis of stress and other affective responses in risky behavior. First, the model analyzes the process of decision making in terms of a set of issues or questions about risk the person tries to answer as he or she copes with new threats, such as remaining in one's house as flood waters begin to lap at the door, or new opportunities, such as the offer of a parcel of shares in an obscure company. According to the model, the person's first question is: "Are the risks serious if I *don't* change?" and the second question is: "Are the risks serious if I *do* change?" (Janis & Mann, 1977, p. 70). Conflict is aroused whenever the person recognizes that there are indeed serious risks from whatever course of action is taken. In sum, it is the perception that serious risks are involved, no matter what the person chooses, that elicits strong feelings of anxiety and emotional stress. Thus, risk perception is one link in the chain of risk and affect.

Second, the three coping patterns commonly used to deal with conflict— defensive avoidance, hypervigilance, and vigilance—involve distinct modes of information processing that are associated with tendencies toward extreme risk-taking behavior (hypervigilance) or tendencies toward careful, deliberate choice (vigilance). The conflict model postulates that each of the three conflict coping patterns is associated with a distinctive level of stress—Defensive avoidance: variable stress levels from low to high as signs of threat become salient; Hypervigilance: extremely high stress level; Vigilance: a moderate level of stress. Stress, in turn, has either a facilitative or a deleterious effect on the quality of information processing, depending upon stress levels. Thus, stress level is a second link in the chain of affect and risk taking.

It must be pointed out that unlike normative decision models, which prescribe a precise assessment of the probability of gains and losses for each choice option, conflict theory does not stipulate decision rules for identifying and selecting the best "option." Conflict theory uses the term "risk" in its common, everyday meaning of "exposure to the chance of injury or loss" (cf. Chapter 1).

The logic of the conflict model and some evidence

The conflict model is concerned with the linkages between three factors: conditions relating to decisional conflict; the level of stress generated by the conflict; and the coping pattern adopted by the decision maker to deal with the conflict. The model is founded on the assumption that decisional conflict is a source of psychological stress. The task of making a vital decision is worrisome and can cause anxiety reactions such as agitation, quick temper, sleeplessness or oversleeping, loss of appetite or compulsive overeating, and other psychosomatic symptoms. Psychological stress arising from decisional conflict stems from three main sources.

First, the person is acutely aware that there are serious risks involved no matter which alternative is chosen, that is, there is arousal of conflict. The decision maker is concerned about the material and social losses that will follow if the chosen course of action turns out badly. In addition, the person is aware that to some extent his or her reputation and self-esteem as a competent decision maker are at stake. Another factor is the expected social cost of undoing a prior decision or breaking a long-standing commitment. The greater the anticipated costs or losses, the higher the decision maker's level of stress. Thus, the model makes important assumptions about the connection between conflict and stress.

But decisional conflict, that is concern over the risks and losses involved in the competing choice alternatives, is only *one* of several causes of the level of stress experienced by the decision maker. Pessimism about finding a better alternative than the imperfect ones already available and a belief that there is insufficent time to search for alternatives *add* to the stress.

The combination of the three conditions—arousal of conflict from awareness of risks involved, pessimism about finding a better solution, and insufficient time available in which to make the decision—is related directly to the level of stress and to the coping pattern used to resolve the dilemma, as set out in Table 7.1. This table shows the cognitive and emotional determinants of five basic patterns of decision making.

The coping patterns are assumed to be functionally related to the nature of the decisional conflict and the degree of stress in the following ways:

1. *Unconflicted adherence*: The decision maker complacently decides to continue whatever he or she has been doing, ignoring information about the risk of losses. Because the person believes there is very little or no risk from continuing with his present course of action, there is no decisional conflict and, accordingly, little or no stress.
2. *Unconflicted change*: The decision maker reacts to a challenge or threat by precipitously changing to a new course of action without giving the matter much thought. The decision maker uncritically adopts whichever new course of action is most salient or most strongly recommended. Because the person believes there is no risk involved in moving directly to a new policy, there is no conflict regarding alternatives and, accordingly, little or no stress.

The remaining three coping patterns function to resolve the decisional conflict, either by evading or escaping from it, or by confronting and attempting to solve the problem.

3. *Defensive avoidance*: The person believes that there are serious risks involved both in staying with the current course of action *and* in moving to a new course of action. Hence there is a classic state of conflict. Stress aroused by the conflict is compounded by pessimism about finding a good solution to the dilemma. In that case the person becomes motivated to reduce the distressing state of high emotional arousal by one or another of the three mechanisms of defensive avoidance. Procrastination enables the person to postpone the decision, turning his attention away from the conflict to other, less distressing matters. Shifting responsibility to someone else ("buck-passing") enables the person to evade the dilemma and provides him with a handy scapegoat should the decision turn out poorly. The invention of fanciful rationalizations in support of one of the choice alternatives is another mechanism for escaping conflict. Stress is warded off by selectively attending to only the good aspects of that alternative and by ignoring or distorting negative information about it. All three forms of defensive avoidance enable the decision maker to escape from worrying about the decision.

4. *Hypervigilance*: The decision maker recognizes that there are serious risks entailed in the competing courses of action. He believes that a better solution might be found. But because he also believes there is insufficent time to search for and evaluate that solution, he experiences a high degree of psychological stress. The person in a hypervigilant state is frantically preoccupied with the threatened losses that seem to loom larger every minute. He searches anxiously for a way out of the dilemma in order to put an end to the stress. He impulsively seizes a hastily contrived solution that seems to offer immediate relief, overlooking the full implications of his choice. The behavior of the decision maker in this type of crisis is marked by a very high rate of vacillation. Other symptoms of hypervigilance include a high degree of emotionality, reduced memory span, and simplistic, repetitive thinking. In its most extreme form, hypervigilance is equivalent to "panic."

5. *Vigilance*: The vigilant decision maker is in a state of conflict, in that he recognizes that there are serious risks associated with the competing alternatives. However, the conditions surrounding the conflict confine psychological stress to a moderate level. The person has confidence about finding an adequate solution and believes there is ample time to do it. The decision maker is accordingly motivated to confront the dilemma head-on. He searches painstakingly for relevant information, assimilates it in a relatively unbiased manner, and evaluates alternatives carefully before making a choice.

The conflict model assumes, then, that extremely low stress and extremely intense stress give rise to defective patterns, while moderate levels of stress are more likely to produce careful decision making. This implies a curvilinear relationship between magnitude of stress and quality of decision making, like the relationship that has been described for emotional arousal and responsiveness to persuasive communications (McGuire, 1985). This postulate, linking the magnitude of stress to the kind and quality of information processing adopted by the decision maker, is readily generalized to a variety of contexts, including political, military, environmental, and economic decisions made in crisis.

Evidence for the relationship between stress level and coping pattern is reviewed by Holsti and George (1975), who discuss the effects of crisis-induced stress on the decisional performance of foreign policy makers. Reviewing the actions of decision makers in the crises leading to World War I, the Cuban Missile crisis, and the Korean War, Holsti, and George conclude that crisis-induced stress produces a reduced time perspective and cognitive rigidity, which leads to a higher value on immediate goals, premature closure, restricted search for alternatives, and less rigorous evaluation of alternatives and their consequences. An analysis by Michael Brecher (1980) of Israel's decision making during the 1967 Six Day War and 1973 Yom Kippur War lends support to some of Holsti and George's (1975) conclusions.

Brecher analyzed 57 decisions made by the Israeli cabinet and Kitchen cabinet during the 1967 and 1973 crises. The independent variable, *stress*, was measured by perceptions of threat, time pressure, and probability of war. Brecher found that as stress rose during each crisis there was an *increased* search for options/alternatives (linear relationship). However, in line with the conflict theory hypothesis, he also found a curvilinear (inverted-U) relationship between stress and group performance in the consideration of policy alternatives. None of the five decisions taken under conditions of low stress showed careful evaluation of alternatives. As stress rose to a moderate level, evaluation of alternatives became *more* careful. Beyond that, as stress became intense, there was a decline in care taken in the evaluation of alternatives. Several points emerge from Brecher's empirical study that bear out conflict theory: changes in stress level are associated with distinctive changes in the quality of decision making procedures, especially in regard to the search for and evaluation of alternatives. Some stress is required to promote extensive search for and careful evaluation of alternatives. However, as stress becomes more intense, decision making becomes less comprehensive and the quality of information processing suffers.

An experiment on the effects of stress on decision making

An impressive demonstration of the decline in cognitive functioning associated with psychological stress is found in Keinan's (1987) experiment on decision making under stress.

Table 7.1.   Determinants of five basic patterns of decision making.

Pattern of coping with challenge	Determinants Subjective beliefs	Level of stress
1. Unconflicted adherence	• No serious risk from current course action	Low: persistently calm
2. Unconflicted change	• Serious risk from current course of action • No serious risk from new course of action	Low: persistently calm
3. Defensive avoidance	• Serious risk from current course of action • Serious risk from new course of action • No better solution can be found	Variable from low to high (predominantly pseudo-calm, with break-through of high emotional arousal when signs of threat become salient)
4. Hypervigilance	• Serious risk from current course of action • Serious risk from new course of action • A better solution might be found • Insufficient time to search for and evaluate a better solution	High: persistently strong anxiety
5. Vigilance	• Serious risk from current course of action • Serious risk from new course of action • A better solution might be found • Sufficient time to search for and evaluate a better solution	Moderate: variations within inter-mediate range, with level depending upon exposure to threat cues or reassuring communications

Source: Based on Janis & Mann (1977), p. 78, with permission. Copyright © 1977 by the Free Press, a Division of Macmillan, Inc.

In Keinan's study, Israeli undergraduates were asked to solve decision problems, for each of which six alternative answers could be searched before choosing the correct one. In one condition subjects were exposed to *controllable stress*. They were told that painful but harmless electric shocks might be administered if they gave incorrect responses to the decision problems. In a second condition, subjects were exposed to *uncontrollable stress*. They were told that the electric shocks might be administered randomly while they worked on the decision problems. In the *no-stress* condition, subjects worked on the decision problems with no mention of shocks.

The first experimental condition captures the situation in a classic decision dilemma: an incorrect choice may produce punishment, and the threat of that punishment induces anxiety and stress. The second experimental condition captures the situation found in many mood induction experiments. The threat of shock, which induces anxiety and stress, is quite unrelated to the person's performance on the decision problem. The stress represents an additional burden plaguing the decision maker while he or she attempts to solve problems. It has much the same function as loud, distracting music or the sound of a noisy jackhammer that occurs while a doctor is trying to decide which medication to prescribe for a patient.

Keinan measured subjects' performance on 15 decision problems, recording the number of items on which they showed premature closure (i.e. made a choice before having seen all six alternatives), scanned the alternatives in a disorganized nonsystematic fashion, and made incorrect responses. Compared with the no-stress condition, subjects in the two stress conditions showed a significantly stronger tendency to choose before seeing all alternatives (approximately four times as often), to scan the alternatives in a nonsystematic fashion, and to choose incorrectly (approximately twice as often). As might be expected, subjects' tendencies to premature closure and to nonsystematic scanning were significantly linked with poor decision performance ($r = -0.34$, $r = -0.49$, respectively). Unfortunately missing from Keinan's report is an indication of whether those subjects who reported feeling most stressed were also most likely to perform poorly on the decisions.

Failure to find any difference between subjects in the two stress conditions might be due to the fact that the situation was equally stressful for both groups and to the overwhelming need to escape as quickly as possible.

Keinan's findings are a nice demonstration that psychological stress—irrespective of whether it stems from concern about the painful consequences of a wrong choice or from concern about an extraneous painful threat—spurs the decision maker to take the risk of choosing before seeing all of the alternatives.

The findings also illustrate another important point about the destructive effects of psychological stress aroused by the prospect of pain and losses in case of a faulty decision. The prospect of pain and suffering, which ought to motivate the decision maker to search and choose carefully, brings about, ironically, the very opposite, producing disorganized and inadequate search activity.

Time pressure as a source of stress

Time pressure is identified by Janis and Mann (1977) as an additional source of stress whenever there is decisional conflict. Extreme time pressure has a deleterious effect on decision making. Abelson and Levi (1985) identify two effects of imposing time pressure on the decision maker—a tendency to rely on one or two salient attributes in making the choice and a tendency to attach greater weight to unfavorable information about choice alternatives and therefore to become more cautious. Wallsten (1980) found that subjects under time pressure typically focus their attention on a few salient cues as they process information before making a choice. Wright (1974) predicted, and found, that subjects under time pressure simplify decision making by focusing on unfavorable information. This enables them to use a simple choice strategy—such as to rule out all alternatives with any flaw or impediment. The effect of this is to make subjects under time pressure more cautious and conservative in their decisions.

Ben Zur and Breznitz (1981) found that subjects chose safer gambles (i.e. gambles characterized by lower potential losses) under high time pressure (8 seconds) than under medium or low time pressure (16 seconds and 32 seconds, respectively). They also found that subjects under high time pressure paid more attention to the probability of losing and amount of possible loss than to the probability of winning and amount of possible gain.

Ben Zur and Breznitz argue that under time pressure the decision maker's main objective is to reduce the threat of future losses. Accordingly, attention is focused on searching negative information in order to rule out potentially damaging alternatives. This portrayal of the decision maker as becoming cautious and risk-avoidant under conditions of time pressure seems to contradict the conflict theory assumption that time pressure promotes jumpy, hypervigilant, panicky behavior.

This issue may be resolved by arranging an experiment in which the decision involves major losses, and time pressure is varied from low to extreme. I would predict that under such conditions, the most anxious decision makers will become *less* rather than *more* cautious.

Charlotte Tan (1985) studied the effects of time pressure on quality of decision making. Her subjects were given a standard amount of time (25 minutes) to find a solution to a decision dilemma, making use of information provided in a separate information booklet.

In the *time pressure* condition, subjects were deliberately hassled by the experimenter's statement: "You have about 25 minutes to complete the dilemma, so that's not much time. You'll have to hurry. Keep your eye on the clock to make sure that you are keeping up." In the *no-time* pressure condition, subjects were told "You have about 25 minutes to complete the dilemma, so that's plenty of time. Don't hurry, just take your time."

As predicted, subjects who were "time-pressured" came up with fewer alternatives to solve the dilemma, and considered fewer consequences (costs and benefits) for each alternative than in the no-pressure situation. Thus, being hurried had the effect of inducing subjects to work less effectively in the time available.

Tan's findings are evidence that it is not time *per se* but rather the perception that it is insufficient for dealing with the decision task, that contributes to impairment of decision-making performance.

Arbitrary and unreasonable imposition of time pressure may itself elicit a variety of affective responses that in turn influence decision making. An example is the explosive response of an employee who is pressured by an impatient boss to make a choice under an impossible deadline.

To sum up this section on the effect of psychological stress on risk taking: The conflict model (Janis & Mann, 1977) postulates that stress and other affective responses infuse decision making. The theory does not specifically address risk-taking behavior. However, it describes risk perception as a condition leading to the arousal of psychological stress, and it analyzes various decision coping patterns for dealing with stress (such as hypervigilance) as likely to lead to impulsive, risky choices. Extreme time pressure, the key antecedent condition for hypervigilance, is identified as a major source of stress in decision making. The conflict model relies on historical case studies as well as laboratory studies for evidence. The model, because it is ambitious in scope and encompasses a wide array of psychological phenomena, is not easily testable. For example, it refers to perception of "serious risks" as the condition for arousal of conflict, but there is no yardstick for determining serious risks. The model also refers to levels of stress associated with each of the conflict-coping patterns, but there is no reliable metric for determing "low stress," "moderate stress," and "high stress." The model, however, makes an important contribution to the analysis of risk taking in that:

1. it places risk taking within the framework of a general model of decision making;
2. it makes important distinctions between at least five different patterns of coping with decision dilemmas, including decisions involving serious risks;
3. for each coping pattern it specifies the factors leading to arousal of stress and describes the effect of different levels of stress on the quality of decision making;
4. the model's focus on highly conflictful, consequential decisions points to the disruptive effects of extreme emotional stress on decision-making and risk-taking activity.

AFFECT AND RISK TAKING

The continuum of affective responses studied in decision-making research spans the gamut from strong, unpleasant emotions, such as anxiety aroused whenever a highly conflictful decision is made, to mild, transient mood states of happiness and gloom, induced by a variety of clever experimental manipulations prior to asking a person to make a decision.

Alice M. Isen and her colleagues have conducted a sustained program of research on the influence of positive affective state on risk-related behavior. Many of the studies employ a standard experimental paradigm. The subjects are psychology students who participate in the study in order to obtain one hour's course credit. At the beginning of the session the experimenter gives some students a McDonald's hamburger coupon (Isen & Patrick, 1983) or a bag of candy (Isen & Geva, 1987) as "a token of appreciation for their participation in the experiment." These modest gifts constitute the affect manipulation—manipulation checks indicate that the gifts put subjects in a good mood (Arkes, Herren, & Isen, 1988). Next, subjects are given 10 poker chips to represent their credit for participating in the study. Then, depending upon the study, the experimenter asks subjects about their willingness to stake their participation credit chips in a roulette game (Isen & Patrick, 1983), the number of chips they are willing to bet (Isen & Patrick, 1983), whether they prefer a small, rather than a large bet (Isen et al., 1984), the probability of winning they require before agreeing to bet (Isen & Geva, 1987), and their betting preferences between pairs of gambles varying in size of potential gains and losses (Isen, Nygren, & Ashby, 1988). The surprising finding that recurs throughout these studies is that subjects induced with positive feelings are generally more cautious and conservative in their risk preferences and risk taking than control subjects. There are, however, exceptions.

Isen and her colleagues point out that the effect of affect on risk taking is complex, and depends on such factors as nature of the risk (gambles, social risks, etc.) the level of risk involved, and whether the potential loss is meaningful or hypothetical. I will describe Isen and Patrick's (1983) study to illustrate some of the features of the work.

Isen and Patrick (1983) tested the idea that positive affect leads to risky behavior only in low-risk situations. In order to manipulate positive affect, some subjects were given a McDonald's coupon, good for a hamburger worth $0.50. They were told by the experimenter that the coupon was a token of appreciation for participating in the experiment. In the neutral affect condition, no coupons were handed out; subjects simply received their instructions.

All subjects were then given 10 poker chips, representing their credit for participating in the study. They were then asked if they were interested in gambling those chips in a game of roulette. They were told: "If you don't want to gamble, of course, you don't have to. You can play it safe and not risk your credit. It's up to you" (p. 196). However, if they chose to bet, subjects could win more chips, which would bring them a prize, or lose all or part of their 10 chips, which would cost them the credit they had earned for participating in the study. The experimenter then manipulated risk level by telling different subjects that the bet available to them held a 17% chance of winning (high risk), a 50% chance of winning (medium risk) or an 83% chance of winning (low risk). Subjects then made up their minds whether they wanted to bet, and, if so, how many of the 10 chips they would wager. The findings, shown in Table 7.2, are interesting.

First, let us compare the number (or proportion) of subjects in the positive affect and neutral affect conditions who chose to gamble on their experimental credit. The findings reveal that positive affect did not have a uniform effect across the three risk conditions. A significantly greater proportion of positive affect subjects than neutral affect subjects chose to bet in the low risk condition (92% versus 31%); approximately equal proportions of positive affect and neutral affect subjects chose to bet in the moderate risk condition (70% versus 75%). A somewhat *smaller* proporation of positive affect subjects than neutral affect subjects chose to bet in the high risk condition (27% versus 44%); thus, positive affect promotes an interest in gambling when the risk of losing is low, has no effect when the risk of losing is moderate, and inhibits interest when the risk of losing is high.

A comparison of the mean amount bet (number of chips wagered, by those who chose to bet) yields a similar pattern of findings. On average, positive affect subjects wagered more chips than the neutral affect subjects in the low risk condition (3.7 versus 1.5), but wagered fewer chips in the high risk condition (0.46 versus 2.6).

Isen and Patrick also report a second study, in which subjects were presented with hypothetical dilemmas, in which the protagonist had either a 20%, 50%, or 80% chance of success on an attractive, but risky, action. Again, subjects who were the happy recipients of a hamburger coupon were compared with controls on their willingness to take the risk *if* they were the protagonist in the story.

Contrary to the findings of the betting study, positive affect subjects did not differ from the neutral affect subjects in willingness to take risk in the low risk

Table 7.2.   Proportion of subjects choosing to bet and mean number of chips bet in a high, moderate, or low risk situation following induction of positive or neutral affect.

Risk condition	Positive affect	Neutral affect
High risk		
Proportion who bet	3/11 (27%)	4/9 (44%)
Mean chips bet	0.46	2.6
Moderate risk		
Proportion who bet	7/10 (70%)	9/12 (75%)
Mean chips bet	4.1	2.8
Low risk		
Proportion who bet	11/12 (92%)	4/13 (31%)
Mean chips bet	3.7	1.5

Source Adapted from Isen & Patrick (1983), p. 198, with permission of the authors and Academic Press, Inc.

(80 % chance) condition (6.60 versus 6.63), but were *more* willing to take the risk in the high risk (20 % chance) condition (5.15 versus 3.30). Clearly, as Isen and Patrick indicate, the strong contrast between the findings obtained from a personal, consequential decision and from a make-believe, hypothetical decision, brings home the point that psychological investigation of the relationship between affect and risk taking cannot be based solely on the study of inconsequential, hypothetical decisions.

Positive affect and risk perceptions and cognitions

The literature on the influence of positive affect on cognitive processes and behavior suggests that positive affect tends to prime positive thoughts and memories. The priming or accessibility model (Fiske & Taylor, 1984) suggests that persons who are happy are more likely to think about positive possibilities and be optimistic in their decisions. Isen and Geva (1987) examined risk preference (and cognitions about risk) as a function of positive and neutral affect. Again, the candy bag method was used to induce positive affect. Subjects were then invited to wager their 10 credit points on a roulette game, in which the experimenter determined the number of chips they could bet, if they chose to bet (all 10 chips in the high risk condition, 5 chips in the medium risk condition, 1 chip in the low risk condition). They were then asked to indicate on a 10-interval scale (0, 0.10, 0.20, ..., 1.00) what the probability of winning would have to be in order for them to bet. They were then asked to write down all their thoughts while deciding on their risk preference. The results (Table 7.3) show that subjects in a positive state were more risk-averse (i.e. insisted on a higher probability of winning) in the high risk and moderate risk conditions (0.68 vs 0.52; 0.65 vs 0.52, respectively), but tended to be more risk-prone in the low risk condition (0.53 vs 0.59). Consistent with this finding, positive mood subjects reported more thoughts about losses and losing in the high risk and moderate risk conditions (24 % vs 12 %; 20 % vs 5 %, respectively) but had fewer thoughts about losing in the low risk condition (6 % vs 20 %).

The results are surprising. According to the priming model, happy people should think about positive possibilities, not negative possibilities, and act accordingly. Isen and Geva argue that *mood maintenance* is the reason. People who feel happy, because they have gained something but now have something to lose, think and behave conservatively. This finding suggests that the need for mood maintenance exerts a powerful influence on cognition and behavior. Isen suggests that the influence of positive affect depends on what it makes the person think about. Clearly, positive affect, as Isen maintains, may cue thoughts about how much one has to lose and about avoidable loss, but may also trigger thoughts about risk taking and winning. The question of what happens when affect maintenance and cueing processes are in opposition merits investigation. The context in which positive affect is elicited—for example, after a string of

Table 7.3. Mean probability of win required in order to bet, and mean number of thoughts about loss (corrected) as a function of affective state and level of risk.

Risk condition	Positive affect	Neutral affect
High risk	$n = 11$	$n = 11$
Mean probability required	0.68	0.52
Mean number of thoughts about loss	24%	12%
Moderate risk	$n = 11$	$n = 13$
Mean probability required	0.65	0.52
Mean number of thoughts about loss	20%	5%
Low risk	$n = 13$	$n = 12$
Mean probability required	0.53	0.59
Mean number of thoughts about loss	6%	20%

Note. High risk = all 10 chips at stake
      Moderate risk = 5 out of 10 chips at stake
      Low risk = 1 chip at stake
Source Adapted from Isen and Geva (1987) pp. 149, 150, with permission of the authors and Academic Press, Inc.

painful losses or in a group setting—may be factors that help determine what people think about and how they respond when faced with a choice of risky or cautious action.

To sum up Isen's findings: When does positive affect discourage risk taking? When the risky decision is meaningful and therefore there is a genuine loss at stake (Isen & Patrick, 1983; also Deldin & Levin, 1986); and when the risk of losing is high, for example, on the order of 0.83 (Isen & Patrick, 1983). In contrast, positive affect encourages preference for risk when the risk is low (or the prospect of loss is not salient) or the cost associated with loss is small or trivial.

Isen's work is impressive because it represents a sustained attack on the question of affect and risk preference/taking. These are important findings, that positive affect does not have the simple effect "common sense" would predict, viz. little concern about risks and a general propensity to take or endorse risky actions. The program has mapped risk-related behavior across one band of the emotional spectrum—mild positive affect. An obvious next step is to examine the strength and pervasiveness of the affect-maintenance principle in a series of parametric studies in which such factors as magnitude of affect, the normal or "background" mood state of the person, magnitude (or meaningfulness) of the win/loss at stake, and nature of the risky action (e.g. whether socially sanctioned or approved) are compared or varied. As an example, it would be important to know how students who are truly happy and elated because they have been accepted into Harvard Law School, received their team's most valuable player award, or won an all-expenses-paid trip to Paris respond when they are then offered high-risk bets. Will they respond cautiously, so as to avoid the possibility of loss and guarantee the maintenance of their positive affect or will their elation flood their attention to the extent that thoughts about possible loss do not come to mind? As another example, it would be worth exploring whether and how the person's normal mood state interacts with the elicitation of positive affect to produce affect-maintenance (or opposing) tendencies in risky situations. The question of whether weak, mild, and strong feelings constitute a continuum as far as risky behavior is concerned is an important issue to be resolved.

A nice example of the possibilities for natural field studies of mood and risk taking is work on the effect of winning or losing an important game on football fans' risk taking. The Ohio Lottery Commission has found that for several days following a victory by the Ohio State University football team, sales of State of Ohio lottery tickets tend to be greater than after the football team suffers defeat. Presumably, the upsurge in gambling on the lottery is a reflection of increased positive mood in the community. It is possible, of course, that the influx of lottery gamblers is from those who bet—and won—on the OSU football team and therefore had money to wager. Arkes, Herren, and Isen (1988), who report this datum, do not see it as a difficulty for the Isen position. The lottery advertisements emphasize massive wins, not losses, and the amount to lose in buying a ticket is dismissed as trivial.

Mood effects on the quality of decision making

The previous discussion dealing with mood effects on risk tasking has been limited to the effect of positive mood—and has not evaluated whether the apparent risk aversion of happy subjects is a function of sound, thoughtful decision making, ill-considered decision making, or neither. As stated earlier, risk taking in greater or lesser degree does not correspond necessarily to devil-may-care adventurism on the one hand and sober rationalism on the other. There is little in the risk-taking work reported in the previous section to help answer the question of whether we should be wary of the arousal of positive (or negative) moods for their deleterious effects on decision making under risk. We turn to the literature on mood effects on decision-making strategies and performance for some leads to answer the question. Again, many of these leads come from the work of Alice M. Isen.

Isen's studies suggest that people who are made to feel good by their success on a perceptual-motor task (Isen & Means, 1983) or by receipt of a small, free gift (Isen et al., 1982) tended to simplify the decision problem and make their decision more quickly than comparison controls. Sometimes this tendency facilitated performance, and sometimes impaired it, depending on the nature of the decision task (Isen, 1987).

Isen et al. (1982) found that subjects in whom good feelings had been induced were significantly more likely to use an intuitive solution to solve a physics problem, leading 72% of them to give an incorrect answer (cf. 40% in the control condition). Similarly, positive mood-induced subjects were more likely to rely on the "availability heuristic" (cf. Tversky & Kahneman, 1974) to solve a problem of numbers in a set, again leading them to give an incorrect answer.

Isen and Means (1983) studied the effects of positive affect on decision making in which there was no correct or incorrect choice. Subjects were asked to select one of six fictitious cars, differing along nine dimensions (e.g. fuel economy, safety record), with information about each placed in a folder. The subjects who had been induced with a positive mood chose much the same cars as the control subjects, but considered fewer dimensions, rechecked less information, and took about half the time to make their choice (11 minutes versus 20 minutes). Thus, people who feel happy tend to simplify a decision problem. Such simplification can, of course, produce sloppy decision making or it can be an efficient strategy to prevent one from becoming bogged down in complex decision situations. In the case of Isen and Mean's subjects, the process appears to have been efficient rather than sloppy—for example, the two dimensions eliminated from consideration were demonstrably of little importance.

Recent work by Isen and others reveals that the simplification tendency shown by subjects in a positive mood is related to integrative organization of problem-related and decision-related material and is conducive to creative problem solving (Isen et al., 1982) and to efficiency in clinical problem solving (Isen, Rosenzweig, & Young, 1991).

Research by Murray et al. (1990) has found that positive mood subjects, relative to others, identify a greater variety of similarities and differences between stimuli, indicative of cognitive flexibility in categorizing information. However, in some cases, such as the processing of persuasive messages, positive mood may lead to poorer task performance (Mackie & Worth, 1989; Worth & Mackie, 1987). These contrasting findings indicate that the effects of mood on cognitive processes are task- and situation-dependent. In the case of tasks that are important, allow for creative processing, and provide feedback, positive mood may stimulate efficient information processing and enhance task performance. But in the case of trivial and uninteresting tasks, positive mood may lead to error-prone heuristics that impede task performance (cf. Isen, 1987; Murray et al., 1990).

Negative affect and decision making

Forgas (1989) extended the study of mood effects on decision making by comparing the effects of positive and negative affect on information search and decision strategies on both personally relevant and personally irrelevant decisions. Mood was manipulated by giving subjects bogus feedback about their performance on a "social adjustment and personality test." Subjects in the positive affect condition were told: "This is very good. You have done much better than the averge score for students in your age group. You obviously have an excellent personality and you find most social situations very easy to handle." Subjects in the negative affect condition were told: "This is very bad," etc. The decision involved a choice between potential partners with whom the subject would work (personally relevant decision) or with whom the *next* subject would work (personally irrelevant decision). Files were produced containing information about eight potential partners on ten features, such as intelligence, friendliness, etc. Thus, the decision was complex.

Forgas found that in their choice of partners, happy and neutral mood subjects preferred partners who had good task skills (e.g. high IQ) while sad subjects preferred partners who had good interpersonal qualities (friendly, likeable). This provides an interesting example of how mood can interfere with the quality of choice. Consider a personnel manager who has had a personal setback which affects his mood. It is possible that, in selecting between candidates for the next position, he will choose on the basis of their friendliness rather than the skills required for the position. Forgas then compared the performance of subjects on four indices:

1. *Decision time*: Happy subjects took less time to decide than either the sad or neutral mood subjects. This finding is consistent with Isen and Mean's (1983) finding that happy subjects reach decisions quickly.
2. *Decision efficiency*: Happy subjects considered fewer irrelevant dimensions and rechecked less information than sad subjects but did not differ from neutral subjects, again consistent with Isen and Means (1983). An interesting finding is that in the sad mood condition, subjects were more efficient when they were dealing with a personally relevant decision than with an irrelevant decision, suggesting that if the choice is important, the person will, to some extent, overcome his or her mood state and perform efficiently.
3. *Information preference*: Happy subjects searched more task-related (cf. social) information than sad subjects, but again did not differ from neutral subjects. Also, when dealing with a personally relevant decision, subjects searched more task-related information than with an irrelevant decision.
4. *Information processing stragegy*: Happy subjects were more likely to search by attribute than sad subjects, but did not differ from neutral subjects. Search by attribute, rather than search by alternative, is an efficient search strategy that enables decision makers to reduce the complexity of decision making (Klayman, 1985).

Forgas's results demonstrate that mood has an effect on the alternative actually chosen in a social decision. People in sad moods tend to choose a partner who will not be a threat (i.e. they choose someone who is friendly rather than someone who is intelligent and competent). The effect of the sad mood was especially marked, compared to positive mood which did not differ consistently in its effects from the neutral mood, perhaps because people's normal state approximates happiness. (This relates to the asymmetry of mood effects, cf. Isen, 1987). As in Isen's studies, positive mood led subjects to be more efficient in their decision making, a sensible strategy given the difficulty of searching an 8×10 matrix of information.

One of the limitations of Forgas's study is its reliance on the bogus feedback method to induce positive, neutral, and negative moods. This method raises the question of whether subjects are influenced more by their mood or by their success or failure on a previous task as they face a new task. It is to be expected that subjects who learn they have "failed" a test of personality and social adjustment will be particularly slow, cautious, and extremely careful to check (and recheck) relevant and possibly irrelevant information before they make a choice. Having been "burned" once, they are highly motivated to prevent a repeat.

Susan Simpson's (1989) thesis at Flinders University addresses this problem by using the reading of a happy, neutral, or sad story as the method of mood induction. The subjects were high school students who were asked to choose an essay topic in a simple decision (2 alternative essays × 5 dimensions) or complex decision (3 alternative essays × 8 dimensions). Consistent with previous findings, subjects in a positive mood were more efficient in their information search than subjects in the neutral condition (i.e. searched and researched less information before making their choice).

In sum, this body of research shows consistently that positive mood is associated with a simplifying style of information search in decision making—faster, more selective, less redundant. There is no indication that this fast-track style of decision strategy leads to sloppy decision making. However, that proposition has not been put to the test in respect to important decisions in which major gains or losses are involved. Such a test would involve the induction of positive and negative mood states followed by administration of a complex decision task for which there are correct or incorrect solutions for better and worse alternatives. In the previous section we noted the greater risk aversion of happy mood subjects. Clearly, their risk aversion is not accompanied by an increase in cautiousness in the way they search information.

Risk taking in depression

Studies of people who suffer from depression are an important source of evidence about the effects of extreme affective states on risk taking. Clinicians point to the close link between clinical depression and deficits in decision making (Klerman, 1980). Depressed patients are characterized by an inability to make decisions and a tendency to depend on others to decide for them. (At the other end of the continuum, case studies of manic patients show that they often make rash and ill-conceived choices during periods of hyperactivity.)

The effect of depression is to lead to a slowing down in decision making, a reluctance to make decisions, and marked tendencies to give greater weight to risks than to benefits, and to practice risk-avoidance in making choices.

Elizabeth Costello (1983) compared 26 depressed women (hospital outpatients) with 26 nondepressed women on how they integrated information about probability and utility of outcomes in making hypothetical decisions. The depressed women required a higher utility before selecting an uncertain alternative. The more depressed the patient, as measured on the Beck Depression Inventory, the higher the expected utility required before taking a risk.

Radford, Mann, and Kalucy (1986) studied a sample of 39 highly depressed patients in the psychiatric ward of a South Australian hospital. The patients were administered, with great difficulty, two hypothetical dilemmas, based on the expectancy-value model (Edwards, 1961). They were asked to rate the attractiveness (utility) and probability of the choice alternatives in a dilemma about study vs travel and in a dilemma about taking a job vs unemployment. In general, the most depressed patients (as measured on the Beck Depression Inventory) were the most "depressed" in their ratings of utilities and probabilites. Also, the most depressed were most reluctant to offer a choice between the two options in order to resolve the dilemma, and if they made a choice usually failed to combine utility and probability ratings correctly to produce a "rational" choice consistent with the expectancy model.

Finally, Pietromonaco and Rook (1987) studied the decision style of two samples of college students — 25 depressed and 44 nondepressed. The students were administered a set of 10 decision scenarios and a list of potential risks and benefits that might follow from making a particular choice. An example of one of the problems is: "You recently purchased a pair of shoes. After wearing the shoes for about a month, you notice that some of the stitches around the sole of the shoe are coming loose. In deciding whether to return the shoes to the store, you consider the following benefits and risks. Potential benefit: You might get your money back or a replacement pair of shoes. Potential risk: You may waste a lot of time and not accomplish anything" (Pietromonaco & Rook, 1987, pp. 401–402).

Subjects were asked to rate the potential benefit and the potential risk on three 7-point scales relating to *importance* of their possibility, the *likelihood* they would occur, and the *feeling* they would have if the benefit (or risk) were to happen. A composite measure was formed to represent *perception* of potential risks and benefits. In general, depressed students rated potential risks *more* highly and potential benefits less highly than nondepressed students. In addition, depressed students were more reluctant than the nondepressed to take the action specified in the scenario (in the shoe example, returning the shoes to the store).

This work on depression is consistent with findings from studies of subjects who are induced into a negative mood and then given risk-related decisions to make. These studies of depressive subjects are consistent with Forgas's (1989) finding that sad subjects take more time to reach decisions, are less efficient in information search (recheck more information), and tend to make nonthreatening, risk-avoidant choices. In sum, the constellation of transient negative mood, stress, anxiety, and severe depression seems to follow a similar pattern in regard to risk taking and decision making. In varying degrees, the constellation is associated with cautious and inefficient information processing, selective attention to risks at the expense of benefits, reluctance to choose, and in many cases, self-defeating choices.

Explanations for the effect of mood on decison making

Two theoretical approaches have featured in the discussion of how mood influences judgment and risk taking. One approach, the mood-memory model, focuses on the effects of mood state on the priming of memory (Fiske & Taylor, 1984) and on access to memories of mood-congruent ideas (Bower, 1981). The other approach focuses on the effects of mood on the selection of information-processing rules (Forgas, 1989) and on decision-coping patterns and heuristics (Janis, 1989; Janis & Mann, 1977).

Mood-memory models

One explanation for the effect of mood on risk taking is the priming of mood-congruent categories that influence subsequent perception and interpretation of risk events. Being in a good mood leads to positive thoughts and being in a bad mood leads to negatively toned ideas (Fiske & Taylor, 1984). The priming process tends to be automatic. Ideas and memories of similar emotional tone tend to be linked in memory. Thus, activation of a positive or negative item automatically primes other positive or negative items. According to the priming model, the effect of a positive mood will be to recall positive items, to prompt one to think about the good consequences of choice alternatives, and to follow through on decisions because one is optimistic. The effect of a negative mood will be to recall negative items, to prompt thoughts about losses and hassles associated with the choice alternatives, and to put off action. (Note: An interesting study would be to make a comparison of decision balance sheets (Janis & Mann, 1977) completed by subjects in a positive mood and in a negative mood. The priming model would predict that positive mood subjects would enter more *gains* in the balance sheet, negative mood subjects would enter more *losses*.)

Happy subjects sometimes take more risks, as a result of being especially optimistic, although as Isen's (1987) work demonstrates, sometimes they take fewer risks. A difficulty for the priming model is Isen and Geva's (1987) finding that subjects in a positive mood and faced with a medium-to-high risk have a greater number of thoughts about loss than those in a neutral mood. Indeed, Isen's findings in general pose difficulties for the model.

There has been less research on negative mood than on positive mood, and so less is known about the usefulness of the priming model in regard to negative mood. The effect of negative mood is more variable than that of positive mood, possibly because people in bad moods try to control and neutralize their mood.

Bower's (1981) network model of mood and memory is a somewhat more elaborate explanation for the effects of mood on cognition. Bower argues that the onset of a mood or emotion brings to mind events and memories linked to that emotion and, as in a network, other mood-congruent or consistent memories are elicited. As a highly fanciful example of a memory net, imagine a subject in a mood experiment who has been put in a good mood by learning that he has topped the class on a test of human performance (dart throwing). Kenny's thoughts (we will call him Kenny) might go like this: "I came out on top! Terrific!... I knew I was okay at pitching, but dart throwing... far out!... Reminds me that the Student Union is having a games night later this semester ... should give it a try... might win big!... You want us to play roulette?... I'm pretty good at darts, aren't I?... And now that I think of it, I'm no slouch at cards... won a couple of dollars when we played poker on vacation... should be a breeze... Put me down for $2... It's my lucky day..."

The network model suggests that affect has a pervasive influence because it elicits clusters of similar, interrelated memories. The model also suggests that the influence of affect should be strongest for highly similar events in the memory network. Thus, in the example of Kenny, his happiness in learning he is tops in darts is more likely to make him remember positive events and successful decisions relating to games and sport rather than events and decisions relating to, say, academic achievement. Johnson and Tversky (1983) indicate that this is not necessarily so. They found that their subjects, who were saddened by the story of a murdered student, showed a significant increase in their risk perception not only about the risk of homicide but also about a wide array of quite unrelated hazards, such as toxic chemical spills, floods, and tornados. Johnson and Tversky's finding that mood tends to flood risk perception in a quite undifferentiated way creates a problem for the network model of mood and memory.

Rule-based models

We have seen that mood-memory models do not fare all that well in accounting for the diversity of findings about mood effects. There is also the problem that risk perception and risk taking related to mood appear to vary substantially according to the nature of the risk, the level of risk, the nature and intensity of the mood, and so on. Thus, the plausibility of simple memory models as an explanation for mood effects is in question.

Forgas (1989) has suggested that a rule-based approach, based on social cognition, may be a more useful way to account for mood effects on complex personal decisions. According to the production systems framework (Pitz, 1977), decision making is a context-dependent social activity governed by rules and strategies that are produced automatically whenever certain antecedent conditions, such as time pressure and affective states, are present. Examples of such automatic rules include "When feeling bad, select an alternative most likely to lead to rewarding outcomes" or "When pushed too hard, do the opposite," "When happy, beware of losses," or "When stressed, reduce information input." According to Forgas (1989), such rules are stored in memory in a priority ordered list, and the highest priority rule relevant to the decision situation is automatically selected. The production system model is very general, but it has the merit of addressing the highly context-dependent, rule-based character of many personal and social decisions. A limitation of the approach is that it has yet to specify which rules will be applied in different mood-related situations.

Janis's (1989) constraints model of policy making includes some of the features of rule-based models of decision making and risk taking. The constraints model identifies some of the conditions under which decision makers tend to rely on three types of simple, error-prone decision rules—cognitive rules, affiliative rules, and emotive rules. The decision maker tends to rely on emotive rules for coping with difficult decisions when he is emotionally stressed, strongly aroused by feelings of anger, elation, etc., or is driven by powerful motives such as lust and greed. Examples of emotive rules include the "retaliate" or "tit-for-tat" rule, which dominates when the decision maker is frustrated or angry; the "can do!" rule, frequently observed among military men when they feel threatened; and the "wow, grab it!" rule, often invoked when frustration gives way to elation at the prospect of a solution, any solution.

SUMMARY AND CONCLUSIONS

The research literature on the relationship between stress, emotional state, and risk taking is sparse and incomplete. Indeed, the question of how emotion influences risk taking behavior comprises two rather different literatures. The first, deriving from case studies of responses to threatening and emergency situations, deals with aversive emotions, stress arousal, and the resolution of painful decisional conflict. The second, deriving from studies of mild, everyday events that induce modest changes in mood, deals with, for the most part, transient positive affect, and its influence in essentially benign situations. The first literature, of which Janis and Mann's (1977) conflict theory is representative, uses studies of historical and political decisions, clinical research, and experiments in which stress is manipulated, to test the deleterious effects of high levels of stress on decision making, and by extension on risk taking. The second literature, of which Alice M. Isen's (1987) work on positive affect and social behavior is the exemplar, uses laboratory studies of undergraduates to investigate the effect of mild increases in positive mood on thought processes, risk perception, and risk taking. This literature has yielded a consistent and intriguing finding that mild positive affect tends to make the person risk-avoidant and cautious under conditions of high risk of meaningful loss. Unlike the first literature, the literature on positive affect has no extension into studies of high levels of positive affect. Little is known about the influence of high levels of positive affect on risk taking and whether highly elated subjects are likely to be risk-avoidant or risk takers.

It is clear that the two literatures do not run in parallel. Also, it is evident that, at least at the level of mild moods, there is not much symmetry between positive and negative mood states in their effects on decision making and risk taking. Negative mood, perhaps because it is an "abnormal" condition, or perhaps because subjects attempt to alleviate the condition, seems to follow a different course and may require a different explanation from positive mood effects. Certainly, the asymmetry between positive and negative mood effects stands as a challenge to any global theory of emotional influences on judgments and decisions.

It is customary to conclude with a call for further research. My conclusion is a call for a wider perspective on the study of affect and risk taking. Such a perspective should encompass longitudinal studies of the relationship between normal mood state and risk-taking propensity, correlational analysis of the relationship between self-reported mood and risk taking (for example, in the so-called "neutral" or control condition of mood experiments), and field studies comparing pre- and post-event risk taking as a function of mood changes produced by personal and shared success or failure.

ACKNOWLEDGMENTS

I am grateful to Joseph Forgas, Alice M. Isen, and the editor for their many helpful and constructive suggestions and comments on the first version of this chapter.

REFERENCES

Abelson, R. P., & Levi, A. (1985). Decision making and decision theory. In G. Lindzey & E. Aronson (Eds.), *Handbook of social psychology*. (3rd ed, pp. 231–310) New York: Random House.

Arkes, H. R., Herren, L. T. & Isen, A. M. (1988). The role of potential loss in the influence of affect on risk-taking behavior. *Organizational Behavior and Human Decision Processes*, **41**, 181–193.

Ben Zur, H., & Breznitz, S. J. (1981). The effect of time pressure on risky choice behavior. *Acta Psychologica*, **17**, 89–104.

Bower, G. H. (1981). Mood and memory. *American Psychologist*, **36**, 129–148.

Brecher, M. (1980). *Decisions in crisis: Israel 1967 and 1973*. Berkeley: University of California Press.

Costello, E. J. (1983). Information processing for decision making in depressed women: A study of subjective expected utilities. *Journal of Affective Disorders*, **5**, 239–251.

Deldin, P. J., & Levin, I. P. (1986). The effect of mood induction in a risky decision-making task. *Bulletin of the Psychonomic Society*, **24**, 4–6.

Edwards, W. (1961). Behavioral decision theory. *Annual Review of Psychology*, **12**, 473–498.

Fiske, S. T., & Taylor, S. E. (1984). *Social cognition*. Reading, MA: Addison-Wesley.

Forgas, J. P. (1989). Mood effects on decision making strategies. *Australian Journal of Psychology*, **41**, 197–214.

Forgas, J. P., & Moylan, S. (1987). After the movies: The effects of mood on social judgments. *Personality and Social Psychology Bulletin*, **13**, 467–477.

Holsti, O. R., & George, A. L. (1975). The effects of stress on the performance of foreign policy makers. *Political Science Annual*, **6**, 255–319.

Isen, A. M. (1987). Positive affect, cognitive processes, and social behavior. In L. Berkowitz (Ed.), *Advances in Experimental Social Psychology* (Vol. 20., pp. 203–253). New York: Academic Press.

Isen, A. M., & Geva, N. (1987). The influence of positive affect on acceptable level of risk: The person with a large canoe has a large worry. *Organizational Behavior and Human Decision Processes*, **39**, 145–154.

Isen, A. M., & Means, B. (1983). The influence of positive affect on decision making strategy. *Social Cognition*, **2**, 18–31.

Isen, A. M., Means, B., Patrick, R., & Nowicki, G. (1982). Some factors influencing decision making strategy and risk taking. In M. S. Clark & S. T. Fiske (Eds.), *Affect and cognition: The 17th Annual Carnegie Symposium on Cognition* (pp. 243–261). Hillsdale, N. J.: Erlbaum.

Isen, A. M., Nygren, T. E., & Ashby, F. G. (1988). Influence of positive affect on the subjective utility of gains and losses: It is just not worth the risk. *Journal of Personality and Social Psychology*, **55**, 710–717.

Isen, A. M., & Patrick, R. (1983). The effect of positive feelings on risk-taking: When the chips are down. *Organizational Behavior and Human Performance*, **31**, 194–202.

Isen, A. M., Pratkanis, A. R., Slovic, P., & Slovic, L. (1984). *The influence of positive affect on risk preference*. Paper presented at the 92nd Annual Meeting of the American Psychological Association, Toronto, Ontario, Canada.

Isen, A. M., Rosenzweig, A. S., & Young, M. J. (1991). The influence of positive affect in clinical problem solving. *Medical Decision Making*, **11**, 221–227.

Janis, I. L. (1959). Motivational factors in the resolution of decisional conflicts. In M. R. Jones (Ed.), *Nebraska Symposium on Motivation* (Vol. 7., pp. 283–311). Lincoln: University of Nebraska Press.

Janis, I. L. (1982). *Groupthink: Psychological studies of policy decisions and fiascoes*. Boston: Houghton Mifflin.

Janis, I. L. (1989). *Crucial decisions: Leadership in policy making and crisis management*. New York: Free Press.

Janis, I. L., & Mann, L. (1977). *Decision making: A psychological analysis of conflict, choice and commitment*. New York: Free Press.

Johnson, E., & Tversky, A. (1983). Affect, generalization and the perception of risk. *Journal of Personality and Social Psychology*, **45**, 20–31.

Keinan, G. (1987). Decision making under stress: Scanning of alternatives under controllable and uncontrollable threats. *Journal of Personality and Social Psychology*, **52**, 639–644.

Klayman, J. (1985). Children's decision strategies and their adaptation to task characteristics. *Organizational Behavior and Human Decision Processes*, **35**, 179–201.

Klerman, G. L. (1980). Overview of affective disorders. In H. I. Kaplan, A. M. Freedman, & B. J. Sadock (Eds.), *Comprehensive textbook of psychiatry* (3rd ed., pp. 1305–1318). Baltimore: Williams and Williams.

Mackie, D. M., & Worth, L. T. (1989). Processing deficits and the mediation of positive affect in persuasion. *Journal of Personality and Social Psychology*, **57**, 27–40.

McGuire, W. J. (1985). The nature of attitudes and attitude change. In G. Lindzey & E. Aronson (Eds.), *Handbook of social psychology* (3rd ed., pp. 136–314). Reading, MA: Addison-Wesley.

Murray, N., Sujan, H., Hirt, E. R., & Sujan, M. (1990). The effect of mood in categorization: A cognitive flexibility intepretation. *Journal of Personality and Social Psychology*, **59**, 411–425.

Payne, J. W. (1985). Psychology of risky decisions. In G. Wright (Ed.), *Behavioral decision making* (pp. 3–23). New York: Plenum.

Pemberton, W. E. (1989). *Harry S. Truman: Fair dealer and cold warrior*. Boston: Wayne.

Pietromonaco, P. R., & Rook, K. S. (1987). Decision style in depression: The contribution of perceived risks versus benefits. *Journal of Personality and Social Psychology*, **52**, 399–408.

Pitz, G. F. (1977). Decision making and cognition. In H. Jungermann & G. de Zeeuw (Eds.), *Decision making and change in human affairs* (pp. 403–424). Dordrecht, Holland: Reidel.

Radford, M. H., Mann, L., & Kalucy, R. S. (1986). Psychiatric disturbance and decision making. *Australian and New Zealand Journal of Psychiatry*, **20**, 210–217.

Simpson, S. (1989). *Mood by task complexity effects on information processing in decision-making*. Unpublished honours thesis, The Flinders University of South Australia, Bedford Park, Australia.

Tan, C. (1985). *The role of conflict, expectancies and individual differences in the decision-making process*. Unpublished master's thesis, The Flinders University of South Australia, Bedford Park, Australia.

Tversky, & Kahneman, D. (1974). Judgments under uncertainty: Heuristics and biases. *Science*, **185**, 1124–1131.

Wallsten, T. S. (1980). Processes and models to describe choice and inference. In T. S. Wallsten (Ed.), *Cognitive processes in choice and decision behavior* (pp. 215–237). Hillsdale, NJ: Erlbaum.

Worth, L. T., & Mackie, D. M. (1987). Cognitive mediation of positive affect in persuasion. *Social Cognition*, **5**, 76–94.

Wright, P. (1974). The harassed decision maker: Time pressures, distractions, and the use of evidence. *Journal of Applied Psychology*, **59**, 555–561.

Chapter 8

Risk taking and health

Nancy E. Adler, Susan M. Kegeles, and Janice L. Genevro
University of California, San Francisco

CONTENTS

INTRODUCTION

In risk-taking behaviors, what is often put at risk is one's health. Behaviors commonly identified as risky (e.g. rock-climbing, driving race cars, sky-diving, and living in areas where there is a substantial risk of natural hazards such as floods or earthslides) increase one's chances of morbidity (i.e. illness and injury) and mortality. In recent years, as more threats to health have been identified, a wide range of behaviors would now be included as risky. For example, smoking cigarettes, which was largely governed by moral and social considerations until

Risk-taking Behavior. Edited by J. F. Yates
© 1992 John Wiley & Sons Ltd

the US Surgeon General's report on smoking in 1964, is now viewed as a health-risking behavior.

In recent years, as morbidity and mortality have come to be related more to chronic conditions which are tied to lifestyle and behavior (e.g. smoking, alcohol use, diet, exercise) rather than to acute conditions, there has been increasing interest in understanding and influencing such behaviors. What characterizes these behaviors is that they are repetitive and ongoing. Further, some health-risking behaviors are associated with use of addictive substances so that changing the behavior may involve different dynamics than averting their onset.

Several theoretical models have been developed specifically to examine health-promoting and health-damaging behaviors. While these derive from broader theories of decision making and risk taking, they are tailored particularly to understanding health-related behaviors. In this chapter we will examine several theoretical models which have been designed specifically to account for health-risking behaviors and consider two particular health problems related to risk taking—AIDS and unwanted pregnancy. These are both important health problems and ones for which theoretical models have been developed based on broader models of risk taking and health.

MODELS OF HEALTH BEHAVIORS

Many of the models of health behaviors that have been developed are consistent with "expectancy-value" theories of behavior. Although various theories differ in terms of specific elements, they share the assumption that individuals weigh the costs and benefits of engaging in a behavior based on their subjective estimates of the likelihood that various consequences will occur as the result of their doing so (or their failing to do so) and the values they attach to those outcomes. Several of the broader theories of choice behavior, such as the Theory of Reasoned Action (Ajzen & Fishbein, 1980), have been applied to understanding health behaviors as well as nonhealth-related behaviors. As will be seen below, models that have been developed specifically to account for the likelihood that individuals will engage in health-promoting or disease-preventing behaviors incorporate the "rational" component of the expectancy-value models, but some have expanded these to include emotional aspects that can emerge when there is a potential threat to one's health and well-being.

The Health Belief Model

The Health Belief Model (HBM) was developed in the early 1950s, and although it is consistent with expectancy-value models, its intellectual roots derive more closely from Lewinian field theory and Tolman's theory of learning (Kegeles, 1980; Rosenstock, 1966; Rosenstock, Strecher, & Becker, 1988). The HBM has provided an important framework for studying the extent to which individuals accept recommendations regarding health care and act on them. This model has been credited with generating more research on health-related behaviors than any other theoretical approach (Rosenstock, Strecher, & Becker, 1988).

The HBM was originally formulated to account for the failure of individuals to take advantage of preventive health services such as inoculations and screening tests (Kegeles, 1980; Rosenstock, 1966). Reflecting the components of an expectancy-value theory, it hypothesizes that behavior depends primarily on the value of a particular goal (e.g. avoidance of a given health threat) to the individual, and on the person's estimate of the probability that a given action (e.g. inoculation, diagnosis) will result in the achievement of that goal (Maiman & Becker, 1974).

As originally formulated, the HBM hypothesized that an individual would not make the decision to undertake a health action aimed at avoiding a specific disease threat unless he or she was psychologically ready to act (see Figure 8.1). Readiness to act was posited to be a function of the individual's perceptions of his or her personal susceptibility to the health threat, the perceived severity of the threat, the perceived benefits of the recommended health action, and barriers the individual foresaw to taking the action. These four elements form the basic components of the HBM.

The HBM originally also included "cues to action" as a determinant of engaging in a health behavior. Cues could be external, such as reminder postcards from a health care provider or a health information campaign in the mass media. Cues could also be internal, such as an individual's perception of his or her bodily states. Cues were hypothesized to be necessary to trigger health action in individuals psychologically ready to act based on their beliefs about personal susceptibility, severity, benefits, and barriers (Rosenstock, 1966). Although some studies have demonstrated that cues are an important predictor of health behavior (e.g. Jones, Jones, & Katz, 1988), this element of the original model has not been consistently included in research conducted using the HBM. Researchers may have been reluctant to include measurement of cues to action because the specific cues that influence a given action may vary considerably between different individuals, and such an idiosyncratic variable may be difficult to assess.

In the years following its introduction, the HBM has been applied to behaviors beyond the realm of preventive health behaviors, including illness behaviors such as coming for follow-up visits for diagnosed conditions or following recommended regimens for the treatment of disease. As a result of these applications, the model has been modified and reformulated. Of the more significant reformulations has been the inclusion of a new element, general motivation for health (Becker & Maiman, 1975). This variable is conceptualized as an individual difference in orientation toward and interest in health, and in perceived control over health matters. In some studies this has been treated as a

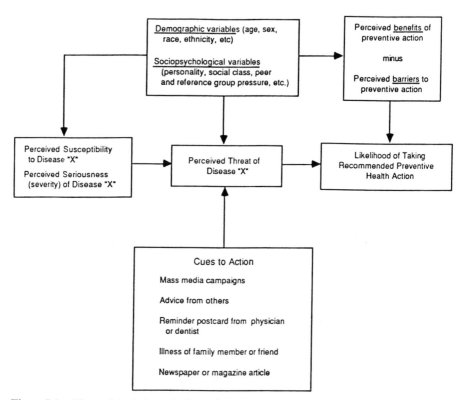

Figure 8.1. The original formulation of the Health Belief Model (from Becker & Maiman, 1975, p. 12, with permission).

single variable and in others it has been separated into two variables, orientation toward health and health locus of control (cf. Becker & Maiman, 1975; Jette *et al.*, 1981). Motivation for health is hypothesized to be stable over time for a given individual and not specific to any particular health condition or disease (Cummings, Jette, & Rosenstock, 1978).

In a more recent reformulation, Rosenstock, Strecher, and Becker (1988) suggested that the concept of perceived self-efficacy that one can perform the preventive behavior (Bandura, 1977, 1986) should be incorporated into the model as an explanatory variable. Rosenstock, Strecher, and Becker argue that the concept of self-efficacy may not have been critical to early applications of the HBM since these applications dealt with circumscribed and fairly simple preventive health behaviors, such as obtaining immunizations. Current uses of the model, however, involve investigation of the relationship between health beliefs and more complex behaviors involved in complying with medical regimens, some of which may be complicated and comprise multiple behaviors, and the changing of lifelong health habits. Given a psychological readiness to act, the probability that individuals actually will engage in a complex or difficult health behavior may be influenced by their belief that they are capable of performing the behavior. Rosenstock and his colleagues, citing evidence of the importance of self-efficacy in the initiation and maintenance of behavioral change, maintain that the explicit addition of perceived self-efficacy to the HBM may help to explain variance in health-related behaviors that was previously unaccounted for by the model (Rosenstock, Strecher, & Becker 1988).

A large number of empirical studies have been conducted using the HBM to explain and predict preventive health behavior, illness behavior, and compliance behavior. One of the most comprehensive reviews on research using the HBM was done by Janz and Becker (1984). The primary criterion they used in drawing conclusions about the empirical value of the HBM was a significance ratio, the ratio of the number of studies in which statistically significant results were reported to the total number of studies. This ratio was calculated separately for the findings related to each of the four major elements of the HBM (perceived personal susceptibility, perceived severity, perceived benefits, and perceived barriers), for prospective and retrospective studies, and for studies in three domains of behavior (preventive health behaviors, sick-role behaviors such as taking prescribed medicines, and clinic utilization). Studies reviewed were selected using the following criteria: (a) publication between 1974 and 1984; (b) contained at least one behavioral outcome measure; (c) only findings relevant to the relationships of perceived personal severity, perceived susceptibility, perceived benefits and perceived barriers are reported; (d) dealt with medical (not dental) conditions; and (e) subjects were adults (Janz & Becker, 1984, p. 3). In the 46 studies reviewed, there was substantial empirical support for the HBM based on high significance ratios for both prospective and retrospective studies across the four HBM dimensions and the three behavioral domains (Janz & Becker, 1984).

The support for the HBM based on this review is not definitive, however. One difficulty in using a significance ratio as a criterion to evaluate the empirical backing for the HBM is that studies that do not report statistically significant findings are less likely to be published. Significance ratios would therefore be biased in favor of a high ratio of significant studies in relation to the total number of studies published, and would not necessarily represent the ratio for studies with significant findings in relation to all studies conducted. In addition, in using a significance ratio rather than conducting a meta-analysis, which provides a rigorous quantitative method for combining results of different studies (Hunter, Schmidt, & Jackson, 1982; Rosenthal, 1984), Janz and Becker do not take into account effect size (i.e. amount of variation in health-related behavior explained by the HBM) in their assessment of the empirical value of the HBM. This is unfortunate since one of the primary criticisms of the HBM has been that although its use "has frequently yielded significant results... the proportion of variance it explains is often lower than expected" (Rosenstock, Strecher, & Becker, 1988, p. 182).

It is, in fact, difficult to compare effect sizes across studies using HBM variables because the operational definitions of the constructs and the measures used vary greatly. One finds substantial discrepancies both across and within studies in the strength of the relationships found between HBM variables and behavioral outcomes. For example, in an application of the HBM to mothers' adherence to a dietary regimen for their obese children, Becker et al. (1977) found that HBM variables in combination explained 49% of the variation in weight change at an initial follow-up visit, which dropped to 22% of the variation in weight change at the fourth follow-up visit for these children. In a study of members of a pre-paid health plan, Leavitt (1979) found that the set of HBM variables accounted for only about 10% of the variation in general clinic utilization.

One factor contributing to the erratic performance of the HBM in accounting for behavior is the wide variation in measures used to assess elements of the model. Because the HBM is based on the supposition that health behaviors relate to specific beliefs regarding that particular behavior, measures are designed that are relevant for each particular behavior. The measures are unique to each study and are not comparable across studies. In addition, the constructs of the HBM have not been operationally defined in a consistent manner, and the constructs themselves have varied from study to study (cf. Jette et al., 1981). Unfortunately, there has been relatively little work done investigating these issues and other psychometric properties of measures of the dimensions of the HBM (Jette et al., 1981).

Some elements of the HBM appear to be more consistently related to behavioral outcomes than do others, but this varies by behavioral domain. In their review, Janz and Becker (1984) found that the construct of perceived barriers was the most consistent predictor of health-related behavior in general. Perceived susceptibility, however, contributed most to understanding preventive health behaviors, while perceived benefits and perceived severity were more useful in explaining sick-role behaviors.

The HBM has been utilized recently in studies examining predictors of dieting and exercising behavior in adolescents (O'Connell et al., 1985); in developing effective education regarding sexually transmitted diseases (Simon & Das, 1984); in identifying the origins and stability of children's health beliefs relative to their mothers' health beliefs and to use of medicines (Bush & Iannotti, 1988); and to improve compliance in emergency room patients (Jones, Jones, & Katz, 1988). Findings from these studies echo the discrepant results discussed earlier. In some cases, specific HBM variables have been found to be significantly related to certain health-related behaviors (e.g. Mullen, Hersey, & Iverson, 1987), whereas in other studies, significant relationships have not been found between outcomes and components of the HBM variables (O'Connell *et al.*, 1985).

Much of the research on the HBM conducted subsequent to Janz and Becker's review has compared the HBM with other theoretical models, such as the Theory of Reasoned Action (Ajzen & Fishbein, 1980), which, as noted earlier, is a more general theory of choice behavior. The Theory of Reasoned Action (TRA) differs from the HBM in two important ways. First, while both models incorporate the individual's view of the consequences of taking or not taking a particular health action, they differ in the range of consequences that are examined. In the HBM the two immediate predictors of action are the extent of the perceived threat to oneself (severity) and perceived benefits of taking the recommended action for averting the threat. These perceived costs and benefits tend to be framed in terms of health-related considerations. In the Theory of Reasoned Action, one of the two key components hypothesized to influence one's intention to engage in the behavior is attitude towards performing the behavior. While attitude towards engaging in the behavior may reflect perceptions of health-related costs and benefits of the action for averting the threat and the degree of threat, other nonhealth-related considerations may also play a role. Because the TRA is broader and can encompass more considerations than the HBM, stronger predictions of intention and behavior should emerge using the TRA. In addition, the TRA incorporates perceptions of other people who are important to the individual regarding whether or not he or she should take the action. The HBM includes social variables in terms of cues that may be socially based but does not explicitly include perceived social norms and expectations that may govern some behaviors.

In a study of the extent to which patients followed recommendations regarding taking prescription drugs, Ried and Christensen (1988) found perceived benefits and perceived barriers, drawn from the HBM, to be significantly associated with compliance. The HBM dimensions, taken together, explained 10% of the variance in the drug-taking compliance variable. When variables representing the elements of the TRA were added to the analysis using hierarchical multiple regression techniques, an additional 19% of the variance in the compliance variable was explained. The authors concluded that the findings of the study "lend support to critics of the HBM who state that the model is insufficiently articulated, and the important determinants [of behavior] are not included" (Ried & Christensen, 1988, p. 283).

One of the aspects of the HBM that has made it appealing to researchers and health care providers alike is that it provides a clear framework for attempts to modify health behaviors. Health behaviors are explained in terms of perceptions and beliefs, and to the extent that these can be altered, behavior should change as well. To demonstrate the utility of this approach, one needs evidence that: (a) components of the model can be modified through targeted interventions and (b) changes in components of the model lead to changes in behavior.

There is mixed evidence on these two issues (Kegeles, 1980). For example, Haefner and Kirscht (1970) randomly assigned subjects to an intervention or control condition. Intervention subjects saw films presenting information relevant to three health problems: cancer, heart disease, and tuberculosis. The films urged some protective action: seeking health exams for all three conditions and, in relation to heart disease, improving diet, exercising, and refraining from smoking. Follow-up questionnaires eight months later revealed that the films were successful in changing some health beliefs (e.g. perceived personal susceptibility and perceived benefits). The intervention also had some effect on behavior. Subjects who saw the films were significantly more likely to report having had a check-up in the intervening period than were the control subjects. In addition, those with more positive belief scores (summed from components of the model) were more likely than those with lower scores to have obtained a check-up. However, the intervention was *not* successful in influencing personal health habits (diet, exercise, and smoking) and reports of these behaviors were unrelated to belief scores from the HBM.

A later study suggests that cues to action may be relatively more potent in influencing behaviors than are the other components of the HBM. Jones, Jones, and Katz (1988) used two interventions to influence compliance with a recommendation to schedule and keep a follow-up appointment among a sample of emergency department patients. The initial intervention at the time of the visit to the emergency room was designed to influence the following variables of the HBM: perceptions of susceptibility to illness complications, the seriousness of complications, benefits of a follow-up appointment, costs of returning, and cues which could prompt a patient to return. The second intervention was a telephone call which provided an abbreviated version of the earlier message. The researchers found that the initial intervention had little effect on beliefs (susceptibility, severity, benefits, costs) and that the telephone call was relatively more effective. They concluded that the telephone cue was "more effective than the clinical intervention in increasing the number of patients who schedule a follow-up appointment, and [was] equally effective in terms of increased appointment-keeping" (Jones, Jones, & Katz, 1988, p. 1183).

Protection Motivation Theory

Protection Motivation Theory, like the Health Belief Model, is a type of expectancy-value model, but focuses on fear as a major motivating factor in health behaviors. In contrast to much of the earlier work on fear arousal which used an affective variable (fear) as the key variable (Hovland, Janis, & Kelley, 1953), this model focuses on the cognitive appraisal process in response to components of a fear appeal message regarding a given health behavior (Rogers,

1983). The theory posits that the motivation to protect oneself mediates the influence of persuasive messages on the intention to engage in a health-relevant behavior. Protection motivation is, in turn, hypothesized to be a function of individuals' appraisals of the severity of the threat if they do not change their behavior, their perceived susceptibility or vulnerability to the threat, and their belief that the recommended action will reduce the threat.

In a later modification of the theory, Maddux and Rogers (1983) added a fourth component to the model: self-efficacy, drawn from Bandura (1977, 1986). A schematic depiction of the model from Rippetoe and Rogers (1987) is presented in Figure 8.2.

To test the theory, Maddux and Rogers (1983) examined responses of cigarette smokers to various communications about the effects of smoking. These communications varied in terms of the extent to which they presented: (a) the likelihood that negative outcomes (lung cancer and heart disease) would result from smoking, (b) how severe such outcomes would be, (c) how beneficial it would be to stop smoking in order to avoid experiencing the outcomes, and (d) how easy or difficult it would be to stop smoking. The manipulation of self-efficacy had the greatest impact on intention to stop smoking, although the manipulation of the perceived effectiveness of ceasing to smoke was also significant. Rippetoe and Rogers (1987) also found support for the model in an experimental study of intentions to perform breast self-examination among a group of college women. This study, which manipulated degree of threat, benefits of breast self-examination, and self-efficacy found that increased threat increased both adaptive and maladaptive responses such as avoidance and wishful thinking. Intentions to perform breast self-exam were greatest under conditions of high threat, high self-efficacy, high response efficacy, and higher levels of beliefs about the health benefits of breast self-examination.

Optimistic bias

The models described above all deal, at least in part, with individuals' evaluations of their own risk status. Unfortunately, individuals are not always accurate judges of the actual risk they face regarding various threats to their health (cf. Chapter 3). Weinstein (1984, 1987) has established the existence of a pervasive bias in people's judgments regarding their susceptibility to illness. Stated simply, individuals think, on average, that they are less likely than the average person to experience health problems. For example, when asked to evaluate their own chances of developing heart disease compared to the chances of other students of the same sex at their university, college students evaluated their own risk to be significantly lower than that of others (Weinstein, 1983). While this may be true of a given individual, it clearly cannot be true of the population as a whole; for some individuals to be at lower risk than average, others must be at higher risk. Weinstein (1987) replicated this finding of the

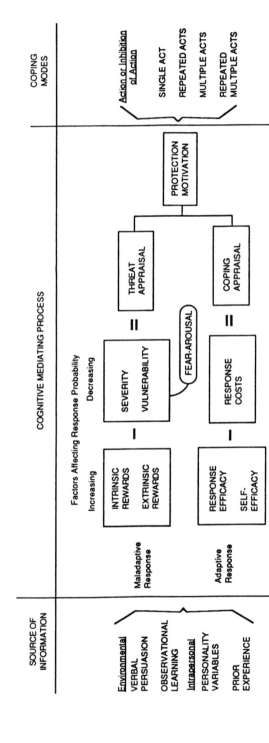

Figure 8.2. Protection-Motivation Theory (from Rippetoe & Rogers, 1987, reproduced by permission of the authors and J. B. Lippincott Co.)

occurrence of "unrealistic optimism" in a more diverse community sample as well. This bias can be reduced by providing subjects with information regarding the actual risk status of the peer group with which the comparisons are made (Weinstein, 1983).

In making their assessments of their own risk, people seem to take into account family history, but are not sensitive to the role that behavioral risk factors play (Weinstein, 1984). In the community sample, Weinstein (1987) found very little correlation between the occurrence of a risk factor and the person's estimate of his or her chances of an unfavorable outcome. Although cigarette smoking correlated with increased perceptions of risk of developing lung cancer, there was only a small correlation between smoking status and perceived risk of other smoking-related health problems such as heart attack and other cancers, and no correlation with perceived risk of stroke. Similarly, there was no relationship between seat-belt use and perceived risk of injury in an automobile accident or between frequency of flossing one's teeth and perceived risk of having gum disease.

Optimistic bias does not seem to occur as a result of defensive denial of risk. Weinstein (1987) found that individuals' perceptions of the seriousness of a hazard were not associated with their tendency to display unrealistic optimism regarding that hazard. Rather, the bias appears to emerge from limitations of cognitive processing of risk factors. Bias appears particularly likely to occur for risks which are seen to be infrequent, with which the individual has had little past experience, and which are perceived to be preventable by actions the person can take. Further, among older subjects, those who have not experienced a given health problem are likely to consider themselves to be less likely to develop it in the future. However, the lack of experience with a health problem in younger people is less likely to increase optimistic bias (Weinstein, 1987).

Optimistic bias may function to dissuade individuals from engaging in protective health actions. This was demonstrated in a study by Burger and Burns (1988) which will be discussed later in the chapter in the section on unwanted pregnancy.

Self-Regulation Theory

Self-Regulation Theory (Leventhal, Nerenz, & Steele, 1984; Leventhal, Safer, & Panagis, 1983) has primarily been applied to understanding illness behavior, such as taking medications for hypertension, and understanding how people respond to health-related communications. Viewed more broadly, it is a theory of how people decide what to do with respect to health behavior in situations in which there is a clear threat because of evidence of a disease state. Unlike the Health Belief Model and the Theory of Reasoned Action, Self-Regulation Theory does not place its only emphasis on cognition. In Self-Regulation Theory, some of the cognitive factors from the Health Belief Model are integrated with emotion-based factors, particularly those related to fear. Self-Regulation Theory posits that generally people are motivated to regulate their behavior to avoid health dangers, and that they actively extract information from their environments and previous experiences to formulate plans and actions to cope with health threats.

Self-Regulation Theory is based upon and extends the "Dual Process Model" (Leventhal, 1970), which postulates that an individual reacts both cognitively and emotionally to health communications. A distinction is made between coping with the danger (the objective threat) and coping with the fear that the communication may arouse (the subjective threat). Leventhal theorized that separate and partially independent information-processing systems influence these two types of responses.

Cognitive processes that are involved with coping with the objective threat have two functions. First, "action plans" for coping with the threat are generated; these plans are based on the cognitive representation of the health threat, which reflects current experience as well as past history. Current experience includes health messages (e.g. from the media and health care providers) and concrete body sensations. Past history includes memories about body experiences and previous health messages, and information about the health status and experiences of friends and family. The second function of the cognitive processes is to perceive and imagine response alternatives. This involves evaluating the benefits and costs of the potential actions the person could take to deal with the threat.

In addition to eliciting these cognitive responses, communications about health threats may also result in emotional reactions of fear, depression, or anger. These emotional responses to subjective threat result from information processing that is particularly responsive to concrete perceptions and is at least partially independent of cognition.

Since cognitive elements and emotional reactions may be independent of each other, separate action plans may be generated to deal with each. The cognitive and emotional reactions (and resulting action plans from each process) can be mutually interfering or mutually facilitating. Interference occurs when the response stemming from the fear reaction is incompatible with the action demanded by the objective task. For example, smokers might avoid lung X-rays if they fear the X-rays will reveal lung cancer, and their response to fear is avoidance. Facilitation occurs when the objective demands are compatible with the fear-motivated responses. For example, an individual may brush his or her teeth because of fear of the pain of tooth decay and dental work.

The Dual Process Model has been extended to become Self-Regulation Theory, which has three general principles: (a) people construct a representation of their illness or the health threat and develop a plan to cope with it; (b) individuals construct both objective representations and coping plans (a danger control process) and subjective representations and coping plans (an emotion control process); (c) a process of evaluation follows coping to determine the adequacy of the representation, the response, and the criterion for evaluation. Leventhal and his colleagues assert that particular attention must be paid to the fit between health messages and individuals' underlying beliefs about health and illness.

Particularly salient in this model is the concept that people hold "common-sense" representations of illness and health, and process new information from health communications and health care providers according to their underlying beliefs about health. For example, Meyer (1980) asked medical patients about various aspects of their experience with high blood pressure (which is asymptomatic) and its treatment. When asked if they agreed or disagreed with the statement "people can't tell when their blood pressure is up," 80% indicated agreement with the statement. Despite this, 88% of these individuals reported that they could tell when their own blood pressure was elevated, relying on internal indicators such as headaches, dizziness, nervousness, and other symptoms. These common sense representations of high blood pressure were very much in existence, even though they were contrary to individuals' more abstract beliefs.

There has not yet been an empirical test of this complex theory in its entirety. However, research findings have supported different aspects of Self-Regulation Theory. The research described above demonstrated the occurrence of common sense representations regarding blood pressure. Another study found that these representations had an influence on responses to symptoms. A study of help-seeking and delay found that, after controlling for age of the patient, those who attributed physical symptoms to aging delayed an average of 16 days before seeking health care, whereas those not making such an attribution delayed only an average of 8 days (Prohaska et al., 1987). Apparently, physical symptoms which are perceived as being due to the aging process are not believed to warrant medical attention as much as do those symptoms which seem to have no such explanation.

In a study examining the dual-process part of the theory, individuals were given one of four anti-smoking communications. The messages varied in the level of fear (high versus low) and in the presence or absence of specific action instructions (Leventhal, Watts, & Pagano, 1967). The high- and low-fear messages contained the same factual material, but the high-fear message also contained a description of an operation for lung cancer. All groups were told what to do (to stop smoking), but only the two action plan groups received detailed concrete information about specific steps to accomplish this. The high-fear message was more effective than the low-fear one in producing short-term changes in attitudes and intentions to quit smoking, while the presence or absence of an action plan did not influence attitudes or intentions. However, in changing long-term behavior it was the presentation of a specific action message that was important: In the absence of an action plan neither high- nor low-fear messages produced long-term behavior changes, and both levels of fear were associated with changes when accompanied by an action plan.

Although the empirical validity of the model is not yet proven, the theory is useful. In pointing out that cognition and emotion may lead to very different action plans, it alerts those who wish to intervene that they should be aware of the potential for interfering effects of the two processes. In addition, it emphasizes the need to understand people's own explanations for health and illness, since these may influence their health behaviors. Leventhal, Safer, and Panagis (1983) suggest ways that the theory can be put in practice in health education programs.

EXAMPLES OF HEALTH PROBLEMS

We have presented several models which have been developed to explain why individuals may engage in health-risking behaviors, or fail to take health-protecting actions. In the following section we examine two health problems, AIDS (Acquired Immune Deficiency Syndrome) and unwanted pregnancy, to show how such models have been used to understand these behaviors.

AIDS

Changing high-risk behaviors is the only means of preventing transmission of human immunodeficiency virus (HIV), the cause of AIDS. Thus, a great deal of research is currently focusing on understanding the factors involved with why people continue to put themselves at risk for contracting HIV, and using this information to develop AIDS prevention programs. Three models of behavior are currently being used to guide research in the area of AIDS risk behavior. One is the Theory of Reasoned Action (Ajzen & Fishbein, 1980), which was not designed specifically for examining health-risking behaviors, but which can be applied to understanding them. The second is the Health Belief Model described earlier, which is a general model of health behavior. The third is a model which has been developed specifically for understanding risk behaviors relevant to AIDS. This model, which incorporates components of the other models, is described below.

The AIDS Risk Reduction Model, ARRM (Catania, Kegeles, & Coates, 1990), identifies three stages individuals may traverse to reduce or change sexual activities which place them at risk for HIV transmission: (a) recognizing that their sexual activities place them at risk for acquiring HIV, and thus labeling their behavior as being risky; (b) making a decision to alter the high risk behavior and committing to that decision; (c) overcoming barriers to enacting the decision. The three stages are neither undirectional nor nonreversible. For example, some people may encounter difficulty in changing their behavior and come to relabel their activities as nonproblematic or reduce their commitment to change. In addition, the stages are not necessarily invariant. For example, some individuals with sex partners who are determined to change risky activities may acquiesce and therefore alter the risk behavior, but nonetheless, may not perceive their previous behavior as risky.

Each stage includes a number of constructs identified in prior research as important for engaging in "healthy" or low-risk behaviors. The ARRM postulates that it may be necessary for an individual to have some degree of distress or anxiety about AIDS to keep traversing the different stages of the model, although overly high levels of anxiety may hinder effective behavior change, and insufficient anxiety about AIDS may not motivate the individual to alter the risky activities. These constructs and the model are described below.

Stage one: identifying and labeling activities as risky

Three variables are hypothesized to contribute to labeling one's behavior as risky. First, knowledge of how HIV is transmitted is a necessary but insufficient condition to identify high-risk activities (Brandt, 1988). Early in the AIDS epidemic, level of knowledge was found to be associated with engaging in risk reduction (Emmons *et al.*, 1987); however, this relationship is not necessarily found in longitudinal analyses of risky behavior (Joseph *et al.*, 1987). Becker and Joseph (1988) have posited a threshold effect of knowledge, whereby information causes some people to alter their behavior, but other variables account for changes above and beyond the initial effects of knowledge.

The second variable is perceived personal susceptibility to AIDS. Parallel to elements in the Health Belief Model, it is assumed that individuals must feel personally vulnerable to contracting AIDS before labeling their behaviors as risky. Because contracting AIDS is perceived universally as being extremely negative, perceived severity is unlikely to contribute substantially to variations in labeling risk or taking actions.

Social norms regarding risk are the third contributing force. Parallel to the normative component of the Theory of Reasoned Action, the ARRM posits that what an individual's reference group considers to be risky sexual practices influences whether he or she labels the behavior as risky. For example, if the prevailing view in an individual's group is that unprotected intercourse is not particularly risky, it is unlikely that he or she will define lack of condom use as risky.

Stage two: commitment to engaging in low-risk activities

Given that an individual has labeled his or her behavior as risky, two types of variables will influence the likelihood that the person will commit to engaging in low-risk behaviors.

First are attitudes about the high- and low-risk activities. Consistent with an expectancy-value model, an individual's decision to reduce risky sexual practices is posited to be determined by his or her analysis of the costs and benefits (positive and negative consequences) of continuing that behavior and of changing the behavior. Perceived enjoyment of the high- versus low-risk activities, perceived efficacy of the advocated low-risk activity in achieving risk reduction, interpersonal costs associated with requesting a change in sexual activities, and the perceived social norms surrounding the low- and high-risk activities are all likely to influence commitment to engage in low-risk behavior. Thus, unlike the Health Belief Model, the costs and benefits an individual considers are not necessarily constrained to those related to health.

Secondly, in accordance with self-efficacy theory (Bandura, 1977, 1982) the ARRM posits that, to adopt low-risk activities, individuals need to feel capable of engaging in activities that will prevent HIV infection. For example, people must feel that they are capable of acquiring condoms and of using them with their partner(s).

Stage three: changing behavior

Two variables are hypothesized to influence the likelihood that the person will act on his or her commitment to change behaviors. The first variable is the individual's sexual communication abilities. To engage in low-risk behaviors, people need to communicate their intentions to their sexual partners. Individuals may be committed to having their partner use condoms, but if they lack the social skills necessary to communicate this to their partners, they will not be able to act on their intentions.

Finally, people may seek informal help and social support from friends and family or professional help from a therapist or physician to reduce risk behavior. For example, help may be sought in learning how to communicate desires to one's sex partner, in discovering enjoyable alternatives to high-risk sexual behaviors, or in finding out where to obtain condoms.

Current status of the model

The ARRM was developed largely for adults regarding sexual risk behavior, although by extension it could be applied to intravenous drug use behavior. The ARRM is currently being used to guide both descriptive and intervention studies with adults and adolescents from various ethnic/racial backgrounds and sexual orientations.

As with some of the previous models, while the ARRM is a useful heuristic model, indicating variables to be examined and targeted for change, it has not been fully validated. Preliminary results from two different pilot studies of adolescent females provide initial supporting evidence for some of the ARRM variables. A study of white, primarily working-class and middle-class females attending a family planning clinic found that greater enjoyment of protected intercourse, stronger self-efficacy beliefs, and greater willingness to request partners to use condoms, were related to the proportion of time adolescents used condoms during intercourse (Catania et al., 1989). A study of white and Hispanic adolescents from varying socioeconomic backgrounds similarly found greater enjoyment of protected intercourse, lesser enjoyment of unprotected intercourse, social norms supporting condom use, and greater sexual communication abilities to be associated with more frequent use of condoms (Kegeles et al., 1989).

Unwanted pregnancy

Some unwanted pregnancies occur as the result of contraceptive failure, and some pregnancies are initially wanted but become unwanted because of changing circumstances (e.g. diagnosis of a genetic defect, abandonment by the partner). However, most unwanted pregnancies result from the failure to use effective contraceptive protection even though pregnancy is not desired.

There have been several studies examining the extent to which the occurrence of unwanted pregnancy can be understood in terms of risk taking. Luker (1975) characterized the behavior of women who experience unwanted pregnancy as reflecting their risk-taking orientation towards pregnancy. Based on interviews with women who were seeking to terminate their pregnancies, Luker suggested that women had a "cost-benefit 'set' toward risk taking" which was determined jointly by the utility they assigned to contraception and to pregnancy. This "set," in combination with a woman's subjective probability of becoming pregnant and of reversing a pregnancy should it occur, was hypothesized to determine her risk-taking behavior regarding exposure to unwanted pregnancy.

Empirical tests of Luker's model have yielded mixed support. Based in part on this model, Rogel et al. (1980) interviewed 120 female teenagers from an inner city hospital family planning and pre-natal clinic. Rogel et al. concluded that the high pregnancy rate in the sample was due to the perception of high costs attributed to contraceptive use (particularly regarding safety and side-effects) which were not balanced by equally strong negative perceptions of the costs of pregnancy. Furthermore, the teens attributed benefits to engaging in sexual activity. The authors suggest a model similar to Luker's but which balances the costs and benefits of contraceptive use with the costs and benefits of the physical intimacy associated with sexual intercourse.

In a different sample of adolescents, Peacock (1982) found no relationship between any of the variables specified in Luker's model and length of contraceptive use. The only variable related to use was perceptions of financial cost. Peacock concluded that contraceptive use is complex and may not be adequately explained by the model. In contrast, Philliber et al. (1986) found support for Luker's model in another sample of adolescent females. Their findings suggested that the most important component of the model for predicting pregnancy risk taking was the adolescent's subjective estimate of the chances that she would become pregnant. In addition to components of Luker's model, three other variables were found to contribute to exposure to unwanted pregnancy: amount of time that the adolescent's family had been on welfare, level of ego development, and higher frequency of prior risk taking regarding possible pregnancy.

In addition to the Luker model, which was specifically designed to account for risk taking regarding unwanted pregnancy, applications of other theories of health and of choice behavior more generally have been used to account for contraceptive behavior. For example, Eisen and Zellman (1986) assessed the four core components of the Health Belief Model in relation to pregnancy and contraception among a sample of adolescents participating in a demonstration health education program: perceived susceptibility to pregnancy, perceived seriousness of pregnancy occurrence, perceived benefits of contraception, and perceived barriers to contraceptive use. Based on data collected before the adolescents participated in the program, significant relationships were found between five indicators of sexual and contraceptive knowledge and components of the HBM.

The model that has been most widely and successfully applied to contraceptive behavior is the Theory of Reasoned Action (Ajzen & Fishbein, 1980). Jaccard and Davidson (1972) found that the two components of the model, attitude towards using birth control pills, and perception of social normative expectations governing their use, were significantly related to intention to use birth control pills (Multiple $R = 0.84$). Fishbein and Jaccard (1973) found significant relationships between attitude towards each of four methods of contraception and intention to use them among college women.

There has been debate about the applicability of such "rational" models to understanding the contraceptive behavior of adolescents. Research has often focused on the influence of sociodemographic variables such as ethnicity or social class, and of personality variables, such as locus of control or alienation. However, a meta-analysis of studies on adolescent contraceptive use conducted by Whitely and Schofield (1986) concluded that there was support for the hypothesis that female adolescents weigh advantages and disadvantages of contraception as well as of pregnancy. This is not to suggest that such processes necessarily result in an optimal decision. Decision-making processes are influenced by the information and misinformation that the young person has. Adolescents may, for example, underestimate the chances they will become pregnant if they engage in unprotected intercourse, or may overestimate the chances of experiencing side-effects if they use a method such as the pill.

In addition, the beliefs that are salient to adolescents may not be those which seem most logical or important from an adult perspective (see Chapter 5, by Fischhoff). For example, in a recent study, contraceptive intentions and behaviors of male and female adolescents were examined in light of the Theory of Reasoned Action (Adler et al., 1990). Adolescents were interviewed as they sought care from adolescent medicine clinics regarding their beliefs, attitudes, perceptions of normative expectations, and intentions to use each of four methods of contraception in the coming year: pills, condoms, diaphragm, and withdrawal. They were reinterviewed a year later regarding their actual use of each method during the intervening year. The results provided support for the model. Intentions were significantly associated with the two components of the model (Multiple Rs ranged from 0.54 for condoms to 0.74 for pills for females and from 0.33 for diaphragms to 0.82 for withdrawal for males).

In the sample described above, it is interesting to examine which beliefs were related to intentions to use given methods and which were not. For example, in relation to condom use, beliefs in the efficacy of condoms to prevent pregnancy and to protect against sexually transmitted disease were not related to the strength of intention to use them. However, controlling for sexual activity, prior condom use, and racial/ethnic background, beliefs that condoms allow for spontaneous sex, are easy to use, and are popular with peers were significantly associated with intentions to use them among both males and females (Kegeles, Adler, & Irwin, 1989). These results suggest that one may be able to modify contraceptive behavior of adolescents, but to do so one must address beliefs that are most central to them. These may not be the beliefs that are traditionally presented in health education interventions (e.g. those regarding the efficacy of a method for preventing pregnancy or disease), but rather those that relate to the physical and social aspects of use.

Actual contraceptive use is a complex behavior. For some methods, it requires the cooperation of the partner, over whose behavior the individual may not have control. In the study of adolescent contraceptive use noted earlier (Adler et al., 1990), intention was significantly but not strongly related to the subsequent behavior. Among females, the relationship of intention with later use was strongest for the pill, over which females have complete control ($r = 0.42$) and least for withdrawal, which depends on male behavior ($r = 0.20$). For males, the pattern was reversed. The strongest correlation of intention and behavior use was for withdrawal, which the male performs ($r = 0.46$), and the weakest was for the partner's use of the pill ($r = 0.10$).

As noted earlier, unrealistic optimism about one's chances of experiencing negative health outcomes may reduce motivation to take protective health actions. This has been demonstrated in relation to contraceptive use. Burger and Burns (1988) found that a sample of female college students were optimistically biased regarding their chances of experiencing an unwanted pregnancy in the next year compared to other females at the same university, average American females their age, and average American females of childbearing age. The greater the bias shown, the less likely they were to be using effective contraception; the correlation between degree of optimistic bias and percentage time using contraception was -0.34 ($p < 0.05$).

CONCLUSION

The models which have been developed to understand health-risking behaviors focus, by and large, on individual risk behaviors. They identify factors which increase or decrease the likelihood that an individual will engage in a specific behavior. This makes sense from the perspective of intervention. The information can be used to develop prevention and health-care programs that seek to increase the likelihood that people will engage in health-protective actions or to decrease the likelihood of their engaging in health-risking behaviors.

At this time, there are no good theoretical models of a broader orientation towards health risk. The available evidence suggests that such models would be difficult to develop. People often seem to be characterized more by inconsistency than by consistency in their orientations towards health risks (Mechanic, 1979). Although relationships have been shown among some behaviors such as use of tobacco, alcohol, and mind-altering drugs (Istvan & Matarazzo, 1984; Kandel & Logan, 1984), there is often little relationship between these behaviors and frequency of engaging in health-promoting actions such as exercising or using seat belts (Harris & Guten, 1979; Williams & Wechsler, 1972).

Some inconsistencies in behavior may derive from limitations on information-processing capacities. Because of these limitations, people simplify complex information and systematic biases enter their judgment (Slovic, Fischhoff, & Lichtenstein, 1987). Limitations on information processing are exacerbated by the uncertainty associated with many of the potential risks to health and the information overload which has emerged concerning possible risks. The public is bombarded by messages about the risks involved in almost every human activity—eating, breathing, being out in the sunshine, engaging in sex. Responses to these threats do not always appear to be associated with a "rational" weighing of the actual harm. As former US Surgeon General C. Everett Koop has noted, "People just have an inappropriate sense of what is dangerous. They get overly upset about minor problems. If you translate the weight and time it takes a laboratory rat to develop bladder cancer to a 200-pound man drinking Fresca (which contains artificial sweeteners), it comes out to about two bathtubs full each day. People dropped Fresca in a minute, but they continued to smoke" (Specter, 1989).

Another reason for inconsistency is that each behavior has its own set of dynamics—that is, factors that encourage its continuation and that create pressures for discontinuation. Concerns about health may be only one factor. Thus, it may not be surprising to see only a modest relationship among different kinds of health-risking and health-protective behavior. Because of this, efforts to change behaviors may be more successful if they focus on a particular behavior than if they try to change a general orientation toward risk taking or health.

SUMMARY

Several models have been developed to understand why individuals take (or fail to take) actions that will protect their health or put it at risk. The most widely used has been the Health Belief Model, which identifies two factors as immediate predictors of the likelihood of engaging in a specific health-promoting or disease-preventing action: the perceived threat of the negative outcome if one fails to take the action and the perceived benefits and barriers associated with taking the action. Later modifications of the model incorporated the concept of self-efficacy in relation to performing the behavior. While this model has generated a great deal of research and has been useful in understanding some health behaviors, it has received mixed support. One concern is that it does not take into account a sufficiently broad set of determinants. The Theory of Reasoned Action, while not specifically a health model, includes social expectations, attitudes towards the action, and perceived costs and benefits that are not necessarily health-related and may account for more variance in health behaviors than does the Health Belief Model. Other models designed to account for health-related behaviors, such as Protection Motivation Theory, include components that overlap with ones in the Health Belief Model, particularly appraisal of threat. Self-Regulation Theory includes affective responses to threat as well as cognitive processes. Complementing the other models is work on optimistic bias, which suggests that individuals tend to underestimate their own susceptibility to health problems, causing systematic bias in the appraisal of threat.

These models have been useful in understanding some of the factors that influence why individuals may take risks in relation to their health and have pointed to ways to modify risk taking. The AIDS Risk Reduction Model, for example, identifies three stages needed to reduce the risk of exposure to the HIV virus. The three stages involve aspects of the health models described in the chapter, including appraisal of risk for acquiring HIV, emotional response to the potential threat, social norms governing the health-promoting or health-risking behaviors, cost and benefits of engaging in the behaviors, and self-efficacy regarding one's ability to take the recommended actions. The final stage, enactment of the behavior, involves more social variables such as communication abilities with one's sexual partner and support from others. These variables have not been included in other models of health behavior.

Finally, in applying "rational" models to understanding exposure to unwanted pregnancy, both the uses and limitations of these models were discussed. A major limitation derives from the fact that individuals are often not consistent in their behavior. This inconsistency derives from: (a) the uncertainty associated with taking any given action and whether or not negative outcomes will result, (b) cognitive and emotional overload that results from awareness of risk in many (if not most) behaviors, and (c) the complex and varied dynamics associated with performing any given behavior.

ACKNOWLEDGMENTS

Preparation of this manuscript was supported in part by a grant from the John D. and Catherine T. MacArthur Foundation Network on Health-Promoting and Disease-Prevention Behavior and US National Institute of Mental Health/National Institute of Drug Abuse AIDS Center Grant No. MH42459.

REFERENCES

Adler, N. E., Kegeles, S. M., Wibbelsman, C., & Irwin, C. E. (1990). Adolescent contraceptive behavior: A decision analysis. *The Journal of Pediatrics*, **116**(3), 463–471.

Ajzen, I., & Fishbein, M. (1980). *Understanding attitudes and predicting social behavior*. Englewood Cliffs, NJ: Prentice Hall.

Bandura, A. (1977). Self-efficacy: Toward a unifying theory of behavior change. *Psychological Review*, **84**, 191–215.

Bandura, A. (1982). Self-efficacy mechanisms in human agency. *American Psychologist*, **37**, 122–147.

Bandura, A. (1986). *Social foundations of thought and action: A social cognitive theory*. Englewood Cliffs, NJ: Prentice Hall.

Becker, M. H., & Joseph, J. G. (1988). AIDS and behavioral change to reduce risk: A review. *American Journal of Public Health*, **78**, 394–410.

Becker, M. H., & Maiman, L. A. (1975). Sociobehavioral determinants of compliance with health and medical care recommendations. *Medical Care*, **13**, 10–24.

Becker, M. H., Maiman, L. A., Kirscht, J. P., Haefner, D. P., & Drachman, R. H. (1977). The health belief model and prediction of dietary compliance. *Journal of Health and Social Behavior*, **18**, 348–366.

Brandt, A. M. (1988). AIDS in historical perspective: Four lessons from the history of sexually transmitted disease. *American Journal of Public Health*, **78**, 367–371.

Burger, J. M., & Burns, L. (1988). The illusion of unique vulnerability and the use of effective contraception. *Personality and Social Psychology Bulletin*, **14**, 264–270.

Bush, P. J., & Iannotti, R. J. (1988). Origins and stability of children's health beliefs relative to medicine use. *Social Science and Medicine*, **27**, 345–352.

Catania, J. C., Coates, T. J., Greenblatt, R., Dolcini, M. M., Kegeles, S. M., Puckett, S., Corman, M., & Miller, J. (1989). Predictors of condom use and multiple partnered sex among sexually active adolescent women: Implications for AIDS related health interventions. *Journal of Sex Research*, **26**, 514–524.

Catania, J. A., Kegeles, S. M., & Coates, T. J. (1990). Towards an understanding of risk behavior: An AIDS risk reduction model (ARRM). *Health Education Quarterly*, **17**, 53–72.

Cummings, K. M., Jette, A. M., & Rosenstock, I. M. (1978). Construct validation of the health belief model. *Health Education Monographs*, **6**, 394–405.

Eisen, G. L., & Zellman, G. L. (1986). The role of health belief attitudes, sex education, and demographics in predicting adolescents' sexuality knowledge. *Health Education Quarterly*, **13**, 9–22.

Emmons, C. A., Joseph, J. G., Kessler, R. C., Wortman, C., & Montgomery, C. (1987). Psychosocial predictors of reported behavior change in homosexual men in at risk for AIDS. *Health Education Quarterly*, **13**, 331–345.

Fishbein, M., & Jaccard, J. J. (1973). Theoretical and methodological considerations in the prediction of family planning intentions and behavior. *Representative Research in Social Psychology*, **4**, 37–51.

Haefner, D. P., & Kirscht, J. P. (1970). Motivational and behavioral effects of modifying health beliefs. *Public Health Reports*, **85**, 478–484.

Harris, D., & Guten, S. (1979). Health protective behavior: An exploratory study. *Journal of Health and Social Behavior*, **20**, 17–29.

Hovland, C. I., Janis, I., & Kelly, H. H. (1953). *Communication and persuasion*. New Haven, CT: Yale University Press.

Hunter, J. E., Schmidt, F. L., & Jackson, G. G. (1982). *Meta-analysis: Cumulating research findings across studies*. Beverly Hills, CA: Sage.

Istvan, J., & Matarazzo, J. D. (1984). Tobacco, alcohol, and caffeine use: A review of their interrelationships. *Psychological Bulletin*, **95**, 301–326.

Jaccard, J. J., & Davidson, A. R. (1972). Toward an understanding of family planning behaviors: An initial investigation. *Journal of Applied Social Psychology*, **2**, 228–235.

Janz, N. K., & Becker, M. H. (1984). The health belief model: A decade later. *Health Education Quarterly*, **11**, 1–46.

Jette, A. M., Cummings, K. M., Brock, B. M., Phelps, M. C., & Naessens, J. (1981). The structure and reliability of health belief indices. *Health Services Research*, **16**, 81–98.

Jones, S. L., Jones, P. K., & Katz, J. (1988). Health belief model intervention to increase compliance with emergency department patients. *Medical Care*, **26**, 1172–1183.

Joseph, J., Montgomery, C., Kirscht, J., Kessler, R., Ostrow, D., Wortman, C., O'Brien, K., Eller, M., & Estileman, S. (1987). Perceived risk of AIDS: Assessing the behavioral and psychosocial consequences in a cohort of gay men. *Journal of Applied Social Psychology*, **17**, 231–250.

Kandel, D. B., & Logan, J. A. (1984). Patterns of drug use from adolescence to young adulthood: I. Periods of risk for initiation, continued use, and discontinuation. *American Journal of Public Health*, **74**, 660–666.

Kegeles, S. M., Adler, N. E., & Irwin, C. E. (1989). Adolescents and condoms: Associations of beliefs with intentions to use. *American Journal of Diseases of Children*, **143**, 911–915.

Kegeles, S. M., Greenblatt, R., Catania, J., Cardenas, C., Gottlieb, J., Coates, T., Dolcini, P., & Miller, J. (1989). *AIDS risk behavior among sexually active Hispanic and Caucasian adolescent females*. Paper presented at the Fifth International Conference on AIDS, Montreal, June.

Kegeles, S. S. (1980). The health belief model and personal health behavior (Book review). *Social Science and Medicine*, **14**, 227–229

Leavitt, F. (1979). The health belief model and utilization of ambulatory care service. *Social Science and Medicine*, **13**, 105–112.

Leventhal, H. (1970). Findings and theory in the study of fear communications. In L. Berkowitz (Ed.). *Advances in social psychology* (Vol. 5). New York: Academic Press.

Leventhal, H., Nerenz, D. R., & Steele, D. F. (1984). Illness representations and coping with health threats. In A. Baum & J. Singer (Eds.), *A handbook of psychology and health* (pp. 219–252). Hillsdale, NJ: Erlbaum.

Leventhal, H., Safer, M. A., & Panagis, D. M. (1983). The impact of communications on the self-regulation of health beliefs, decisions, and behavior. *Health Education Quarterly*, **10**, 3–29.

Leventhal, H., Watts, J. C., & Pagano, F. (1967). Effects of fear and instructions on how to cope with danger. *Journal of Personality and Social Psychology*, **6**, 313–321.

Luker, K. (1975). *Taking chances*. Los Angeles: University of California Press.

Maddux, J. E., & Rogers, R. W. (1983). Protection motivation and self-efficacy: A revised theory of fear appeals and attitude change. *Journal of Experimental Social Psychology*, **19**, 469–479.

Maiman, L. A., & Becker, M. H. (1974). The health belief model: Origins and correlates in psychological theory. *Health Education Monograph*, **2**, 336–353.

Mechanic, D. (1979). The stability of health and illness behavior: Results from a 16-year follow-up. *American Journal of Public Health*, **69**, 1142–1145.

Meyer, D. (1980). *The effects of patients' representation of high blood pressure on behavior in treatment*. Unpublished doctoral dissertation, University of Wisconsin, Madison.

Mullen, P. D., Hersey, J. C., & Iverson, D. C. (1987). Health behavior models compared. *Social Science & Medicine*, **24**, 973–981.

O'Connell, J. K., Price, J. H., Roberts, S. M., Jurs, S. G., & McKinley, R. (1985). Utilizing the health belief model to predict dieting and exercising behavior of obese and nonobese adolescents. *Health Education Quarterly*, **12**, 343–351.

Peacock, N. (1982). Contraceptive decision-making among adolescent girls. *Journal of Sex Education and Therapy*, **8**, 31–34.

Philliber, S., Namerow, P. B., Kaye, J. W., & Kunkes, C. H. (1986). Pregnancy risk taking among adolescents. *Journal of Adolescent Research*, **1**, 463–481.

Prohaska, T. R., Keller, M. L., Leventhal, E. A., & Leventhal, H. (1987). Impact of symptoms and aging attribution on emotions and coping. *Health Psychology*, **6**, 495–514.

Ried, L. D., & Christensen, D. B. (1988). A psychosocial perspective in the explanation of patients' drug-taking behavior. *Social Science and Medicine*, **27**, 277–285.

Rippetoe, P. A., & Rogers, R. W. (1987). Effects of components of protection-motivation theory on adaptive and maladaptive coping with a health threat. *Journal of Personality and Social Psychology*, **52**, 596–604.

Rogel, J., Zuehlke, M. E., Petersen, A. C., Tobin-Richards, M., & Shelton, M. (1980). Contraceptive behavior in adolescence: A decision-making perspective. *Journal of Youth and Adolescence*, **9**, 491–506.

Rogers, R. W. (1983). Cognitive and physiological processes in attitude change: A revised theory of protection motivation. In J. Cacioppo & R. Petty (Eds.), *Social psychophysiology* (pp. 153–176). New York: Guilford Press.

Rosenstock, I. M. (1966). Why people use health services. *Milbank Memorial Fund Quarterly*, **44**(3), 94–127.

Rosenstock, I. M., Strecher, V. J., & Becker, M. H. (1988). Social learning theory and the health belief model. *Health Education Quarterly*, **15**, 175–183.

Rosenthal, R. (1984). *Meta-analytic procedures for social research*. Beverly Hills, CA: Sage.

Simon, K. J., & Das, A. (1984). An application of the health belief model toward educational diagnosis for VD education. *Health Education Quarterly*, **11**, 403–418.

Slovic, P., Fischhoff, B., & Lichtenstein, S. (1987). Behavioral decision theory perspectives on protective behavior. In N. D. Weinstein (Ed.), *Taking care: Understanding and encouraging self-protective behavior* (pp. 14–41). Cambridge, UK: Cambridge University Press.

Specter, M. (1989, 12 May). Seeing risks everywhere. *San Francisco Chronicle*, p. 17.

Weinstein N. D. (1983). Reducing unrealistic optimism about illness susceptibility. *Health Psychlogy*, **2**, 11–20.

Weinstein, N. D. (1984). Why it won't happen to me: Perceptions of risk factors and susceptibility. *Health Psychology*, **3**, 431–457.

Weinstein, N. D. (1987). Unrealistic optimism about susceptibility to health problems: Conclusions from a community-wide sample. *Journal of Behavioral Medicine*, **10**, 481–500.

Whitely, B. E., & Schofield, J. W. (1986). A meta-analysis of research on adolescent contraceptive use. *Population and Environment*, **8**, 173–203.

Williams, A. F., & Wechsler, H. (1972). Interrelationship of preventive actions in health and other areas. *Health Services Reports*, **87**, 969–977.

Chapter 9

Risk taking and accident causation

Willem A. Wagenaar
Leiden University

CONTENTS

INTRODUCTION

The problem

The question addressed in this chapter is whether misperceived risk, or consciously accepted risk, is a major source of accidents. The question originates from my experience that frequently in accident reports, or in law suits that follow accidents, the actors in the drama are accused of underestimating or

Risk-taking Behavior. Edited by J. F. Yates
© 1992 John Wiley & Sons Ltd

accepting grave risks in an irresponsible manner. Examples are the capsizing of the *Herald of Free Enterprise*, the stranding of the *Esso Valdez*, the drama in the Heizel Stadium in Brussels. By trying and convicting those who were instrumental in causing the accidents, the suggestion is created that these people made a culpable mistake either by misperceiving obvious risks, or by willfully accepting those risks. My own impulse, after reading hundreds of accident histories, is that those who are running risks cannot always be said to have taken those risks, because they were simply not in the position to make the appropriate analysis. The problem is therefore not one of risk taking, and consequently risk communication is not the solution that will prevent similar accidents in the future. The following pages contain a less impulsive analysis of this problem.

A definition of risk

First we should agree about what we mean by "risk" and "risk taking." There is a wide variety of interpretations of these terms, which blocks a meaningful discussion (cf. Chapter 1).

On one end, "risk" is interpreted to mean "probability of an undesired event." An example of this use is found in *Living with risk*, a source book published by the British Medical Association. Here it is said that "the way that most scientists believe the word should be used is as an expression of the *probability*—the likelihood—that something unpleasant will happen. If the consequence of throwing a six when you roll a dice [sic] is that you receive an electric shock, then there is a one-in-six *risk* of being shocked." This definition does not imply any risk awareness, and even less a conscious analysis that produces such awareness. Risk defined as probability may exist even when one doesn't know about it. Since in my view "risk taking" presupposes risk awareness, this definition precludes a discussion of risk taking as a source of accidents.

A more neutral definition of risk is used by Yates (1990), who argued that there is no single definition. Rather, risk should be viewed as a multidimensional concept that, as a whole, refers to the prospect of loss. The dimensions that contribute to this prospect are: loss probability, the maximum possible loss, the expected loss, the semivariance of all losing options, and the variance among all options. Risk is the prospect of a loss, characterized by one or more of these dimensions. The nature of this definition is statistical: the computations can be done afterwards, or by another person, so that the person who actually *runs* the risk is not aware of the prospect. Hence it remains possible that risk is present without being felt. In this context it is only meaningful to talk about risk taking as consciously accepting a course of action after the identification and characterization of a prospect of loss.

An even more abstract definition of risk is used by those who focus on the process of analyzing risky prospects, without any reduction of the results to one risk notion. An example is presented by Fischhoff in Chapter 5 of this book. Fischhoff's approach suggests that the study of risk taking should consider that risky decisions may be the result of a probabilistic decision process entailing several activities: identification of possible courses of action; identification of consequences; evaluation of the attractiveness (or unattractiveness) and chances of the consequences; combination of all the previous assessments and choosing according to that combination. It is not clear whether a closer study of these activities requires a separate notion of risk additional to the notions featured in each of the activities. Risk may be nothing else than a feeling, concomitant with an analysis comprising some or all of the decision activities listed above. Without a further definition of risk, it can then be said that risk taking is following the course of action selected at the end of a probabilistic process.

For the present purpose I will combine the second and third approaches: risk is a multidimensional characterization of a negative prospect, obtained in a process of probabilistic decision making. The problem discussed in this chapter is whether accidents occur because risk characterizations are unrealistic, or because courses of action are accepted in the full realization that other options had a less negative risk characterization.

The source of the problem

The question as defined above is rarely asked, because it is often assumed that the answer is known to be affirmative. This is obvious from the many attempts to convince car drivers to drive safely, or employees to work safely. Many of us have seen the huge signs at the entrances of industrial plants, indicating the number of days worked without accidents. These signs are aimed at motivating workers to cause no accidents. Another example is the multitude of posters used to the same end (see Figure 9.1). Industrial psychologists are often hired either to select those people who will cause no accidents, or to indoctrinate those selected not to cause accidents. Many analyses of risk-taking behavior (cf. Chapter 4) and of accident proneness have revealed that there is a relationship with personality characteristics. The selection mechanism might therefore work. But there is no relationship between risk taking and the intellectual capabilities required for probabilistic analyses. Hence, it is doubtful whether indoctrination attempts will ever be successful.

The notion that risks, identified after the occurrence of accidents, were accepted after a conscious analysis, may have emerged from a confusion between normative and descriptive models. The normative model of decision making assumes that all available alternatives are considered, their consequences evaluated with respect to probability and utility, which are subsequently combined into some expression of the attractiveness of the expected outcome. Within the framework of such models, much attention was paid to the ways in which people conceptualize alternative choices, the ways in which

Figure 9.1   A poster that is supposed to discourage risk taking.

probabilities can be inferred from related indicators, the ways in which utilities are derived and handled. Less attention was paid to the conditions in which people will engage in such detailed analyses, instead of acting automatically, following their gut feeling, or accept the first choice that is offered. Still the widespread industrial interest in risk-taking behavior is based upon this acceptance of the normative decision model as a true description of human behavior. Millions of dollars are spent on campaigns that take conscious risk consideration for granted.

The logic behind such campaigns is compelling especially because accident scenarios usually look very silly; it is often hard to believe that the actors in the drama did not consider the risk of the approaching doom that in hindsight is seen by everyone. Hence, since the actors could not have failed to consider the negative consequences of their actions, they must have misperceived or accepted the risk. This notion of mishap following a consciously considered risk is not limited to managers and officials; Hovden and Larsson (1987) reported that in a representative sample of Swedes between 18 and 70 years of age, 90% agreed that *risk taking* is the major source of accidents.

But this belief may be a result of hindsight wisdom, and nothing else. One reason to question the decision-making model as a description of what goes on in everyday operator behavior is the fact that industrial safety campaigns based on making people more "safety conscious" have had no appreciable effects (cf. Heinrich, 1931; Kletz, 1985; Planek, 1982).

Individual and societal decision making

The possibility that people engage in most of their everyday behavior without a conscious consideration of the associated risks, and that therefore many accidents cannot be attributed to misperceived or accepted risk, is worth investigating. But it will be necessary to distinguish here between societies and organizations on one hand, and individual people on the other. Societies and organizations may be involved in decision processes that contain an organized investigation and evaluation of risks. Risk evaluation might even be enforced by statutory law. But this does not mean that individuals, engaging in risk activities, will also consider the risks prior to their actions, nor even that individuals feel that risk evaluations *ought* to be made in such cases. Some evidence about this may be obtained from two studies by Slovic, Fischhoff, and Lichtenstein (1985), and Slovic, Lichtenstein, and Fischhoff (1984), both referenced by Slovic (1987). These studies considered the factor-analytic representation of subjective risk, which tends to contain two major factors: "Dread Risk," which stands for the perceived lack of control, catastrophic potential, and inequitable distribution of fatal consequences; and "Unknown Risk," which stands for hazards that are unobservable, unknown, new, and that have delayed effects (see Chapter 3). In the third quadrant of this plane there are risks that score low on both "dread" and "unknown." Typical examples are riding bicycles, recreational boating, downhill skiing, home swimming pools, use of chainsaws, smoking, drinking. Compared to the other three quadrants, where we find water fluoridation, diagnostic X-rays, DNA-technology, Starwars, nuclear reactors, general aviation, and large dams, it can be said that the third quadrant represents more individual behavior, the other quadrants more societal behavior. This dissociation is further exemplified when we look at two other factors emerging from the analyses: desire for strict regulation to reduce risk, and signal potential, defined as "the degree to which an accident involving that hazard was judged to serve as a warning signal for society." It appears that hazards in the third quadrant load low on these factors, whereas hazards in the other quadrants load high on them. Apparently, people make a distinction between individual and societal hazards. They seem to feel that risk considerations do not apply to individual actions in the same way as to societal issues.

The allegation that accidents are caused by misperception of risk or by excessive risk taking usually involves the individual actors in an accident scenario. This can be concluded from the fact that preventive measures take the form of warning individual people about risks. Therefore I will first discuss the relation between accidents and individual risk taking. In later sections I will address the problem of risk taking by organizations as a whole.

CONSCIOUS DECISIONS VS ACTION SCHEMATA

Some theory

The model of actions being preceded by risk considerations is not psychologically plausible as a general model when we talk about individuals instead of organizations, and when we talk about everyday behavior instead of the taking of once-in-a-lifetime decisions. It is widely accepted that much of our everyday behavior is automatized, and runs without continuous attentional control (cf. Shiffrin & Schneider, 1977). Possibly this automated behavior is controlled by a hierarchy of stored schemata (cf. Norman, 1981). My schema for going home after work may contain the following steps: leaving the office, finding my car, getting on the road, following the way home, parking the car, entering home. Each of these steps in this "mother schema" is itself a "daughter schema." Getting on the road involves opening the car, putting my things in the car, getting seated, belting myself up, getting the engine started, backing out of the parking lot, joining the traffic stream. These steps contain again "granddaughter schemata": starting the engine involves finding the car key, inserting it, turning it, waiting till the engine is heated (I drive a diesel), turning the key again, listening whether the engine catches on (eventually repeating some of the previous steps). Each of the steps involves a finely tuned perceptual-motor program, for example inserting the car key without really looking. On an ordinary day no step in this hierarchical organization involves a decision based on risk considerations. Only at the transitions a conditional check is applied, just to see whether the progress is according to plan. If not, automatic control is stopped; the ensuing problem must be solved at a higher level. Reason's (1990) GEMS model describes how the transition from automatic control to conscious problem solving takes place when exceptional circumstances arise. Problem-solving activities might involve risk considerations, but these are mostly acute and restricted to the few options that present themselves in the emergency. In ordinary conditions these considerations will rarely occur. For instance, the overtaking of other cars, or the crossing of intersections, are guided by pre-arranged schemata with built-in decision criteria that have evolved on the basis of experience, and that are not subjected over and over again to conscious risk analyses.

Two examples: stopping at traffic lights and stopping for children

A study by Jørgensen (1988) is illustrative of what may go on in the heads of drivers performing such normal tasks as stopping at a traffic light. If, at the moment a traffic light turns amber, you are close to the light and driving fast, you will not brake, but assume the light can be passed before it turns red. If you are distant and driving slowly, you will stop, knowing that you cannot pass the light in time. In a plot of speed versus distance, these two regions are separated by a straight line, because speed and distance can be traded off in a linear fashion. However, the braking characteristic of a car is curvilinear: the necessary stopping distance increases exponentially with speed. The result is that there exists a zone, called the dilemma zone, in which you could brake and stop before the crossing line, or continue and cross before the light turns red. However, drivers can never be certain that they are in the dilemma zone, because the time-distance relationship is not perfectly obvious. For instance, at an intersection one has never crossed before, one cannot know how long the amber period will be. Jørgensen used this feature in a simple experiment on an intersection with signals controlled by a pedestrian-actuated button. When a car approached with sufficient speed to be in the dilemma zone, the experimenter pushed the button and observed the driver's reaction. Out of 50 cars, no driver attempted a braking maneuver. Jørgensen interpreted this result to mean that in this situation, although there is uncertainty, and hence a need for a probabilistic analysis that leads to a decision, a fixed routine is applied. The rule would be that one does not stop unless there is *certainty* that the light cannot be reached before it turns red. Carstensen (1983; cited by Jørgensen, 1988) suggested that accidents at traffic signals are to a large extent due to the fact that many road users rely exclusively on behavioral rules that assume the proper functioning of signals and the respect of other road users for the signals, making no attempt to evaluate the risk themselves. In fact, the issue is not resolved. We do not know whether risks are considered in those instances in which drivers cause accidents because they fail to stop at traffic lights. But Jørgensen's results are certainly not encouraging.

Another suggestion of fixed behavior schemata is provided by a group of traffic researchers at the University of Nottingham (cf. Howarth, 1988). They studied the interaction between the behavior of children crossing an intersection and drivers approaching that intersection. Their expectation was that drivers are aware of the fact that child pedestrians are less predictable than adults, and that drivers, knowing this, would therefore take special care in the presence of children. In reality, they found that fewer than 10% of the drivers took any action at a time that would allow avoiding a child stepping from the curb unexpectedly. Those who took action would still not be able to stop their cars in time, because their actions were insufficient. When the car reached the ultimate point at which action could be taken by the driver, 80% of the children had already taken an avoidance action. Statistics show that in the remaining stage of the encounter an additional 19.999 % of the children take action, while only 0.001 % do not. Thus, the entire responsibility for accident avoidance is borne by the children.

Likewise, it was shown that in a school area drivers maintained the same average speed, irrespective of the presence or absence of child pedestrians waiting to cross the road. They simply continued with an average of 60 kph, leaving a distance to the curb of 1.2 meters.

What do these data mean? Are all drivers murderous fanatics, prepared to kill innocent children? Or should we assume the alternative, which is that drivers are not using any subjective considerations of risk, despite all exhortations of safety eduction and propaganda; that they maintain a routine behavioral pattern based on the experience that children intending to cross the road take appropriate action? The propaganda about children's unpredictability is at odds with their actual behavior. It seems that driver behavior reflects the routine shaped by reality, rather than some conscious risk evaluation that would take into account the propagated unpredictability and vulnerability of children.

The only hole in this argument is that drivers may perform the full analysis, but base their judgment on the conviction that children along the roadside do not require extra caution. Howarth (1988) gives the counterargument that after an accident it is often claimed that the child "was running heedlessly into the road so that there was nothing the driver could do to avoid the accident." Such an excuse, if accepted, proves, according to Howarth, that people generally believe the propaganda and not the factual statistics which, if expressed in a similar way, would say: "There was nothing the driver could do to prevent the accident because our contention that this child behaved heedlessly is backed by the well-established fact that five-year-old children only succeed in avoiding 99.999 % of potential accidents" (p. 531). Again we must accept that research in this area has not yet revealed what is going on in the heads of drivers. Howarth's interpretation is more or less a proof through "reduction ad absurdum." In principle it is possible that the risk perception of drivers is shaped by reality, in which accidents rarely occur. But certainly the observations do not support the view that the widespread publicity about the risks of children in traffic has affected driver behavior.

The interesting aspect of Jørgensen and Howarth's studies is that they are not restricted to accidents. The apparently reckless behavior of drivers is not only present in few fatal encounters; conscious risk evaluation seems to be lacking all the time. Thus, it appears that accidents are not atypical occurrences in which risk was handled in a manner totally different from all other cases in which nothing happened. The difference between safe crossings and accidents resides in the behavior of the children, not in the risk considerations of drivers.

Two models of risk taking

The process of decision making, as represented in the various constituent activities proposed by Fischhoff (see above) will tell us little about risk taking when in actual practice risk takers are showing routine behavior that is not based on a conscious analysis of the situation. There are a few models of risk taking in everyday situations that do not assume a full analysis of decision problems. I will discuss two of these: *risk homeostasis theory* (Wilde, 1982), and *zero-risk theory* (Näätanen & Summala, 1974, 1976).

"Risk homeostasis theory" is a name that has caused unnecessary confusion. The simple thought is that behavior in risky situations is determined by a desire for cost minimization; cost estimations are derived from ongoing experience, not from a formal and ever-repeated analysis. Take the example of selecting driving speed, as presented in Figure 9.2. With increasing speed the cost of travel time goes down, while the cost of risk is going up. The sum of these costs reaches a minimum value at a speed S1. The two cost functions need not be exact representations of reality. They only summarize experience accumulated across

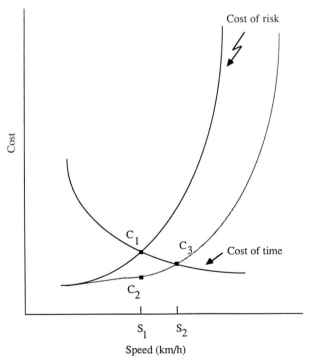

Figure 9.2 Graphical illustration of risk homeostasis theory.

a large set of similar situations, for instance, "driving on a motorway in heavy rain." The speed S1 will be selected in every situation that is recognized as belonging to this set. Now imagine that a new safety measure is introduced, that shifts the cost-of-risk function to the right. It could be the introduction of a new type of asphalt that reduces the splashing of rain. If drivers do not detect the change, and go on driving at the speed S1, the cost of risk will decline from C1 to C2. The new asphalt would have caused a risk reduction. On the other hand, when drivers appreciate the new situation correctly, they will realize that the minimum cost is now reached at a higher speed, S2. This will not be immediately obvious, but through experience drivers may understand that going a little bit faster does not create the problems they used to have before. At the speed S2 the cost of risk C3 is between C1 and C2. This means that a certain proportion of the expected risk reduction is lost through the adaptive behavior of the road users. It is misleading to state that *risk* is kept constant, because it clearly is not.

The misnomer "risk homeostasis theory" has caused violent discussions, because it suggests that no safety measure will ever help to reduce risks, when people maintain their old preferred risk level. One argument against this position was that risk can only be kept constant when it is the basis on which behavior is selected. This is, however, rather unlikely, as I also have argued above. But the whole discussion is beside the point; nothing is kept constant according to the theory; only *cost* is kept *minimal*.

Risk homeostasis theory explains how behavior can be in accordance with risks, even subjectively perceived risks, without an ever-repeated process of conscious risk evaluation. Misperception of risk may occur when cost functions are unrealistic. Conscious risk acceptance will occur when the cost of going slow becomes extremely high. An example is the maneuver of the *Herald of Free Enterprise* (see below), making a complete rudder turn at full speed, which would endanger any roll-on, roll-off ferry boat, even when the bow doors are shut. The reason for this irresponsible maneuver was that the ship had left Zeebrugge five minutes late, but was due to arrive 15 minutes early in Dover. Many of us will have the same experience that being late for a meeting seems a good enough excuse to speed or to run traffic lights. According to risk homeostasis theory, the cure for such unwanted behavior is not simply telling people to stick to the rules. Their behavior is automatic, and based on vast experience. Telling them that their experience is wrong may not be credible; replacing experience by theoretical considerations may even be impossible. Other ways of influencing behavior, suggested by the theory, are to make the situation safer without it being noticed; or to affect the cost-of-risk function, for instance, by imposing control and punishment; or to affect the cost-of-time function by making traffic delays a socially acceptable excuse for being late.

The second theory that is proposed to explain risk taking in everyday situations is Näätanen and Summala's *zero-risk theory*. The essence of the theory is that people seek situations in which they do not experience any risk. In

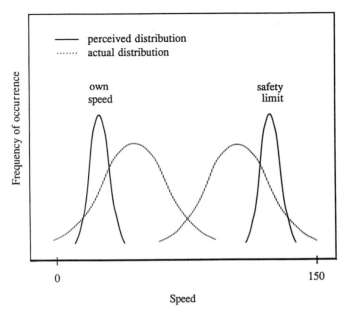

Figure 9.3   Graphical illustration of zero-risk theory.

reality there may still be considerable risk, but this is not noticed. As an example, the selection of speed is portrayed in Figure 9.3. The left-hand curve represents the perceived variation in driver behavior; the right-hand curve the variation of the speed limit. The graph shows that within the selected range of speed it is impossible to reach the danger region. Thus, there is zero risk, represented by a considerable safety margin between the two curves. Additionally, it is assumed that people are motivated to keep the safety margin as small as possible. The representation differs from reality in two ways; the distributions are too narrow, and their means are dislocated. As a consequence, the two curves will in reality be overlapping, which means that the selected behavior may very well bring the driver into the danger region.

Many different processes may lead to a right-hand shift of the selected speed. An environmental change that seems to push the safety range to the right will increase the perceived safety margin. Since people are motivated to keep the margin at a minimum, they will react by increasing their speed. A decrease of one's own variability through accumulated skill will also increase the perceived safety margin. The same is true for a decrease of the variability in the danger region, for instance, because one feels better protected against the errors of other road users.

The forces that play a role in this model are perceptual, experiential, and motivational. A realistic consideration of risk is not involved. Suggestions for measures that may restrict the risk of driving are therefore not based on the idea that risk perception, or even the cost-of-risk function, should be affected. Drivers are supposed to use any opportunity for decreasing the safety margin. Any perceived improvement of driving conditions, any experience of prolonged safe traffic participation, any perceived decrease in the variability of behavior of other participants, will lead to a perceived widening of the safety margin. The reaction will be to increase speed in order to keep the margin small.

Behavioral decision theory provides room for risk control skills on the part of road users. Risk homeostasis theory replaces risk control by cost control. Zero-risk theory even disclaims the existence of cost control: drivers will always select speeds at which no risk or prospective loss is envisaged, while in reality the risk or prospective cost of a loss is considerable. The only way to prevent risk taking is by *enforcing* wide safety margins. In the example this means: imposing speed limits.

Both theories agree with respect to the limited role of conscious risk evaluation, and that risk reduction measures should not be directed at influencing the process of *risk evaluation*, but at influencing *habits*: "Whilst the risk of an accident may be very much in the mind of the accident researcher, it may not be in the mind of participants in the activity being studied. Most people who engage in activities with some level of associated risk will have successfully and safely carried out these activities on hundreds and perhaps thousands of previous occasions. Under these circumstances, it seems more likely that their behavior will be directed by task-related events and goals, which have a much higher frequency of occurrence than accidents" (McKenna, 1988, p. 479). "Automatization of the driving task and avoidance learning make it possible that most of driving eventually becomes a habitual activity based largely on automatized control of safety margins in partial tasks. No consideration is normally given to risks" (Summala, 1988, p. 497). Attempts at influencing risk taking are further discussed in the next section.

WARNINGS ON DANGEROUS PRODUCTS

In this section I could have attempted to present the vast literature on the effects of warnings. However, the best summary has already been given by Slovic (1987) in his short discussion on the usage of seatbelts. The bottom line of that discussion is that admonitions to wear seatbelts simply do not work. About 20% of road users wear seatbelts voluntarily; 50% will use them if it is made mandatory by law. No amount of warning will improve upon this number; only control and punishment will. Instead of repeating this literature, I will present a few examples from our own research.

Our group at Leiden University has conducted a number of studies concerning the design and use of warning labels on dangerous products used by professionals (Souverijn, 1989) and lay persons (Venema, 1989). The Dutch

National Centre for Information on Poison receives around 4000 queries a year about acute poisoning by cleaning fluids and do-it-yourself products. Probably there are many more cases. This is why we were asked to study the effects of warning labels on these products. We interviewed 779 people in the age range of 12 to 79 years. Of these, 97% claimed that they read warnings on dangerous products, although 40% added that they read warnings only if the product was new to them. Similar percentages were found for professional vermin-killers and farmers.

Such outcomes indicate only that people are generally aware of the fact that some chemicals are dangerous, and that it is socially desirable to read warning labels. However, in an observation study it transpired that people were not behaving in accordance with such beliefs. In a home-economics fair we organized a stand in which new products were introduced. We invited visitors to try the new products. The products were Green-Free (a vermin-killer for plants), Texatok (a vermin-killer for unpainted wood), Verf-Fix (a paint remover), and Candle-Light (a fuel for fondue sets). The participants were asked to try the newly designed bottles and cans through actual use, such as spraying a plant, and refueling the burner. The instructions on the label included the use of gloves, not sniffing at the bottle, closing the can after usage, extinguishing the fire before refueling. The environment was a simple kitchen mock-up, that provided all the necessary tools, such as apron, gloves, etc. The observed behaviors are portrayed in Table 9.1.

Despite people's expressed attitudes towards reading labels on new products, they were in fact reading labels in a minority of the cases. This result may be caused by the presence of the experimenter. However, it is not clear how the presence of an experimenter could have compensated for breathing poison, or for the explosion of a stove that is refueled while burning. Also, the experimenter's presence could have worked as an additional social control. However this may be, the danger of the situation was obvious. Therefore, the failure to take some simple precautions, even *after reading* the instructions, is remarkable. Table 9.1 shows that some people took precautions spontaneously, without reading the label. Actual reading of labels led to a significant increase of following the instructions, but the effects were far from maximal.

Table 9.1. Behavior of visitors trying out new products in a home-economics fair.

| Product | N | Reading label (%) | Following instructions | |
			Spontaneously (%)	After reading (%)
Green-Free	104	31	22	60
Texatok	104	13	45	70
Verf-Fix	180	39	24	54
Candle-Light	166	29	87	98

Why did our subjects not read the labels? Of those not reading the labels 55 % said they forgot. Habitually neglecting warnings was mentioned by 8 %. Not seeing the label was mentioned by 14 %. Thus, in 77 % of the cases, not reading the labels had nothing to do with conscious decisions, but rather with routinized behavior. Also, this result does not suggest that neglecting warnings has anything to do with the presence of an experimenter. Not using gloves, or not extinguishing the open fire of the burner, was explained by routine behavior (it's never necessary, I forgot, I never do that, I hate gloves) in 57 % of the cases.

The relation between beliefs, attitudes, and behavior is apparently weak. This has been noted before (e.g Midden, 1986; Nuttin, 1975). It is easier to change attitudes than behavior. If perceptions of risk, revealed by attitudes, are used in a conscious risk evaluation that precedes behavior, this lack of relationship is hard to explain. However, if behavior is mainly determined by pre-arranged routines, it is easy to understand that a change of risk-attitudes would only result in behavioral change if the existing routines were broken down and replaced by new routines.

Once a certain degree of dissociation between attitudes and behavior is assumed, another question emerges: How can we be certain that these attitudes existed prior to the investigation, instead of being the product of the investigation? Attitude measurement and the assessment of subjective risk share this problem of engaging subjects in questions that might be totally new to them. Most subjects are very willing to oblige the experimenters, and will therefore reply to questions as well as they can. But this does not mean that they have considered such questions before, and even less that their replies constitute a psychological reality. What evidence is there that people do of their own account engage frequently (or at all) in the type of risk evaluation prescribed by normative theories? Most of the experiments we have been conducting in the past 20 years bring subjects to situations in which their responses, no matter what they are, cannot be interpreted in another way than to mean that risk evaluation takes place. This constraint is true for the old choice-among-gambles situation, for the heuristics and biases studies, for the risk-factor investigations, and even for process-model experiments. None of these paradigms guarantees that the type of process proposed by our theories does really occur outside our experimental settings. In the next section I will therefore look more closely at some accident histories, to disclose whether risk considerations are found in the descriptions of how the accidents happened.

ACCIDENT HISTORIES

Scenario analysis

Accidents are usually studied retrospectively; that is, the situations in which accidents may occur are represented by the subset of those situations in which accidents did actually occur. There is no control group of situations in which no accidents occurred. This is unfortunate, because it is quite possible that there is a fundamental difference between those dangerous situations that developed into an accident and those that did not. The difference might even be in the amount or type of risk consideration that took place. The distinction between at least two modes of operation, the routine application of fixed behavioral patterns, and the conscious consideration of risk, leads to the prediction that perceived risk (or subjective risk) and actual accident rates (objective risk) are unrelated, or even inversely related: "Perceived risk is likely to generate awareness of danger and avoidance of accident involvement, whereas danger which is not perceived will tend to result in accidents" (Jørgensen, 1988, p. 660). Thus, if in everyday life people are avoiding risks that therefore rarely materialize, while they are hit by risks they never really considered, the study of accident scenarios will reveal that people generally fail to appreciate the risks that are facing them. One could argue that for this reason accident scenarios are not the appropriate material for the study of risk taking. The counterargument is exemplified by Howarth's (1988) study of child–car encounters. The unresponsiveness of drivers is universally present, in safe and fatal encounters alike. The subset of fatal encounters studied as accidents would not cast a false light upon the population of all encounters. Another counterargument is that the study of behavior that leads to accidents is valuable, even if that behavior is exceptional. If routine behavior is the major source of accidents, then it is still true that measures for the prevention of accidents should not assume a continuous assessment of risks.

The capsizing of the *Herald of Free Enterprise*

From the hundreds of accident scenarios that were analyzed by our group at Leiden University, I will take just one to elucidate the points made above. It is the much discussed capsizing of the *Herald of Free Enterprise*, a roll-on, roll-off ferry boat sailing between Zeebrugge in Belgium and Dover in England (CHMSO, 1987). In the accident 180 people died because the ship toppled over within a few minutes. At the inquest it transpired that the bow doors, through which the cars enter the ship, had been left open, so that seawater had free access to the car decks. It was the assistant bosun's task to close these doors, but this functionary had taken a nap, and did not wake up in time. There were no alarm lights, signaling the open bow door on the bridge. The captain had applied for such lights, but the request had been turned down with the argument that a senior officer should monitor the closing of the doors, and that therefore there was no possibility of the doors staying open. In fact, the ship's crew had adopted a "negative checking" system: functionaries did not control one another, but assumed that all was well as long as there were no alarms. The first officer, responsible for the supervision of the assistant bosun, had left the car deck before the closing of the door could take place, because he had some more urgent duties. This urgency was again due to a chronic shortage of staff.

Another aspect of the accident had to do with the question of why the water entered through the open doors, which were several meters above sea level. Here it appeared that the *Herald* was originally designed for the Dover–Calais connection. The ramp in Zeebrugge differed from the ramp in Calais; at high tide it was not possible for the cars to reach the upper deck. Therefore, the nose of the ship had been lowered a few meters through the filling of the ballast tanks. The ballast pumps did not have a sufficient capacity for emptying the tanks in a short time. The *Herald* had docked in Zeebrugge five minutes late, but was requested to arrive in Dover 15 minutes early. Therefore, there was no time for waiting till the ballast tanks were empty. Instead, the *Herald* left the harbor with the nose 3 meters down, and at full speed, which created a high bow wave. And so the *Herald* capsized, in perfect weather, and on a practically waveless sea.

A summary of the events is presented in Figure 9.4. Each branch of the tree is an event, and each lense-shaped figure a logical AND. Some of the events that were discussed above are identified in the tree. The interesting aspect of the accident is that the actions immediately preceding the capsizing were, although extremely dangerous, not the result of a deliberate acceptance of risks. The assistant bosun failed to wake up, but not because he thought the risk was acceptable. The captain failed to notice the open bow doors, but not because he thought he could risk it. The first officer applied the negative checking routine without consideration of the risk that the whole ship might perish. On the contrary, the accident scenario is so complicated, stretches out over such a long period of time, and involves so many actors, from the car deck to the upper management levels of the company, that no one could have predicted that such an accident could happen. If interviewed about the possible causes of major accidents with ferries, even the experts would list only such conditions as storm, collision with other traffic, grounding, fire, shifting cargo, explosion, and the like. Nobody would include a sleeping assistant bosun. Accidents like the one with the *Herald* have been called "inconceivable events" (Oestberg, 1984) or "impossible accidents" (Wagenaar & Groeneweg, 1987). The disturbing aspect of impossible accident scenarios is that, since they cannot be foreseen, they are never considered as representing risks. Here we encounter again the mechanism noted by Jørgensen (1988): Accidents that are reckoned to belong to the possible outcomes may be avoided, impossible accidents are not, and are therefore bound to occur. It is quite likely that major accidents in comparatively sophisticated systems will all be of the impossible type, that follow a scenario that was never envisaged, and definitely not considered by those making the last fatal steps at the sharp end of the system. Our main question, whether accidents are the result of misperceived risk, or consciously accepted grave risk, could be rephrased as: Are there other than impossible accidents? A more extensive analysis of accident scenarios could provide the answer.

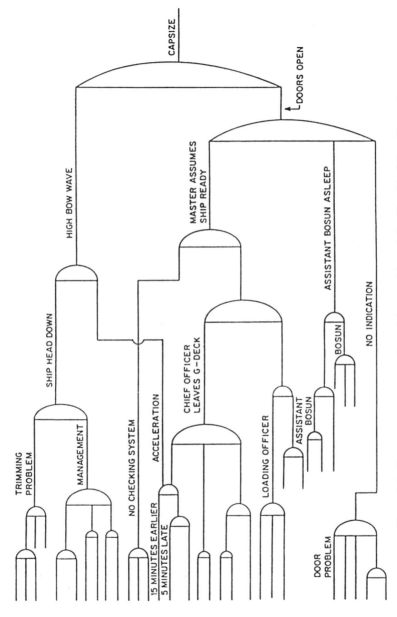

Figure 9.4 Event tree representation of the capsizing of the *Herald of Free Enterprise*.

57 accidents at sea

Our group in Leiden studied a large number of histories of accidents that happened at sea (Wagenaar & Groeneweg, 1987); police shooting accidents (Groeneweg & Wagenaar, 1986); accidents in oil exploration and production (Groeneweg & Pleit-Kuiper, 1987); accidents in electricity transport (Van de Roovaart, 1987); and accidents in intensive care wards (Wagenaar, Souverijn, & Hudson, in press). All accidents were represented by means of event trees, such as the one presented in Figure 9.4. The role of risk taking was specifically studied in an analysis of 57 accidents at sea that were reported by the Dutch Shipping Council, the Dutch legal authority dealing with the judiciary investigation of accidents at sea (Hagenzieker & Wagenaar, 1987). Each accident was described in an elaborate report to the Council, sometimes covering well over 100 pages.

The rationale of our analysis was that risk taking presupposes the consideration of risk, and that risk consideration, in turn, presupposes a few of the decision stages proposed by Fischhoff (see above). It is essential that the risk taker has sought or received the relevant information. The second stage is that the risk taker has recognized that there is a problem. These two stages are necessary conditions, because there can be no risk taking without awareness of a problem. Conscious preference for a risky option presupposes a few more stages, in which there is an investigation of the available choices, of their possible consequences, and of how these consequences are to be valued. Finally, there is a stage at which, following some decision rule, risks are compared, and accepted or rejected.

Accident histories with the level of detail as present in the reports of the Dutch Shipping Council allowed us to ascertain with some degree of confidence whether the responsible actors went through the various stages of decision making. The outcome of this analysis is presented in Table 9.2, which reads as follows: in 17 of the accidents information about the risk was not available, which means that the evaluation did not go beyond the first stage; in 21

Table 9.2. Where the consideration of risk stopped in 57 accidents at sea presented to the Dutch Shipping Council in the years 1984 and 1985.

Stage	Number of accident scenarios in which the risk evaluation (would have) stopped at a particular stage	(%)
1. Seeking or receiving information	17	21
2. Recognizing there is a problem	21	27
3. Listing of options	12	15
4. Investigation of consequences	16	20
5. Evaluation of consequences	13	16
6. Acceptance of risk	1	1

accidents it was not recognized that there was a problem, etc. The total adds up to 80, because in some accidents the analysis was defective at more than one stage. Problems with coding of the defects occurred mainly between Stages 4 and 5, and therefore do not affect the argument (cf. Wagenaar, 1990, for discussion of coding reliability). Here are some examples that were classified in the various categories:

1. *Seeking or receiving information*: The light on the telegraph was broken; maps were obsolete; danger warning was not received because the radar was switched off.
2. *Not recognizing there is a problem*: The captain assumed he.would not need a pilot.
3. *Listing choices*: The rules specified that no extra man was required on the bridge; hence this option was never considered.
4. *Investigation and evaluation of consequences*: Captain says that rules were silly; skipper claims it is all right to predict encounters without plotting; captain says the probability of an accident was negligible.
5. *Acceptance of risk*: Captain says the risk of a collision was smaller than the risk of a grounding.

Only in the one case classified under "Acceptance of risk" was there a full analysis and understanding of the negative result that finally came out. The risk was accepted because the alternative choice was judged to be riskier. In the end the Council decided that this judgment had been wrong.

This inventory lends little support to the notion that accidents occur because risks are evaluated and accepted by those directly involved. In 21 % of the cases the information about the imminent danger was not even available. In another 27 % the information was received, but the situation was not recognized as problematic. Thus, in 48 % of the cases there was definitely no decision preceded by a conscious analysis. In a further 15 % the error was in not considering the alternative that would have solved the problem. Thus, there was no misperceived risk, or a conscious rejection of a less risky alternative. In a further 36 % of the cases it is not totally clear what happened. The consequences were either not foreseen, or the likelihood of disaster was underestimated. In case the consequences were not at all foreseen, it is quite possible that action was taken on a routine basis, again without consideration of any risk. A skipper who even at the inquest claims that encounters between ships can be predicted without plotting the positions would probably also not have considered the risk during the actual maneuver. Therefore, I assume that those errors classified under "Evaluation of consequences" represent cases that were handled without a conscious analysis of the risks. Hence, in a total of 83 % of the cases errors were not due to a calculated acceptance of risk. In other words: most of the accidents were of the "impossible" type; those involved were completely taken by surprise.

Levels of operation

The examples listed above raise questions with respect to the locus of decision making. The employment of out-of-date maps prevents a captain from being warned against wrecks that have recently gone down. Thus, on the spot, the captain cannot evaluate the risk of sailing near wrecks. However, the use of out-of-date maps might itself also be the result of a decision, taken much earlier in the process. This decision might have been based on risk considerations.

The broader issue, hidden behind this problem, is the definition of levels of operation. The routine behavior of drivers, captains, operators, and all those who cause accidents at the sharp end of the system, is often preceded by some less routine-like planning. Van der Molen and Boetticher (1988) distinguish three levels in their model of driving behavior: the operational level, which describes the ongoing behavior during actual driving; the tactical level, describing incidental decisions such as overtaking and stopping at traffic lights; and the strategic level, at which long-term decisions are taken, such as route choice, and choice of average speed.

A similar distinction among levels of operation was introduced by Rasmussen (1982, 1983). He distinguished skill-based behavior, which runs mostly automatically; rule-based behavior, which operates through the application of consciously chosen but fully pre-programmed rules; and knowledge-based behavior, under which all sorts of conscious problem solving are grouped.

It is tempting to combine these two tripartitions by equating the operational level with skill-based behavior, the tactical level with rule-based behavior, and the strategic level with knowledge-based behavior. One rationale for this equation would be that in both systems risk evaluation is absent at the bottom level, and fully present at the top level. The two systems differ with respect to the amount of risk evaluation that takes place at the middle level. Van der Molen and Boetticher assume some sort of quick-and-dirty risk assessment, while Rasmussen excludes any type of risk assessment that is not incorporated in fixed rules. A possible reconciliation is obtained by assuming that any amount of risk assessment at the tactical level operates through the application of fixed decision rules, such as rules for overtaking other traffic, based on perceived distances and velocities. The creation and adaptation of such rules would then occur at the top level.

The three-level organization is fully compatible with risk homeostasis theory and zero-risk theory. The recognition of the actual situation as belonging to a set for which a behavioral pattern is already established occurs at the middle level. The execution of the fixed pattern is at the bottom level; the adaptation to new situations occurs at the top level. Additionally, the full cycle of a decision process leading to explicit assessments of risks can also be executed at the top level of operation.

The distinction among levels of operation can be applied to accident histories, such as the capsizing of the *Herald of Free Enterprise*. The routine actions of the assistant bosun and the deck officer are to be placed at the bottom level. The captain's decisions, such as to leave with the nose down in order to gain 20 minutes, are taken at the intermediate level. Management decisions, such as understaffing, the use of a ship not designed for that route, and the chronic acceptance of too short turn-around times, are taken at the top level. The three levels of operation are in this manner spread across time, and across levels of the organization. The top level has to do with management decisions high up in the organization, a long time before accidents occur. These decisions lead to a repertoire of policies that serves as a limiting condition for middle management. The middle level has to do with the selection of actual plans from these established policies, from a few days till a few hours before the accident. The bottom level has to do with the execution of plans at the work floor immediately preceding the accident.

Our initial question, "Are accidents caused by faulty risk assessments?" is possibly answered differently for the various levels of an organization. There is little evidence that risk assessment occurs at the bottom level; hence inadequate risk considerations by the actors directly involved are rarely among the causes of accidents. At the intermediate level the actors in the drama apply rules of the if... then type, which means that the application is dictated by the circumstances. A specific assessment of the risk involved does not take place every time the rule is applied. But the generation and maintenance of these if... then rules is under the control of conscious deliberations at the top level. In this way if... then rules may embody faulty risk assessments, even when the rule is thereafter applied without any consideration of the risks involved. Finally, at the top level, there are many deliberations that may well involve a consideration of risk, tradeoffs between safety and costs, and willful acceptance of calculated risks.

It is obvious that the accident histories described in accident reports, and considered in our analysis of accidents at sea, will contain almost exclusively behavior at the two lower levels. Behavior at the top level is localized in entirely different sections of an organization, and occurs at a time that may antedate the accident by many years. It is therefore no surprise that so little conscious risk taking was observed. But this does not mean that the outcome is trivial or meaningless, because the tenet that risk taking rarely occurs at the operational level is not universally accepted. Many industrial organizations still attempt to improve the accident statistics by advertising safety awareness to employees on the shop floor. Our conclusion that consideration of risk occurs mostly at the strategic level means that risk communication, as a means to prevent accidents, could most profitably be directed at those levels of an organization where strategic planning is executed. Only knowledge-based behavior can be modeled by consideration of risk.

The use of this newly gained insight is easily demonstrated when we consider the example of the *Herald of Free Enterprise*. There are many useful opportunities for risk communication, once the top level of the organization is identified as our target.

- The captain's decision to leave at full speed is a less promising target for improvement than the tight time schedules that prevail in most ferry lines. It should be possible to convince shipowners, harbor authorities, or national governments that the turn-around time of ferry boats should be made longer. This will probably require the construction of more berths, but that is easier to achieve than a change of behavior in all those instances in which under time pressure a crew may adopt dangerous procedures.
- Banning the irresponsible use of the ballasting facility will save fewer lives than forcing top management to monitor on a regular basis the practices that result from their decisions. Shipowners must realise that a regular audit of operational procedures is needed, because otherwise they cannot know the side-effects of their managerial decisions. Technical safety audits are by now almost universally accepted for nuclear power plants. There is no reason to exempt ferry boats, with their considerable killing potential, from such obvious practices. The lack of an auditing routine is a more serious flaw than the adoption of a dangerous ballasting trick.
- Adopting international rules about the closing of bow doors will have less effect than adopting rules about the quality of organizations that are licensed to operate public transport systems. Risk-communication efforts could be directed at national governments, in order to convince them that safety requirements should extend to the top levels of an organization, where the actual risk management takes place. Bus drivers, train drivers, and ship masters are selected and thereafter examined according to strict rules. But their managers, who may cause much greater havoc, are not.

Of course, following these recommendations may be more costly than telling people on the shop floor not to cause accidents. Even though the effect of risk evaluation may be large at the strategic level and negligible at the operational level, cost-effectiveness can in the end be the limiting factor. Naturally, the resources that can be spent on the promotion of safety are not infinite. But this issue is not relevant to the present discussion: even though changes at the strategic level are costly, this still does not mean that accidents are caused by risk acceptance or risk misperception at lower levels. Risk communication directed at the lower levels, although relatively cheap, will have little effect.

CONCLUSION

Are accidents caused by risk-taking behavior? My answer is yes, but not at the level of those directly involved at the sharp end of systems. The behavior of people walking in the streets, driving their cars, doing their regular jobs on a routine basis, may be among the causes of almost all accidents. But these people rarely consider these accidents in advance: they run risks, but they do not take them.

Much more risk evaluation occurs at the blunt end of the system, where the planners are, the designers, the managers, the authorities that make decisions in lieu of millions of others. But these evaluation processes are rarely considered in accident histories, rarely adapted after the occurrence of accidents, and rarely the target of risk communication programs, possibly because the illusion that most risks originate at the operational level is so strong.

I am not arguing that those who drive too fast, who cut corners in executing prescribed procedures, or who use dangerous materials without reading instructions, are right. Only, these people do not evaluate risks, and therefore it cannot be argued that their way of evaluating risk is wrong and needs to be improved. Even the argument that not considering risks at this level is something that should be changed through risk communication is not really tenable. Most activities are necessarily executed at the bottom level of automated behavior, where there simply is no room for consideration of risks.

I would urge those who address themselves to risk-taking behavior to verify that those who were perceived to take risks had really been engaged in any form of risk consideration. At the end, risk taking is the cause of almost all accidents. But it is not always easy to find those who took the risks; too often they are confused with those who ran the risks.

SUMMARY

The issue addressed in this chapter is whether accidents are caused by misperception of risk and the conscious acceptance of risk. Many industrial programs to raise the risk awareness of workers seem to be based upon this assumption.

The answer to the question is based upon the conviction that the large majority of our everyday actions are automatically controlled, instead of being the result of conscious decisions. At least two risk theories, risk homeostasis theory and zero-risk theory, allow the development of more or less standardized behavioral patterns that render everyday risk evaluation superfluous.

The effects of automatic behavior in dangerous situations are illustrated by a number of examples: stopping at traffic lights, slowing down in areas with children, reading and reacting to warnings on dangerous products.

The analysis of accident scenarios, such as the scenario causing the capsizing of the *Herald of Free Enterprise*, reveals that the behaviors leading to accidents occur at three levels: operational (routine shop floor behavior), tactical (incidental decisions), and strategic (planning and long-term decisions). Although error at all levels leads to accidents, a conscious evaluation of risks can be expected only at the strategic level. Therefore, the question, "Are those directly involved in the causation of accidents misperceiving or knowingly accepting risks?" should be answered in the negative. They are not, because they function at the operational level. However, the more general question, "Are accidents preceded by misperception or conscious acceptance of risks?" should be answered positively. Those who are responsible at the strategic level, often far removed from the accident both in time and space, have the opportunity to evaluate risks. Risk communication, when aimed at a decline of accident rates, should be directed at those who operate at the strategic level.

REFERENCES

Carstensen, G. (1983). Faerdselsuheld i bytrafik—en analyse af 29 uheld påen radialgade. *Danish Council of Road Safety Research*, Notat 5/1983, Lynbgy 1983 (in Danish).

Groeneweg, J., & Pleit-Kuiper, A. (1987). *Causes of accidents in the Dutch Petroleum Company*. (Report 87-13). Leiden: Leiden University, Centre for Safety Research.

Groeneweg, J., & Wagenaar, W. A. (1986) *Oorzaken en achtergronden van foutieve geweldsaanwendingen door de politie*. (Report 86-9). Leiden: Leiden University, Centre for Safety Research.

Hagenzieker, M., & Wagenaar, W. A. (1987) *Beslissen en risico-acceptatie aan boord van schepen: Riskant gedrag op zee?* (Report 87-15). Leiden: Leiden University, Centre for Safety Research.

Heinrich, H. W. (1931). *Industrial accident prevention* (4th ed. with D. Petersen & N. Roos, 1980). New York: McGraw-Hill.

Hovden, J., & Larsson, T. J. (1987). Risk: Culture and concepts. In W. T. Singleton & J. Hovden (Eds.), *Risks and decisions*. New York: Wiley.

Howarth, C. I. (1988). The relationship between objective risk, subjective risk, behaviour. *Ergonomics*, **31**, 527–535.

Jørgensen, N. O. (1988). Risky behaviour at traffic signals: A traffic engineer's view. *Ergonomics*, **31**, 657–661.

Kletz, T. A. (1985). *An engineer's view of human error*. Rugby: The Institution of Chemical Engineers.

McKenna, F. P. (1988). What role should the concept of risk play in theories of accident involvement? *Ergonomics*, **31**, 469–484.

Midden, C. J. H. (1986). *Individu en grootschalige technologie*. Unpublished doctoral dissertation, Leiden University, Leiden.

MV Herald of Free Enterprise, Report of Court No. 8074, formal investigation. (1987). London: HMSO.

Näätanen, R., & Summala, H. (1974). A model for the role of motivational factors in drivers' decision making. *Accident and Prevention*, **6**, 243–261.

Näätanen, R., & Summala, H. (1976). *Road user behavior and traffic accidents*. Amsterdam: North-Holland.

Norman, D. A. (1981). Categorization of action slips. *Psychological Review*, **88**, 1–15.

Nuttin, J. J. (1975). *The illusion of attitude change*. London: Academic Press.

Oestberg, G. (1984). Evaluation of a design for inconceivable event occurrence. *Materials and Design*, **5**, 88–93.

Planek, T. W. (1982). Home accidents: A continuing social problem. *Accident Analysis and Prevention*, **14**, 107-120.

Rasmussen, J. (1982). Human errors: A taxonomy for describing human malfunction in industrial installations. *Journal of Occupational Accidents*, **4**, 311-335.

Rasmussen, J. (1983). Skills, rules, and knowledge: Signals, signs, and symbols, and other distinctions in human performance models. *IEEE Transactions on Systems. Man. and Cybernetics*, **3**, 257-268.

Reason, J. T. (1990). *Human error*. Cambridge, UK: Cambridge University Press.

Shiffrin, R. M., & Schneider, W. (1977). Controlled and automatic human information processing II: Perceptual learning, automatic attending, and a general theory. *Psychological Review*, **84**, 127-190.

Slovic, P. (1987). Perception of risk. *Science*, **236**, 280-285.

Slovic, P., Fischhoff, B., & Lichtenstein, S. (1985). Characterizing perceived risk. In R. W. Kates, C. Hohenemser, & J. X. Kasperson (Eds.), *Perilous progress: Managing the hazards of technology*. Boulder, CO: Westview.

Slovic, P., Lichtenstein, S., & Fischhoff, B. (1984). Modeling the societal impact of fatal accidents. *Management Science*, **30**, 464-474.

Souverijn, A. M. (1989). *Etikettering van Bestrijdingsmiddelen*. (Report 89-29). Leiden: Leiden University, Centre for Safety Research.

Summala, H. (1988). Risk control is not risk adjustment: The zero-risk theory of driver behavior and its implications. *Ergonomics*, **31**, 491-506.

Van der Molen, H. H., & Boetticher, A. M. T. (1988). A hierarchical risk model for traffic participants. *Ergonomics*, **31**, 537-555.

Van de Roovaart, B. (1987). *Ongelukken bij opwekking en transport van energie*. (Report 87-14) Leiden: Leiden University, Centre for Safety Research.

Venema, A. (1989). *Productinformatie ter preventie van ongevallen in de privesfeer*. (Report 1989-69). The Hague: Institute for Consumer Research.

Wagenaar, W. A. (1990). Risk evaluation and the causes of accidents. In K. Borcherding, O. I. Larichev, & D. M. Messick (Eds.), *Contemporary issues in decision making*. Amsterdam: North-Holland.

Wagenaar, W. A., & Groeneweg, J. (1987). Accidents at sea: Multiple causes and impossible consequences. *International Journal of Man–Machine Studies*, **27**, 587-598.

Wagenaar, W. A., Souverijn, A. M., & Hudson, P. T. W. (in press). Safety management in intensive care wards. In B. Wilpert & T. Qvale (Eds.), *New technology, safety, and systems reliability*. London: Erlbaum.

Wilde, G. J. S. (1982). The theory of risk homeostasis: Implications for safety and health. *Risk Analysis*, **2**, 209-225.

Yates, J. F. (1990). *Judgment and desision making*. Englewood Cliffs, NJ: Prentice Hall.

Chapter 10

Risk taking, design, and training

Gordon F. Pitz
Southern Illinois University at Carbondale

CONTENTS

INTRODUCTION

Mary and Jim have saved enough money to build their dream house. Their favorite feature in the design for the house is a loft above the living area, reached by a spiral staircase. Their architect has serious reservations about the safety of the loft and staircase, especially considering the couple's two small but very active children. Mary and Jim refuse to believe the risk of accident is significant. They hope to prevent danger to the children by training them to recognize the risks and to behave appropriately when using the staircase. Thus, they want to go ahead with the loft as designed. They discover, however, that local building codes prohibit spiral staircases of the sort they have in mind, and require railings around the loft that Mary and Jim believe would be unsightly. Mary and Jim appeal to the city council for a variance, arguing that they have evaluated the risk, they accept it, and the decision to build the staircase or not should be theirs.

This brief scenario illustrates the concerns of this chapter. How does one assess the risk posed by something like a loft or staircase? What options does the architect have in responding to the risk? What are the behavioral implications of decisions made by the architect? Is it possible to reduce risk by modifying people's behavior, and if so, how does one create a suitable training program for achieving that goal? Can a regulatory agency reduce the potential for accident and injury through regulation, and should it even try?

The scope of the chapter includes problems that might be faced by a designer who is concerned about risk. The concern may be for equipment that is potentially hazardous to the user or to bystanders, or for environments in which accidents might occur. The latter might include living space or work places. The range of problems is broad, and the nature of the risks is varied. There are significant psychological, social, and political differences among the risks of driving an automobile, using a chain saw, working in a chemical plant, or selecting a site for toxic waste disposal. The problems can be addressed at many levels, and from many perspectives. The chapter makes no effort to be comprehensive. The focus is on the decision-making process, although, as Wagenaar has pointed out in Chapter 9, not all risk-taking behavior is the result of deliberate decisions made by the person who engages in risky behavior. I summarize the findings of research within the framework of behavioral decision theory, bearing in mind the limitations of this research. Several earlier chapters have provided relevant discussions of risk-taking behavior. I discuss ways in which this material might illuminate the issues that concern a designer.

The discussion will consider risk and design from the point of view of three groups of people: first, managers or designers who must consider the potential for accident or injury when making decisions; second, people who use the equipment or who live in or work in the space created by the designer, and who are affected by the designer's decisions; third, a group I refer to as "society-at-large," whose concerns are usually expressed through regulatory agencies and the elected officials who appoint these agencies. In the example used to introduce this chapter, the architect is a member of the first group, Mary and Jim are members of the second group, and the city council represents the concerns of the third. Decisions are made by members of all of these groups. Managers and designers make decisions about the design of systems that might be hazardous; users make decisions about how to respond to the hazards; society-at-large decides how to regulate the risk and how to enforce the regulations.

While the primary concern of this chapter is with problems faced by the manager and the designer, it is impossible to respond adequately to their problems without considering the perspectives of the other parties. For example, a lack of restrictions on hazardous building materials, or user ignorance of such hazards, may present designers with otherwise avoidable dilemmas. Design problems are system problems in the largest sense. The equipment or space is part of a system that includes the user, and this system itself is part of a broader social and cultural context. The context places constraints on the design of the system, and is sensitive to events that occur within the system (see Nadler, 1985, for a related discussion). The architect cannot respond effectively to the problem of the loft and staircase without anticipating decisions made by the other parties: Mary, Jim, their children, the city council, and others.

Descriptive and prescriptive theory

Behavioral decisions theory usually takes two forms (cf. Chapter 2, by Neumann & Politser). First, the theory provides a descriptive account of people's behavior, seeking to explain observed decisions in terms of general psychological principles. Second, it offers normative prescriptions in the form of advice to the decision maker, and seeks to improve the quality of decisions (see Fischhoff, Svenson, and Slovic, 1987, for a review of behavioral decision theory in the context of environmental hazards). In evaluating the research, it is important to bear in mind its goals. Descriptive research does not necessarily show how decisions ought to be made, while prescriptive theory is not necessarily accurate as a description of behavior. Nevertheless, while one can make a distinction between descriptive and prescriptive goals, they interact; one cannot discuss one without reference to the other. Furthermore, there are broader issues to be considered when discussing risk, issues that transcend the usual scope of prescriptive and descriptive theory.

First I deal with descriptive concerns, the psychological analysis of human behavior. The principal focus is on the behavior of users of systems, as it might affect decisions made by managers and designers. However, many of the conclusions apply to the behavior of managers and designers, too, for architects and engineers are subject to the same principles of behavior that affect the owner of a house or the driver of an automobile. Three descriptive questions might be addressed by behavioral decision theorists: (a) How do people in each of the three groups I have identified perceive and evaluate risks? (b) How do these people behave in risky situations? (c) How do responses to risk change when designers, managers, or regulators adopt certain approaches to the management of risk?

The second focus of the chapter is the prescriptive one. There is a growing interest in procedures designed to help decision makers. Formal methods of decision analysis have been developed that can be helpful in complex situations. Decision analysis is especially useful when the decision maker would like to achieve goals that seem to be incompatible, or when the consequences of some alternatives are highly uncertain. Such conflict and uncertainty is a salient characteristic of problems of risk. The decision maker must balance her concerns for minimizing costs, preserving freedom of choice, and improving safety. She must also consider the potentially serious consequences of outcomes that might have only a small probability of occurring. Decision aids will be most useful to those who design and manage the equipment or facility, but one might also seek ways to improve decisions made by users and by the regulatory bodies that set general policies.

UNDERSTANDING BEHAVIOR IN THE FACE OF RISK

A person's response to a risky situation involves several stages, stages that may interact, but which reflect different psychological processes (MacCrimmon & Wehrung, 1986). He must first recognize and then evaluate the risk; the recognition and evaluation may occur automatically, or may be the result of conscious deliberation. If the risk is considered significant enough, he must respond to the risk, perhaps by attempting to leave the situation, by trying to change the situation, or by ignoring the risk. Usually a person will monitor the effect of his actions, and modify his response accordingly.

Perceptions of risk

Discussions of risk are often bedeviled by disagreements over the magnitude of the risk that exists. Consumer groups believe that all-terrain vehicles pose significant dangers to children who drive such vehicles, while purchasers may fail to perceive any risk. Owners of a manufacturing plant may refuse to acknowledge any health risk to their employees, while the employees believe that the risks are serious. Designers of systems and members of regulatory agencies often expend much effort to estimate accurately the degree of risk presented by a situation. Users must either rely on their own intuitions, or take at face value the evaluations provided by others. The gap between intuitions and expert assessment is often large (see Fischhoff, 1989).

One source of the differences lies in the definition of risk (see Chapter 1, by Yates & Stone). Expert assessments usually focus on the potential for loss, which includes the probability of the loss occurring and the magnitude of the loss in terms of death, injury, or monetary costs. There is a great deal of evidence that a nonexpert's sense of risk depends on more than the probability and magnitude of the loss. Numerous psychometric studies (e.g. Slovic, MacGregor, & Kraus, 1987; Vlek & Stallen, 1981) have identified factors that contribute to perceived risk. Perceived risk may depend on such obvious factors as the potential degree of damage, but also on dimensions such as the unfamiliarity of the consequences, the involuntary nature of exposure to the risk, the uncontrollability of the damage, and the degree to which the hazard could have been foreseen. The sense of control that a person feels in a situation may be a particularly important factor. For example, Rumar (1988) found that the perceived risk in driving an automobile is typically low, since in most situations the driver has control, and receives no feedback to suggest that there is any risk. For many, flying seems very unsafe because one has no control over one's fate once in the air.

A different research direction has addressed emotional reactions to risky situations. The potential for serious loss generates a variety of emotional reactions, not all of which are necessarily unpleasant; there is a fine line between fear and excitement. Investigators have examined factors related to such affective concepts as "danger" or "fear." Psychometric procedures can be used to identify relevant dimensions (e.g. Riemersma, 1988, on determinants of perceived safety, or Rohe & Burby, 1988, on social determinants of fear). The same methods can be used to differentiate affective reactions that may be difficult to disentangle (e.g. Herzog & Smith, 1988, on the difference between mystery and danger). Again, a major determinant of perceived risk and of affective reactions to risky situations seems to be a person's sense of control, or the lack thereof.

An important design principle has been proposed by Newman (1972), who was concerned with the sense of safety that people feel in residential areas. His theoretical concept of "defensible space" specifies the conditions under which people feel safe from assault. The concept remains rather fuzzy, and some attempts to test precise predictions have failed (Nomoyle & Foley, 1988). Nevertheless, the theory and experimental tests of the theory help to define factors that are critical in determining perceptions of risk and danger. The concept of defensible space may have potential implications that are broader than the design of housing projects; it would be interesting to see if the concept is related to the sense of control that has been identified as an important determinant of perceived risk.

One problem with efforts to identify environmental correlates of perceived risk or danger is that the effect of any particular stimulus variable is likely to be highly dependent on context (Moran & Dolphin, 1986). Better than a simple catalog of relevant factors would be a more general theory that predicts affective responses in any risky situation. The foundation for such a theory may be found in a model proposed by Purcell (1986). Purcell suggests that people match the features of a situation to their representation of past experience, and that affect is produced when a significant discrepancy is noted. The affect may be positive—interest or excitement—or negative. To understand how such a process operates, it is necessary first to introduce other theoretical concepts.

Current cognitive theory suggests that knowledge is represented as a collection of complex associational networks, referred to variously as prototypes, scripts, or schemas (see Anderson, 1985). These networks represent generalized concepts that summarize past experience. New experiences are interpreted and understood by relating them to existing schemas. Affect, then, may occur when there is a mismatch or discrepancy with the schema that a situation elicits. Although concerned with positive affect such as interest and attraction, Purcell's theoretical idea has more general application. In some situations, where risks are already encoded as part of schematic knowledge, activation of a schema causes the risk to be recognized, but with little associated affect. Brown and Groeger (1988) use such an account to explain how automobile drivers assess risks. Recognition of a hazard depends upon the identification of well-learned indicators that initiate a risk-avoidance response (see Hoyos, 1988). In other cases, perceived risk may represent a deviation of situational features from the expectations induced by the schema. These may be the cases in which strong emotional responses accompany the sense of risk.

Before the research on risk perception is used to guide design decisions, one must recognize its limitations. For example, Arabie and Maschmeyer (1988) point out that individual differences have usually been neglected. They suggest that researchers need to examine differences in the weights that people assign to various factors. Research on individual differences in risk perception (see Chapter 4, by Bromiley & Curley) has not yet addressed this issue systematically. Kishchuk (1987) has criticized risk perception research for its emphasis on correlational studies and for insufficient analysis of the causal relationship between risk factors and perceived risk. It has not been demonstrated, for example, that one can modify the perception of risk by changing one of the important factors.

Another weakness of psychometric studies is that they often divorce the perception of risk from behavior in a risky environment. Factors that affect a person's considered assessment of risk in a psychometric experiment may be unimportant when he is required to respond to actual risk. In many cases, recognition of a risk must occur while the person performs some task that places other demands on information-processing capabilities. The driver of an automobile must recognize the presence of hazards while concentrating on the task of driving (Hoyos, 1988). In these situations, reactions are likely to reflect automatic response processes rather than thoughtful deliberation.

The distinction between automatic responses that occur without deliberate thought and responses that depend on the explicit consideration of salient factors is an important one. Skills and habitual behaviors, such as driving an automobile or using a familiar piece of equipment, involve very little conscious attention. Such behavior is very different from deliberate analysis. When investigators ask for judgments of the probability of some risky outcome, they are primarily tapping a person's memory for facts. Howarth (1988) suggests that such conscious verbal knowledge mostly reflects social stereotypes. By contrast, risk-taking responses in familiar situations are controlled by the tacit knowledge that underlies skilled or routine behavior.

There have been criticisms of the risk perception literature from other perspectives. The research is heavily dominated by psychological studies that explore relevant cognitive factors, but which ignore the sociological and political context that conditions the perception of risk. Clarke (1989) discusses many of these political processes, as they were found to operate in an accident involving the leak of dioxin in a state office building. It is not possible to explain the different perceptions of various parties to the events without considering their political motivations and cultural backgrounds.

While Clarke's account of risk perception provides interesting insights, he also exhibits a common misunderstanding of behavioral decision theory that is worth noting. It is easy to confuse the descriptive and normative goals of the research. The research shows that there are major discrepancies between the risk assessments of experts and nonexperts; this is a descriptive statement. Clarke incorrectly assumes that the investigators must be stating a normative conclusion: that nonexperts are mistaken, and decisions about risk should rely on the formal assessments of experts. The conclusion drawn from the literature by most behavioral researchers is, if anything, the opposite. Since formal risk assessments so often ignore factors that lay people find important, it is foolhardy to base decisions only on formal assessments.

There is a relationship between the descriptive and normative issues that will be explored in more detail later in the chapter. For now I simply note that experts and nonexperts interpret risk in different ways. Is one way more "correct?" Does the fact that one is an "expert" impart a greater importance to one's judgments, or is the expert mistaken in ignoring others' opinions? Before these questions can be answered, it will be necessary to develop a framework within which an answer can be derived.

Designers, then, should be aware of users' responses to risk at three levels. First, it is possible to identify the factors that are related to deliberate assessments of risk. These factors involve more than the probabilities and costs of potential outcomes. One common factor seems to be the perceived degree of control a person has in affecting the outcome. Also important may be the concomitant affective reactions such as danger or fear, which may reflect deviations of a perceived situation from schemas based on prior experience. Third, behavioral responses to risk may reflect different processes, especially when a user is skilled in using the equipment or familiar with the situation that produces the risk. Of primary importance in these latter situations are learned indicators of hazard that trigger largely automatic responses involved in skilled behavior. Since behavior of this sort occurs only after prolonged experience or practice, the hazard indicators are likely to be highly situation specific.

Responses to risk: SEU theory

From the point of view of managers, designers, and regulatory agencies, other people's perceptions of risks are important primarily in so far as they are predictive of behavior. It may be helpful to know that the user of a piece of equipment believes it to be hazardous. It is more useful to know what the person will do with the equipment. A useful starting point in the analysis of behavior is an old and often maligned theory of decision making, Subjective Expected Utility (SEU), which was introduced in Chapter 2 by Neumann and Politser. SEU theory is still widely employed by authors who view risk taking as a decision-making process (e.g. Oppe, 1988). There are some serious limitations to SEU as a descriptive theory; nevertheless, it provides a valuable perspective on users' behavior.

Consider the following oversimplified example. When faced by a risky situation, a person may adopt procedures to reduce the risk, or may choose to ignore the risk. A construction worker who uses a piece of equipment that can cause eye injuries can use safety goggles, or ignore the danger (of course, she may have other options such as quitting the job). The probability of injury is much lower if she wears safety goggles, but it is not eliminated altogether. Thus, there are four scenarios that might unfold:

1.   Worker uses safety goggles and is injured.
2.   Worker uses safety goggles and is not injured.
3.   Worker ignores the risk and is injured.
4.   Worker ignores the risk and is not injured.

An analysis of the problem according to SEU theory is illustrated in Figure 10.1. The utility of scenarios 1 and 3 depends on the undesirability of being injured: the expected costs, the anticipated pain and inconvenience, and so on. The utility of scenarios 1 and 2 depends on the discomfort (physical or psychological) attendant on wearing safety goggles. The probability of avoiding injury when wearing goggles is P, and the probability of avoiding injury otherwise is Q, with P much larger than Q. The utility of avoiding injury, relative to being injured, is A, and the utility of not wearing goggles, relative to the discomfort of wearing them, is G. A is usually greater than G. The utility of scenario 1, presumably the worst of the outcomes, is set arbitrarily at zero. Assuming that A and G can be combined additively, the utility of the scenarios 2, 3, and 4 is A, G, and A + G respectively.

The expected utility for wearing goggles is P * A, and the expected utility for not wearing goggles is (Q * A) + G. Although P is larger than Q, and A is larger

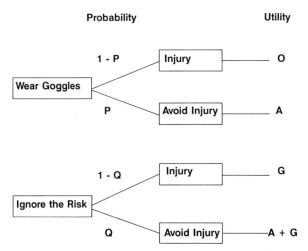

Figure 10.1. SEU analysis of the decision to wear safety goggles. The expected utility of wearing goggles is $((1 - P) \times 0) + (P \times A) = P \times A$. The expected utility of ignoring the risk is $((1 - Q) \times G) + (Q \times (A + G)) = G + (Q \times A)$.

than G, the second expected utility might be greater than the first if G (the utility for not wearing goggles) is large enough. In other words, if the worker dislikes the safety goggles enough, she will not wear them. The decision will also depend on the utility of avoiding injury (or the disutility of being injured), and on the relative magnitude of the perceived probabilities, P and Q. From this perspective, anything that increases the utility of not wearing goggles, or reduces the utility of avoiding injury, will make it more likely that the worker will ignore the risk. Similarly, anything that increases the perceived probability of avoiding injury when not wearing goggles, or reduces that perceived probability when wearing goggles, will increase her inclination to ignore the risk.

Phrased this way, the SEU analysis might seem trite. Certainly there are enough free parameters in the analysis to make *a priori* predictions of behavior difficult or impossible. When the theory is formulated in a sufficiently precise way, it is often shown to be false. Nevertheless, the theory still provides a good first approximation to behavior in most situations. Many observed phenomena make sense from the perspective of SEU theory. More importantly, perhaps, no alternative theory has the same generality of application. In a discussion of risk taking by traffic participants, van der Molen and Bötticher (1988) recommend using SEU to predict choices among behavioral alternatives, and they criticize other theories for their inability to make quantitative predictions. They further suggest that the best way to use the theory is to consider the hierarchy of choices that are available. This hierarchy includes choices made at strategic, tactical, and operational levels. Risk-taking behavior might be predicted at any of these levels.

Consider the effects on behavior of such factors as additional benefits or workers' compensation for employees who face risky environments, or who are injured because of risks inherent in the workplace. Such benefits increase the utility associated with risky behavior, since they provide a gain in the event that injury occurs. In Figure 10.1, the benefit serves to reduce the relative value of A. Thus, the expected utility for wearing safety goggles will be reduced more than the expected utility for ignoring the risk. One would then expect employees to select the risky option more often. There is evidence that exactly this effect can be observed. Chelius (1977) reported that higher levels of workers' compensation benefits are associated with a higher rate of occupational injury. He argued that the goals of accident prevention and alleviation of financial hardship resulting from injury may be in conflict, for anything that promotes the latter hinders the former. The data suggest that workers will take greater risks than they would if the entire cost of accidents were theirs to bear (see also Burton, 1983).

An analysis of behavior in terms of SEU theory will be helpful only if one realizes that the utility of an outcome is a function of many factors. There may be social pressures on a person not to follow safety procedures. For example, it took many years for face masks to become acceptable items of equipment for hockey goalies. Companies sometimes punish or threaten to punish employees who cause expensive delays by responding to warning signals; such pressure may have been responsible for many accidents, including the downing of the Korean Air flight 007 over the Soviet Union, and the Challenger shuttle explosion. A useful exercise for any designer or manager is to list the factors that might affect the utility of the decision maker's options.

Risk homeostasis theory

An interesting theoretical idea with close connections to SEU theory is the theory of risk homeostasis (RHT), which was discussed in Chapter 9, by Wagenaar. Developed in the context of automobile safety (see Wilde, 1988), RHT has some interesting implications for risk-taking behavior in general. In the terminology of SEU, RHT proposes that, as environments are made safer, the perceived probability of injury is reduced, and thus the expected utility of risky behavior is increased. For this reason, efforts to reduce risks, for example by constructing safer highways, may be self-defeating. These efforts increase the expected utility of risk-taking responses by lowering the perceived probability of accident, thereby increasing the frequency of risky behaviors. The increased frequency of risk taking may offset any reduction in accidents produced by the original improvements.

In Wilde's (1988) description of RHT, he assumes that people have a "target level" for risk, a level at which they estimate that the ideal balance of benefits and costs is achieved. This is not the same formulation as the presentation I have given in terms of SEU theory. Rather than considering behavior to be a matter of decision making, Wilde proposes that the process operates at a more automatic, preattentive level. Drivers try to attain their target level by modifying their behavior as the perceived level of risk changes (hence the term "homeostasis"). Wilde's formulation is subject to criticisms that do not apply to the SEU version (see Janssen & Tenkink, 1988). For example, McKenna (1988) uses the findings of research on risk perception to argue that people would find it impossible to maintain risk at a desired level.

Adams (1988) notes that almost all of the data cited in support of RHT use accident statistics before and after safety improvements, and points out the limitations to such data when testing a theory that emphasizes perceived risk. However, an ingenious and more valid test of RHT was described by Streff and Geller (1988). These authors studied the behavior of subjects wearing or not wearing seat belts while driving go-carts (a within-subject comparison), and while driving to the experimental site (a between-subject comparison). They found no evidence for risk compensation between subjects in time to travel to the experimental site. Within subjects, however, when subjects switched from non-seat belt to seat belt conditions, they did increase their driving speed, as predicted by RHT.

Regardless of the final disposition of RHT, the ideas suggested by Wilde have important implications for anyone who must manage risks. Adams (1988) argues that RHT points up a need for a new agenda in managing risks and improving safety: designers and managers should be less concerned with protecting people from themselves, a goal which may be impossible to achieve, and more concerned about the distribution of involuntary risks. This issue is properly a concern for prescriptive decision theory, which will be addressed below.

Limitations to SEU theory

There are many reasons why a simple SEU model of risk taking is inadequate as a descriptive theory. The model suggests that people employ a largely rational approach to risk taking, in that choices will be consistent with beliefs and values. There is plenty of evidence that people's behavior is often quite irrational (see Neumann & Politser, Chapter 2). The implication that decision makers can integrate probabilities and utilities in the deliberate manner implied by the theory is clearly inconsistent with what is known about cognitive processes. Descriptive analyses of decision making suggest that decision makers adopt a variety of strategies for dealing with their limited ability to process complex information (Montgomery & Svenson, 1989). In the area of safety, van der Colk (1988) suggests that traffic accidents result from the conflict between the demands of the traffic system and the cognitive capabilities of road users, and argues that drivers' limited ability to process information, rather than deliberate choice, is the basis for accidents.

Some changes in risky behavior may reflect changes that occur at a purely automatic level. While the changes might be predictable from SEU theory, the deliberate assessment of options that is implied by the theory is unlikely. Weinstein, Gubb, and Vautier (1986) tried to increase seat belt use by making the link to personal risk more salient. Changes in frequency of use were observed, but interviews did not elicit any increase in spontaneous references to seat belt use and risk. The implication is that automatic behavior changed, while deliberate thought processes did not. If changes in the utility of wearing seat belts occurred, they did so at an automatic level.

Part of the problem, then, is that many so-called risky decisions are not deliberate decisions at all. The distinction between automatic and deliberate behavior was raised in a previous section. SEU theory is usually presented as a theory of deliberate choice. In many ways, however, a person's responses to risky situations are more likely to result from learned habits that are automatic, and of which he is unaware. Wagenaar makes a related point in Chapter 9, distinguishing between habitual behavior at the "sharp end" of the system and deliberate decisions at the "blunt end." A response may be inconsistent with the person's beliefs and values, and hence inconsistent with SEU theory. If, however, the response occurs automatically, then simply pointing out the inconsistency is unlikely to be effective in changing his behavior.

Some automatic responses reflect habits that have been acquired by a user, such as an established routine that ignores safety procedures. Automatic behavior is also an important characteristic of skilled behavior, an activity that has been practiced to the point where one would be considered an "expert." Skill in this context includes not only motor performance such as driving an automobile, but cognitive skills, including problem solving, that involve only mental activities. Skilled performance can be described by rule-based theories that specify actions to be performed given some set of stimulus conditions. The stimulus conditions and the actions can be arbitrarily complex. Indeed, a feature that differentiates skilled experts from novices is the ability to interpret situational factors at an increasingly abstract level (Anderson, 1981).

From the point of view of the designer, the most important characteristic of skilled and habitual behavior is that it can be carried out with very little conscious attention. Safety procedures that depend on deliberate consideration of a warning are likely not to be effective unless the warning disrupts the normal routine. Desirable behavior is best incorporated into the skilled activity. A second important principle is that acquiring a skill, and hence modifying a skill, takes extensive practice. Thus, training programs are not likely to change routine behaviors if they consist of occasional seminars devoted to a discussion of safety procedures.

One other implication for designers follows from the previous discussion. Since behavior tends to follow automatic rules in well known situations, then when the situation changes suddenly, one will seek out that which is familiar. In emergencies, a person will look for situational features or other people that are easily recognized. Behavior will then reflect learned responses to those features or people. Sime (1985), for example, has shown how evacuation behavior in a fire is determined by familiarity with an exit or with people who are nearby. A designer who wants to know how a user will react to an unexpected incident must consider which situational features are likely to trigger automatic responses.

The distinction raised here between automatic and deliberate processes may be one of the most important points that a manager or designer must consider when evaluating behavior in the face of risk. The most significant differences are summarized in Table 10.1. Some implications of the distinction for design practice have already been suggested; others will be discussed later in this chapter.

One must conclude that a designer who wishes to predict the behavior of users in a risky situation should proceed at two levels. An analysis in terms of SEU theory may provide useful insights into deliberate decisions, and these decisions might be changed by modifying the user's subjective probabilities or utilities for outcomes. The analysis must be supplemented, however, by a concern for automatic forms of behavior that reflect long-term learning processes and familiar environments. Automatic behavior is likely to be highly variable among individuals, and from one situation to another. The designer must discover what rules have been acquired by users in a given context. Changing automatic patterns of behavior will require extensive practice or training. Changing behavior through training is a topic to be discussed in a later section of this chapter.

MANAGING RISK

Once a designer has an understanding of users' responses to risk, there are several steps that can be taken to manage the risk. She can inform users of known dangers, implement training programs to promote safety, design the system in such a way that errors are minimized, or incorporate elements into the design that are responsive to errors and accidents when they occur. In this section I discuss psychological principles that are relevant when considering any of these steps.

Providing information about risk

The use of labels and warnings to combat potential hazards is a controversial procedure for managing risk. Too often they are seen as a way for manufacturers to avoid responsibility for unreasonably risky products. Nevertheless, labels serve a useful purpose, either in warning of risks that cannot be prevented, or in

Table 10.1. Automatic versus deliberate behavior.

	Summary of the differences	
	Automatic	Deliberate
Access to Awareness	Individual may not be aware of actions	Individual is aware of actions
Degree of Control	Little conscious control	Controlled behavior
Attentional Demands	Attention not required	Attention required
Distractability	Little interference	Actions easily disrupted
Response Determinants	Learned stimulus patterns	Knowledge, beliefs, values
Speed of Response	Relatively fast	Relatively slow
Speed of Learning	Slow: requires extensive practice	Can be rapid under appropriate conditions
Training Approaches	Define explicit behaviors to be modified	Teach problem-solving skills or new knowledge
Areas of Application	Habitual behavior	Problem solving in novel situations
	Expert behavior	Deliberate decision making
	Experienced users	
Relevant Theories	Rule-based theories	SEU theory of choice
	Production system models	Neo-associationist theories

providing users of a product with the freedom to make their own decisions. Obviously, labels will be successful only if the information they contain is read and understood by members of the intended audience. Assuming that a designer is genuinely concerned about providing information (an assumption that is not always warranted), there are several steps that should be taken to ensure that the labels are effective.

The first concern is to ensure that the labels are read by the intended user. The earlier discussion of skilled behavior suggests that warnings will have little effect on the way one performs a familiar task. When confronted with unfamiliar equipment or facilities, however, a person is likely to pay attention to, and even look for, relevant information. Wogalter, Desaulniers, and Brelsford (1986) found that people are more willing to read labels concerning a consumer product if the product is perceived as hazardous to begin with. People then expect to find warnings close to the product, and they do not find that warnings detract from the appearance of the product. The conclusion seems to be that the user must have some prior reason to believe that the warning is important before attending to it. A warning sign in a building, for example, is likely to be ignored if the person for whom it is intended has no reason to expect the situation to be unsafe.

Once read, the label must be understood. Research on the processes of attention, recognition, and understanding offers some rules that are relevant to the design of warning labels. A review of these aspects of cognitive theory has been provided by Ryan (1987). Some of the relevant suggestions concern the surface structure of the warnings, the way in which the idea to be conveyed is translated into words. For example, studies of reaction times indicate that positive assertions are processed more easily than negative ones. Warnings that provide explicit instructions on what to do will be more effective than labels that warn of actions that are dangerous. The manual for my new computer contains the warning, "Make certain you are using the correct version of MS-DOS for your particular system"; the warning is not very helpful. Fortunately, on a different page is the clear statement, "Genuine generic Microsoft DOS 3.3 or later is the only DOS you should use!" My favorite example of useless warnings that provide only negative information is the baggage check receipt issued by many airlines, which states without further explanation, "This is not the luggage ticket described by Article 4 of the Warsaw Convention."

For the reader, the meaning of a message depends on its relationship to other knowledge that he possesses. The person who reads a warning label will interpret it in terms of his existing knowledge of the product or the situation. A similar principle applies to the author of a message; the form of the message will depend on the author's prior knowledge. Every sentence contains an implicit reference to information that the author assumes is known already, together with new information that the author wishes to convey to the reader. For example, the previous sentence makes the assumption that you the reader know what kind of "sentence" I am talking about, and understand who the '"author" and "reader" are. If the author and the reader of a warning message do not share common background information, the message will not be understood.

A major source of difficulty in creating comprehensible warnings is the different background of the designer and the audience, for the designer then makes unwarranted assumptions about the readers' prior knowledge. Pity the purchaser of a computer who reads the warnings cited above who has never heard of DOS. Since most designers are well-educated and relatively affluent, labels are often designed so that they can be understood only by the well-educated and more affluent members of society. Many companies and agencies address the problem by employing people with backgrounds similar to the intended users; migrant workers are sometimes charged with writing warnings for pesticides, for example. However, in addition to the fact that poorer and less-educated users of a product are less likely to understand a warning, they are less likely to seek information in the first place (Hadden, 1986).

There are other ways to warn people of hazards besides labels. One alternative is to rely on users' memory of past experiences to provide the necessary information. Research findings by Buck and Turpin (1988) suggest a useful general principle. In their study, when information about unlikely events was available either from memory of past events or by an explicit warning on a display, the latter resulted in slower but more accurate responses. The findings suggest once again the importance of the distinction between highly learned skilled responses and deliberate action. One should rely on extensive practice to provide a user with the appropriate warnings if speed of response is important. Otherwise, explicit messages that are processed deliberately are more likely to be effective.

The US National Research Council (1989) has published a thorough review of risk communication that should be studied by anyone who is concerned about these issues. They emphasize the importance of two-way communication to promote understanding; the communicator of information should make it possible for the receiver of the information to provide feedback and ask questions. They also emphasize the role of the receiver's own knowledge in framing his understanding of a message. The conclusions of the report are summarized in two checklists, one for use by managers, the other a guide for the recipient of the information. The only weakness of the report may be an assumption of commonality of interests among the two parties, the communicator and the receiver, and a failure to consider the political conflicts that seem inevitably to confuse discussions of risk.

These research findings and conclusions will be irrelevant, of course, if the provider of the information is more concerned with protecting his own interests than with informing the audience. Relevant information on hazards is often difficult to obtain by those who need it (Brown, 1985). Providing information, either to workers, to consumers, or to society-at-large, seems to run counter to normal managerial inclinations, except sometimes as a device for avoiding litigation. Perhaps for this reason, workers and consumers often mistrust any information that is provided. The issues involved in designing labels and warnings thus go beyond human factors considerations; there are sociological, legal, and political concerns that the designer must confront. A good discussion is provided by Hadden (1986). She evaluates current policies governing labeling, and offers several suggestions for change. A thorough review of many problems involved in risk communication is given by Covello, von Winterfeldt, and Slovic (1986). The importance of recognizing the conflicting goals of managers, users, and regulators is a topic to be considered later, when I discuss methods for analyzing decisions that these parties make.

Training the user

In discussing training it is useful to divide the process into three stages (see Goldstein, 1986, for a general review). A manager must determine the training needs, design the training program, and evaluate its results. The needs assessment should lead to a definition of training goals and an identification of the individuals to be trained. Once the needs have been defined, the selection of a training program is itself a decision-making problem: one must select the program that offers the best return in improved performance at the smallest cost. Finally, the effectiveness of the program should be evaluated in terms of the needs that were defined at the first stage.

Some of the relevant concerns at all three stages are best left for a discussion of normative approaches to decision making. Later in the chapter I present a framework that can help a manger to address some of the critical questions: Is there sufficient need for training to justify the expense of a training program? Which program is likely to produce the best results? Does a particular program meet the objectives that have been set for it? In this section I discuss some issues that are descriptive in nature.

Consider two situations in which one might want to employ programs that train individuals to deal with risk. In the first case, a city council is concerned by the large number of accidents caused by high school students who drive at a high rate of speed through the city. The council has suggested that a program of driver education should be designed to address the problem. In the second case, the owner of a chain of record stores believes that the managers of his branch stores are not sufficiently adventurous in selecting and promoting new record titles. He hopes that a managerial training program might encourage the managers to be more daring. In the first case the concern is expressed as a desire to reduce risk taking; in the second case the concern seems to be to increase risk taking. There are reasons to expect that in both cases the people who are seeking to change others' behavior will be disappointed.

First, there are problems with the goals articulated by both the city council and the store owner. Training programs are most effective when concrete behavioral objectives are defined. When, for example, a clearly defined behavior that promotes safety, such as wearing a hard hat, can be identified, a reinforcement program that monitors and rewards the behavior can be very effective (Cohen, Smith, & Anger, 1979). On the other hand, it makes little sense to establish such abstract goals as training drivers to "take fewer risks," or training store managers to "take more risks." It may be relatively easy to specify concrete objectives for the student drivers. Setting behavioral goals for the store manager will be harder, and a different approach will be required.

As noted earlier, some aspects of risk taking are habitual, and occur without deliberate thought. We might seek to increase the frequency of habits that reduce the chance of accidents, or eliminate habits that lead to accidents. There are well-established methods for teaching any behavior that can be given explicit definition. For example, Geller, Lehman, and Kalsher (1989) present a simple approach to promoting safer work settings. They list three critical features of the approach: (a) the identification of "activators," that is, incentives that elicit a response or disincentives that discourage responses, (b) the definition of the behavior that is to be changed, and (c) the specification of the consequences, the rewards or punishments, that will modify the behaviors. In the case of the student drivers we would ask, what activators now lead to their driving fast? What specific responses do we want drivers to learn? What incentives can we use to discourage speeding and encourage safer driving habits? There are some obvious practical difficulties in the approach, but if driver education programs follow the principles listed by Geller, Lehman, and Kalsher, they have a greater chance of success.

A more serious problem with such programs becomes apparent when the focus changes from concrete behaviors to the ultimate goal, which, presumably, is a reduction in accidents. There is little evidence that behaviors learned in driver training have desirable long-term effects on such goals as accident reduction (e.g. Struckman et al., 1989). Similarly, the overall effect of training programs on occupational safety is not always a positive one (Vojtecky & Schmitz, 1986). In other words, it is possible to modify habitual behaviors that are related to risk taking, but to show that such changes lead to fewer or less serious losses is more difficult.

When the risk-taking behavior to be modified is more deliberate, a different approach is required. SEU theory suggests that one might improve deliberate decisions by providing users with the ability to conceptualize a problem in terms of options and outcomes, and by improving their judgments of the likelihood and severity of outcomes. The store managers' inventory decisions might profit from this approach. Optimal risk taking by a manager consists of balancing two kinds of errors, failing to attract customers because the records in stock are too dull, and antagonizing customers because the inventory departs too far from community standards. The managers need a procedure that would help them find the right balance.

In a later section of this chapter, and in other chapters of this volume, a normative framework for decision making is described that can (and often does) form the basis for a managerial training program. Indeed, this book might be used as part of an effort to improve risky decision making by managers and designers. Unfortunately, not much is known about how to improve judgment and decision making (see Chapter 3, by Yates & Stone), and the effectiveness of training programs that promote normative approaches to decision making remains as yet unknown.

Modifying the design: user-centered design

Training the user or providing information about risk are sufficient responses only if the designer has no control over the degree of risk. In most situations it is possible to modify the design of a product or system to minimize the risks that it presents. Unfortunately, the designer works under constraints that limit her ability to create a safer or less error-prone product. The primary goal of any design is to ensure that the product works, accurately and safely. Achieving this goal, however, demands an assessment of the design from the point of view of the user. It is often impossible for the designer to adopt such a perspective, for her knowledge and experience are different from, and usually more extensive than, the user's. Good design that minimizes the risk of error and injury demands a greater concern for the user than is typically evidenced.

To understand how a user responds to a product or system, it is helpful to introduce the concept of a mental model. Like the theoretical concept of a schema, a mental model refers to generalized knowledge that a user has acquired. There is no universally accepted clear distinction between the terms. In general, a schema represents a person's static, conceptual knowledge, whereas a mental model refers to his understanding of the dynamic relationships among elements of his environment. The relevant elements include the person's conception of himself, and of the things and people with which he interacts (see, e.g. Johnson-Laird, 1983). When interacting with complex systems, a user develops a model of how the system operates in terms of the relationships among its components and between the system and external elements. The model of the system may be neither complete nor accurate when compared with the system itself. Nevertheless, the model will encompass everything the user believes he needs to know about the system.

Learning to edit text with a word processor provides a simple example of a mental model in operation. For example, using cut and paste commands is tricky until one acquires the concept of a buffer that holds the deleted material. It is not necessary to know the word "buffer," or to understand how it is realized in the computer, but one must have a functional understanding of its operation in order to use the editor effectively.

A major cause of error and accident is the development of mental models that provide a grossly inaccurate representation of the system. Brehmer (1987) has examined people's ability to control complex processes with which they are unfamiliar. The problems of control that most people encounter arise from inappropriate models of the system that they develop. By recognizing the importance of mental models, designers can develop more effective procedures for preventing errors. A few authors have addressed the question of how this can be done.

In a discussion of the design of computer systems, Norman and Draper (1986) employ the concept of "user-centered system design." They point out how important it is to understand mental models, not only the models developed by users of the system, but also the model that the designer employs when building the system. Systems design embodies, implicitly or explicitly, a model of the user; design decisions will be driven by the designer's assumptions about the abilities and predispositions of the user. The most effective designs are those that employ realistic models of the user. The concept of user-centered design is extended by Norman (1988) in a delightful and thought-provoking analysis of product design. Norman provides a simple and perhaps obvious set of rules for designing objects that are safe and easy to use, together with many examples of everyday objects that violate these obvious rules. His proposals are summed up in two principles: "Make sure that (1) the user can figure out what to do, and (2) the user can tell what is going on."

The designer begins her task of creating a system or a product with her own mental model. The most significant element of this model should be a consideration of the mental model that users develop when interacting with the system. That is, the designer must try to understand the system as it is interpreted by a user. The user's model is established in part by his past experience prior to encountering the system, and in part by his direct experience with the system. Thus, there are three different concepts that need to be considered by the designer: the designer's own model of the system, the system image (the concept that emerges from the physical structure), and the mental model of the system that is constructed by the user.

It is important to note that users establish their own models from the system image, not from the design model. Thus, it is the designer's responsibility to ensure that users can develop models that are consistent with the design model. To do this, she has to consider the image that the system presents. This is best done by observing users as they interact with the system. The analysis can take place informally, by asking users to describe their understanding of the system. A formal method for assessing and monitoring users' models has been described by Coury (1987). Multidimensional scaling, a procedure for measuring a person's "cognitive space," is used to track changes in performance and reveal the relationship between a hypothetical model and the person's performance.

While Norman and Draper (1986) developed their ideas in the context of computer system design, their proposal has significant implications for the design of any system that presents serious risks to users or to others. Consider, for example, the design of a chain saw. A novice user of a chain saw is likely to form a mental model based on his experience with hand saws. Nothing in his conceptual model suggests the hazards that might result from a kick back, when the saw is forced backwards into the user's face if not employed carefully. For the user to understand how and when such an accident may occur, he must acquire a model of the forces that are created as the chain passes through wood. While the manual for a saw may warn of the hazard, rarely does it attempt to provide the user with a model of the process that would make the hazard predictable.

One problem with a user-centered approach is that there may be many users of a single system, and the users' models may differ significantly. The designer must then decide among a number of approaches to individual differences, for example, (a) design for the most frequent user, (b) design for the user who is least expert, or (c) design for the user whose errors are likely to be most costly. The problem is yet another example of the need for the designer to make decisions that require tradeoffs among conflicting goals. The next major section addresses such decisions at a general level.

Designing for error

In some systems it is impossible to prevent errors and accidents from occurring. Complex systems such as aircraft and power plants will eventually break down, or their operators will make mistakes. In this case one can only hope to develop procedures that will handle the errors and minimize their negative effects. The concept of user-centered design is relevant when considering how the designer proposes to handle accidents and errors. Again, the designer will have her own model of the system and the users will have their model. The relationship between the two will determine in large part how safely and gracefully the system can deal with errors.

Norman and Draper's (1986) ideas are closely related to an analysis of error handling offered by Ramussen and Goodstein (1987). These authors describe two common approaches to managing risk by designing the system to handle errors. In one approach the designer's analysis of potential errors leads to results that are stored in the system as automated control actions. In other words, the designer attempts to anticipate all possible failures. In the other approach a system analysis is designed to provide advice to operators during disturbances. According to Rasmussen and Goodstein, neither approach is satisfactory:

"Both ... run the risk of giving trivial answers in frequent situations and wrong answers in rare events—and therefore can lead to a loss of operators' confidence" (p. 669). The authors suggest that the designer should not program responses and countermeasures for the users of a system. Instead, the users should have access to the designer's conceptual models, from which they can make their own decisions. Discussing the design of power plants, they assert, "Allow the operators to function as their [the designers'] extended arm in coping with the plant." The burden is then placed on the user to decide on an appropriate response. The advantage to this approach is that the user's decision can be based on all of those factors that might be relevant: design considerations that were part of the original system model, the user's updated knowledge of plant status, and her accumulated operational experience.

To implement Rasmussen and Goodstein's proposal it would be necessary for the designer to provide users with information that is rarely available. Users must understand not only how each component of the system works, but also why it has been designed that way—how each feature of the design serves the overall goals of the system. Designers may find the exposure of their own thought processes to be threatening, but the idea of establishing an intellectual partnership between designers and users is well worth pursuing.

Based on a descriptive analysis of the behavior of potential users, a variety of recommendations for design practice have been derived. A summary of these recommendations is provided in Table 10.2, together with reference to appropriate sections of the chapter. The next section takes a different approach. Every suggestion in Table 10.2 requires the designer or manager to make some difficult decisions. There are general comments that can be made about decision making, and these will be examined from the point of view of prescriptive decision theory.

DECISIONS ABOUT RISK

Whatever one's approach towards managing risks, problems arise that must be solved by the designer or the manager. Someone must determine what warnings are necessary, whether a training program for users might help, whether to design a less hazardous but more costly system, and how to handle errors when they occur. As a general rule, there are no correct answers to these problems. Inevitably, there are important goals that are incompatible: the designer must make tradeoffs between safety and costs, between aesthetics and ease of operation, between flexibility and freedom of choice for the user. Since one can never simultaneously maximize the attainment of incompatible goals, there is always room for criticism of any decision the designer makes. In addition to the conflict, there is an inevitable uncertainty about the future; one can never say with confidence that all possible hazards have been eliminated or that any given

Table 10.2. Summary of recommendations for design practice.

1. Consider the determinants of perceived of risk

   Automatic reactions:
      Responses to learned indicators of potential risk
      Affect induced by departures of events from expected schemas   Section: "Perceptions of Risk"

   Deliberate risk assessment:
      Experts use the probability and cost of potential outcomes
      Nonexperts mostly use perceived lack of control   Section: "Perceptions of Risk"

2. Consider the determinants of responses to risk

   Automatic responses:
      Skilled or habitual behavior based on prior learning   Section: "Limitations to SEU Theory"

   Deliberate decisions:
      An analysis based on SEU theory   Section: "Responses to Risk: SEU Theory"

3. Decide among ways to manage the risk

   Provide information to users:
      Provide some *a priori* reason to look for warnings or information
      Make information understandable in terms of users' prior knowledge
      Positive statements are better than negative statements   Section: "Providing Information About Risk"

   Provide training of users:
      Specify behavioral objectives
      Identify incentives that promote current behavior
      Develop contingencies for modifying behavior
      Use approaches based on normative theory for changing
        deliberate decision processes   Section: "Training the User"

   Modify the design:
      Understand the user
      Consider the image presented by the system
      Explore the user's mental model of the system
      Allow the user to understand the designer's intentions   Section: "Modifying the Design: User-Centered Design"

outcome will occur. When unexpected losses occur, society looks for someone to blame; the idea that there can be "unintended consequences" of a design decision is hard to accept (see Pidgeon, Blockley, & Turner, 1986). The conflict and uncertainty can generate a fear of taking responsibility for one's own actions, which can lead managers to avoid, delay, or delegate decisions. Unfortunately, choosing to delay or to delegate is itself a decision, and in the long run there is no way to avoid responsibility. The best approach, then, is to develop a mechanism for addressing such problems that is sensitive to the concerns raised in this paragraph.

The first step is to acknowledge that, in the real world, one does not solve such problems, one merely exchanges them for other problems—a maxim referred to by committees on which the author has served as Pitz's Cynicism Principle. In large part, coping with risk is the same thing as choosing between options, each of which is characterized by advantages and disadvantages. This does not mean that one must accept an apparently exhaustive set of options; there is always room for the creative generation of new choices (Pitz, Sachs, & Heerboth, 1980). Nor does it mean that one must make continuous tradeoffs between all pairs of attributes; some goals or objectives may be so important that they cannot be compromised. It does mean, though, that designers and managers need to be aware of what they must give up on one dimension when they adopt a solution that offers gains on another dimension.

Decision analysis with multiple objectives

Expected utility (EU) theory (see Chapter 2, by Neumann & Politser) was originally developed to provide guidance for decision making in the face of risk. The essence of the theory is to express the decision maker's attitude towards risk in terms of a utility function. There are serious limitations to EU theory as a prescriptive theory, however, as noted by Neumann and Politser. An extension of EU theory that incorporates the techniques of multiattribute utility theory, or MAUT (Keeney & Raiffa, 1976), can be more useful in practice. MAUT was designed specifically to deal with problems that require tradeoffs between conflicting objectives. The decision maker's objectives are expressed as a set of attributes, which are measures that might be used to assess the degree to which an option promotes a certain objective. In the simplest form of MAUT (e.g. Edwards & Newman, 1982), the available options are evaluated on each relevant attribute, weights are assigned to the attributes that reflect their importance, and a linear model is used to calculate an aggregate utility for each option. More complex procedures are available that incorporate uncertainties about future outcomes as probabilities, and permit the calculation of expected utilities.

Detailed descriptions of multiattribute decision analysis have been given by

Pitz and McKillip (1984) and von Winterfeldt and Edwards (1986). There are several other approaches to decision making that differ in their details but are similar in spirit, including cost-benefit analysis and multicriterion decision analysis. Many of my comments apply to any formal method for combining multiple attributes.

To illustrate the procedures, assume that the designer of a kitchen appliance is concerned about keeping costs low, maintaining the safety of the equipment, avoiding legal liability, and creating an attractive object. These goals might be expressed by attributes such as manufacturing costs, likelihood of injury, legal exposure, and attractiveness. If these attributes are not sufficiently clear, they can be decomposed into more precisely defined quantities. The attributes then provide a multidimensional framework for evaluating designs.

The analysis can be described in four stages, although in practice these stages overlap, and they certainly do not imply a fixed progression through the analysis. First, the decision maker's understanding of the problem must be expressed in terms of the formal structure demanded by the analysis (a set of options, attributes, and possible outcomes). Second, the decision maker's preferences and beliefs must be quantified; beliefs about possible outcomes are expressed as probabilities, while preferences and values are expressed as utility functions for the attributes. Third, a mathematical solution to the problem is derived. Finally, the sensitivity of the solution to changes in the analysis is explored, and a tentative choice is identified.

In the first stage the decision maker defines the problem in a systematic way. It is not uncommon for the systematic problem definition to lead to new insights that point towards a solution. In the second stage the decision maker provides piecemeal judgments of the various components of the problem. The question of whose values and whose beliefs should be employed at this stage is a complex one that cannot be addressed here. The third stage is purely mechanical. The fourth stage, the sensitivity analysis, provides an opportunity for the decision maker to explore other judgments. Often the sensitivity analysis leads to changes in the original description of the problem. The final solution is achieved by seeking convergence through several iterations of the whole process.

A simple example can be used for illustration. Mary, Jim, and the architect, who were introduced at the beginning of the chapter, are discussing the height of the railing around the loft. Mary and Jim want the railing to be lower for aesthetic reasons. The architect wants to make it higher for safety reasons. The problem can be described in terms of two attributes, aesthetic attractiveness and the likelihood of accident. The disagreement boils down to the question, how much reduction in attractiveness is each party willing to accept in order to achieve a given increase in safety? The answer to this question will determine the weights to be used in a MAUT analysis, and the analysis can then be used to identify the optimal railing height. The optimal height will, of course, be different for parties who do not agree on acceptable tradeoffs.

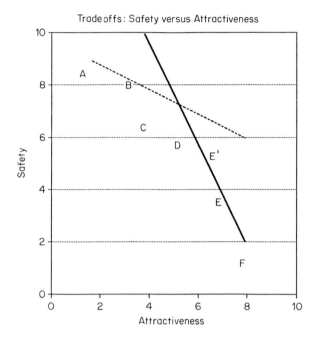

Figure 10.2. Hypothetical options that vary in attractiveness and safety. The best option depends on the relative weights of the two attributes: B is best if the weight for safety is twice that for attractiveness; E is best if the weight for attractiveness is twice that for safety. Option C will be unacceptable under any circumstances. Option E' is a variant of E that is clearly preferred to E. The solid line connects equally preferred options for someone who assigns a higher weight to attractiveness. The dashed line connects equally preferred options for someone who assigns more weight to safety.

Figure 10.2 illustrates the kind of analysis that might be appropriate. A variety of solutions, A through F, have been evaluated in terms of their safety and attractiveness, each factor measured on an arbitrary scale from zero to ten. In general, as attractiveness increases, safety is reduced. No single alternative can be said to be best; the optimal choice depends on the tradeoff the decision maker is willing to make between the two attributes. The flatter line in Figure 10.2 represents options that would be equally attractive for someone who assigns safety twice the weight of attractiveness; for this person, no option is as good as B. The steeper line represents options that would be equally attractive for someone who gives attractiveness twice the weight of safety; the two options E and E' are best for this individual. It may be noted that option C should be rejected by everyone. Compared with B, it offers too little gain in attractiveness for a large decrease in safety; compared with D, it offers too small an increase in safety for a large decrease in attractiveness.

The analysis does not restrict the decision maker to choosing between available options. It can also be used to evaluate potential options that do not yet exist. Option E' represents a possible improvement the architect has suggested for option E. For a very small reduction in attractiveness, it is possible to achieve a large gain in safety. E', then, would be preferred to the original version of E for someone who assigns a large weight to attractiveness. However, if the decision maker assigns a larger weight to safety, so that his overall preference is for option B, then the possible improvement in E would be irrelevant.

The use of computers for decision analysis has greatly extended the usefulness of the process, especially during the final stage, the sensitivity analysis. The computer makes it possible to modify the analysis and receive immediate feedback concerning the effect of the changes. In this way, the decision maker can develop a more complete understanding of the dynamics of the problem, and continue to explore possible solutions until an acceptable decision is discovered. The use of sensitivity analysis for decision making is in many ways like the use of simulators for systems design; one can make hypothetical changes and explore their effects. The difference is that in the decision analysis it will be the decision maker's beliefs and preferences that are modified at the hypothetical level.

Advantages of formal decision analysis

There are numerous evaluations of MAUT as a procedure for addressing problems of risky decision making. Elsewhere (Pitz, 1987) I have discussed MAUT-based decision aids for medical decision making, specifically for those problems that involve genetic risks. I concluded that there has been no definitive demonstration that decision aids are effective in personal decisions of this sort. However, there is enough indirect evidence to suggest that the procedures can be helpful. From a very different perspective, a monograph published by the International Atomic Energy Agency (1987) reviews decision making in response to accidents in nuclear facilities. The authors of the monograph state, "When the costs of error are high, when the issues are complex and decisions have to be justified in detail, formal techniques for analyzing the processes leading to decisions have now largely supplanted intuitive methods."

The major advantage to decision analysis is that it provides a systematic procedure for helping decision makers think about all relevant concerns. For the designer, the analysis serves as a framework for exploring the implications of changes that might be made in assumptions underlying the design. The analysis in Figure 10.2 will show how the optimal design changes as the relative importance of safety and aesthetics is changed. When used as a decision tool by policy-setting agencies, decision analysis can force members of the agency to consider society's values explicitly. Some risks seem to be regarded by society as more important than others; earthquake, fires, and airline accidents generate more concern than do emphysema and automobile accidents; sometimes society seems to be willing to spend far more money to save a life in one context than in another (Lind, 1988). This is not necessarily irrational or undesirable, but, as Lind points out, it is the job of the analyst to point out these implications of social policy. A formal decision analysis forces decision makers to ask whether the implications of their decisions are consistent with their values.

The value of a formal analysis might be illustrated by reference to the decision concerning training programs that were discussed earlier. Consider the typical driver education program. High schools in the US may offer such programs because they are mandated by state law, or because school boards decide to include them in the curriculum. In either case, some agency has decided that the program is worthwhile. Rarely, however, is there an explicit consideration of the benefits to be gained and the costs incurred by the program. As noted, evaluations of driver education programs are often pessimistic concerning the effect of the program on accident rates. Those responsible for the program may attempt to justify it in other ways, for example, as demonstrating that the agency cares about safe driving, or modifying student attitudes towards safety. By using a formal analysis, the decision makers are forced to make explicit, at least among themselves, how important such goals are to them, and how likely a program is to lead to the achievement of such goals.

Limitations of decision analysis

There are, of course, many technical difficulties in applying formal decision analysis to decisions involving risk. The analysis requires an unambiguous problem structure, an exhaustive and realistic set of scenarios by which accidents and other failures might be predicted, and explicit evaluations of each scenario. The disarmingly simple form of Figure 10.2 disguises a great deal of preliminary analysis. Particularly serious problems arise when trying to incorporate all possible outcomes into the analysis. Perrow (1984) argues that a formal analysis of complex systems systematically underestimates the likelihood of accidents. When components of a system interact in unexpected ways, joint failures in each system create accidents that could never have been anticipated. For some systems, Perrow argues, disaster is inevitable; yet, since a formal decision analysis does not consider the unanticipated, the decision maker is inevitably misled.

Decision analysis is not well suited to decisions that must be adapted dynamically as the situation changes. In the usual form of analysis, the decision maker is presented with a fixed set of options among which a choice must be made; once the decision has been made the problem is over. Connolly (1988) contrasts this "tree felling" approach to decision making, which treats actions as isolated events, with a "hedge clipping" approach, in which each small decision is followed by a reevaluation and modification of the overall plan. The latter is more characteristic of managerial and design decision making.

Some decision makers might resist formal analysis for different reasons. In their study of risk taking, MacCrimmon and Wehrung (1986) found that managers tried to avoid making an explicit decision. They preferred to adjust the situation, seek additional information, or delay or delegate the decision. One can argue that the decision to delay or to delegate is still a decision, and that this decision is also subject to the scrutiny of a formal analysis. It is less likely, however, that a manager will be willing to endure long and careful deliberation prior to taking such action.

One also must recognize that, while decisions are unavoidable, an evaluation of immediately available options can sometimes blind one to more creative solutions. In a discussion of risk analysis in a historical context, Clark (1980) retells an old folk story. Suitors who seek the hand of a beautiful princess are taken to a room with two doors. Behind one door is the princess; behind the other is a man-eating tiger. One suitor, trained in risk assessment, conducts a careful analysis, chooses the door with the highest expected utility, and is eaten by a low-probability tiger. A second suitor takes a course in tiger training, opens both doors, tames the tiger, and marries the princess—or perhaps it was the other way round. Clark's point is that the best strategies for coping with risk are those that are capable of responding to unknown factors. There is no reason in principle why a formal analysis cannot reflect such a goal, but in practice it may be difficult to build such abstract concerns into the analysis.

While some criticisms of decision analysis are valid, others seem to reflect a misunderstanding of the methods. Pidgeon, Turner, and Blockley (1987) suggest that decision analysis promotes unwarranted assumptions of "rationality" in decision making. While this may be true of some naïve exponents of decision analysis, it is not an assumption made by most experienced analysts. Indeed, the purpose of the analysis is to alleviate the irrational judgments people will make if left to their unaided intuitions. Downs and Larkey (1986) review decision analysis and other analytic methods for policy decision making. They focus, however, on simple EU methods rather than on the more useful MAUT procedures. They also fail to recognize the value of recent computer-based methods for exploring decision problems through decision analysis (see, e.g. Pitz & McKillip, 1984, Chapter 9). They agree that one strength of decision analysis lies in forcing decision makers to think about their problem thoroughly, but find the quantitative, calculational aspect of the analysis to be unimportant. In reaching this conclusion, they ignore the value of the sensitivity analysis as a tool for exploring problems.

Some authors object to the use of analytic method when the welfare of society as a whole is at stake. Perrow (1984), for example, argues that analyses ignore such concerns as the equity of the distribution of costs and benefits. While this criticism may accurately describe the way in which some analyses are used, it is important to understand that there is nothing in the methods themselves that prevents the decision maker from incorporating social values. A MAUT analysis of risk can readily incorporate such goals as equity of distribution of risk. In fact, such an analysis may be helpful in pointing out the incompatibility of equity with other goals that society might value (Keeney, 1984).

A topic that has generated some dispute is the problem of differences of opinion among parties to a decision. A decision analysis can deal with such disagreements by using the analyses as a vehicle for discussion and negotiation. Opposing parties can modify the analysis and explore the implications of their disagreements (see Pitz & McKillip, 1984). There is some evidence that disagreements are reduced in this way (Aschenbrenner & Kasubek, 1978; Gardiner & Edwards, 1975). The approach is effective, however, only when the parties agree on the basic structure of the problem. For problems that reflect enduring political and cultural differences, the approach is not likely to be effective (Lathrop & Linerooth, 1984; Linerooth, 1984). For one thing, each side to a dispute begins by using a different language to frame the problem (Hilgartner, 1985). Industry and labor, for example, hold contradictory beliefs about social relationships, government control, severity of risks, and the assumptions that should guide policy. It is unlikely that representatives of each side could agree on a common structure for analyzing a problem.

The issue that Hilgartner raises suggests another dilemma that faces proponents of decision analysis. The sole criterion employed in evaluating an analysis is its consistency with the values of the decision maker. The only possible "wrong" response in analysis is one that is incompatible with some other. This leads to the question, are decision makers free to express any set of internally consistent values, or is there some higher principle than consistency? Is a company president free to make decisions about hazardous designs without considering the potential for injury to users if she states that such a concern is of no importance? There has been very little concern expressed in the literature with such ethical issues. In the final section of the chapter I explore some ideas that might lead to a better definition of the role of decision analysis.

Decision analysis is a developing technology, and many of its weaknesses are likely to be alleviated with further development. Pidgeon (1988) considers some of the limitations of decision analysis, and discusses alternative strategies for decision making. These include problem-structuring techniques that generate a richer set of scenarios, an explicit evaluation of the incompleteness of the analysis, and placing value on the controllability and flexibility of options. All of these strategies can be seen as modifications rather than replacements of the formal analysis.

This section has touched on many issues that are related to the formal analysis of risk. By way of a summation, Table 10.3 lists in summary form the advantages of a formal analysis, and the problems and difficulties that limit the

Table 10.3. Advantages and difficulties of formal decision analysis for risky decision making.

Advantages
   Provides a systematic procedure for considering relevant issues.
   Provides a framework for exploring the implications of a decision.
   The procedure forces decision makers to consider their values explicitly.
   Disagreements may be reduced, provided parties agree on the problem structure.

Difficulties
   The analysis requires an unambiguous problem structure.
   Managers may try to avoid making an explicit decision.
   Disagreements may reflect political or cultural differences:
      These are not readily reconciled by formal analysis alone.
   The analysis may discourage a search for more creative solutions.
   The method is not well suited to situations in which decisions change dynamically.
   Guidance is restricted to pointing out inconsistencies among judgments:
      There is a need for an ethical or moral foundation for the analysis.

applicability of the analysis. The final section is an attempt to set the issues listed in Table 10.3 in a broader context.

BEYOND FORMAL ANALYSIS

Everyone who is concerned about decision making and risk eventually faces issues broader than those discussed so far. Political and ethical questions arise that are difficult to handle with formal methods of analysis. For example, how do we strike a balance between aesthetics and human well-being, or between protecting people from harm and preserving freedom of choice? Where do we set the dividing line between guaranteeing that every case is treated equitably and preventing flexible responses to new problems? How much responsibility should manufacturers assume for accidents that might be due to the careless use of hazardous products? How do we deal with the moral outrage that sometimes seems to inhibit rational thinking, yet which provides the ultimate justification for many decisions? Those who offer advice about risky decision making cannot ignore these moral, social, and political concerns.

   Consider the political implications of decisions that a designer might make. Attempts to reduce or manage risk will be interpreted in light of their political connotations. Why, for example, would a company be concerned about making the workplace safer? Does the company's behavior reflect humanitarian concerns for its employees, or is it inspired only by the selfish concerns of management? Are all changes in the workplace a manifestation of the conflict between capital and labor? Both the humanitarian and the Marxist interpretations are no doubt overly simplistic. Knights, Willmott, and Collinson (1985) present a series of accounts of job design in terms of political, economic, and social forces, which are worth studying by anyone who would manage risks in the workplace. Sincere efforts by a manager or designer will always be interpreted within the framework of such concerns.

An important aspect of attitudes towards risk is one's feelings about *responsibility*: to what degree are individuals thought to be responsible for the outcome of their actions? Is a manufacturer responsible for a consumer's failure to read warning labels? Is a designer responsible for the impact of a decision on someone other than her client? Is society-at-large responsible for the well-being of its members? Our answers to these questions create a framework within which both descriptive and prescriptive analyses are conducted (Douglas, 1985). In any analysis of decisions about risks, the results of the analysis will be determined in large part by the answer to the question: Who is responsible for potential loss?

A possible resolution to the issue of responsiblity is provided by the distinction between automatic and deliberate behavior that has emerged several times in this chapter. One might argue that responsibility is something one assumes at the deliberate level. Since the manager or designer makes design decisions at a deliberate level, she should assume responsibility for any automatic behavior elicited by the product or the system. Eliminating the dangers of, say, a lawn mower, which may elicit habitual and dangerous behavior in many users, would be the responsibility of the designer. On the other hand, if hazards can be shown to be the result of deliberate risk taking by the user, then the user, not the designer, assumes the responsibility.

Unfortunately, such a simple distinction breaks down when faced with problems in which some hazards can only be eliminated at the cost of introducing other potential losses. What does one do when a safety feature makes it impossible for some users, for example the elderly, to use a product? I have suggested earlier that decision analysis, which provides a formal method for establishing tradeoffs, might provide the tools for dealing with such problems. Some authors, however, deny any value to formal analysis when the hazards are socially significant. For example, Morone and Woodhouse (1986) find analytic solutions to be inappropriate for problems that place people at risk of death. They suggest that it may be morally offensive to state explicitly that a certain number of deaths would be an acceptable tradeoff for given savings in cost or convenience. Issues of this sort, they argue, should be resolved through extended political argument. For other authors the preferred approach to problems of risk is to allow a free market to set standards. Discussing risk in the workplace and the role of agencies such as the US Occupational Safety and Health Administration (OSHA), Viscusi (1983) objects to setting standards that limit the freedom of action of a consumer or an employee.

The issue here is not whether one agrees with Morone and Woodhouse or with Viscusi. It is not even clear on what grounds one would compare approaches so different as the free market, the poltical process, and formal decision analysis. Nevertheless, the arguments of these authors should not be ignored by anyone who recommends an approach to decision making based on formal analysis. The analysis needs a firmer moral foundation than it has heretofore received. Decision analysts have always felt secure because of the axiomatic underpinning of their procedures: the validity of the result can be *proved* mathematically! My point is that logical validity is not necessarily enough.

One basis for a stronger foundation is offered by Sagoff (1985). In a discussion of ethical issues in risky decision making, he contrasts arguments that are based on moral outrage about specific incidents (Bhopal, Three Mile Island, or the Challenger disaster, for example) with analytic approaches that measure costs and benefits and seek to optimize the difference. Sagoff presents the argument as one of moral intuition versus economic efficiency. It can be phrased more broadly: it is a conflict between intuitive forms of understanding that tend to be driven by emotional forces, and analytical understanding that is more coldly rational. Sagoff suggests that there is a place for both in discussions of risk and decision making.

Sagoff argues that moral intuitions and engaged concerns should drive the decision processes at the extremes; we should not demand an analytic proof of the unacceptability of the Bhopal disaster. On the other hand, the analytic, detached approach should drive decisions at the fine-grained level; how high should a safety railing be? At what age should a person be allowed to drive an all-terrain vehicle? At this level the intuitive evaluation of options is too crude, too sensitive to biases. In other words, one might allow nonanalytic, moral, or emotional considerations to set the boundaries within which the analysis will operate, and look to the analytic process to settle disputes within those boundaries.

How might this work in practice? There are two stages at which a decision maker can establish the moral boundaries of acceptable choice. One can state the limits within which factors are free to vary when the problem is first defined. At this stage, however, the decision maker's moral concerns may not even be well defined, so it may be better to suspend early intuitive judgments. The exploratory stage of the decision analysis, the sensitivity analysis, is a second point at which such concerns may enter. It is at this stage that one discovers the implications of one's judgments for action. If apparently acceptable tradeoffs lead to the selection of a choice that is unacceptable for intuitive reasons, one must find out why the judgments have this consequence. Considered analysis may lead to a revision of one's intuitions, or else may force a change in the form of the analysis.

Of course, this solution to the debate still leaves a great deal of room for argument; one person's moral outrage will be someone else's acceptable trade-off. It does, however, resolve some of the dilemmas discussed throughout the later sections of this chapter. The point at which a formal analysis of options leads to a choice that violates fundamental human values, whether these are the values of the designer, the user, or society-at-large, is the point at which the analysis must be rejected. Within those limits, one should feel free to consider in the cold light of rational assessment questions of the kind: How much risk of accident are we willing to accept in order to enjoy the benefits of a more attractive or less expensive or more exciting alternative?

SUMMARY

This chapter deals with risk from the point of view of a decision maker, who might be a manager or a designer or a user of a product or system. Recommendations are presented for those who are concerned about accidents, injuries, or other serious losses that might occur as users interact with the system. Descriptive decision theory makes it possible to predict users' behavior; prescriptive theory provides a framework within which decision problems faced by managers or designers can be analyzed and evaluated.

Behavior in risky situations involves recognizing and evaluating risk, and responding to that risk. Both deliberate and automatic forms of behavior need to be considered. Automatic behavior is habitual, and often involves complex skills. Automatic responses are acquired only through extended practice, and are likely to change slowly. Deliberate behavior involves the intentional considerations of available options. Provided one can initiate such deliberation, changes in behavior can be produced by changing the decision maker's beliefs and values. SEU theory, while not entirely adequate as a descriptive theory of decision making, provides a good first approximation to deliberate behavior. By examining users' beliefs about future outcomes, and the value they place on those outcomes, it is possible to anticipate their choices.

The behavior predicted by SEU theory will not necessary be the same as the behavior predicted by an analysis of automatic processes. In general, deliberate choices occur only when the situation contains no clear stimulus to elicit an automatic response, or when a feature of the situation prompts deliberate thought. Thus, designers must consider how a system or product will be interpreted by users. Managing potential risks requires a careful balance of training, information presentation, and modification of the system design.

In other words, dealing with risk is itself a problem of risky decision making. Decisions are made difficult by uncertainties about future outcomes and by conflicting goals that require tradeoffs to be made. Problems are said to involve risk when the uncertainties are significant, and when some of the tradeoffs create the possibility of serious loss. The prescriptive form of decision theory provides an approach to solving problems of this sort. While formal methods of decision theory such as MAUT have been subject to some criticism, no alternative approach has received such widespread acceptance. By setting the decision analysis within a context that reflects the decision maker's fundamental values, it is possible to obtain the benefits of a formal analysis without losing sight of moral or ethical concerns.

ACKNOWLEDGMENTS

I am grateful for the help of John Wallace in reviewing the literature for this chapter, and for comments made by readers of an earlier draft: JoAnn Pitz, Alan Vaux, and Frank Yates. They are, of course, absolved of any responsibility for weaknesses in the final version.

REFERENCES

Adams, J. G. U. (1988). Risk homeostasis and the purpose of safety regulation. *Ergonomics*, **31**, 407–428.

Anderson, J. R. (1981). *Cognitive skills and their acquisition*. Hillsdale, NJ: Erlbaum.

Anderson, J. R. (1985). *Cognitive psychology and its implications* (2nd ed.). New York: Freeman.

Arabie, P., & Maschmeyer, C. (1988). Some current models for the perception and judgment of risk. *Organizational Behavior and Human Decision Processes*, **41**, 300–329.

Aschenbrenner, K. M., & Kasubek, M. (1978). Challenging the Cushing syndrome: Multiattribute evaluation of cortisone drugs. *Organizational Behavior and Human Performance*, **22**, 216–234.

Brehmer, B. (1987). Development of mental models for decision in technological systems. In J. Rasmussen, K. Duncan, & J. Leplat (Eds.), *New technology and human error* (pp. 111–121). Chichester, England: Wiley.

Brown, I. D., & Groeger, J. A. (1988). Risk perception and decision taking during the transition between novice and experienced driver status. *Ergonomics*, **31**, 585–597.

Brown, M. S. (1985). Disputed knowledge: Worker access to hazard information. In D. Nelkin (Ed.), *The language of risk* (pp. 67–96). Newbury Park, CA: Sage.

Buck, L., & Turpin, B. A. M. (1988.) Comparing two methods of informing operators about what might happen next. *Ergonomics*, **31**, 161–171.

Burton, J. F., Jr. (1983). Compensation for permanent partial disabilities. In J. D. Worrall (Ed.), *Safety and the work force* (pp, 18–60). New York: I.L.R. Press.

Chelius, J. R. (1977). *Workplace safety and health*. Washington, DC: American Enterprise Institute.

Clark, W. C. (1980). Witches, floods, and wonder drugs: Historical perspectives on risk management. In R. C. Schwing, & W. A. Albers (Eds.), *Societal risk assessment: How safe is safe enough?* (pp. 287–313). New York: Plenum.

Clarke, L. (1989). *Acceptable risk?: Making decisions in a toxic environment*. Berkeley: University of California Press.

Cohen, A., Smith, M. J., & Anger, W. K. (1979). Self-protective measures against workplace hazards. *Journal of Safety Research*, **11**, 121–131.

Connolly, T. (1988). Hedge clipping, tree felling, and the management of ambiguity. In L. R. Pondy, R. J. Boland, & H. Thomas (Eds.), *Managing ambiguity and change* (pp. 37–50). New York: Wiley.

Coury, B. G. (1987). Multidimensional scaling as a method for assessing internal conceptual models of inspection tasks. *Ergonomics*, **30**, 959–973.

Covello, V. T., von Winterfeldt, D., & Slovic, P. (1986). Risk communication: A review of the literature. *Risk Abstracts*, **3**, 171–182.

Douglas, M. (1985). *Risk acceptability according to the social sciences*. New York: Russell Sage Foundation.

Downs, G. W., & Larkey, P. D. (1986). *The search for government efficiency*. New York: Random House.

Edwards, W., & Newman, J. R. (1982). *Multiattribute evaluation*. Newbury Park, CA: Sage.

Fischhoff, B. (1989). Risk: A guide to controversy. In National Research Council (1989).

Fischhoff, B., Svenson, O., & Slovic, P. (1987). Active responses to environmental hazards: Perceptions and decision making. In D. Stokols & I. Altman (Eds.), *Handbook of environmental psychology* (pp. 1089–1133). New York: Wiley.

Gardiner, P. C., & Edwards, W. (1975). Public values: Multiattribute utility measurement for social decision making. In M. F. Kaplan & S. Schwartz (Eds.), *Human judgment and decision making* (pp. 1–38). New York: Academic Press.

Geller, E. S., Lehman, G. R., & Kalsher, M. J. (1989). *Behavior analysis training for occupational safety*. Newport, VA: Make-A-Difference, Inc.

Goldstein, I. L. (1986). *Training in organizations*. Monterey, CA: Brooks-Cole.

Hadden, S. G. (1986). *Read the label: Reducing risk by providing information*. Boulder: Webster Press.

Herzog, T., & Smith, C. A. (1988). Danger, mystery, and environmental preference. *Environment and Behavior*, **20**, 320–344.

Hilgartner, S. (1985). The political language of risk: Defining occupational health. In D. Nelkin (Ed.), *The language of risk* (pp. 25–66). Newbury Park, CA: Sage.

Howarth, C. I. (1988). The relationship between objective risk, subjective risks and behavior. *Ergonomics*, **31**, 527–535.

Hoyos, C. G. (1988). Mental load and risk in traffic behavior. *Ergonomics*, **31**, 571–584.

International Atomic Energy Agency (1987). *Techniques and decision making in the assessment of off-site consequences of an accident in a nuclear facility*. Vienna: IAEA.

Janssen, W., & Tenkink, E. (1988). Risk homeostasis theory and its critics: Time for an agreement. *Ergonomics*, **31**, 429–433.

Johnson-Laird, P. N. (1983). *Mental models*. Cambridge, MA: Harvard University Press.

Keeney, R. L. (1984). Evaluation of mortality risks for institutional decisions. In P. C. Humphreys, O. Svenson, & A. Vari (Eds.), *Analysing and aiding decision processes* (pp. 23–38). Amsterdam: North-Holland.

Keeney, R. L., & Raiffa, H. (1976). *Decisions with multiple objectives*. New York: Wiley.

Kishchuk, N. A. (1987). Causes and correlates of risk perception. *Risk Abstracts*, **4**, 1–4.

Knights, D., Willmott, H., & Collinson, D. (1985). *Job redesign: Critical perspectives on the labour process*. Aldershot, Hants, England: Gower.

Lathrop, J., & Linerooth, J. (1984). The role of risk assessment in a political decision process. In D. C. Humphreys, O. Svenson, & A. Vari (Eds.), *Analysing and aiding decision processes* (pp. 39–68). Amsterdam: North-Holland.

Lind, N. C. (1988). Hazards schmazards! *Risk Abstracts*, **5**, 51–52.

Linerooth, J. (1984). The political processing of uncertainty. *Acta Psychologica*, **56**, 219–232.

MacCrimmon, K. R., & Wehrung, D. A. (1986). *Taking risks: The management of uncertainty*. New York: Free Press.

McKenna, F. P. (1988). What role should the concept of risk play in theories of accident involvement? *Ergonomics*, **31**, 469–484.

Montgomery, H., & Svenson, O. (1989). *Process and structure in human decision making.* New York: Wiley.

Moran, R., & Dolphin, C. (1986). The defensible space concept: Theoretical and operational explication. *Environment and Behavior,* **18**, 396–416.

Morone, J. G., & Woodhouse, E. J. (1986). *Averting catastrophe: Strategies for regulating risky technologies.* Berkeley, CA: University of California Press.

Nadler, G. (1985). Systems methodology and design. *IEEE Transactions on Systems, Man, and Cybernetics,* **15**, 685–697.

National Research Council (1989). *Improving risk communication.* Washington, DC: National Academy Press.

Newman, O. (1972). *Defensible space.* New York: Macmillan.

Nomoyle, J. B., & Foley, J. M. (1988). The defensible space model of fear and elderly public housing residents. *Environment and Behavior,* **20**, 50–74.

Norman, D. A. (1988). *The psychology of everyday things.* New York: Basic Books.

Norman, D. A., & Draper, S. W. (Eds.) (1986). *User centered system design.* Hillsdale, NJ: Erlbaum.

Oppe, S. (1988). The concept of risk: A decision theoretic approach. *Ergonomics,* **31**, 435–440.

Perrow, C. (1984). *Normal accidents: Living with high risk technologies.* New York: Basic Books.

Pidgeon, N. F. (1988). Risk assessment and accident analysis. *Acta Psychologica,* **68**, 355–368.

Pidgeon, N. F., Blockley, D. I., & Turner, R. A. (1986). Design practice and snow loading—lessons from a roof collapse. *The Structural Engineer,* **64A, 65A,** 67–71, 236–240.

Pidgeon, N. F., Turner, R. A., & Blockley, D. I. (1987). Hazard assessment in structural engineering. In N. C. Lind (Ed.), *Reliability and risk analysis in civil engineering* (Vol. 1, pp. 358–365). University of Waterloo, Canada: Institute for Risk Research.

Pitz, G. F. (1987). Evaluating decision aiding technologies for genetic counseling. In G. Evers-Kieboms, J.-J. Cassiman, H. van den Berghe, & G. d'Ydewalle (Eds.), *Genetic risk, risk perception, and decision making* (pp. 251–278). New York: Alan R. Liss.

Pitz, G. F., & McKillip, J. (1984). *Decision analysis for program evaluators.* Newbury Park, CA: Sage.

Pitz, G. F., Sachs, N. J., & Heerboth, J. (1980). Procedures for eliciting choices in the analysis of individual decisions. *Organizational Behavior and Human Decision Processes,* **26**, 396–408.

Purcell, A. T. (1986). Environmental perception and affect. *Environment and Behavior,* **18**, 3–30.

Rasmussen, J., & Goodstein, L. P. (1987). Decision support in supervisory control of high-risk industrial systems. *Automatica,* **23**, 663–671.

Riemersma, J. B. J. (1988). An empirical study of subjective road categorization. *Ergonomics,* **31**, 621–630.

Rohe, W. M., & Burby, R. J. (1988). Fear of crime in public housing. *Environment and Behavior,* **20**, 700–720.

Rumar, K. (1988). Collective risk but individual safety. *Ergonomics,* **31**, 507–518.

Ryan, J. P. (1987). Cognitive aspects of hazard warning. In L. S. Mark, J. S. Warm, & R. L. Huston (Eds.), *Ergonomics and human factors: Recent research* (pp. 188–194). New York: Springer-Verlag.

Sagoff, M. (1985). Sense and sentiment in occupational safety and health programs. In D. Nelkin (Ed.), *The language of risk* (pp. 179–198). Newbury Park, CA: Sage.

Sime, J. D. (1985). Movement towards the familiar: Person and place affiliation in a fire

320

entrapment setting. *Environment and Behavior*, **17**, 697–724.

Slovic, P., MacGregor, D., & Kraus, N. N. (1987). Perception of risk from automobile safety defects. *Accident Analysis and Prevention*, **19**, 309–373.

Streff, F. M., & Geller, E. S. (1988). An experimental test of risk compensation: Between-subject versus within-subject analyses. *Accident Analysis and Prevention*, **20**, 277–287.

Struckman, J., David, L., Adrian, K., & Williams, A. F. (1989). Comparative effects of driver improvement programs on crashes and violations. *Accident Analysis and Prevention*, **21**, 203–215.

van der Colk, H. (1988). Risky behavior resulting from bounded rationality. *Ergonomics*, **31**, 485–490.

van der Molen, H. H., & Bötticher, M. T. (1988). A hierarchical risk model for traffic participants. *Ergonomics*, **31**, 537–555.

Viscusi, W. K. (1983). *Risk by choice: Regulating health and safety in the work place*. Cambridge, MA: Harvard University Press.

Vlek, C. A. J., & Stallen, P. J. (1981). Judging risks and benefits in the small and in the large. *Organizational Behavior and Human Performance*, **28**, 235–271.

Vojtecky, M. A., & Schmitz, M. F. (1986). Program evaluation and health and safety training. *Journal of Safety Research*, **17**, 57–63.

von Winterfeldt, D., & Edwards, W. (1986). *Decision analysis and behavioral research*. New York: Cambridge University Press.

Weinstein, N. D., Gubb, P. D., & Vautier, J. S. (1986). Increasing automobile seat belt use: An intervention emphasizing risk susceptibility. *Journal of Applied Psychology*, **71**, 285–290.

Wilde, G. J. S. (1988). Risk homeostasis theory and traffic accidents: Propositions, deductions and discussion of dissension in recent reactions. *Ergonomics*, **31**, 441–468.

Wogalter, M. S., Desaulniers, D. R., & Brelsford, J. S. (1986). Hazardousness and warning expectations. In *A cradle for human factors* (pp. 1197–1201). Santa Monica, CA: Human Factors Society.

Epilogue

Risk-taking behavior is rich and varied, as this book has made abundantly clear. Each chapter has summarized and critically evaluated what is known about some particular aspect of this behavior. Some risk-taking phenomena seem peculiar to specific tasks or contexts, such as risk appraisal or risk responses in the presence of stress. However, a careful reading of the chapters reveals themes that cut across several domains. One purpose of this epilogue is to highlight and explicate some of these overarching themes, ones that seem especially important. As acknowledged by the authors themselves, there are many things we do not yet understand about the nature of risk-taking behavior and how to improve its effectiveness. So another aim of this epilogue is to bring attention to some of the unresolved scientific and practical risk-taking issues the contributors have uncovered, issues that should be examined carefully in future research and development efforts.

DELIBERATIVE VS NONDELIBERATIVE RISK TAKING

Implicit in the term "risk *taking*" is the idea that risk-taking behavior is deliberative. That is, it is assumed that the risk taker consciously contemplates how he or she should act, taking into account risk as well as, perhaps, other considerations. This assumption is especially prominent in decision-theoretic analyses of risk taking (e.g. in Chapter 2, by Neumann and Politser; in Chapter 3, by Yates and Stone; in Chapter 5, by Fischhoff; and in Chapter 6, by Davis, Kameda, and Stasson). However, there are common behaviors which at first glance appear to result from deliberative consideration of risk, but upon more careful analysis are found not to be so determined. Examples are actions that are the immediate causes of certain accidents (discussed by Wagenaar in Chapter 9) and practices that damage one's health (described by Adler, Kegeles, and Genevro in Chapter 8). Thus, we are led to acknowledge two major classes of risk-taking behavior: deliberative and nondeliberative. As indicated, in the former class, the person literally decides how to act, weighing risk against other factors. In the latter, the person's actions do not take risk into account; it is as if the risk taking were inadvertent. The only reason for calling such behavior "risk

Risk-taking Behavior. Edited by J. F. Yates
© 1992 John Wiley & Sons Ltd

taking" at all is that an observer viewing the situation in which it occurs would likely say that risk is present.

Deliberative risk taking has been studied extensively for a long time, and that effort has been rewarded by increasingly successful explanations for the behavior. In contrast, because until recently nondeliberate risk taking has not been recognized explicitly, we know little about it. Thus, high—if not paramount—on the risk-taking research agenda should be determining explanations for nondeliberative risk-taking behavior. This endeavor promises to be an interesting enterprise.

The study of nondeliberative risk taking would probably benefit from a recognition that there are at least two aspects to the problem. The first is why the person involved does not recognize the given situation as an occasion for explicitly choosing how to act, rather than proceeding according to habit or a schema. As implied by Pitz in Chapter 10 and articulated more directly by Ronis, Yates, and Kirscht (1989), one plausible reason is that the individual sees nothing in the situation that is out of the ordinary. Equivalently, this is a claim that one instigator of decision episodes—of which deliberative risk-taking instances are a special case—is the unusualness of the situation, say, a new barricade on a well-traveled road. The second essential feature of the nondeliberative risk-taking problem is that the actor fails to see the risk that is acknowledged by others. As noted by Yates and Stone in Chapter 3, recognizing the presence of risk is an important part of risk appraisal more generally. The hypotheses suggested in Chapter 3 might be a reasonable starting point in attempts to understand this neglected phenomenon.

The deliberative vs nondeliberative risk taking distinction has significant practical implications. Reducing mishaps—if not precluding them—should be a major responsibility of designers, policy makers, and managers. As emphasized by Wagenaar in Chapter 9 and Pitz in Chapter 10, how this goal is approached ought to differ radically according to whether the actions that contribute to setbacks are deliberative or nondeliberative. For instance, strategies predicated on an assumption of deliberation would emphasize such things as improving probability judgments and changing incentives (e.g. personal liability for injuries resulting from at-fault accidents). Such strategies are useless when the focal actions are determined nondeliberatively. Instead, it seems that a "risk behavior engineer" would have two options in these cases. First, steps could be taken to make nondeliberative actions into deliberative ones, and then to encourage the "proper" consideration of risk (e.g. requiring loan officers to state and justify their risk appraisals before granting loans). Alternatively, nondeliberation can be taken for granted and the situation structured to yield suitable outcomes regardless. This strategy is akin to the user-centered design discussed by Pitz in Chapter 10. A concrete, minimal example is the "child-proofing" to which parents of two-year-olds often subject their houses—plugging electrical outlets, blocking stairs, and so on.

CHOOSING RISKS VS HANDLING RISKS

Virtually all analyses of risk taking apply to situations where the person is depicted as choosing between two or more specified alternatives, for instance, selecting one investment opportunity rather than another, or engaging in some health-threatening habit such as taking drugs vs abstaining from drug use. Nevertheless, several recent studies (discussed briefly by Yates and Stone in Chapter 1 and reviewed more extensively by Bromiley and Curley in Chapter 4) have found that this perspective is too limited. In particular, examinations of risk taking in naturalistic situations have revealed another common mode of behavior that sometimes has been dubbed "risk handling." In this mode, rather than merely selecting among the options that just happen to present themselves, the individual more aggressively tries to formulate options that reduce risks without sacrificing advantages. For example, individuals adopting this risk-handling stance while pondering drug use vs abstinence would seek a third option that satisfies their cravings but does not carry addiction risks. Because risk handling has been recognized for such a short time, we do not yet have models or even broadly descriptive data about this behavior. Thus, risk handling also must be a high-priority research topic for the next several years.

ORIGINS OF RISK TAKING VARIABILITY

A major thread running through the book is that not every person experiences and deals with risk the same way, even in identical situations. Characterizations of risk-taking behavior often simply take such variability as a given factor, with little or no attempt to explain it. For instance, expected utility theory (Neumann and Politser, Chapter 2) allows for either risk aversion or risk seeking, as encoded in different but equally admissable utility functions. But the theory simply does not address the question of *why* Person A's utility function is different from Person B's. Other work on individual and group differences in risk-taking dispositions has revealed an even richer variety of distinctions in how people respond to risk. Nevertheless, as noted by Bromiley and Curley in Chapter 4 and Fischhoff in Chapter 5, throughout all scholarship on risk-taking behavior there has been remarkably little attention devoted to the issue of where such distinctions originate. Hopefully, work over the next few years will correct this oversight.

GENERALIZABILITY OF RISK TAKING RESEARCH

Several chapters in this book have expressed concerns that are, essentially, methodological. Implicitly, those chapters urge a healthy (and sobering) skepticism about how much we can trust the conclusions we have inferred from years of research on risk taking. There is no reason to doubt the internal consistency of that work. But there might well be some question about the generality of what we have observed. Consider the example of people's risk judgments. Most of our conclusions about such assessments have been derived from subjects' measured responses to hypothetical situations, obtained in carefully controlled laboratory settings. Both Wagenaar (Chapter 9) and Pitz (Chapter 10) note that people often have had little experience with situations that resemble the ones they are asked to consider. Thus, those individuals' responses might have little connection with the risk-taking behavior that is ultimately of interest. There is a striking parallel between the present issues and those involving contingent valuation, whereby people are asked to indicate how much they would pay for hypothetical goods and services, such as pollution controls that would improve air quality (cf. Cummings, Brookshire, & Schulze, 1986). It is known that such valuations are highly unreliable, being easily affected by such things as question formulation.

In Chapter 7, Mann speculates that the defensibility of our conclusions about risk taking could be compromised by other considerations besides subjects' unfamiliarity with the situations they are asked to ponder in paper-and-pencil tasks. Specifically, he argues that there is reason to suspect that the actual risk-taking behavior observed in comfortable, low-stakes, laboratory settings differs in kind, not just degree, from that which occurs in the often stressful, high-stakes, real-world contexts to which we would like to generalize. But trying to find out whether misgivings about generality are warranted is no mean feat. High-fidelity studies in many of the risk-taking settings of practical concern are difficult, if not impossible, to perform in an ethical yet controlled manner. For instance, we cannot conceive of exposing individuals to the possiblity of serious injury solely for the purpose of studying their risk-taking behavior. In Chapter 6, Davis, Kameda, and Stasson note related but different feasibility constraints on research about risk taking in groups. For example, countless real-world groups, such as parole boards, executive committees, and research review panels, wrestle with and resolve weighty risk issues daily. However, privacy concerns preclude the examination of how they go about their work, or even how *well* they accomplish their tasks. Clearly, to meet these challenges, risk researchers must seek and exploit creative field and quasi-experimental techniques.

RECOMMENDATIONS FOR RISK TAKING

The literature on risk taking is replete with implicit and explicit recommendations for how that behavior could be improved. What "improved" means is that the incidence of serious adverse outcomes resulting from people's actions would be reduced. Ideally, these recommendations should be accompanied by justifications for believing that such improvements would be realized. Wagenaar's analysis of accident causation in Chapter 9 illustrates that detailed examination of justifications can be informative and ultimately, perhaps, lead to more effective strategies for reducing adverse outcomes. A consideration of expected utility theory, as a basis for decision-analytic guidance for risk taking (Neumann and Politser, Chapter 2, and Pitz, Chapter 10), provides another instructive example.

The core of utility theory addresses the tradeoff between uncertainty and value. In its normative role, utility theory says that the appropriate tradeoff procedure is embodied in the multiplication operation entailed in expectations. For instance, suppose a certain surgical treatment promises a 15% chance that a patient will be left with permanent, low-level chest pain. Effectively, utility theory says that this feature should contribute to the acceptability of the surgical option according to

$$(0.15) \times u(\text{Low-level pain})$$

where u denotes the patient's utility function for various health states.

Why does utility theory not say that the above contribution should correspond to

$$f(0.15) + v(\text{Low-level pain})$$

or

$$w(\text{Low-level pain})^{g(0.15)}$$

or some other combination of functions of the outcome probabilities (e.g. f and g) and values (e.g. v and w)? As discussed by Neumann and Politser in Chapter 2, one answer to this question is provided by axiomatizations like von Neumann and Morgenstern's (1947). Suppose a risk taker feels that it is important to decide in such a way that his or her decisions never contradict the principles embodied in the von Neumann–Morgenstern axioms. Then von Neumann and Morgenstern's theorem says that choosing so as to maximize expected utility (which implies multiplicative uncertainty-value tradeoffs) will assure consistency with those principles. More recently developed axiomatic treatments of risky choice, of the kind studied by Camerer (1989), imply guarantees of consistency with similar though somewhat different sets of principles. (See Machina, 1989, for an analysis of the normative implications of some of the newer utility models.)

To reiterate the question posed by Pitz in Chapter 10, what is so important about preserving consistency with a particular set of choice principles (see also Yates, 1990, Chapter 9)? To be sure, there is a certain intellectual appeal to such consistency. Nevertheless, confronted with the possibility of losses that can actually hurt—the essence of risk—most people want the assurance of something more substantial. It can be demonstrated that decision rules like expected utility maximization can prevent losses of the sort entailed in exploitative "books" or "material traps" (cf. Machina, 1989; Winkler, 1972; Yates, 1990). These are cycles of transactions in which a decision maker is caused to repeatedly suffer material losses because a victimizer (or the situation) exploits that individual's persistent violation of some given choice principle, such as transitivity. But how often are people actually exposed to material trap conditions? No one knows. It is possible, however, that such conditions virtually never occur. If so, why should we go to the bother of protecting against them by deciding according to expected utility?

The point of this discussion is not to call into question the usefulness of applying expected utility-based decision rules or any other specific risk-taking recommendation. Instead, the aim is to suggest that risk specialists consider subjecting every prospective recommendation to a four-part justification test. Implicitly or explicitly, every recommendation is intended to address some particular negative result of faulty risk taking (or perhaps several of them), for instance, material trap victimization. The proposed test would focus on each such result:

Possibility   Is there reason to expect that the focal negative result could occur in the given situation or in similar situations generally? For instance, should we anticipate that potential material trap conditions are widespread, such that, if a risk taker's choices violate utility theory principles, that individual actually will be victimized?

Seriousness   If the negative result did occur, would its consequences be serious or only minor? For example, even if a utility theory violator did succumb to the potential traps in a given setting, might the setbacks be only mild ones?

Susceptibility   Given how the risk taker behaves naturally, how likely is it that his or her actions actually would cause the negative result to occur? Again continuing our example, how probable is it that a given individual really would take risks in a manner that disagrees with utility theory?

Remedial Costs Are the costs of carrying out the recommended "preventive treatment" for the negative result high or low? In our illustration, is it easy to determine and follow the dictates of utility theory (say, in decision analysis), or is such an exercise a major undertaking?

All four of these quesitons are important, but especially the last one. This is because every risk taker has limited resources and because typically several recommendations compete for those resources. For example, a risk taker not only might consider trying to act according to expected utility, but also contemplate improving risk taking by seeking better likelihood judgments or value assessments (Yates and Stone, Chapter 3), by deliberating actions in groups (Davis, Kameda, and Stasson, Chapter 6), or by developing better task performance skills (Pitz, Chapter 10). And since the risk taker likely cannot afford to do all these things, some difficult choices among them must be made. Answers to the above test questions for all the proposed remedial options should allow the risk taker to proceed most sensibly.

The actual, concrete resolution of various tradeoffs presents special chal lenges for risk takers and those who advise them. One such tradeoff is that between risk itself and the other considerations that exist in a given risk-taking situation, for instance, the benefits of the prospective actions. To declare that one person is risk-averse while another is risk-seeking amounts to saying that the former individual demands better "other considerations" in the risk vs other-considerations tradeoff than does the latter. Interestingly, expected utility theory (Neumann and Politser, Chapter 2) is mute on how this tradeoff should be resolved. That is, it is perfectly acceptable within utility theory for a person to be risk-averse, risk-seeking, or risk-neutral. But is there any sense in which a risk taker could be unjustified or "wrong" in how he or she balances risk against other factors? Equivalently, should experts on risk taking offer advice about such matters and, if so, on what basis should they do so? Risk takers themselves seem to seek such counsel when they ask questions like, "Am I being too conservative here?"

Another kind of tradeoff encountered in some risky situations is implicit in the social dilemmas faced by policy makers and designers (Wagenaar, Chapter 9, and Pitz, Chapter 10). It is equivalent to choosing between exposing one group of people to risks rather than another. An example: It is possible to produce cars that virtually eliminate the risk of death from, say, rear-end collisions. But with today's technology, the cost of such cars would be so prohibitive that few people could afford to buy them. One effect of choosing to go ahead and produce only these safer cars would be throwing thousands of auto workers out of their jobs because of the resulting lower car sales. Generalizing from past experience, this would, in turn, result in greater poverty and crime, as some of the displaced workers turn to illegal activities in their struggle to survive economically. Eventually, it is inevitable that at least some number of people would die from the associated illnesses and criminal victimiza- tion. Conceivably, as many lives—or more—would be lost in this indirect manner than from the rear-end collisions that were the focus of attention initially. About whose lives should the policy makers and designers be more concerned, the potential auto crash victims or the potential victims of economic and social disruption? As before, on what bases should the implied tradeoffs be made? It is unclear that questions like these are answerable, scientifically, at least (Pitz, Chapter 10). But they are certainly an essential topic for future work on risk-taking behavior.

THEORY DEVELOPMENT

As each chapter in this book has testified, there is a wide variety of theories of risk-taking behavior. Such a circumstance normally leads us to wonder why there are so many theories and which is the "best." In this instance, however, a thoughtful reading of the chapters makes it apparent that these are not the right questions to pose. Perhaps the primary reason there are so many theories of risk taking is that the behavior itself is so broad; different theories tend to address different elements of the behavior. Accordingly, in most cases distinct risk theories (e.g. SEU theory vs risky shift models) do not contradict one another, since they are offered as explanations for very disparate phenomena. This accounting for the current state of affairs does not mean there is no need for further development and improvement in risk-taking theories. Quite the contrary seems to be true.

Perhaps foremost on the theory development agenda should be the generation of a risk-taking "supertheory." Such a theory would integrate what is known about what occurs in various narrow, specific phases of the typical risk-taking episode. It would also highlight what *needs* to be known.

One simple conception of the phases that constitute a risk-taking cycle is as follows:

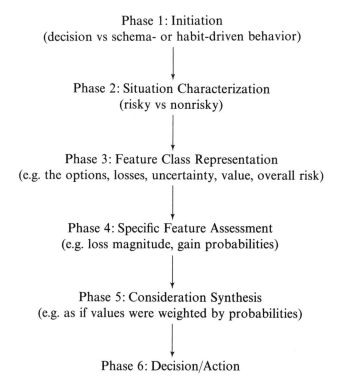

Phase 1: Initiation
(decision vs schema- or habit-driven behavior)

Phase 2: Situation Characterization
(risky vs nonrisky)

Phase 3: Feature Class Representation
(e.g. the options, losses, uncertainty, value, overall risk)

Phase 4: Specific Feature Assessment
(e.g. loss magnitude, gain probabilities)

Phase 5: Consideration Synthesis
(e.g. as if values were weighted by probabilities)

Phase 6: Decision/Action

Despite its impoverishment, even this skeletal broad view of what might happen in a risk-taking episode brings to the fore significant issues that warrant attention.

Thus, for example, in Phase 1, the risk taker effectively classifies the given situation as one that requires a decision or can be driven by a preexisting schema or habit, a process that, as noted above, is quite poorly understood. In Phase 2, assuming that a decision opportunity has been acknowledged, the individual either recognizes or ignores the presence of risk, another activity that, as emphasized before, is not well studied. In Phase 3, the person constructs a representation that has "slots" for such situational features as losses, uncertainty, overall risk, and the very options themselves (see Chapter 3). These are the kinds of features that are assumed in models like utility theory (Chapter 2, by Neumann and Politser), risk homeostasis theory (Chapter 9, by Wagenaar), or the theory of reasoned action (Chapter 8, by Adler, Kegeles, and Genevro). In Phase 4, the risk taker assesses the actual status of these features for the given situation with which he or she is faced, say, the chances and seriousness of wrongly convicting defendant Smith. In Phase 5, the risk taker somehow synthesizes various (typically conflicting) considerations, yielding a final decision or action in Phase 6.

It seems that risk-taking research in particular disciplines has placed special emphasis on only some of the above phases. For instance, work in economics and traditional, "mainstream" decision theory has often concentrated on Phase 5, in developments like utility theory and prospect theory (Neumann and Politser, Chapter 2). However, a "supertheory" of the kind that might soon emerge would settle a most important but rarely raised issue: What is the relative significance of occurrences in the various phases of risk-taking episodes? That is, which phases explain the lion's share of the variance in people's actual, real-world risk taking? Relatedly, if we want to improve risk-taking behavior most dramatically, on which phases should we focus our attention? Along with all the other issues identified here and throughout the book by the contributors, these questions assure that risk-taking research will be lively and exciting for some time to come.

REFERENCES

Camerer, C. (1989). An experimental test of several generalized utility theories. *Journal of Risk and Uncertainty*, **2**, 61–104.

Cummings, R. G., Brookshire, D. S., & Schulze, W. D. (1986). *Valuing environmental goods: An assessment of the contingent valuation method*. Totowa, NJ: Rowan & Allanheld.

Machina, M. J. (1989). Dynamic consistency and non-expected utility models of choice under uncertainty. *Journal of Economic Literature*, **27**, 1622–1668.

Ronis, D. L., Yates, J. F., & Kirscht, J. P. (1989). Attitudes, decisions, and habits as determinants of repeated behavior. In A. R. Pratkanis, S. J. Breckler, & A. G. Greenwald (Eds.), *Attitude structure and function* (pp. 213–239). Hillsdale, NJ: Erlbaum.

von Neumann, J., & Morgenstern, O. (1947). *The theory of games and economic behavior* (2nd ed.). Princeton, NJ: Princeton University Press.

Winkler, R. L. (1972). *Introduction to Bayesian inference and decision.* New York: Holt, Rinehart, and Winston.

Yates, J. F. (1990). *Judgment and decision making.* Englewood Cliffs, NJ: Prentice Hall.

Author index

Subject index